LYLE
Price Guide to
American Furniture

LYLE
Price Guide to American Furniture

ANTHONY CURTIS

A PERIGEE BOOK

While every care has been taken in the compiling of information contained in this volume, the publisher cannot accept liability for loss, financial or otherwise, incurred by reliance placed on the information herein.

All prices quoted in this book are obtained from a variety of auctions in various countries during the twelve months prior to publication and are converted to dollars at the rate of exchange prevalent at the time of sale.

The publishers wish to express their sincere thanks to the following for their involvement and assistance in the production of this volume.

ANTHONY CURTIS (Editor)   CATRIONA DAY (Art Production)

EELIN McIVOR (Sub Editor)   ANGIE DEMARCO (Art Production)

ANNETTE CURTIS (Editorial)   NICKY FAIRBURN (Art Production)

A Perigee Book
Published by The Berkley Publishing Group
A division of Penguin Putnam Inc.
375 Hudson Street
New York, New York 10014

Copyright © 1998 by Lyle Publications
Cover design by Jack Ribik

First edition: June 1998

Published simultaneously in Canada.

The Penguin Putnam Inc. World Wide Web site address is
http://www.penguinputnam.com

Library of Congress Cataloging-in-Publication Data

Curtis, Tony, 1939–
   Lyle price guide to American furniture / Anthony Curtis.—1st ed.
      p.   cm.
   "Lyle Publications/A Perigee book."
   Includes index.
   ISBN 0-399-52410-X (pbk.)
   1. Furniture—United States—Catalogs.   I. Title.
NK2405.C87   1998
749.213'075—dc21   98-9793
                                          CIP

Printed in the United States of America

10   9   8   7   6   5   4   3

INTRODUCTION

It is significant that, when most people hear the word 'antiques', their mind immediately flicks not to glassware, ceramics, silver or the like, but to a Chippendale chair, or a Regency commode - in short, a piece of furniture.

For furniture is, and always has been, the backbone of the antiques trade, and deservedly so. What else can you sleep on, sit on, eat your dinner on, store your clothes, books, linen in, which, moreover, if treated well, will last for ever, and, if made well, will actually increase in value as time goes on? It is something we all need, as even the law recognises, for when the debt collectors come to relieve you of all your worldly goods, they are nevertheless legally obliged to leave you a bed, a chair and a table.

The necessities apart, it is hardly surprising that furniture holds such a fascination and interest for us. It has been with us since earliest times, and from earliest times there has been a constantly changing and adapting range of styles and pieces. It is surely this richness and diversity as much as anything else that enchants us.

American furniture is no different in this respect from any other tradition. Obviously, in the beginning, its design was heavily influenced by European styles. European pieces were brought over by the first settlers, but the fact that one already sees a 'Pilgrim

The Hollingsworth family Chippendale carved walnut high chest-of-drawers, matching dressing table and side chair, by Thomas Affleck, Philadelphia, 1765-75, the high chest in two sections on acanthus carved cabriole legs with claw and ball feet, 42in. wide, the dressing table with a long thumbmolded drawer over three small drawers, 48in. wide. Sold at Christie's, New York for an amazing $2,972,500.

Fathers' chair, table or whatever, shows that almost as soon as the immigrants set foot on American soil, their furniture began to develop its own characteristics.

Of course European influence did not just get up and go away. Leading figures in American furniture design and manufacture such as Duncan Phyfe, were, almost two centuries after the Pilgrim Fathers, still first generation immigrants, who would take European ideas and modify them to suit the domestic market. This happened to the extent that the same term would come to mean two very different things, depending on what side of the Atlantic you were. 'Chippendale', for example, in an English auction catalog as often as not means made by TC himself, or at least his workshop. On the other hand, he would, except by general inspiration, have had absolutely nothing to do with most of the myriad pieces which bear his name in America. Similarly, the bulk of American Queen Anne furniture was emphatically not made during her short reign, but often as much as two centuries later.

This is, of course, not to say that America was devoid of its own ideas, though perhaps because the European tradition was constantly bolstered by the influx of new immigrants, it took a while for a truly characteristic style to develop. It was really not until the 19th and early 20th centuries that this finally emerged, and in all its forms it had one salient feature - its simplicity. Perhaps this was a result of the American pioneering spirit: it is not easy to trek across vast tracts of difficult and often hostile territory and break new frontiers without at least some damage to your delicate bonheur du jour. Even back in the comfortable East it was easy to identify with the courage and tenacity of the pioneers, especially as traditional furniture styles of the period seemed to be going right over the top in the form of Gothic and Rococo Revival.

The American styles which emerged, whether Shaker, Eastlake, Limbert, Roycroft, Mission or Arts and Crafts, all had in common a rejection of the elaborate and heavily ornamented forms of the time, and apart from William Morris, from whom the Arts & Crafts movement drew its inspiration, did not have counterparts of similar importance on the other side of the Atlantic.

Furniture is much less susceptible than other collecting fields to the vicissitudes of the market, perhaps because of its intrinsic usefulness and the fact that the craftsmanship and materials which have gone into making the pieces give them a worth of their own. It is therefore a particularly rich field for investment, and when dipping into this book you may well be surprised to find how much your heirlooms or even your past purchases have grown in value since you acquired them.

CONTENTS

American Periods...... 11
Furniture Designers 13
Beds 20
   Federal...... 23
   Herter...... 27
   New England...... 28
   Sheraton 28
   Stickley 29
Blanket Chests 30
Bookcases 37
   Stickley 40
Boxes 42
Bureaux 52
   Federal 54
Cabinets 57
Candle Stands 60
   Chippendale 64
   Federal 68
   New England 70
Canterburys 72
Chairs 73
   Corner Chairs 73
   Dining Chairs 76
      Chippendale 82
      Federal 88
      New England 90
      New York 91
      Queen Anne 94
      Shaker 100
      Stickley 101
      William & Mary 102
      Windsor 103
   Easy Chairs 108
      Stickley 113
   Elbow Chairs 115
      Chippendale 117
      Federal 119
      Massachusetts 120
      New England 121
      Queen Anne 122
      Stickley 124
      William & Mary 126
      Windsor 127
   High Chairs 130
   Lolling Chairs 132
   Rocking Chairs 136
      Shaker 138
      Stickley 139
      Windsor 139
   Wing Chairs 140
      Chippendale 140
      Federal 145
      Queen Anne 147

Chests 150
   Dower 152
   Six Board 153
Chests of Drawers 154
   Chippendale 156
   Chippendale, Connecticut 158
   Chippendale, Massachusetts 160
   Chippendale, New England 166
   Chippendale, Pennsylvania 167
   Federal 168
   Federal, Massachusetts 170
   Federal, Mid Atlantic States 171
   Federal, New England 172
   Federal, New Hampshire 174
   New England 175
   Queen Anne 177
   Shaker 178
   Stickley 179
Chests on Chests 180
Chests over Drawers 186
Clocks 188
   Banjo 188
   Mirror Clocks 192
   Pillar & Scroll 193
   Shelf 196
   Tall Case 202
   Wall Clocks 208
Corner Cupboards 210
   Chippendale 213
   Federal 214
   Federal Mid-Atlantic States 215
   Federal, New England 216
   Federal, Pennsylvania 217
Cradles & Cribs 218
Credenzas 219
Cupboards 220
   Hutch 226
   Wall 227
Desks 228
   Federal 231
   Kneehole 232
   Slant Top 234
      Chippendale 235
      Chippendale, Connecticut 236
      Chippendale, Massachusetts 237
      Chippendale, New England 241
      Chippendale, New Hampshire 244
      Chippendale, Pennsylvania 244
      Chippendale, Philadelphia 244
      Chippendale, Rhode Island 245
      Federal 246
      Queen Anne 247
      William & Mary 248

Stickley 250
Display Cabinets 252
Fireplace Furniture 254
Fireplaces 258
High Chests of Drawers 260
Highboys 267
Kas 272
Linen Presses 273
Lowboys 274
Miniature Furniture 278
Mirrors 283
Pianos 294
Screens 296
Secretaries 298
   Chippendale 300
   Classical 301
   Federal 302
   Federal, New England 305
   Federal, Massachusetts 306
   Sheraton 308
Settees & Couches 310
   Chippendale 316
   Classical 318
   Federal 325
   Spindle Back 331
   Stickley 334
Shelves & Brackets 336
Sideboards 339
   Federal 342
   Federal, Massachusetts 344
   Federal, New England 347
   Federal, Philadelphia 348
   Limbert 348
   Stickley 349
Stands 351
   Drink Stands 356
   Etagères 356
   Light Stands 356
   Magazine Stands 357
   Music Stands 358
   Plant Stands 358
   Smoking Stands 359
   Umbrella Stands 359
Step Back Cupboards 360
Stools 364
   Stickley 368
Suites 369
Tables 374
  Breakfast Tables 374
  Card Tables 376
   Chippendale 378
   Classical 380
   Federal 384
   Federal, Massachusetts 388
   Federal, New England 390

Federal, New York 391
Center Tables 392
Dining Tables 394
Dressing Tables 396
   Cabriole Leg 402
Drop Leaf Tables 410
   Chippendale 413
   Federal 417
   Queen Anne 419
   Queen Anne, Massachusetts 421
   Queen Anne, New England 422
   Queen Anne, New York 424
   Queen Anne, Pennsylvania 424
   Queen Anne, Rhode Island 424
Drum Tables 425
Gateleg Tables 426
Hutch-Chair Tables 428
Large Tables 430
Library Tables 436
Occasional Tables 439
   Stickley 444
Pembroke Tables 446
   Chippendale 448
   Federal, Baltimore 450
   Federal, Connecticut 450
   Federal, Massachusetts 450
   Federal, Mid Atlantic States 451
   Federal, New England 451
   Federal, New York 451
Pier Tables 454
Serving Tables 457
Side Tables 460
Sofa Tables 462
Tavern Tables 463
   New England 465
   William & Mary 466
Tea Tables 467
   Chippendale 468
   Queen Anne 472
   Tray Top 473
Work Tables 474
   Classical 476
   Classical, Massachusetts 478
   Classical, New York 480
   Federal 484
   Federal, Massachusetts 486
   Federal, New York 489
   Shaker 491
Tall Chests 492
   Chippendale 494
   Federal 496
   Queen Anne 496
Wardrobes & Armoires 498
Washstands 500
Wine Coolers & Cellarets 504

ACKNOWLEDGMENTS

Auction Team Köln, Postfach 50 11 68, D–5000 Köln 50 Germany
Bearnes, Rainbow, Avenue Road, Torquay TQ2 5TG
Boardman Fine Art Auctioneers, Station Road Corner, Haverhill, Suffolk CB9 0EY
Bonhams, Monpelier Street, Knightsbridge, London SW7 1HH
Bonhams Chelsea, 65–69 Lots Road, London SW10 0RN
Bonhams West Country, Dowell Street, Honiton, Devon
Butterfield & Butterfield, 220 San Bruno Avenue, San Francisco CA94103, USA
Butterfield & Butterfield, 7601 Sunset Boulevard, Los Angeles CA 90046, USA
Christie's (International) SA, 8 place de la Taconnerie, 1204 Genève, Switzerland
Christie's Monaco , S.A.M, Park Palace, 98000 Monte Carlo, Monaco
Christie's Scotland, 164–166 Bath Street, Glasgow G2 4TG
Christie's South Kensington Ltd., 85 Old Brompton Road, London SW7 3LD
Christie's, 8 King Street, London SW1Y 6QT
Christie's East, 219 East 67th Street, New York, NY 10021, USA
Christie's, 502 Park Avenue, New York, NY10022, USA
Christie's, Cornelis Schuytstraat 57, 1071 JG Amsterdam, Netherlands
Christie's, SA Roma, 114 Piazza Navona, 00186 Rome, Italy
Christie's Swire, 2804–6 Alexandra House, 16–20 Chater Road, Hong Kong
Christie's Australia Pty Ltd., 1 Darling Street, South Yarra, Victoria 3141, Australia
William Doyle Galleries, 175 East 87th Street, New York, NY 10128, USA
Du Mouchelles Art Galleries Co., 409 E. Jefferson Avenue, Detroit, Michigan 48226, USA
Eldred's, Box 796, E. Dennis, MA 02641, USA
Andrew Hartley Fine Arts, Victoria Hall, Little Lane, Ilkely
Giles Haywood, The Auction House, St John's Road, Stourbridge, West Midlands, DY8 1EW
Locke & England, 18 Guy Street, Leamington Spa CV32 4RT
Locke & England, Sale Rooms, Walton House, 11 Parade, Leamington Spa CV32 4DG
Phillips Manchester, Trinity House, 114 Northenden Road, Sale, Manchester M33 3HD
Phillips Son & Neal SA, 10 rue des Chaudronniers, 1204 Genève, Switzerland
Phillips West Two, 10 Salem Road, London W2 4BL
Phillips, 11 Bayle Parade, Folkstone, Kent CT20 1SQ
Phillips, 49 London Road, Sevenoaks, Kent TN13 1UU
Phillips, 65 George Street, Edinburgh EH2 2JL
Phillips, Blenstock House, 7 Blenheim Street, New Bond Street, London W1Y 0AS
Phillips, Marylebone, Hayes Place, Lisson Grove, London NW1 6UA
Phillips, New House, 150 Christleton Road, Chester CH3 5TD
Schrager Auction Galleries, 2915 N Sherman Boulevard, PO Box 10390, Milwaukee W1 53210, USA
Selkirk's, 4166 Olive Street, St Louis, Missouri 63108, USA
Skinner, Bolton Gallery, Route 117, Bolton MA, USA
Sotheby's, 34–35 New Bond Street, London W1A 2AA
Sotheby's, 1334 York Avenue, New York NY 10021
Sotheby's, 112 George Street, Edinburgh EH2 2LH
Sotheby's, Summers Place, Billinghurst, West Sussex RH14 9AD
Sotheby's, Monaco, BP 45, 98001 Monte Carlo
Peter Wilson, Victoria Gallery, Market Street, Nantwich, Cheshire CW5 5DG
Wooley & Wallis, The Castle Auction Mart, Salisbury, Wilts SP1 3SU

(Sotheby's)

AMERICAN PERIODS

PILGRIM STYLE – 17TH CENTURY
This earliest distinguishable American style was derived from Renaissance and 17th century English models. Items were massive, rectilinear and of simple basic construction. Tables were mainly trestle based or gateleg; chairs were comprised often of posts and spindles with rush seats or had hard slat backs. Typical was the Wainscot chair, which, with its solid back and columnar turned legs, was based on Elizabethan models.

WILLIAM & MARY 1690–1725
This style was introduced into America at the end of the 17th century, and was essentially a New World version of the baroque. Chairs had scroll, spiral and columnar legs, surfaces were richly decorated, painted or veneered, and walnut and maple replaced oak as the major working media. Innovations at this time included the butterfly table, and tea and dressing tables also became popular.

COUNTRY 1690–1850
This term is used to describe most simple furniture made between the late 17th and late 19th centuries, which combined both fashionable and more conservative features. As the name suggests, it was supposed to be made by rural artisans, who modified more sophisticated designs to suit rural homes, but some was also made in cities. Pine and maple were the principal woods and surfaces were often painted, with very sparse decoration. Often, features of various styles were combined, those being chosen for ease of crafting. Thus turned William & Mary legs persisted long after they were no longer fashionable elsewhere, and cabriole legs are very rare. Windsor and slat back chairs are perhaps two of the most characteristic products of the Country style.

QUEEN ANNE 1725–50
This followed the English Queen Anne style, with elegant curving forms. Walnut, cherry and maple were the most popular woods, and mahogany began to be imported from around 1750. Finely decorated candlestands and tea-tables with tripod, cabriole bases are typical of this period, and folding games tables and large, drop-leaf tables also emerged at this time.

CHIPPENDALE 1750-80
This was more conservative than its English counterpart and reflected earlier 18th century trends such as ball and claw feet, which were already démodé in London. Designs were much lighter than those of the Queen Anne period and forms became more ornamental. Intricate chair backs, including the ladder back, now became popular. Mahogany was by now the favored wood.

During this period different regional preferences became apparent. Craftsmen in Newport, Rhode Island, for example, followed the classical style more closely, with fluted and reeded columns and legs, whereas their Philadelphia counterparts produced more elaborately carved rococo pieces.

FEDERAL 1780–1820
This was the American answer to neoclassicism. Most furniture of the period will be described as either Sheraton or Hepplewhite, although it is difficult to establish how much American craftsmen actually depended on their designs. In any case, the suggestion that there is a vast difference between them is also somewhat spurious.

The later Federal period saw a much more literal borrowing of Greco-Roman motifs, and the French influence of the Empire Style, whether it came direct or filtered through England, is also apparent. New forms, such as the work table, appeared. Side tables too became popular as did chair backs with a center splat carved with classical motifs such as urn and feather or a series of columns. After 1800, however, chair designs became simpler. The Grecian couch found its modern counterpart as a daybed. Duncan Phyfe was one of the best and most sought after exponents of the Federal style.

SHAKER FURNITURE 1790-1900
This furniture was made by the Shaker religious sect living in Massachusetts, New York and a few other states, and was in the finest tradition of country design. Its heyday lasted from 1820–70 and the furniture is characterized by its simplicity and utility. Form was subsidiary to function. Many pieces reflect the agricultural nature of the Shaker communities, such as tables for sorting seeds. Pine and maple were again the principal woods. Surfaces were unadorned and painted, legs were turned and slender.

EMPIRE 1815–40
The delicacy of early neo-classicism gave way now to heavier classical forms with more

emphasis on outline than on carved detail. In the Empire style, undulating scrolls typically balanced heavy geometric shapes with ornamentation carved in high relief. Mahogany, rosewood veneers and marble were common materials. A French emigré, Charles Henri Lannuier, was among the first to introduce the style to America in the first years of the 19th century. His work combined late Louis XVI and Empire designs and was characterized by the use of gilded caryatids on tables and chairs.

19TH CENTURY REVIVAL STYLES
GOTHIC REVIVAL 1840–1890

In its early stages the Gothic Revival was mainly expressed in decoration, with the use of details imitating historical ornament, such as quatrefoils, trefoils, tracery etc. Designs tended to be extravagant and florid and by the 1850s designers were turning rather towards Norman, Romanesque and Elizabethan models.

A further surge of neo-Gothicism came in the 1870s. This took a much simpler and functional form, and followed the purist theories of William Morris in trying to return to genuinely medieval designs. Walnut, oak and cherry were the woods most used, and decoration consisted of simple turned or cut out elements.

ROCOCO REVIVAL 1840–70

The Rococo Revival, also referred to at the time as the Louis XIV style, reached America around 1840 and persisted for about thirty years. It took a much bolder form than the 18th century style on which it was based, with ornament carved in very high relief on forms which were very 19th century in taste. Ornamentation consisted of florid roses, leaves, vines, scrolls and shells, all richly carved on curving forms, with mahogany, rosewood and walnut as the preferred media. The main output of pieces in this style was concentrated in New York, Boston and Philadelphia, though there were makers all over the States. It was a style favored for 'Social' furniture, such as sofas, the newly introduced tête à têtes, center tables etc. The period too saw an increasing use of upholstery as techniques advanced and comfort became all important.

RENAISSANCE REVIVAL 1850–90

While it began as early as 1850, this is often looked on as a reaction to rococo. Features of both Renaissance and 18th century neoclassical style were combined on straight rectilinear forms. Porcelain and bronze plaques were often incorporated as embellishments, and popular motifs included flowers, medallions, classical busts, caryatids etc, combined with architecturally derived features such as pediments and columns. Light woods, such as walnut, were favored. Pieces were produced both by skilled craftsmen in New York, and mass produced in midwest factories, notably Grand Rapids.

EASTLAKE STYLE 1870–90

This was one of the styles conceived as a rejection of the flamboyance of most of the preceding 'revivals'. It was named for Charles Lock Eastlake, an influential English architect who advocated a return to simple, honest furniture, where there was a basic relationship between form and function.

17th century forms were recalled, and to avoid the simple repetition of classical motifs, new inspiration was sought for decoration from Middle Eastern and Far Eastern sources. Eastlake believed in letting the natural wood grain speak for itself and preferred oak, cherry and rosewood and walnut when not heavily varnished. Later, however, the movement fell away from his high standards, and a great deal of poor quality furniture was produced.

MISSION, AND ARTS & CRAFTS 1900–1925

These again were reactions against much of the design of the 19th century. The Mission style purported to be based on the furniture supposedly found in the old Franciscan Missions in California and was seen as a revival of medieval and other functional designs. It was, broadly speaking, the American expression of the British Arts & Crafts Movement.

Most pieces were executed in oak, forms were rectilinear and functional, the construction simple, often with obvious signs of handwork, such as exposed mortice and tenon joints. Chair backs consisted chiefly of flat vertical or horizontal splats. One of the most important proponents of the style was Gustav Stickley, who was uncompromising in the austerity of his pieces. His brothers, working Grand Rapids, turned out pieces in a similar style, though they were more flexible in their approach to decoration.

AMERICAN
FURNITURE DESIGNERS

THOMAS AFFLECK

Thomas Affleck was born and trained as a cabinet maker in Edinburgh.

He emigrated to America and from 1763 worked in Philadelphia. He worked very much in the contemporary English style, putting his own gloss on Chippendale's designs.

Among his most famous pieces are a set of chairs made for the Senate and House of Representatives whilst Philadelphia was the nation's capital. He died in 1795.

JOHN HENRY BELTER

(1804-1861)

The name of John Henry Belter is synonymous with the American Rococo Revival style. He emigrated to New York from Württemberg, Germany, in 1844, quickly establishing himself as a leading craftsman in the city. He devised a means of using iron cauls and steam to bend and laminate rosewood. The strength thus obtained allowed the use of decoration by intricate piercing and carving of leaves, grapes, vines and bouquets. He also devised a machine for cutting arabesques on chairbacks.

Belter employed many German carvers who emigrated to America during the 1840s, and they brought with them superb skills in naturalistic carving.

THOMAS BROOKS

Thomas Brooks (1811-87) was a New York cabinet maker who from around 1865 produced pieces in the Louis XVI style. He was also known as a maker of Eclectic furniture, which as the name suggests, combined styles and decorative motifs from various periods. A bookcase made by Brooks was presented to Jennie Lind in 1850 and this combines rococo, baroque, Caroline and Renaissance motifs.

CHARLES A. COOLIDGE

Charles Coolidge (1858-1936) was a Boston architect who also designed furniture, desks, chairs and tables in Romanesque and American Colonial styles.

PETER COOPER

Peter Cooper (1791-1883) was the American industrialist and philanthropist who was credited with making America's first metal rocking chair at Trenton NJ sometime in the 1860s. The frame of strap metal was painted in imitation of tortoiseshell and had a continuous button-upholstered seat and back and padded armrests.

CORSET BACK CHAIR

This was an American style of armchair with a high upholstered back curving in at the sides to give a waisted effect. It was at the height of its popularity around 1850.

COTTAGE FURNITURE

This simple furniture was promoted by Andrew Jackson Downing (1815-1852), an American architect and landscape gardener, who advised the working class to furnish their homes with simple, inexpensive and nicely painted 'cottage furniture'. This was cheaply made in factories and then quickly painted by specialists who perfected freehand brushwork and stenciling until it became a routine.

The style also found favor with the wealthier sections of society, who ordered their pieces carefully painted by accomplished artists. The decoration consisted mainly of flowers, birds, vines and fruit, which could be embellished by touches of gilding. This was sometimes also applied to give the illusion of three-dimensional carving. Tables usually had plain or spool turned legs, while the matching spindle-back chairs often featured cane seats. Cottage furniture continued in vogue for some thirty years until the 1880s.

ALEXANDER DAVIS

Alexander Davis (1803-92) was an American architect and associate of A. J. Downing, who designed both buildings and furniture in the gothic style. He had an eye for the picturesque effects of material and the qualities of light and shadow. He was much influenced by the English Gothic Revivalist A. W. Pugin, but adapted these ideas to modern furniture needs.

THE DOMINY FAMILY

This talented family of East Hampton, Long Island, produced three generations of craftsmen, who, from circa 1760-1840, produced clocks and furniture of fine quality. They received their training under what was believed to be a family apprenticeship system. Nathaniel IV became a clockmaker, as did his grandson, Felix, while his son, Nathaniel V, concentrated on cabinet making. The family workshop produced pieces mainly in cherry and local maple, with white pine or tulipwood for drawer bottoms and backboards. There was little carved embellishment, but many pieces were painted, and while some shapes reveal a surprising sophistication, this coexisted with a certain rural naivete.

DUNLAP

The Dunlaps were a prominent family of New Hampshire cabinet makers, who through four generations produced designs which combined traditional elements with the fashion of the day. Samuel II (1751-1830) was one of the fourth generation who worked mainly in maple, and often used a deeply carved shell motif as embellishment.

EASTLAKE

Charles Lock Eastlake (1836-1906) was an English furniture designer and architect who promoted the English Gothic style which became popular both in England and America. He advocated the use of oak, with peg joinery and simple rectangular designs. His pieces emphasised the beauty of the wood grain, and he disliked the use of French polish or other varnish effects. Decoration was usually linear and incised. Many imitators, particularly in America, followed his style, but produced shoddy pieces which he would have abhorred.

GEORGE ELMSLIE

George Grant Elmslie (1871-1952) was a Scottish born architect who was a member of the Prairie School, and worked for a time in Chicago with Frank Lloyd Wright and George Maher. Between 1895 and 1909 he worked as chief draughtsman for the architect Louis Sullivan. His furniture designs were notable for their rich, flowing ornamental detail, often incorporating geometric motifs as organic parts of the structure.

FROTHINGHAM

Benjamin Frothingham (fl c1756-1809) was the son of a joiner with a shop in Milk Street, Boston. Benjamin set up his own shop in Charlestown in 1754, but this was burned down by the British, along with some 25 other cabinet makers' homes and shops on June 17 1775, at the time of the battle of Bunker or Breed's Hill. Frothingham had already seen military service during the French and Indian wars, and now joined the revolutionary forces. He was wounded at Bethlehem PA and by the end of the war had risen to the rank of major. During Washington's triumphal tour of New England, he called on Frothingham in Charlestown to honor one of his most distinguished officers.

Frothingham returned to cabinet making, working in a modified Chippendale style which he adapted to the emerging Federal fashion.

JOHN GODDARD

The eldest son of Daniel and Mary Goddard, John (1724-85) was apprenticed to Job Townsend in Newport, RI. At 21, he became a free man on termination of his apprenticeship, and a year later he married Townsend's daughter Hannah. In 1748 he bought land on the corner of Washington and Willow Street, where he built a house and cabinet shop.

Only three forms are actually documented to Goddard, and these are all slant-front desks. A few others, including dressing tables, have been authenticated to him. Characteristic of his style was the incorporation of a variety of elements within a self-contained, compact design. He is also known for what came to be known as the Goddard foot, a bracket foot sloping outwards beyond the vertical edge of the object.

GRAND RAPIDS FURNITURE

This was a term loosely used for the cheap, factory-produced furniture produced in Grand Rapids, Michigan, from about 1850. The city was to become an important center of furniture making during the 1870s, when many immigrant craftsmen settled there and began producing commercial editions of varying styles of furniture, from Colonial through Louis XVI to Art Nouveau. Their products were exported throughout the North and South American Continent.

CHARLES GREENE

Charles Sumner Greene (1868-1957) was an American architect who practised in Pasadena.

From 1893 he worked with his brother, Henry Mather Greene (1870-1954) designing furniture influenced by Japanese and Mission styles. Their work was also influenced both by Josef Hoffmann and Gustav Stickley, but by 1904 their furniture had evolved into a highly personal style. Intricate structure revealed in a decorative way became their hallmark, and their particular blend of oriental design, (for example 'cloud' shapes) and Art Nouveau meant that their work was easily distinguishable from anything else being produced at the time.

EPHRAIM HAINES

Ephraim Haines (1755-1837) was a Quaker who was apprenticed to the cabinet maker Daniel Trotter in Philadelphia in 1791. He married his master's daughter and inherited the business after the death of Trotter in 1800. His pieces reflect neo-classical style, and the main part of his output consisted of chairs. He was also a successful entrepreneur and alongside his cabinet making activities he specialised in selling timber, the rare exotic woods which were in great demand by cabinet makers throughout the city.

GEORGE HENKELS

George Henkels (1819-1883) was a Philadelphia cabinet maker who worked mainly in the rococo and gothic styles. His preferred materials were rosewood, walnut, mahogany, satinwood and maplewood, and one of his best remembered commissions was a low bed, with ornate side canopy and draped hangings, which he made for the Swedish singer, Jenny Lind..

HERTER BROS.

Christian (1840-1883) and Gustave (fl 1848-1880) were German born half brothers who set up as furniture manufacturers in New York around 1865. Their output had a characteristic style, the chairs often with bulbous-topped front legs, tapering to ring-shaped ankle and trumpet foot. Their tables often had marble tops with the end panels carved in low relief. Many slipper chairs were made, often in ebonised maple, with deeply cushioned round seats and small backs. These could also be inlaid with wave, floral and leaf motifs.

Cherrywood was another favored material, and in the 1870s and 1880s they produced furniture in the Japanese and Eastlake styles.

Gustave returned to Germany around 1870, leaving Christian to take over. He in turn retired around 1880.

GEORGE HUNZINGER

George Hunzinger (fl. 1850-1890) was a German-born furniture manufacturer working in New York. He was noted for his chairs, and developed a number of adjustable and folding designs which he patented in the 1860s. In 1876 he obtained a patent for a steel mesh model. The textile covered mesh pioneered by Hunzinger became something of a hallmark of late 19th century design.

Hunzinger chairs are frequently marked under the seat, and this adds to the value of each piece.

He also worked frequently in the Renaissance Revival style; pieces in this style with unusually shaped arms and legs are often more desirable than plainer examples.

JOHN JELLIFF

John Jelliff (1813-90) was an American cabinet maker working in Newark NJ. He produced furniture in the gothic, rococo and Louis XVI Revival styles, and was also noted for his Renaissance Revival style armchairs in rosewood, with broad, buttoned seats, and trumpet-shaped legs. In the 1870s he made a number of small parlor tables, mainly in rosewood, with exotic wood inlay on the tops.

KNOLL

Hans Knoll came to the United States from Germany in 1937, and set up as a furniture manufacturer in New York in 1939. The firm became known as Knoll Associates in 1946. They produced furniture designed earlier by Mies van der Rohe, for example his Barcelona chair. Later known as Knoll International, they continue to produce good quality pieces in contemporary styles.

LANNUIER

Charles Honoré Lannuier (fl. c 1805-19) was a French born cabinet maker who worked in New York and became that city's most fashionable exponent of the Empire style, with which he combined late Louis XVI designs.

His gilt caryatids on tables and chairs gave his pieces great elegance, and other cabinet makers followed his example, albeit with more restraint.

LIMBERT

Charles Limbert was a furniture designer and maker, working in Grand Rapids, Michigan, around 1900–10. He must have been well acquainted with the two Stickley brothers, George and Albert, who were also active in the town at that period, and Limbert's output owes much to the inspiration of Gustav Stickley.

Limbert worked mainly in the Mission style, named from the furniture supposedly found in the Franciscan missions in California. His work is characterized by its simple, sturdy design, with exposed pegs and tenon ends often as the only decoration.

FRANK LLOYD WRIGHT

(1867-1959)

Frank Lloyd Wright began as a Prairie School architect, who also designed furniture. From 1887 he worked in Chicago, where he designed architectural style furniture, sometimes built-in, which was quite a revolutionary concept for the time. As early as 1906 he designed metal office furniture for his innovative Larkin Building in Buffalo, and all his pieces were characterized by their simplicity. His early output was mostly handmade, but later he came to prefer the clean lines of machine made pieces.

Wright had a profound effect on design world-wide, particularly on the members of the group who were to found De Stijl during the years 1914-1916.

SAMUEL MACINTYRE

Samuel McIntyre (1757-1811) was an American cabinet maker, carver, architect and designer who worked in Salem MA, at that time something of a center for the production of fine furniture. His output was very much in the Federal style, and his pieces were of superb quality. He also carved for other cabinet makers. His most popular motifs were bellflowers, cornucopiae, fruit baskets and grape clusters.

GEORGE WASHINGTON MAHER

G. W. Maher (1864-1926) was an American architect, who as a member of the Prairie School, also designed furniture. In the 1880s, he shared an office with Frank Lloyd Wright and George Elmslie in Chicago. He designed a number of private houses, sometimes decorating complete interiors with a single motif, e.g. thistles, hollyhocks or lions.

MARCOTTE & CO.

This New York firm of furniture makers was established in 1861 by Louis Marcotte, a French-born cabinet maker who emigrated to America in 1854, taking with him examples of French furniture. He was noted for his butterfly motifs in shaded woods and mother of pearl stars on his furniture. By 1861 he had become a leading New York designer. His company was known in the 1860s for its pieces in the Louis XVI style, often finished in black and gilt. Mother of pearl and marquetry were often used for back panels, and suites were frequently upholstered in satin. Later, however, the firm began to produce furniture in the Eastlake style.

ARTHUR & LUCIA MATHEWS

Arthur (1860-1954) and Lucia (1870-1955) Mathews were a husband and wife team of painters and furniture designers working in San Francisco, where they owned a furniture shop employing some 50 craftsmen. Between 1906 and 1920 they collaborated with the cabinet maker Thomas McGlynn to produce very decorative art furniture where shallow relief carving was often enriched with elaborate painted designs. Arthur would usually design the whole shape of a piece, while Lucia painted its decorative surface. They preferred rich and muted colors, for example, poppies, leaves and figures in greens and orange, incised on drawer fronts, sides and perimeters. Art Nouveau and Oriental influence can also be seen. The popularity of their work diminished after the First World War.

JOSEPH MEEKS & SONS

This firm of New York cabinet makers was established in 1797 and opened a showroom in New Orleans in 1835. Their period of greatest popularity was during the 1850s and 1860s, and they produced rococo style parlor furniture, richly decorated and gilded.

MISSION FURNITURE

The Mission style of furniture which was immensely popular around the beginning of the 20th century was essentially the major American expression of the Arts & Crafts style which had recently evolved in England.

Its name derives from the fact that it was supposed to reflect the style of furniture found in the old Franciscan missions of California, and it was seen as a revival of medieval and functional designs.

Most pieces were made in oak, and the forms were rectilinear and as simple and functional as possible. Obvious signs of handiwork, such as exposed mortice and tenon joints were characteristic of the style. Mission furniture was often used in furniture schemes alongside Tiffany glass, Navajo rugs and Morris chairs.

The style flourished until around 1920, and mass-produced pieces are often found.

MITCHELL & RAMMELSBERG

From the 1860s onward, the Midwestern states began to provide real competition to the furniture makers on the Eastern seaboard. The firm of Mitchell and Rammelsberg was founded in Cincinnati in 1844, and within twenty years had grown to become the largest furniture business in the entire United States. They were noted for their good, solid, inexpensive furniture, with deep carving to emulate European sixteenth and seventeenth century styles. Many of their designs were inspired by B. J. Talbert, and featured angular brackets, spindles and trestles, while their Eclectic pieces combined Renaissance Revival and rococo elements.

Most pieces are stenciled with the maker's name.

GEORGE NAKASHIMA

George Nakashima is an American of Japanese ancestry who moved to New Hope, Pennsylvania in 1943 where his striking craftsmanship soon won him considerable attention. He combines both Japanese and traditional American elements in his designs, and pays particular attention to the natural grain and forms of the wood.

DUNCAN PHYFE (1768-1854)

Duncan Phyfe was born in Scotland and came to the States with his parents in 1783-4. Within ten years he had established his own shop in New York, where he was still in business in 1840.

His name is synonymous with high quality furniture, mainly at first in the Sheraton and Regency style, but afterwards showing French Directoire and Empire influence.

Common motifs which appear on his work include reeding, lyre, ribbons, swags and acanthus.

QUAINT FURNITURE

Apart from furniture produced by G. & A. Stickley, the Quaint, or fanciful style was the name also given to the Art Nouveau style which flourished between c. 1895–1905. It combined elements of Anglo-Japanese, Arts & Crafts, Glasgow School and Continental Art Nouveau furniture and was characterized by painted and inlaid floral motifs, heart-shaped apertures and ornate hinges.

With regard to decoration, 18th century forms were often used as the basic inspiration. Cabinets and armchairs had thin legs, and often six or eight of them, with low stretchers.

Especially popular were versions of the Windsor chair and asymmetrical sofas. The woods used were mainly polished rosewood, fumed oak and cheap woods stained green or purple.

At its best Quaint furniture was restrained in form and decoration, whereas cheaper imitations tended to be over elaborate. Names of designers and manufacturers associated with the style include William Birch, George Ellwood, J S Henry and E G Punnett.

ANTHONY QUERVELLE

Anthony Quervelle (1789-1856) was a Parisian émigré who arrived in Philadelphia in 1817, and started to produce cabinet work of outstanding quality. He worked in the Empire style, but added features such as specimen marble tops to tables, and restrained leaf carving, to make his pieces particularly elegant. He received commissions from the White House where he made three center tables for the East Room.

BENJAMIN RANDOLPH
(fl c 1750-90)

Benjamin Randolph was another Philadelphia furniture maker who lived through turbulent times and adapted dramatically to meet the prevailing circumstances. He became a dispatch rider for General Washington, and sold his city property and cabinet maker's tools to move to New Jersey, where he produced pig iron at the Speedwell Furnace.

After the war he again reverted to cabinet making, working in the Philadelphia Chippendale style.

HENRY RICHARDSON

Henry Richardson (1836-1886) was a Boston architect who insisted on architecturally designed furniture which would complement the other fittings and structure of his overall designs. His styles were much influenced by the writings of Talbert and Eastlake. His pieces tended to be large and of sound construction, with simple, graceful outlines. Many pieces were probably designed by his staff, without his personal input. Later pieces tended to follow American Colonial style.

CHARLES ROHLFS

The career of Charles Rohlfs (1853-1936) had a couple of false starts as an actor and a designer of cast iron stoves, before he set up as a furniture maker in Buffalo, NY, around 1890.

He favored simple, plain, linear styles, often with unusual carved decoration, which tended to follow the patterns suggested by the wood grain.

Such forms perhaps led him to the Art Nouveau style in which he also came to work. He exhibited successfully at the International Exposition of Modern Decorative Arts in Turin in 1902, and the Louisiana Purchase International Exposition of 1904. A couple of uncharacteristically formal pieces of his were even made for Buckingham Palace.

Rohlfs supervised the design of many office suites and domestic interiors, and employed about eight craftsmen who implemented his designs. His custom made pieces are marked *R*, enclosed in a rectangular frame of wood saw, with date under, either burnt or incised into the frame. Rohlfs retired circa 1925.

ROYCROFT

Elbert Hubbard (1856–1915) was an American soap manufacturer who became fired with enthusiasm for the Arts & Crafts movement after a visit to Britain in 1894. In 1895 he established the Roycroft shops, a craft community based in East Aurora, NY, to produce pieces in the Arts & Crafts style.

Thus they were one of the major manufacturers of Mission style furniture, mainly in oak and mahogany, often with leather seats and copper studs on armchairs. They also produced, between 1905–12, a kind of deck chair, with three slats in the back, which was known as the Morris chair. Their pieces were known as Aurora Colonial Furniture from 1905. In 1908 a copper workshop was set up, making bookends, trays, inkwells etc. Following his visit to England, Hubbard also bought a printing press, on which he printed some fine books, such as The Song of Songs, on handmade paper.

WILLIAM SAVERY

William Savery (172-88) was a Quaker joiner and cabinetmaker who had a shop at the Sign of the Chair below Market on Second Street in Philadelphia. He produced fine, sturdy pieces in the Chippendale style for Philadelphians who liked their furniture to be practical as well as elegant.

JOHN & THOMAS SEYMOUR

This father and son emigrated to America from England, settling in Falmouth, Maine, in 1784. Ten years later they moved to Boston, where they prospered as cabinet makers, as did many craftsmen who made furniture in advanced foreign styles.

Their pieces show the clear influence of Sheraton and Hepplewhite, and are often distinguished by ivory inlay. Other decorative devices typical of the Seymours include narrow dovetails and finely cut tenons, imaginative carved and inlaid decoration, rich veneers and delicate banding. Cupboard interiors are often painted light blue. They frequently featured tambour doors on their pieces, and also made many items in satinwood, mahogany and maple, often combining more than one type of wood in a single piece.

In 1804, Thomas opened a furniture warehouse on Common Street, Boston. Records show that John Seymour died at the age of eighty in August 1818.

STICKLEY

The Arts & Crafts Movement found one of its greatest exponents in the USA in Gustav Stickley (1857–1942). He was the eldest of six brothers who all went into furniture making, though he at first trained as a mason.

In his youth he designed mainly chairs in the American Colonial style, but in 1898 he founded the firm of Gustav Stickley of Syracuse, New York, which specialized in the Arts & Crafts or Mission style of furniture (from the furniture supposedly found in the old Franciscan missions in California). He also published a magazine 'The Craftsman' which popularized this new style.

Like Art Nouveau, of which this was the American version, the style was seen as being a return to the simple functional style of the medieval period. Oak was the most popular wood, and construction was simple, often with obvious signs of handiwork, such as exposed mortice and tenon joints. Chairbacks were usually constructed as a series of flat vertical or horizontal boards.

Interestingly five of the brothers went into the same line of business, and the relationship between them seems to have been a highly political one. George and Albert worked in Grand Rapids, Michigan from 1891, and formed the firm of Stickley Bros. Co. around 1901. Their furniture is similar to the Craftsman style, often characterized by through tenons, but it was generally inferior in quality in terms of wood, design and finish. It was marketed as Quaint Furniture. They also produced independent designs similar to English cottage furniture.

The other two brothers, Leopold and J. George, were at first employed by Gustav but left his employment to found L. & J.G. Stickley at Fayetteville, in 1900. They too based their designs on Craftsman furniture, sometimes using veneers and laminated members, and their pieces are identifiable by the name L. & J.G. Stickley in red. They were open to other influences, however, which may help to account for their survival, and made furniture designed by Frank Lloyd Wright, the Morris chair, and by 1914 were turning out reproduction furniture as well.

When one refers to 'Stickley' it is undoubtedly Gustav who springs most readily to mind. Certainly he was the most original designer of the family, he was also the purist, and his pieces are often austere in their unadorned simplicity. His brothers were perhaps more realistic in seeing that their products also had to find a market, and they were readier to compromise in terms of putting some embellishments on the basic style. It may have been Gustav's unwillingness to compromise his ideals that led to the break with Leopold and J. George, and it may also be why, by 1915, he was bankrupt. He attempted to soldier on, selling new lines based loosely on 18th century styles, or in bright colors, but to no avail. It was left to L. & J.G. to buy him out in 1916, when the business became the Stickley Manufacturing Co. Under this name it is still active, chiefly producing American Colonial reproduction furniture in cherrywood.

THE TOWNSENDS

The Townsend dynasty of cabinet makers was established in Newport, Rhode Island, by Job (1699-1765) and his brother Christopher (1701-73). It was perpetuated by Job's son Edmund (1736-1811) and Christopher's son John (1721-1809, and collectively they became known as the Newport School.

They worked in a baroque style, and, together with his son in law, John Goddard, Job Townsend created a style characterised by the use of block fronts, often decorated with shell motifs.

The use of the block front in fact reached its highest artistic level in Boston and Newport and reflects design theories transmitted to Colonial Americans through the immigration of Continental or English craftsmen. It survived here long after the taste for block fronted furniture had declined abroad.

Newport shell carving is also unique, with generous volutes terminating at the lower edges.

Classical carved mahogany and mahogany veneer bedstead, Mid Atlantic States, 1825–35, with reeded raked crest above spiral carved columns, 79in. wide. (Skinner) **$1,265**

Child's bed, circa 1820, in tiger maple with acorn finials. (Eldred's) **$357**

A classical mahogany sleigh bed, New York, 1820–1840, on rectangular molded feet and casters, 60³/₄in. wide. (Christie's) **$2,250**

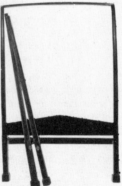

One of a pair of mahogany Mission oak beds, possibly Roycroft, circa 1912, 42in. wide. (Skinner) **$1,000**

A Chippendale mahogany tall post bed, Goddard-Townsend School, Rhode Island, circa 1770, 54in. wide, 86in. high. (Skinner) **$8,750**

A Victorian carved walnut high-post bedstead, Southern States, 19th century, with rectangular molded tester above molded tapering posts, 65in. wide. (Christie's) **$3,220**

A red-painted high-post bedstead, Texas, mid-19th century, the rectangular tester above octagonal tapering headposts, 52¹/₂in. wide. (Christie's) **$3,910**

George III style mahogany tester bed, raised on Marlborough legs, approximate height 94¹/₂in. (Skinner Inc.) **$2,500**

An American late classical mahogany tester bedstead, mid 19th century, by D. Barjon, on columnar feet with casters and shaped rails, 74¹/₄in. wide. (Christie's) **$7,101**

A classical mahogany sleigh bed, Philadelphia, 1820–1840, the serpentine head and foot board each with scrolling crestrail terminating in swans' heads, 78in. long.
(Christie's) $4,600

A good dark green and red-painted maple and poplar lowpost bedstead, Pennsylvania, early 19th century, with ball finials on turned posts, 47½in.
(Sotheby's) $690

George Nakashima walnut slab double bed, New Hope, Pennsylvania, circa 1960, raised on three shaped blade boards, walnut slab footboard, inscribed signature, 82¹/₈in. long.
(Skinner) $8,050

A rare red-painted cherrywood and pine, child's bedstead, American, first half 19th century, has full set of cotton crocheted hangings, width 36in.
(Sotheby's) $4,000

Late 18th/early 19th century pine deception bedstead, Penn., in the form of a slant-front desk with four sham graduated long drawers, the back enclosing a hinged bedstead, 48in. high, 93in. long. (Christie's) $1,100

American maple faux bamboo bed, circa 1880, headboard, footboard, side rails, turned finials, incised details, 72½in. long. (Skinner Inc.) $1,150

An Empire grain painted tall post bed, possibly Mahantango Valley, Penn., circa 1825, 51in. wide. (Skinner Inc.) $4,500

Late 19th century American walnut bed of Eastlake influence, 58½in. wide. $2,000

Mission oak double bed with exposed tenons, circa 1907, 58½in. wide.
(Skinner) $3,100

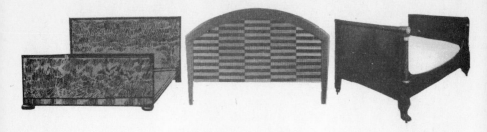

An Art Deco burl and ash bed, American, circa 1930, 4ft. 6in. wide. $950

"Tady" headboard, designed by Ferruccio Tritta, produced by Studio Nove, New York, offset geometric design marquetry of walnut and ebony, 63$\frac{1}{2}$in. wide. (Skinner Inc.) $1,500

A classical mahogany bedstead, Duncan Phyfe, New York, 1815–1833, the paneled head and foot boards with cylindrical crest rails, 58$\frac{3}{4}$in. wide. (Christie's) $11,500

A fine paint decorated cannon-ball bedstead, probably Eastern Connecticut, circa 1840, the whole exuberantly sponge-painted with patterns of red dots on a yellow-gold ground, 54$\frac{1}{4}$in. wide. (Sotheby's) $4,600

Painted and stencil decorated turned low post bed, New England, 1830–45, old red ground with black accents and gold stenciled decoration, 51in. wide. (Skinner) $920

An unusual paint decorated bedstead, Pennsylvania or Ohio, mid 19th century, the tall shaped headboard flanked by block and baluster-turned headposts, 53in. wide. (Sotheby's) $7,188

One of a pair of Arts & Crafts inlaid beds, attributed to Herter Bros., circa 1870, oak burl and other veneers, 26$\frac{1}{2}$in. wide.   (Two) $2,500

Fine Aesthetic inlaid, gilt-incised and carved walnut and burled walnut three-piece bedroom suite by Herter Brothers, New York, circa 1880. (Butterfield & Butterfield) $25,000

Tall post cherry and maple bed, probably Connecticut, circa 1780, old refinish, 47$\frac{1}{2}$in. wide. (Skinner) $4,025

FEDERAL

A late Federal figured maple bedstead, 62in. wide, overall. $3,750

A late Federal carved mahogany bedstead, the footposts on brass ball feet, 57in. wide. $16,000

A Federal maple and birch tall post tester bed, New England, circa 1820, 57in. wide, 80in. long. $6,500

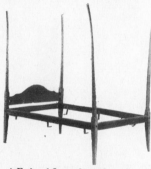

A Federal figured maple and pine 'pencil-post' bedstead, New England, circa 1800, with octagonal flaring posts with 'lamb's-tongue' corners, 4ft. 3in. wide.
(Sotheby's) $12,650

A good Federal red-stained birchwood, maple and pine four-poster bed, New England, circa 1800, with four flaring octagonal posts, 4ft. 4in. wide.
(Sotheby's) $3,162

A late Federal turned maple bedstead, Pennsylvania, circa 1830, with acorn finials on reel- and vase-turned posts, 4ft. 4in. wide.
(Sotheby's) $2,587

Early 19th century Federal painted walnut pencil-post bedstead, North Carolina, 52½in. wide, overall.
$7,250

A Federal turned curly maple four-post bedstead, American, circa 1815, having an arched tester, 6ft. 7in. long.
(Sotheby's) $5,500

A Federal carved mahogany four-post bedstead, Mass., circa 1820, 76in. long, 47¼in. wide. $10,000

A Federal inlaid birch and mahogany high-post bedstead, possibly New Hampshire, 1800–1820,
the rectangular arched headboard flanked by ring-turned headposts on square legs continuing to
reeded, ring, baluster and urn-turned footposts above square tapering line-inlaid legs with spade
feet all surmounted by an arched tester, 57in. wide.
(Christie's) $2,070

FEDERAL

A Federal mahogany high-post bedstead, Mass., 1790-1810, with D-shaped headboard, 53½in. wide. **$7,000**

A Federal maple highpost bedstead, New England, 1800-20, 54in. wide. **$7,250**

A Federal figured maple and ebonized high-post bedstead, Mass., 1810-20, 59in. wide. (Christie's) **$1,750**

A Federal birchwood and maple four-post bedstead, New England, circa 1810, on tapered feet, with tester. (Sotheby's) **$7,500**

A late Federal carved mahogany high post bedstead, Massachusetts, 1810-1820, the footposts spiral turned with acanthus and waterleaf carved inverted balusters, 58in. wide. (Christie's New York) **$3,500**

A late Federal carved cherrywood four-post bedstead, probably New York, circa 1825, 53¼in. wide. **$10,000**

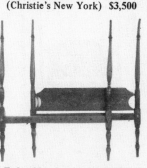

A fine Federal figured mahogany four-post bedstead, Philadelphia, circa 1800, the horizontal box tester on flaring ring-turned supports, 6ft. 8in. long. (Sotheby's) **$2,300**

Federal birch carved red painted tall post tester bed, probably Massachusetts, 1815-20, ring turned head posts and shaped headboard, 73in. long. (Skinner) **$13,800**

A good Federal brown-painted birchwood and pine bedstead, North Coast New England, circa 1810, the octagonal headposts centering a pitched pine headboard, 4ft. 5in. wide. (Sotheby's) **$11,500**

FEDERAL

Federal birch red stained canopy bed, New England, circa 1815, original finish, 54in. wide. (Skinner) $4,025

A Federal carved maple high-post bedstead, Mass., 1790-1810, 57in. wide. $12,500

A fine Federal carved mahogany bedstead, Philadelphia, circa 1800, having a shaped headboard, 7ft. long. (Sotheby's) $20,000

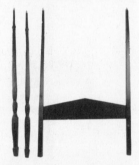

A Federal carved mahogany four-post bedstead, American, probably Salem, Massachusetts, 19th century, the feet with foliate caps, 80in. long. (Sotheby's) $3,000

Federal mahogany tall post bed, New England, circa 1800, square tapering headposts flank head board, reeded footposts, 55in. wide. (Skinner Inc.) $2,850

A Federal turned birchwood bedstead, New England, circa 1820, with flaring octagonal head posts centering an arched pine headboard, 45in. wide. (Sotheby's) $2,070

A late Federal turned and figured maple bedstead, American, possibly Southern, 1830, the turned, molded egg-shape finials above ring-turned flaring posts, 4ft. 7in. wide. (Sotheby's) $5,750

Federal eagle-carved mahogany four poster bedstead, attributed to Joseph Barry, Philadelphia, Pennsylvania, circa 1820, on vase-form feet, 63³/₄in. wide. (Sotheby's) $26,450

A late Federal carved mahogany four-poster bedstead, New York, first quarter 19th century, the headposts and footposts reeded and waterleaf-carved, 69in. wide. (Sotheby's) $2,875

An Aesthetic inlaid and gilt-decorated ebonized bedstead, attributed to Herter Brothers (1865–
1905), New York City, circa 1880, the headboard with a stepped crest centered by a scalloped rail
over a spindle-turned gallery above a tulip-inlaid frieze flanked by floral and linear incised and
gilded stiles further flanked by similar galleries and similar stiles each surmounted by a gilt and
incised turned finial, all over three conforming gilt and incised panels flanked by shaped and
similarly embellished brackets above similarly incised and inlaid side rails continuing to a
footboard with a ring and columnar turned crest, 63in. wide.
(Christie's) $4,600

HERTER

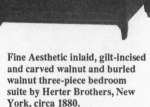

An American 'Aesthetic Movement double bed, in the manner of the Herter Brothers, New York, circa 1880, the headboard with a carved pierced, gilt and ebonised cresting, 5ft. wide.
(Sotheby's) $4,000

Fine Aesthetic inlaid, gilt-incised and carved walnut and burled walnut three-piece bedroom suite by Herter Brothers, New York, circa 1880.
(Butterfield & Butterfield)
$25,000

Fine American Renaissance figured maple and rosewood three-piece bedroom suite comprising a bedstead, nightstand, and dresser, by Herter Brothers, New York, circa 1872.
(Butterfield & Butterfield)
$15,000

NEW ENGLAND

A green-painted maple pencil-post bedstead, New England, circa 1800, with four tapering octagonal posts centering a pitched red-stained pine headboard, 55$\frac{1}{2}$in. wide.
(Sotheby's) $6,900

Painted tall post bed, Northern New England, 1825–35, with original tester, headboard and side rails, original red paint with black accents, 52in. wide.
(Skinner) $3,335

A very rare maple folding pencil-post bedstead, New England, 1770–1800, the tapered and faceted head posts centering the original shaped pine headboard, 4ft. 4in. wide.
(Sotheby's) $5,750

SHERATON

American Sheraton four-post double bed, in maple with turned posts, 83in. high.
(Eldred's) $825

Antique American Sheraton field bed in maple with pine headboard, turned posts, with canopy, 50in. wide.
(Eldred's) $1,650

Antique American Sheraton field bed, in cherry, vase and ribbed posts, original bowed tester and pine headboard, approx. 52in. wide.
(Eldred's) $1,760

STICKLEY

Fine and rare Gustav Stickley child's bed, original deep brown finish, Gustav red decal, 35½in. wide.
(Skinner) **$8,050**

L. & J.G. Stickley davenport bed, circa 1912, no. 285, seat rail slides out opening to a bed, 77in. long.
(Skinner Inc.) **$2,100**

A Gustav Stickley spindle-sided baby's crib, no. 919, circa 1907, 56½in. long.
$2,250

A Gustav Stickley oak bed, designed by Harvey Ellis, 59½in. wide.
(Skinner) **$37,000**

An L. & J. G. Stickley slatted double-bed, signed with red (Handcraft) decal, 58in. wide.
(Skinner) **$1,500**

Gustav Stickley double bed, circa 1907, no.. 923, tapering vertical posts centering five wide slats, signed, 57½in. wide.
(Skinner Inc.) **$4,000**

L. & J. G. Stickley oak double bed, Fayetteville, New York, circa 1910, signed, 50in. high, 58in. wide.
(Skinner Inc.) **$7,500**

L. & J. G. Stickley oak daybed, model 291, 1906–1912, the square slatted end set with an angled rattan woven headrest, 6ft. 4in. long.
(Butterfield & Butterfield) **$1,265**

Pair of Gustav Stickley oak twin beds, 40in. wide.
(Skinner) **$6,250**

A polychrome-decorated poplar blanket chest, Pennsylvania, dated 1796, the hinged rectangular top opening to a well, the case painted with a central lozenge with the initials *CAHR* and the date *1796*, the molded base below on ogee bracket feet; painted allover in tones of white, green and red on an ocher field, 4ft. 4in. wide. (Sotheby's) $6,612

A rare Pilgrim century carved maple and pine two-drawer blanket chest, Hadley-Hatfield area, Massachusetts, 1700–1720, the rectangular cleated hinged top opening to a well above a case with three inset panels and two drawers below; the front of the case decorated with scrolling vines with tulips and strapwork, the two outer panels carved with tulips and each centering the initial *K K*, centering a flowerhead- and tulip-carved panel, the sides of the case with two inset panels and the stiles continuing to form flattened ball feet. Interior of lid bears an inscription, *Peter Butler*, 47in. wide. (Sotheby's) $48,300

Pine blanket chest, probably New England, early 19th century, refinished, replaced brass, 38¹/₂in. wide. (Skinner Inc.) $850

Pine pigmented blanket chest, probably Watervliet, New York, circa 1810, the case with thumbmolded top, 39in. wide. (Skinner) $1,035

Antique American lift-top blanket chest in pine, painted black, two drawers, bracket feet, 37in. wide. (Eldred's) $700

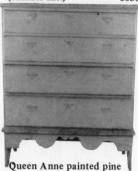

Queen Anne painted pine blanket chest, New England, circa 1750, the molded lift lid above case of two false and two working thumb molded drawers, 40in. wide. (Skinner Inc.) $7,500

A William and Mary red-painted poplar one-drawer blanket chest, Connecticut, 1700-1750, the hinged molded top above two false drawers and one long drawer 40in. wide. (Sotheby's) $3,162

A grain-painted blanket chest, New England, 1760–1780, on bracket feet, the drawers sponge grained and mustard colored, the case sponge grained and red, 43³/₄in. wide. (Christie's) $6,900

Antique American blanket chest, in curly maple with lift top, three false drawers over two full-length drawers, bracket base, 37¹/₂in. wide. (Eldred's) $2,970

Painted pine blanket chest, probably Western Massachusetts, 1730–50, with original ball feet, half round moldings, 36in. wide. (Skinner) $4,025

Grain painted blanket chest, New England, second quarter 19th century, all-over ocher and burnt umber simulated mahogany graining, 38in. wide. (Skinner Inc.) $1,750

American lift-top blanket chest, in old brown grain paint with stenciled decoration, 38in. long. (Eldred's) $770

Painted and decorated pine blanket chest, Pennsylvania, circa 1786, the polychrome painted rectangular hinged molded edge top with molded bread board ends opening to a compartment with a till, length 4ft. 3³/₄in. (Butterfield & Butterfield) $5,463

Salmon grain painted pine blanket chest, New England, late 18th century, 42in. wide. (Skinner) $2,000

An extremely rare William and Mary blue- and red-paint-decorated pine two-drawer blanket chest, Eastern Massachusetts, 1700–50, with a hinged rectangular top opening to a well, 39¹/₂in. wide. (Sotheby's) $129,000

A painted and decorated blanket chest, York County, Pennsylvania, late 18th/early 19th century, the rectangular top with molded edges centering two red and green painted pinwheel motifs, 47in. wide. (Christie's) $29,900

A Queen Anne painted pine two-drawer blanket box, the lift-lid above three false drawers and two working drawers, probably Mass., circa 1750, 38³/₄in. wide. (Skinner) $3,000

A rare William and Mary green- and brown-painted poplar and pine one-drawer blanket chest, Long Island, New York, 1700–50, 41¹/₂in. wide. (Sotheby's) $8,050

American two-drawer lift-top blanket chest, in pine with old red stain, molded top edge, shaped bracket base, 45in. wide. (Eldred's) $302

A Country Chippendale tiger maple blanket chest, New England, circa 1760, 37³/₄in. wide. $11,875

American blanket chest, in pine with old brown finish, molded upper and lower edges, paneled sides and front, 41½in. wide. (Eldred's) **$1,760**

A Chippendale blue painted and decorated blanket chest, signed Johannes Rank, Dauphin County, 1794, the blue painted rectangular top with two orange bordered square reserves, 51½in. wide. (Christie's) **$5,700**

Painted pine blanket box, possibly New York, early 19th century, the lift top opens to a well with open till, 47in. wide. (Skinner Inc.) **$3,900**

Painted pine blanket chest, New England, circa 1750, old red paint, replaced brasses, 38¾in. wide. (Skinner Inc.) **$1,875**

A Chippendale mahogany blanket chest, labeled by William Savery (1721–1787), Philadelphia, circa 1760, the hinged rectangular molded top above a compartment fitted with a till and two secret short drawers, 48in. wide. (Christie's) **$5,000**

A Chippendale poplar blanket chest, New England, circa 1780, 37¾in. wide. (Skinner) **$1,175**

American lift-top blanket chest, 18th century, in maple with tiger maple top, three drawers with molded fronts and brass escutcheons, 39in. wide. (Eldred's) **$935**

An inlaid walnut blanket chest, Lancaster County, Pennsylvania, dated *1772*, the exterior centering two raised lozenge panels with molded surrounds, 48¾in. wide. (Christie's) **$5,520**

A red pine painted joined blanket chest, America, circa 1820, 37½in. wide. **$1,000**

Late 18th/early 19th century painted pine blanket chest, Penn., 50in. wide.
(Christie's) $4,100

Antique American lift-top blanket chest in pine with two drawers, scrolled bracket base, 44in. wide.
(Eldred's) $242

A red painted blanket chest, possibly Pennsylvania, 19th century, the rectangular top with batten edges, 43in. wide.
(Christie's) $2,400

A carved pine blanket chest, signed *Ship Eagle, E. O'Brien, Curling Master*, dated *1859*, the rectangular hinged lid opening to a well, 43½in. long.
(Sotheby's) $12,650

A paint-decorated pine diminutive blanket chest, New York State, dated *1829*, the rectangular molded hinged lid opening to a well with a till, 43in. long.
(Sotheby's) $67,400

An unusual carved and red-painted pine blanket chest, New England, circa 1800, the hinged rectangular top above a conformingly-shaped case, 4ft. wide.
(Sotheby's) $3,450

A paint decorated pine six-board blanket box, New England, early 19th century, the top, front and sides grain-painted with red and yellow reserves, 37¼in. long.
(Sotheby's) $8,050

A grain-painted and stencil-decorated pine blanket chest, Pennsylvania, circa 1825, the hinged rectangular top opening to a well fitted with a till, 4ft. 1in. wide.
(Sotheby's) $4,312

A William and Mary walnut blanket chest, Pennsylvania, early 18th century, the molded hinged lid opening to an interior with till with hinged cover, 47½in. wide.
(Sotheby's) $3,000

Child's painted and decorated blanket box, Pennsylvania, first quarter 19th century, decorated with red, yellow, black and green, 15in. wide.
(Skinner Inc.) $12,500

A fine paint decorated pine blanket chest, Pennsylvania, circa 1820, the whole in original painted and vinegar-grained decorations, 39¼in. wide.
(Sotheby's) $13,800

A fine paint decorated two-drawer dower chest, Pennsylvania, circa 1830, the whole grain-painted in orange and yellow, 46in. wide.
(Sotheby's) $12,650

Paint decorated poplar blanket box, probably Pennsylvania or Ohio, early 19th century, 35½in. wide.
(Skinner) $15,000

Early 19th century grain painted blanket box, New England, 38¼in. wide.
(Skinner) $950

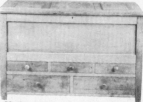

Shaker cherry blanket box, South Union or Pleasant Hill, Kentucky, circa 1840, on turned legs, 20½in. wide.
(Skinnner) $1,955

A sulphur inlaid walnut blanket chest, attributed to Peter Holl (d. 1775) or Peter Holl II (d. 1784), Pennsylvania, dated 1765, 51½in. wide.
(Christie's) $19,550

A red, green and yellow-painted pine blanket chest, Pennsylvania, circa 1790, the hinged rectangular top decorated with two pinwheels, 43in. wide.
(Sotheby's) $5,750

A blue-painted and polychrome-decorated pine blanket chest, Windsor Township, Northern Berks County, Pennsylvania, dated 1787, 4ft. 2in. long.
(Sotheby's) $11,500

Painted pine blanket box, probably Connecticut River Valley, circa 1840, the rectangular hinged top opens to an interior with lidded till, 25¾in. high.
(Skinner) $1,750

A Chippendale walnut blanket chest, Pennsylvania, 1760–1780, the rectangular hinged lid over a conforming case with a molded base, on bracket feet, 51¾in. wide.
(Christie's) $2,420

A polychrome-decorated brown-painted pine blanket chest, signed by Johannes Rank or Ranck, Jonestown, Pennsylvania, circa 1795, 4ft. 3½in. wide.
(Sotheby's) $9,775

Painted pine blanket box, probably New Hampshire, first half 19th century, original blue paint, one original pull, 45¾in. wide.
(Skinner Inc.) $1,750

A fine and very rare blue-green and white-painted pine blanket chest, attributed to Johannes Spitler, Shenandoah County, Virginia, circa 1800, 4ft. wide.
(Sotheby's) $74,000

A grain painted blanket box, the molded lift-top on dove-tailed base and cut-out bracket feet, Conn., circa 1850, 40½in. wide.
(Skinner) $800

Country **Federal** grain and putty decorated blanket chest, Central Massachusetts, circa 1820, 38in. wide.
(Skinner) **$5,250**

Late 18th/early 19th century Chippendale tiger maple two drawer blanket chest, New England, 38¾in. wide.
(Christie's) **$3,300**

Antique American lift-top two-drawer blanket chest, in pine with snipe hinges, original brasses, 41in. long.
(Eldred's) **$715**

A rare Queen Anne carved and painted pine and maple child's blanket chest with drawer, Connecticut, possibly Guilford-Saybrook area, 1740–70, 19³/₄in. wide.
(Sotheby's) **$2,415**

A paint-decorated poplar and maple blanket-chest, Pennsylvania, 19th century, the hinged and molded rectangular top opening to a compartment fitted with a till, 38⁵/₈in. long.
(Christie's) **$17,000**

A William and Mary grain-painted blanket-chest, Connecticut, 1725–1735, the case with applied molding with two sham and two long drawers, 41¹/₂in. wide.
(Christie's) **$3,250**

Painted blanket chest, New England, circa 1830, the top opens to paper lined interior, with lidded molded till above two drawers, 39in. wide.
(Skinner Inc.) **$4,400**

Grain painted pine blanket chest, probably New England, 18th century, the over-hanging top with thumb molded edge, 42in. wide.
(Skinner Inc.) **$3,150**

Grain painted pine blanket chest, New England, 18th century, the molded top overhangs a dovetailed case with a well, 43¼in. wide.
(Skinner Inc.) **$30,000**

A Classical mahogany veneered desk-and-bookcase, American, 1810–1830, in three sections; the detachable cornice with a broken pediment centered by a carved and gilded eagle finial above a rectangular frieze; the upper case fitted with four glazed and interlaced doors; the lower case with a rectangular medial shelf above a banded and veneered long sliding fall-front door opening to a compartmented interior over two paneled doors, all flanked by paneled doors, 84¼in. wide. (Christie's) $14,950

Limbert miniature book-case with heart cut-out gallery, circa 1910, 24in. wide. $1,880

Arts and Crafts bookcase, Jamestown, Ohio, circa 1912, cut out gallery flanked by two cabinet doors, 51½in. wide. (Skinner Inc.) $2,000

A classical mahogany library-case, New York, 1810–1830, on foliate-carved and gadrooned bun feet, 47½in. wide. (Christie's) $4,700

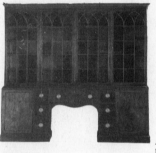

An Aesthetic ebonized and inlaid cherrywood book-case by Herter Bros., N. Y., circa 1880-85, 63½in. wide. $16,500

A Federal mahogany bookcase, Philadelphia, 1790–1810, the two bookcase sections each with double cupboard doors glazed in a Gothic-arch pattern enclosing adjustable shelves, on a molded base, 119in. wide. (Christie's) $27,000

A classical mahogany desk-and-bookcase, probably New York, circa 1820–1840, the upper section with cove-molded pediment above a crossbanded frieze over a pair of Gothic-glazed cupboard doors, on acanthus-carved paw feet, 45½in. wide. (Christie's) $5,000

Shop of the Crafters inlaid bookcase, Cincinnati, Ohio, 1906, with pierced detail over two glass doors, 28¼in. wide. (Skinner) $2,500

Renaissance Revival walnut and burl walnut bookcase, circa 1875–85, with wooden shelves, 55¼in. wide. (Skinner) $1,955

A small Chippendale maho-gany desk bookcase, Mass., circa 1780, 34in. wide. (Skinner) $17,500

BOOKCASES

Renaissance Revival walnut bureau bookcase, circa 1870, drop-front desk enclosing a fitted interior, 51in. wide. (Skinner) $1,850

A very fine Federal inlaid mahogany breakfront bookcase, Salem, Massachusetts, circa 1800, in two parts, on tapering legs, 5ft. 7³/₄in. wide. (Sotheby's) $125,000

Tiger maple glazed desk and bookcase, Ohio, mid 19th century, refinished, 38in. wide. (Skinner) $2,310

A classical carved and figured mahogany bookcase cabinet, probably New York State, circa 1830, the upper section with shaped pediment, 62in. wide. (Sotheby's) $4,025

A classical figured mahogany bookcase, Mid-Atlantic States, probably Philadelphia, circa 1840s, in three parts, width of mid-molding 7ft. 8in. (Sotheby's) $5,750

A small Federal carved cherry glazed bookcase on chest, probably Connecticut, circa 1800, the upper case with moulded and dentiled broken pediment, 32½in. wide. (Skinner) $48,000

Rare Limbert two-door bookcase, tapered sides, arched base, paneled sides, corbels, three adjusting shelves, 36in. wide. (Skinner) $3,105

A late Federal figured mahogany breakfront bookcase, New York or Philadelphia, circa 1815, in two parts, 6ft. wide. (Sotheby's) $24,150

Classical mahogany veneer glazed bookcase, New England, circa 1840, the five-shelved upper case above recessed paneled doors, 48½in. wide. (Skinner) $2,990

STICKLEY

L. & J. G. Stickley two-door bookcase, style no. 645, circa 1912, 49in. wide. (Skinner) $4,400

L. & J. G. Stickley three door bookcase, circa 1906, no. 647, gallery top and exposed key tenons over three doors, unsigned, 70in. wide. (Skinner) $6,250

L. & J.G. Stickley two-door bookcase, attributed, original finish with vibrant quarter-sawn oak, replaced back, 45in. wide. (Skinner) $1,610

A rare and important Gustav Stickley inlaid two door bookcase, designed by Harvey Ellis, circa 1903-1904, signed with red decal in a box, 55¾in. wide. (Skinner) $62,000

L. & J. G. Stickley single door bookcase, circa 1907, no. 643, gallery top with exposed key tenons over single door, 36in. wide. (Skinner) $3,100

Gustav Stickley double door bookcase, Eastwood, New York, circa 1907, gallery top over two doors each with eight panes, 48in. wide. (Skinner Inc.) $3,100

An L. & J. G. Stickley two-door bookcase, no. 654, circa 1910, 50in. wide. (Skinner) $4,400

L. & J. G. Stickley two door bookcase, Fayetteville, New York, circa 1907, unsigned, (escutcheons replaced) 42in. wide. (Skinner Inc.) $5,000

A Gustav Stickley two-door bookcase, no. 718, signed with large red decal, circa 1904-05, 54in. wide. (Skinner) $6,250

STICKLEY

L. & J. G. Stickley narrow bookcase with adjustable shelves, circa 1912, no. 652, 22in. wide.
(Skinner) $3,100

A two-door oak bookcase, twelve panels to each door, by Gustav Stickley, circa 1904, 48in. wide.
(Skinner) $9,300

A Gustav Stickley oak bookcase, the door with wrought iron lock plate and drop loop handle, 98cm. wide.
(Christie's) $3,100

L. & J. G. Stickley single door bookcase with keyed tenons, no. 641, circa 1906, 36in. wide.
(Skinner) $3,750

Rare and early Gustav Stickley oak two-door bookcase, No. 510, circa 1901, overhanging top above two twelve-pane doors with mitered mullions, 58¹/₂in. wide.
(Skinner) $14,950

Gustav Stickley leaded single door bookcase, designed by Harvey Ellis, circa 1904, no. 700, 36in. wide. $12,500

Onondaga double door bookcase, by L. & J. G. Stickley, circa 1902-04, 56½in. high.
(Skinner) $3,500

Gustav Stickley oak bookcase, designed by Harvey Ellis, Model 700, circa 1904, an arched valance below, 4ft. 10in. high.
(Butterfield & Butterfield) $9,775

Gustav Stickley leaded two-door bookcase, designed by Harvey Ellis, circa 1904, no. 716, 42¾in. wide.
(Skinner) $3,750

An unusual stenciled and painted 'Theorem' box, American, probably New England, mid 19th century, with hinged lid opening to a compartmented interior with slide, 9³/₄in. wide.
(Sotheby's) **$2,200**

An extremely fine and rare paint decorated basswood domed top document box, probably Albany, New York State, early 19th century, 12in wide.
(Sotheby's) **$29,900**

An inlaid maple tea-caddy, American, possibly mid-Atlantic, 1780-1800, the rectangular hinged lid with line-inlaid and crossbanded edges centering an inlaid conch, 7¹/₂in. wide.
(Christie's) **$345**

A pine pipe box, American, dated *1723*, with upswept cresting centered by a flowerhead above a rectangular box with shaped top carved with a flowerhead, 12¹/₂in. high.
(Christie's) **$1,980**

A Federal inlaid mahogany tea-caddy, New York, 1790–1810, the rectangular hinged top with rounded recessed corners with inlaid fluting centering an inlaid conch, 6in. wide.
(Christie's) **$1,650**

A black-painted pipe-box, American, 18th century, with recessed carved heart and pierced C-scrolling crest, 20in. high.
(Christie's) **$4,400**

An unusual painted metal figural cigar box, American, late 19th century, height 9³/₄in.
(Sotheby's) **$3,220**

A rare Chippendale walnut spice chest, Pennsylvania, late 18th century, the door opening to an arrangement of fifteen small drawers fitted with brass pulls, 15¹/₄in. wide.
(Sotheby's) **$9,900**

A painted and decorated shopkeeper's bag sorter, American, late 19th century, 16in. high.
(Christie's) **$863**

BOXES

An unusual carved and painted pine and ash key basket, probably Pennsylvania, circa 1830, painted with sprays of red blossoms and green vines, 6¼in. high.
(Sotheby's) $1,955

A very fine paint decorated tinware canister attributed to the Filley Family, Connecticut, early 19th century, 8⅜in. high.
(Sotheby's) $4,945

Oval carrier, probably Canterbury, New Hampshire, circa 1840–70, pine, maple and ash (?) handle, original yellow paint, three fingers, 9⅜in. diameter.
(Skinner) $28,750

A fine paint decorated tinware deed box, Connecticut, early 19th century, painted with brilliantly colored red, yellow and green blossoms and buds, 10in. wide.
(Sotheby's) $3,738

A Chippendale brass-mounted mahogany serpentine-front letter box, probably American, circa 1785, the sloped lid opening to a divided well, 13in. high.
(Sotheby's) $1,430

Rosewood cased surgical set, circa 1870, by G. Tiemann Co., 67 Chatham Street, N.Y., NY, containing approximately sixty-eight instruments in fitted velvet compartments.
(Eldred's) $1,980

Baltimore and Ohio railroad wallpaper covered hat box, dated *Newburyport June 7, 1833*, 16in. wide.
(Skinner) $11,000

A leather key basket, probably Richmond, Virginia, early 19th century, the black oval basket decorated in silver and gold stitches, 4¾in. high.
(Sotheby's) $2,070

One of two wallpaper covered hat boxes, Old Hickory, circa 1840, printed in pink, brown and green on blue ground, 183/4in. wide.
(Skinner) (Two) $5,175

43

BOXES

A painted and decorated trinket trunk, Lancaster County, Pennsylvania, 1800–1840, the rectangular blue-painted box with domed lid, 5½in. high. (Christie's) **$5,750**

Shaker peg rack and divided oval carrier, 20th century, rack 69in. long, carrier 10½in. long. (Skinner) **$575**

Painted pine and oak writing box, probably Massachusetts, early 18th century, the pine overhanging rectangular hinged slant lid, 18in. wide. (Skinner) **$10,350**

A carved and painted pine and mahogany fire box, Pennsylvania or Virginia, dated *1861*, the open square form with turned columnar supports, dated *1861*, 7³/₈in. wide. (Sotheby's) **$1,610**

A turned painted and decorated saffron box, Joseph Long Lehn, Pennsylvania, 1849–1892, cylindrical footed, the cover with turned finial embellished with strawberries, 4⁵/₈in. high. (Christie's) **$1,495**

A carved walnut saltbox, Eastern Pennsylvania, early 19th century, the rectangular slanted and hinged lid opening to two wells, 10¾in. long. (Sotheby's) **$862**

A whalebone and sealskin box, American, possibly Connecticut, second quarter 19th century, the domed hinged rectangular lid with sealskin covering, 9³/₄in. wide. (Christie's) **$1,150**

A wallpaper covered oval box, Pennsylvania, circa 1841, the interior lined with newspaper 'Hannover Gazette' dated *March 11, 1841*, 9in. high. (Christie's) **$1,380**

A carved and painted poplar sewing box, Lehigh County, Pennsylvania, circa 1840, the rectangular hinged top fitted with an oblong pin cushion, 10¾in. long. (Sotheby's) **$1,035**

A painted and polychrome-decorated pine documents box, American, probably Pennsylvania, late 18th/19th century, 10in. long.
(Sotheby's) $1,000

A paint-decorated pine document box, New England, early 19th century, the lid painted with a flower- and leaf-filled basket in shades of green and red on a yellow ground, 13¼in. long.
(Sotheby's) $8,337

A yellow painted and fruit decorated slide-lid box, Pennsylvania, 19th century, the rectangular sliding lid decorated with a flowering strawberry plant and rosebud, 5½in. wide.
(Christie's) $27,600

Carved and stained wood display cabinet, America, 19th century, with geometric, animal and floral decoration, alligatored surface, 16½in. high.
(Skinner) $316

A wallpaper covered comb box with comb, Pennsylvania, 19th century, the semi-circular box covered in gray paper with geometric designs, 5¼in. high.
(Christie's) $1,380

A hat box, New England, circa 1830, covered in a blue, white and beige-glazed wallpaper depicting Castle Garden, New York Harbor, 21⅜in. long.
(Sotheby's) $6,900

Large Shaker oval box, probably New Lebanon, New York, 19th century, with original pumpkin paint, six finger, 15in. long.
(Skinner) $8,050

An unusual painted pine tea caddy, probably New England, 19th century, the top painted with a swooping bird grasping bellflower swags, 9in. long.
(Sotheby's) $3,450

A painted and decorated poplar trinket chest, Jacob Weber, Pennsylvania, 1840–1850, with hinged lid decorated with a single yellow and orange tulip, 4¾in. high.
(Christie's) $17,250

Patriotic inlaid mahogany box, dated *1864*, 9¼in. wide. (Skinner) **$2,090**

A painted maple lap desk, New York State, circa 1840, 19in. wide. (Christie's) **$2,200**

A smoke grained dome-top box, American, circa 1830, 18¼in. long. (Skinner) **$1,200**

Whalebone and black painted wooden hinged box, early 19th century, with whalebone presentation plaque *HAJ*, 13¼in. long. (Skinner) **$1,380**

A fine and unusual paint decorated domed top document box, New England, mid 19th century, 13¾in. wide. (Sotheby's) **$2,645**

Painted and decorated dome top box, America, circa 1830, grain painted in brown over red and decorated with panels of leafage, 76.5cm. long. (Skinner Inc.) **$850**

A fine painted and decorated document box, initialed *EMD*, probably New England, 19th century, with a white-painted heart escutcheon, the sides with two white houses, height 6¼in. (Sotheby's) **$1,265**

A Mic-Mac oval porcupine quill box, American, 19th century, the oval bark lid with stitched porcupine quill decoration, 5½in. long. (Christie's) **$483**

A fine painted and decorated pine utility box, New York, early 19th century, the rectangular top painted with a view of St. Stephen's Park, 12¾in. wide. (Sotheby's) **$2,090**

A knife box, America, 19th century, rectangular form with outward flaring sides and shaped ends. (Skinner) **$700**

A pine hinged-box, American, 19th century, oval with iron sliding lock and bracket front, 17¼in. wide. (Christie's) **$220**

A Federal figured maple tray, New England, 1790–1810, with a flaring gallery and shaped divider pierced to form a handle, 13½in. wide. (Christie's) **$4,620**

Oak and pine carved and painted Bible box, Massachusetts, circa 1700, 26in. wide.
(Skinner) $25,300

Rare miniature painted shaker box, Enfield, New Hampshire, dated *March 1836*, painted yellow, 7.3cm.
(Skinner Inc.) $23,000

Joined oak and yellow pine box, Connecticut or Massachusetts, circa 1700, 27in. wide.
(Skinner Inc.) $12,100

Round baleen box, America, mid 19th century, sides engraved with patriotic devices, ship at sea, building and leafy vine borders, $8^{3}/_{8}$in. diameter.
(Skinner Inc.) $400

An unusual painted chip-carved box, American, probably Pennsylvania, early 20th century, the rectangular top with hinged lid opening to a compartmented interior, $19^{1}/_{2}$in. wide.
(Sotheby's) $1,650

A paint-decorated dome-top box, probably New England, 19th century, the top painted with a green, red and white oval reserve, 21in. long.
(Sotheby's) $2,875

A rare tooled leather key basket, probably Shenandoah Valley, Virginia, mid 19th century, the shaped sides heightened with decorative tooling, $8^{1}/_{2}$in. high.
(Sotheby's) $1,955

Mahogany and exotic wood veneered box, America, 19th century, with fan design and whale bone escutcheon, 12in. wide.
(Skinner) $413

Yellow painted oval Shaker carrier, probably Harvard, Massachusetts, late 19th century, three fingered box with carved handle.
(Skinner Inc.) $6,600

A painted and stenciled pine box, American, 1844, oval, vinegar painted, $11^{1}/_{2}$in. diameter.
(Christie's) $220

Rare painted wood ship's box, with decoration of the 'Ship Flying Fish', $18^{1}/_{2}$in. long.
(Eldred's) $605

A bird's-eye maple roll-top lap desk, America, circa 1820, tambour roll above fold-out writing leaf and single drawer, 9 x 14in.
(Skinner) $1,000

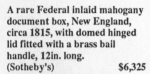

A rare Federal inlaid mahogany document box, New England, circa 1815, with domed hinged lid fitted with a brass bail handle, 12in. long.
(Sotheby's) $6,325

A fine paint decorated pine domed top box, New England, early 19th century, the top and sides painted with large, vigorous loose circles, 24¼in. wide.
(Sotheby's) $10,350

A paint-decorated pine small trunk, probably Massachusetts, early 19th century, with a domed lid painted in red, yellow, white and black, 13in. long.
(Sotheby's) $68,500

Painted and marquetry inlaid mahogany ladies' jewelry cabinet, America, dated *1905*, with spring loaded drawer, lower compartment with painted reserve of American shield, 18¼in. wide.
(Skinner) $633

A pair of Federal burl walnut and tiger maple veneered knife urns, probably Philadelphia, 1800–1810, the squared domed top with veneered panels divided by patterned stringing with acorn finials, 28in. high.
(Christie's) $5,750

A carved and painted pine hanging wall box, New England, probably Connecticut, mid/late 18th century, the shaped rectangular backplate chip-carved with two stylized flowerheads, 15¾in. high.
(Sotheby's) $1,035

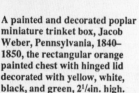

A painted and decorated poplar miniature trinket box, Jacob Weber, Pennsylvania, 1840–1850, the rectangular orange painted chest with hinged lid decorated with yellow, white, black, and green, 2¼in. high.
(Christie's) $5,750

Art Crafts Shop copper and enamel jewelry box, Buffalo, New York, circa 1905, original bronze patina with green, red and yellow enamel floral decoration, 8¾in. long.
(Skinner) $2,185

A miniature grain-painted blanket chest, inscribed John A. Forney, Pennsylvania, 1800–1820, the rectangular hinged lid opening to an interior fitted with a till, 19½in. wide.
(Christie's) $5,175

Gilt decorated box, 19th century, front inscribed *Tainter's Boston Express*, 9in. wide.
(Skinner) $575

Bird's-eye maple, tiger maple and cherry miniature blanket box, probably New England, early 19th century, 8in. wide.
(Skinner) $2,300

Hinged oak box with glass lining, attributed to Stickley Bros., Michigan, circa 1910, 15½in. wide. $1,000

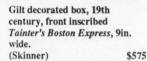

An ivory and whalebone-inlaid mahogany pipe box, probably New England, early 19th century, the initials *E.H.* above a drawer with a turned ivory pull, 14³/₄in. high.
(Sotheby's) $21,850

Two wallpaper covered hat boxes, Pennsylvania, 19th century, both covered in multicolored paper with stylized foliate and geometric motifs, 8¹/₂in. and 9¹/₄in. high.
(Christie's) $748

A grain-painted and comb decorated toy milk cupboard, Lancaster, Pennsylvania, circa 1875, the rectangular top surmounted by a scalloped gallery with carved turkey, 9in. wide.
(Christie's) $5,750

Painted pine wood box, northern New England, first half 19th century, original light green paint, 40in. wide.
(Skinner) $1,725

A walnut and yellow pine tabletop slant-lid desk, Southeastern Pennsylvania, probably late 18th century, case fitted with three short drawers over two long drawers, 29in. wide.
(Christie's) $1,380

A painted and decorated trinket trunk, Lancaster County, Pennsylvania, 1800–1840, the rectangular dark blue-painted box with dome lid, 4⁵/₈in. high.
(Christie's) $3,680

A painted and grained pine blanket box, New England, circa 1810.
(Skinner) $1,550

A paint-decorated bird's eye maple jewel box, probably New England, initialed *MN*, early 19th century, 14½in. long.
(Sotheby's) $2,300

Painted decorated miniature chest, possibly Pennsylvania, circa 1820, polychrome shells and strawberries, 12¾in. wide.
(Skinner) $13,800

Shaker butternut woodbox, mid 19th century, the hinged lid with rounded edge on dovetail constructed box, 24½in. wide.
(Skinner) $4,600

A Chippendale inlaid walnut desk-box, Salem, Massachusetts, 1750–80, the hinged molded rectangular top decorated with stringing and centered by a compass star over a conforming case enclosing an elaborately fitted interior, 22½in. wide.
(Christie's) $7,000

Wood box, purchased at Canterbury, New Hampshire, pine, iron hinges and hooks, chest with hinged lid and one drawer, 23¾in. wide.
(Skinner) $3,220

A Federal inlaid ash and mahogany document box, probably Pennsylvania, 1790-1810, elaborately inlaid with bands of diagonal inlay centering a compass star and two fans in a shaped reserve, 20in. wide.
(Christie's) $3,000

A birch pipe box, America, late 18th/early 19th century, shaped back and single thumb-molded drawer, 14¼in. high.
(Skinner) $650

A joined chestnut butter box, Pennsylvania, possibly Oley Valley, Berks County, 1800–1840, the rectangular form with applied molded and notched surround on three sides, 16in. wide.
(Christie's) $403

Wallpaper covered wooden hat box, America, circa 1840, of oblong form, the fitted lid covered with Castles in Spain pattern, 11½in. high. (Skinner Inc.) $4,000

Wavy birch footed box, New England, early 19th century, with ivory escutcheon and shaped skirt, 14in. wide. (Skinner) $546

An inlaid and painted Masonic box, Lawrence, Massachusetts, dated 1858, the rectangular box decorated with Masonic symbols, 7¼in. wide. (Skinner) $1,000

A painted and decorated miniature blanket chest, Centre County, Pennsylvania, late 18th/early 19th century, the rectangular red-painted hinged lid with molded edge above a conforming case, 17¼in. wide. (Christie's) $4,370

Four oval Shaker boxes, America, 19th century, each with fitted lid (minor imperfections). (Skinner Inc.) $4,000

A paint-decorated pine and poplar small butter firkin, probably New Jersey, circa 1775, of circular form with fitted lid, the top decorated in polychrome with a flowerhead, 5in. diameter. (Sotheby's) $4,600

A painted and decorated document box, attributed to Heinrich Bucher, Reading, Bucks County, Pennsylvania, 1770-1780, the hinged domed lid lifting to an open compartment, 13in. wide. (Christie's) $7,500

Red painted pine lidded wall box, America, late 18th/early 19th century, 12in. wide. (Skinner) $1,495

A painted and decorated bentwood 'Bucher' box, Pennsylvania, circa 1830, oval red painted box with fitted lid decorated with white freehand tulips, 4½in. high. (Christie's) $1,610

Classical mahogany and bird's-eye maple bureau, New England, 1825–30, old refinish, 40½in. wide.
(Skinner)　　　　$1,840

Chippendale cherry serpentine bureau, probably Massachusetts, circa 1780, the overhanging molded top with serpentine front, 19¾in. wide.
(Skinner)　　　　$42,550

Classical mahogany, cherry and mahogany veneer carved bureau, probably New York State, circa 1825, 47in. wide.
(Skinner)　　　　$633

American Empire bureau, 19th century, in pine with bird's eye maple drawers, scrolled backsplash, two stepped drawers over four drawers, 45½in. wide.
(Eldred's)　　　　$550

A Federal mahogany and mahogany veneer bureau, possibly carved by Samuel F. McIntire, circa 1810, 42½in. wide.　　$4,375

Antique American Sheraton four-drawer bureau, circa 1800, in mahogany and maple, back splash, cock beaded drawers, shaped apron, peg feet, 39½in. wide.
(Eldred's)　　　　$750

A Federal mahogany and mahogany veneer bowfront bureau, circa 1800, 35½in. wide.　　　　$1,500

Classical tiger maple bureau, probably New England, circa 1825, incised beaded drawers flanked by ring-turned columns, 47in. wide.
(Skinner)　　　　$2,415

A Chippendale cherry and pine four-drawer bureau on ogee bracket feet, Conn., circa 1780, 39½in. wide.　　　　$5,300

American Sheraton bowfront bureau, in mahogany with cookie corners, four drawers with veneered fronts, 43in. wide. (Eldred's) **$1,210**

Classical mahogany carved and veneered bureau, Massachusetts, circa 1825, brasses replaced, 40.5in. wide. (Skinner) **$1,495**

American four-drawer bureau, in maple, replaced top, tiger maple drawer fronts, ogee bracket base, 39$^{1}/_{2}$in. wide. (Eldred's) **$990**

American Sheraton six-drawer bureau, in mahogany with tiger maple drawer fronts, scrolled backsplash, and turned legs, 47in. wide. (Eldred's) **$770**

Reproduction Hepplewhite four-drawer bureau, in mahogany with satinwood drawer fronts, brass and enamel pulls, French feet, 42in. wide. (Eldred's) **$1,430**

American Sheraton four-drawer bowfront bureau, in mahogany with shaped front and cookie corners, cockbeaded drawers with satinwood banding, 21in. wide. (Eldred's) **$935**

American Hepplewhite bowfront bureau, in cherry with four drawers, drawer fronts with tiger maple banded inlay, 39$^{1}/_{4}$in. wide. (Eldred's) **$1,430**

Classical mahogany and mahogany veneer carved bureau, probably Salem, Massachusetts, circa 1820, 40in. wide. (Skinner) **$3,105**

American four-drawer bureau, circa 1800–20, in mahogany with cookie corners, cockbeaded drawer fronts and wooden pulls, 41$^{1}/_{2}$in. wide. (Eldred's) **$605**

FEDERAL

Federal mahogany inlaid bowfront bureau, New England, circa 1800, old brasses, 38.75in. wide.
(Skinner) $2,070

Federal mahogany veneer inlaid bow front bureau, Massachusetts or New Hampshire, circa 1800.
(Skinner) $4,312

Federal bird's-eye maple and mahogany veneered bow-front bureau, New England, early 19th century, 41¼in. wide.
(Skinner Inc.) $1,300

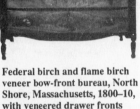

Federal birch and flame birch veneer bow-front bureau, North Shore, Massachusetts, 1800–10, with veneered drawer fronts flanked by divided reeded columns, 42in. wide.
(Skinner) $3,680

Federal cherry and tiger maple veneer bow-front bureau, probably Keene, New Hampshire, 1800–15, the top edge and cockbeaded drawers outlined in crossbanded mahogany veneer, 40in. wide.
(Skinner) $8,050

Federal mahogany veneered bowfront bureau, Pennsylvania, early 19th century, replaced brasses, signed on back *W.H. Spangler, Ephrata. Pa.*, 42in. wide.
(Skinner Inc.) $2,000

Federal mahogany veneered inlaid bureau, New England, circa 1810, drawer front cross-banded in curly maple, 39½in. wide.
(Skinner Inc.) $1,625

Federal mahogany and mahogany veneer bowfront bureau, probably Massachusetts, circa 1810, 39½in. wide.
(Skinner) $2,200

Federal bird's-eye maple veneer and cherry bowfront bureau, New England, circa 1820, four cockbeaded graduated drawers, 39½in. wide.
(Skinner) $1,380

FEDERAL

Federal mahogany and mahogany veneer bureau, Massachusetts, circa 1815, 43in. wide. (Skinner) **$690**

Federal cherry inlaid bureau, Vermont or Connecticut, circa 1810, the rectangular top with applied beaded edge, 42¼in. wide. (Skinner) **$1,955**

Federal mahogany veneer and cherry inlaid bowfront bureau, Connecticut River Valley, circa 1800, 41in. wide. (Skinner Inc.) **$4,400**

Federal cherry bureau, Massachusetts, circa 1810, with cockbeaded drawer surrounds and replaced brass, old refinish, 36½in. wide. (Skinner) **$1,725**

Federal mahogany and tiger maple bowfront bureau, probably Massachusetts, 1815–25, top with bowfront and ovolo corners and crossbanded edge, 40¼in. wide. (Skinner) **$2,530**

Federal cherry inlaid bowfront bureau, southeastern New England, circa 1800, case of four cockbeaded drawers on inlaid base of flaring French feet, 39¼in. wide. (Skinner) **$2,760**

Federal mahogany inlaid bowfront bureau, probably New York, circa 1800, the rectangular inlaid top with bowed front, 41¾in. wide. (Skinner Inc.) **$2,000**

Federal mahogany and mahogany veneer inlaid bowfront bureau, Massachusetts, circa 1790, 40in. wide. (Skinner) **$2,475**

Federal mahogany and veneer bureau, New Hampshire, 1815–25, with stringing, beaded and inlaid drawers and escutcheons, saw tooth skirt, 41½in. wide. (Skinner) **$1,150**

A Federal inlaid mahogany bureau-desk, possibly Virginia, 1800–1820, the molded rectangular top above a conforming case fitted with a cockbeaded fall-front sliding and felt-lined lid embellished with paired paterae inlay, each enclosed by string and quarter-fan inlay opening to a compartmented interior centered by a patera-inlaid prospect door all above a similarly embellished door flanked by four string-inlaid, cockbeaded and graduated short drawers over a shaped skirt, on splayed French feet, 47¼in. wide.
(Christie's) $12,650

Renaissance Revival walnut and marquetry side cabinet, late 19th century, 65in. wide.
(Skinner) $1,725

Renaissance Revival ebonized and gilt metal mounted cabinet, fourth quarter 19th century, inset with porcelain plaques, 19½in. wide.
(Skinner) $1,000

A Neo-Grec ebonized and gilt-decorated breakfront cabinet, New York City, 1870-1890, the rectangular top with gilt-decorated turned gallery.
(Christie's) $14,500

American two-part kitchen cabinet, in walnut, upper section with beveled cornice and beaded molding above two three-light doors, probably Pennsylvania, 48in. wide.
(Eldred's) $1,100

Gustav Stickley smoker's cabinet, circa 1907, over-hanging top above single drawer and cabinet door, 20in. wide.
(Skinner) $2,500

A Gustav Stickley oak music cabinet, the ten pane single door with amber glass, circa 1912, 47¼in. high.
(Skinner) $3,700

Antique American paneled cabinet, from the Starret House of Warren, Maine, built circa 1831, in pine with yellowish-brown grain paint, 49in. wide.
(Eldred's) $1,045

Two-part kitchen cabinet, 19th century, in pine with traces of old blue paint, upper section with three shelves and molded surround, 45in. wide.
(Eldred's) $990

Oak liquor cabinet with copper slide, probably Michigan, circa 1910, with fitted compartments, unsigned, 40¾in. high.
(Skinner Inc.) $875

Renaissance Revival walnut cabinet, third-quarter 19th century, carved broken pediment crest with bust of Shakespeare, 54¹/₂ in. wide. (Skinner Inc.) $5,125

An Aesthetic Movement amboyna and ebonized side cabinet, the rectangular top with mirrored and shelved superstructure, above two frieze drawers, 70in. wide. (Christie's) $9,693

A mahogany dental cabinet by the American Cabinet Co., Two Rivers, Wisconsin, the upper part with three glazed-door compartments, 40¹/₄ in. wide. (Christie's S. Ken) $1,700

A Federal apple-green painted tulip poplar cabinet with drawers, Pennsylvania, circa 1825, the rectangular top with shaped splashboard, width 42¹/₄ in. (Sotheby's) $5,750

An American Renaissance inlaid maple and walnut console cabinet, circa 1870, the rectangular top with incurvate sides with outset canted corners and applied molded edge, 4ft. 2in. wide.(Butterfield & Butterfield) $2,070

A Federal walnut cabinet on chest, Pennsylvania, 1800-1820, in two sections, the upper cabinet with molded cornice above two recessed panel covered doors, on French feet, 41¼ in. wide. (Christie's New York) $12,350

L. & J.G. Stickley Handcraft cabinet, single drawer over door, arched base, interior intact, Handcraft decal, 29in. high. (Skinner) $2,990

Renaissance Revival ebonised, rosewood and marquetry side cabinet, late 19th century, with handpainted porcelain plaques, 57in. long. (Skinner) $1,955

A grain-painted poplar side cabinet, Pennsylvania, circa 1830, the oblong top surmounted by a scrolling three-quarter gallery, 45¹/₂ in. wide. (Sotheby's) $8,050

Aesthetic Movement ebonised and parcel-gilt folio cabinet, fourth quarter 19th century, 40½in. wide.
(Skinner) $1,380

American Aesthetic movement rosewood, marquetry and parcel gilt side cabinet, circa 1875–85, Herter Brothers, New York, 66¾in. wide.
(Skinner Inc.) $21,800

American Dutch-style bombe-fronted walnut and oak glazed display cabinet, 6ft. wide, 7ft. 6in. high. (Giles Haywood) $2,000

An Arts & Crafts oak cabinet with repousse hammered copper panels, circa 1900, 31¾in. wide.
(Skinner) $1,250

Painted pine wall cabinet, America, early 18th century, the rectangular case with applied double arched molding, 18in. wide.
(Skinner Inc.) $4,625

Rare classical mahogany veneer artifact cabinet, Boston, circa 1820, upper case with ratchets to receive shelves, lower case has ten graduated pull-out drawers, 44in. wide.
(Skinner Inc.) $4,150

Renaissance Revival rosewood, marquetry and gilt-incised cabinet, third quarter 19th century, with inset hand painted porcelain plaques, 59½in. long.
(Skinner) $3,910

Grain painted pine lawyer's cabinet, the panel doors opening to reveal thirty-eight compartments, New England, circa 1800, 33in. wide. $4,500

Tiger maple glazed cabinet, New York or New Jersey, circa 1825, the flat carved molded cornice above two glazed doors, 41in. wide.
(Skinner) $5,175

A Chippendale mahogany tilt-top candlestand, Philadelphia, 1760–1780, the circular dished top tilting and turning above a bird-cage support over a ring-turned and compressed ball pedestal, on a tripartite base with cabriole legs and pad feet, 28½in. high, 19in. diameter. (Christie's) $19,550

A Chippendale mahogany
bird cage candlestand, Phila.,
circa 1760, 27½in. high.
                $8,000

Federal mahogany veneer tilt-
top candlestand, Connecticut,
early 19th century, 19³/₄in. wide.
(Skinner) $1,100

A tripod cherry candlestand
with candle drawer, Mass.,
circa 1760, 25½in. high.
                $9,500

A Chippendale carved
mahogany dish-top birdcage
candlestand, Philadelphia, circa
1770, on three downswept legs
ending in snake feet, 23in.
diameter.
(Sotheby's) $1,725

A rare Federal lignum vitae tilt-
top candlestand, New England,
circa 1800, the square top with
shaped sides, 19³/₄in. wide.
(Sotheby's) $3,737

Federal cherry inlaid and
carved tilt top candlestand,
Connecticut River Valley, early
19th century, with an oval
central reserve inlaid with flame
birch veneer, 18¹/₈in. wide.
(Skinner) $4,400

Federal cherry and maple
carved candlestand, New York
or Connecticut, early 19th
century, with double beaded
table top edge, 15⁵/₈in. wide.
(Skinner) $575

A William and Mary red-
painted maple and oak
candlestand, New England,
1700–50, the circular top above
a square flaring pedestal and an
X-form base, 15in. diameter.
(Sotheby's) $1,035

Chippendale cherry
candlestand, Connecticut, circa
1780, square top with vase-
shaped post on cabriole legs
with pad feet, 16¹/₄in. wide.
(Skinner) $880

Turned leg painted candle stand, 18th century, the circular top with chamfered edge, 12¾in. diameter.
(Skinner) $2,300

A Federal inlaid mahogany candlestand on a vase-turned pedestal, 1790-1810, 29½in. high. $3,250

Painted maple, cherry and ash candlestand, New Hampshire, 18th century, original red wash on base, 27in. high.
(Skinner Inc.) $5,500

A fine Queen Anne satinwood-inlaid mahogany tilt-top candlestand, New York, circa 1790, the circular top inlaid with a central flowerhead, 21in. diameter.
(Sotheby's) $4,025

Shaker painted cherry candlestand, New Lebanon, New York, 1820-40, the square top above a turned tapering classic center post and tripod base, 25¾in. high.
(Skinner) $28,750

A paint decorated papier-maché and pine tilt-top candlestand, attributed to the Litchfield Manufacturing Co., Litchfield, Connecticut, mid 19th century, 28in. high.
(Sotheby's) $2,875

Mahogany veneered octagonal tilt top candlestand, Rhode Island, early 19th century, cross banded veneer and cockbeading in outline, 28¾in. high.
(Skinner Inc.) $2,350

Shaker maple candlestand, probably Mt. Lebanon, New York, circa 1830, the circular top on a ring-turned tapering stem, 19¼in. diameter.
(Skinner) $1,725

Federal painted and decorated candlestand, probably New England, on a tripod base with an arris leg, mid 19th century, 28in. high.
(Skinner Inc.) $1,050

CANDLE STANDS

A Chippendale walnut dish-top stand, Phila., 1770-90, 20¾in. diam. (Christie's) $10,325

Painted birch **candlestand**, possibly Shaker, New England, 1830–1845, all over original red paint, 26½in. high. (Skinner Inc.) $3,780

A classical mahogany tilt-top candlestand, N.Y., circa 1820/40, 30¾in. high. $1,750

A Chippendale turned mahogany birdcage candlestand, Pennsylvania, circa 1780, the circular dished top tilting and rotating above a birdcage support, 21in. diameter. (Sotheby's) $1,610

A William and Mary cherrywood and turned maple candlestand, New England, 1700–40, the circular top with chamfered edge above a ring-turned hourglass-shaped standard, 24½in. high. (Sotheby's) $4,600

A Queen Anne figured mahogany dish-top candlestand, Philadelphia, Pennsylvania, circa 1750, tilting above a turned flaring compressed ball standard, 23½in. diameter. (Sotheby's) $12,650

Shaker cherry candlestand, Mt. Lebanon, New York 1830-40, the circular top with quarter round edge on a chamfered rectangular support, 19¾in. diameter. (Skinnner) $20,700

A William and Mary maple candlestand, possibly Dunlap School, Southern New Hampshire, early/mid 18th century, on T-shaped trestle base, 23½in. high. (Christie's) $4,025

A turned maple candlestand, Shaker, circa 1830, the square top above a turned flaring standard on three downswept legs, 25in. high. (Sotheby's) $1,035

A Chippendale mahogany tilt-top candlestand, Pennsylvania, 1750–1770, the circular dished top tilting and turning above a bird-cage support over a ring and baluster-turned pedestal, on a tripartite base with cabriole legs and pointed slipper feet, 27¾in. high, 19½in. diameter. (Christie's) $11,500

CHIPPENDALE

A Chippendale mahogany dish-top candlestand, Massachusetts, circa 1780, the circular dished top tilting above a ring-turned urn-form standard, 27¼in. high. (Sotheby's) $4,600

A fine Chippendale birchwood serpentine-top candlestand, Massachusetts, circa 1780, the oblong top with serpentine sides, 16½in. wide. (Sotheby's) $7,475

Chippendale painted candlestand, New England, circa 1780, the square top with incised border and concave corners, 25¾in. high. (Skinner) $862

A Chippendale carved and figured mahogany birdcage candlestand, Philadelphia, circa 1795, ring-turned and urn-form standard above three downswept legs, 23¾in. diameter. (Sotheby's) $28,750

A Chippendale figured mahogany tilt-top candlestand, Massachusetts, circa 1770, on three cabriole legs, ending in snake feet. (Sotheby's) $2,070

A Chippendale turned and figured mahogany candlestand, Pennsylvania, 1760–80, the circular hinged dished top tilting and revolving above a birdcage support, 21in. diameter. (Sotheby's) $2,875

A Chippendale carved mahogany dish-top candlestand, Philadelphia, Pennsylvania, circa 1765, the circular top tilting and revolving above a bird-cage support, 24½in. diameter. (Sotheby's) $129,000

A Chippendale carved and figured mahogany serpentine-top candlestand, Salem, Massachusetts, circa 1780, on C-scroll-carved cabriole legs, 27½in. high. (Sotheby's) $35,650

A Chippendale red-stained maple tilt-top candlestand, Pennsylvania, circa 1800, the circular top tilting and revolving above a birdcage support, 20½in. diameter. (Sotheby's) $3,450

CHIPPENDALE

Chippendale mahogany dish top inlaid candlestand, Connecticut River Valley, late 18th century, 26in. high.
(Skinner Inc.) $6,530

A rare Chippendale carved mahogany tilt-top birdcage candlestand, New York, circa 1775, on leaf-carved cabriole legs, 25¹/₂in. diameter.
(Sotheby's) $12,650

A Country Chippendale cherry carved candlestand, Connecticut, circa 1780, the square tray top with applied molded edge, 26in. high.
(Skinner) $3,800

A Chippendale turned and figured walnut birdcage candlestand, Pennsylvania, circa 1760, on cabriole legs ending in snake feet, 22in. diameter.
(Sotheby's) $11,500

A Chippendale mahogany tilt-top candlestand, Salem, Massachusetts, circa 1790, the hinged oval top tilting above a ring-turned standard and urn-form support, 27¹/₂in. high.
(Sotheby's) $1,150

A Chippendale mahogany tilt-top candlestand, New England, circa 1770, the oval top tilting above a ring-turned flaring standard, 16¹/₄in. wide.
(Sotheby's) $1,725

A Chippendale turned and figured walnut candlestand, Philadelphia, circa 1770, the circular dished top swiveling and tilting above a birdcage support, 18¹/₂in. diameter.
(Sotheby's) $3,737

Chippendale cherry and tiger maple candlestand, Connecticut River Valley, 1770-90, with cherry tray top, tiger maple pedestal and tripod base, 25.5in. high.
(Skinner) $16,100

A very fine and rare Chippendale cherrywood scalloped-top candlestand with drawer, attributed to the Chapin family, East Windsor or Hartford, Connecticut, circa 1785. (Sotheby's) $85,000

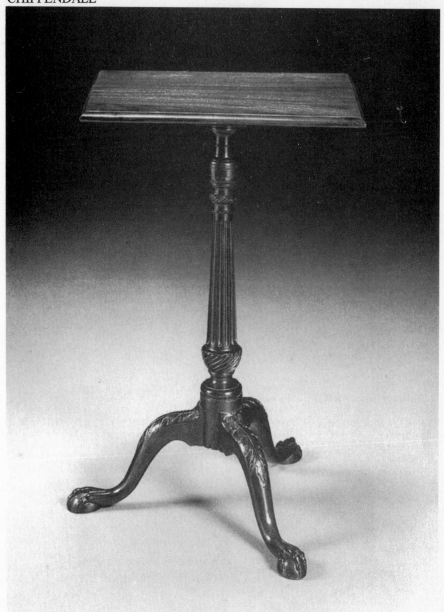

A Chippendale carved mahogany candlestand, Massachusetts, 1760–1780, the molded rectangular top above a tapering fluted column and spiral-reeded vase-turned pedestal, on a tripartite base with cabriole legs with leaf-carved knees terminating in ball-and-claw feet, the top replaced, 15½in. wide.
(Christie's) $3,450

FEDERAL

Federal painted cherry dish top candle stand, possibly Massachusetts, late 18th century, top 16½in. diameter.
(Skinner) $4,025

Federal cherry candlestand with drawer, Connecticut, circa 1790, old cherry color top with molded edge, 16.75in. wide.
(Skinner) $19,550

A Country Federal mahogany and cherry inlaid candlestand, Upper Connecticut River Valley, 1800, 28½in. high.
(Skinner) $1,625

A Federal painted birchwood tilt-top candlestand, New England, circa 1810, the oval top tilting above a vase-form standard, on downcurving legs, 29½in. high.
(Sotheby's) $4,025

Federal maple candlestand, southeastern New England, late 18th century, the square top on a vase and ring turned post and tripod cabriole leg base, 25in. high.
(Skinner) $805

A Federal cherrywood candlestand, Connecticut River Valley, 1790–1810, the circular porringered top above a ring and baluster-turned support, 17½in. diameter.
(Christie's) $8,050

A Transitional Federal turned cherrywood candlestand, New England, circa 1800, the square top on ring-turned baluster-form support, 16in. wide.
(Sotheby's) $575

A Federal maple candlestand, New England, circa 1805, oblong top with rounded corners above a ring-turned urn-form standard, 18in. wide.
(Sotheby's) $460

A Federal turned mahogany candlestand, Massachusetts, circa 1800, the rectangular top with shaped corners, 28¼in. high.
(Sotheby's) $1,035

68

FEDERAL

A Country Federal birch candlestand, possibly New Hampshire, circa 1810, 27¼in. high.
(Skinner) $400

A Federal inlaid cherrywood candlestand, Connecticut River Valley, 1790-1810, 26¾in. high. $20,000

A late Federal carved mahogany tilt-top candlestand, New York, 1815-1835, on saber legs, 30½in. high. (Christie's)
                    $1,500

A Federal turned and figured mahogany tilt-top birdcage candlestand, Pennsylvania, circa 1810, on a ring-turned standard with urn-form support, 20in. diameter.
(Sotheby's) $575

Federal cherry inlaid tilt top candlestand, Concord, Massachusetts area, circa 1780, 14½in. wide.
(Skinner) $5,462

Federal mahogany tilt top candlestand, Boston or North Shore, Massachusetts, circa 1790, the serpentine top with canted corners and molded edge, 19in. wide.
(Skinner) $4,025

A Federal mahogany tilt-top candlestand, Western New Hampshire, circa 1810, oval top on an incised vase and ring turned stem, 22in. wide.
(Skinner) $5,000

A Country Federal tiger maple inlaid tilt top candlestand, New England, circa 1810, the rectangular top with ovolo corners, 28¼in.high.
(Skinner) $1,350

Paint decorated Federal candlestand, New Hampshire, attributed to the Dunlap family of cabinetmakers, 1780-1810, 26½in. high.
(Skinner Inc.) $10,000

NEW ENGLAND

Grain painted candlestand, New England, early 19th century, faux rosewood, 25¹/₄ in. high. (Skinner Inc.) **$2,530**

A fine and rare paint decorated candlestand, New England, circa 1820, 28¹/₂ in. high. (Sotheby's) **$13,800**

Federal tiger maple candlestand, New England, early 19th century, refinished, 27¹/₂ in. high. (Skinner Inc.) **$1,875**

A fine and rare red-painted and turned tripod candlestand, Northeastern New England, 1750–75, the octagonal molded top above a tapered urn-form and ring-turned standard, 17¹/₂ in. diameter. (Sotheby's) **$24,150**

A Chippendale mahogany tilt-top candlestand, New England, 1760–80, on three downswept legs ending in snake feet, 22in. wide. (Sotheby's) **$1,610**

A Chippendale cherrywood candle-stand, New England, 1760–1780, the circular top above a column and urn-turned pedestal and tripartite base with cabriole legs, 28in. high. (Christie's) **$3,800**

Chippendale mahogany candlestand, New England, late 18th century, the circular top on a vase and ring turned post, top diameter 16in. (Skinner) **$1,380**

A fine and rare Federal paint decorated maple candlestand, New England, probably Vermont, early 19th century, 16in. wide. (Sotheby's) **$55,200**

Maple candlestand, New England, late 18th century, with shaped top and cabriole legs ending in arris pad feet, 26³/₄ in. high. (Skinner) **$633**

NEW ENGLAND

A painted pine candlestand, New England, circa 1780, 27in. high, 20in. diam. $1,750

Tiger maple candlestand, New England, 19th century, the square molded top above a turned pedestal, 16¼in. wide. (Skinner) $1,150

Federal cherry candlestand, New England, early 19th century, refinished, 16½in. diameter (Skinner Inc.) $1,250

Tiger maple and cherry candlestand, New England, early 19th century, the square top with canted corners above a turned maple pedestal, 27½in. high.
(Skinner) $402

Classical cherry carved tilt-top candlestand, New England, circa 1825, vase and ring turned and spiral carved post on three scrolled legs, 22in. wide.
(Skinner) $1,150

A Chippendale turned and figured mahogany candlestand, New England, circa 1780, on downswept legs ending in peaked ovoid snake feet, 28½in. high.
(Sotheby's) $8,050

Federal maple and birch candlestand, New England, circa 1800, molded top above vasiform post ending in curving legs, 15⅝in. diameter.
(Skinner) $1,495

A Federal tiger maple candle-stand, New England, circa 1810, top 17 x 17½in.
(Skinner) $1,650

Windsor cherry candlestand, New England, early 19th century, the circular top on vase and ring-turned post, 18½in. diameter.
(Skinner) $1,840

Federal mahogany canterbury, probably New York, 1820's, pulls appear original, 19in. high. (Skinner Inc.). **$2,050**

Late 19th century natural wicker music stand, by Heywood Brothers. (Skinner) **$200**

A Federal inlaid mahogany canterbury, American, circa 1810, of rectangular form, the upper section with five slightly arched transverses, 17$^{1}/_{2}$in. wide. (Sotheby's) **$1,495**

A Federal mahogany canterbury, attributed to Duncan Phyfe, New York, circa 1805, each side fitted with a striped mahogany molded panel with a roundel on each end, 23in. wide. (Sotheby's) **$7,475**

One of a pair of mahogany canterburys, attributed to Duncan Phyfe, New York, 1810–1815, each with bamboo-turned rails and crossed dividers, 19$^{1}/_{8}$in. wide. (Christie's)(Two) **$16,100**

A Federal inlaid mahogany canterbury, American, probably Boston, Massachusetts, circa 1810, of rectangular form, on ring-turned tapering legs, 19in. wide. (Sotheby's) **$4,600**

A classical figured maple canterbury, New York, mid/late 19th century, the rectangular frame headed by ring-turned ball finials, 19in. wide. (Christie's) **$6,900**

A rare Federal mahogany canterbury, Boston or New York, circa 1815, the four turned uprights centering scrolled transverses, 20in. wide. (Sotheby's) **$3,750**

A classical mahogany canterbury, New York or Boston, 1800-1820, the open rectangular case fitted with four bowed compartments, 28in. wide. (Christie's) **$2,750**

Antique corner chair, 19th century, in mahogany with plume-carved central back rail, pierced splat backs. (Eldred's) $495

Red stained maple roundabout chair, New England, early 19th century, old surface. (Skinner) $690

An important Chippendale carved and figured mahogany corner chair, New York, circa 1760, 16¾in. high. (Sotheby's) $63,000

Chippendale cherry corner chair, probably central Massachusetts, circa 1780, 31in. high. (Skinner) $1,840

William and Mary painted Roundabout chair, New England, 18th century, the shaped backrest and chamfered crest ending in scrolled handholds. (Skinner) $800

A Chippendale maple corner chair New England, circa 1765, the molded crest centering a carved fan above a shaped arm column-turned supports. (Christie's) $10,350

Chippendale cherry roundabout commode chair, refinished, 32¾in. high. (Skinner Inc.) $2,000

Queen Anne walnut commode roundabout chair, Philadelphia, Pennsylvania, 1740–60. (Skinner) $920

George II walnut corner armchair, mid 18th century, 31in. high. (Skinner) $1,610

Chippendale mahogany corner chair, New England, circa 1780. (Skinner) **$1,760**

Antique American corner commode chair in maple, square legs, slip seat, 32in. high. (Eldred's) **$300**

Chippendale walnut commode chair, 1760, with pierced splat, above a deep scrolled skirt. (Skinner) **$1,430**

Queen Anne walnut roundabout chair, possibly Rhode Island, last half 18th century, the shaped crest projects above a scrolled back rail ending in circular handholds. (Skinner) **$4,312**

A Queen Anne maple corner chair, New England, 1760–1780, the shaped crest above spurred arm rests with rounded handgrips, rush seat with exposed corners, 30in. high. (Christie's) **$863**

William and Mary turned corner chair, New England, early 18th century, original black paint, old leather upholstered seat over original splint seat. (Skinner) **$7,475**

Chippendale mahogany carved roundabout chair, New England, circa 1780, the shaped back rest continuing to scrolled arms. (Skinner) **$2,530**

Turned maple red painted comb-back corner chair, New England, 18th century, the scrolled crestrail on four split balusters. (Skinner) **$1,725**

A fine Queen Anne carved mahogany corner chair, Massachusetts, circa 1750, the reverse-scrolling crest above concave spurred arms. (Sotheby's) **$43,700**

Roundabout maple chair, New England, 18th century, old refinish, 30in. high. (Skinner Inc.) **$5,650**

Painted roundabout writing armchair, New England, mid 18th century, with black over red paint. (Skinner) **$1,035**

Red stained maple and ash roundabout chair, New England, 1780–1800, with traces of red paint. (Skinner) **$748**

A Chippendale carved walnut roundabout chair, Rhode Island, 1760–1780, with a serpentine slip-seat and cabriole front leg carved with a scallop shell and pendant bellflower, 31³/₄in. high. (Christie's) **$53,000**

A Queen Anne carved walnut balloon-seat corner chair, Newport, Rhode Island, 1740–65, the U-shaped back ending in scrolled handholds. (Sotheby's) **$20,000**

A Queen Anne walnut and maple rush-seat corner chair, New England, 1740–60, the arms surmounted by a shaped crest on turned flaring columnar supports. (Sotheby's) **$1,840**

A fine Queen Anne walnut balloon-seat corner armchair, Boston, Massachusetts, circa 1760, the shaped crest on a concave armrest. (Sotheby's) **$13,800**

A fine and rare Chippendale carved mahogany corner armchair, New York, New York, circa 1770, the convex molded crest with scrolled hand holds. (Sotheby's) **$20,700**

Painted turned roundabout chair, New England, 18th century, the shaped backrest continuing to circular handholds. (Skinner) **$1,495**

Set of four Federal mahogany shield-back side chairs, probably Rhode Island, circa 1790, the molded arched crest rail above a pierced urn and drape splat. (Skinner) $2,530

Set of eight classical tiger maple and maple dining chairs, probably New England, circa 1830, the concave cresting above a horizontal splat on turned raked stiles and caned seat. (Skinner) $2,645

Set of four classical mahogany and mahogany veneer 'gondola' side chairs, probably New England, circa 1825, the concave scrolled cresting above a vasiform splat and raked stiles. (Skinner) $1,150

Anglo/American joined maple and oak low-back chair, 1665–95. (Skinner) $10,925

Pair of Grecian style decorated side chairs, probably Baltimore, Maryland, circa 1830. (Skinner) $805

An 18th century mid American red walnut dining chair, the balloon shaped back with solid vase splat. (Phillips) $3,380

Frank Lloyd Wright mahogany and upholstered side chair, circa 1955, for Heritage-Henredon Furniture Co., medium finish with brushed green vinyl upholstery, unsigned. (Skinner) $805

A pair of paint decorated side chairs with plank seats, Maine, early 19th century, the crest rail painted with two green and brown pears and red and brown oak leaves. (Sotheby's) $6,900

A red-painted slat-back sidechair, Southern York County, Pennsylvania, late 18th/ early 19th century, centering four graduated shaped slats flanked by cylindrical stiles. (Christie's) $1,380

Classical mahogany carved Grecian style side chair, Boston, circa 1820, the figured mahogany crest above a drapery carved splat. (Skinner) $977

A pair of stenciled and paint decorated maple caned seat side chairs, Baltimore, Maryland, circa 1825, each with a wide horizontal crest rail. (Sotheby's) $3,163

A red-painted fancy sidechair, Lancaster County, Pennsylvania, 1810–1820, the tablet crest with green and white painted rose decoration. (Christie's) $1,840

Walnut carved side chair, Newport, Rhode Island, circa 1750, old refinish, 39in. high. (Skinner) **$8,050**

A pair of classical paint-decorated, parcel-gilt and brass-mounted side chairs, Baltimore, Maryland, circa 1820. (Sotheby's) **$1,265**

Turned chair, Boston, 1710–25, turned finials above block turned stiles flanking a leather upholstered back. (Skinner) **$4,888**

An important paint-decorated turned and carved maple rush-seat side chair, attributed to Thomas Gaines, Ipswich, Massachusetts, 1740–70. (Sotheby's) **$23,000**

Pair of Renaissance Revival rosewood side chairs, attributed to Pottier and Stymus, circa 1865, 35in. high. (Skinner) **$920**

One of a set of four classical mahogany carved dining chairs, probably Massachusetts, circa 1820, the slightly rectangular crest bordered by carved beading. (Skinner)
(Four) **$1,610**

One of a set of six antique American Empire dining chairs, in mahogany with horizontal splat back, saber legs and carved stiles. (Eldred's) (Six) **$1,870**

Set of four Lifetime dining chairs, No. 129, quarter-sawn oak with original seats in good condition. (Skinner) **$690**

Worshipful Master's chair, New Hampshire, 1850–70, painted black with gold highlights, back with pressed wood rosettes. (Skinner) **$633**

Turned and painted side chair, possibly Hudson River Valley area, last half 18th century. (Skinner) $2,185

Pair of antique American Sheraton fancy chairs, in old yellow paint with stenciled decoration and rush seats. (Eldred's) $660

Cherry side chair, Connecticut, 1775–1800, with shaped crest and block and ring turned legs. (Skinner) $690

Greene and Greene mahogany chair, executed in the workshop of Peter Hall for the D.B. Gamble House, Pasadena, California, circa 1908. (Skinner) $10,000

Pair of classical side chairs, attributed to John and Hugh Finley, Baltimore, circa 1820, painted light yellow with gilt and black painted fruit filled compôtes. (Skinner) $747

One of a set of six antique American saber-leg side chairs, with cane seats. (Eldred's) (Six) $743

Cherry ladder-back side chair, Deerfield region, 1785–1810, with projecting ears, double curved crest. (Skinner) $690

Pair of birch Transitional side 18th century, Newburyport, Massachusetts area, raked molded terminals and broad splat. (Skinner) $1,840

Cherry turned and carved side chair, Connecticut, circa 1780, with pierced splat and Spanish feet. (Skinner) $805

Painted maple 'Carver' side chair, probably Connecticut, late 18th century, with turned finials, (Skinner) **$1,265**

Pair of antique American Sheraton fancy chairs, with stenciled decoration, rush seat. (Eldred's) **$358**

American Sheraton rush-seat fancy chair, in tiger maple. (Eldred's) **$330**

Very important inlaid walnut and ebony chair, designed by Greene & Greene, executed in the workshop of Peter Hall for the living room of the Robert R. Blacker house, Pasadena, California, circa 1907. (Skinner Inc.) **$37,400**

A pair of painted and decorated fancy sidechairs, Schaefferstown, Lebanon County, Pennsylvania, early 19th century, each with tablet crest centering two red and gold painted rosettes. (Christie's) **$2,530**

A Pilgrim century turned birchwood rush-seat spindle-back side chair, American, 1690–1730, the back surmounted by pointed flattened-ball finials. (Sotheby's) **$1,035**

One of a pair of classical brass inlaid rosewood sidechairs, attributed to William Seavers, Boston, circa 1810, 32¼in. high. (Christie's)
 (Two) **$1,265**

A pair of turned maple slat-back side chairs, Delaware River Valley or Philadelphia, circa 1740, each with ball finials above turned stiles, 45¼in. high. (Christie's) **$17,250**

Maple crooked back side chair, Boston area, 1740–50, with original leather upholstered seat. (Skinner) **$25,300**

A set of six Chippendale style carved mahogany side chairs, circa 1880, in the Philadelphia manner. (Sotheby's) $2,760

A set of eight turned maple and polychrome-decorated rush-seat side chairs, New York, circa 1820, each with projecting stiles centering three-graduated horizontal backrests. (Sotheby's) $2,300

CHIPPENDALE

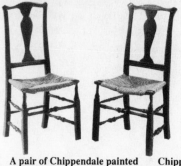

Chippendale mahogany carved side chair, Massachusetts, circa 1780, the serpentine crestrail with carved terminals.
(Skinner) $2,300

A pair of Chippendale painted maple rush-seat side chairs, New England, 1750–80, each with a serpentine crest.
(Sotheby's) $1,150

Chippendale mahogany carved side chair, Connecticut, circa 1780.
(Skinner) $1,092

The Maris-Gregg family Chippendale carved mahogany sidechair, Philadelphia, 1760-1780, the serpentine crest with carved acanthus leaves terminating in carved scrolled ears and centering a carved lobed shell.
(Christie's) $74,000

A pair of Chippendale carved mahogany sidechairs, Philadelphia, 1760–1770, the bow-shaped crestrail centering a carved shell flanked by molded and scrolled ears above a pierced scrolled and interlacing splat.
(Christie's) $27,600

A carved Chippendale mahogany sidechair, attributed to James Gillingham, Philadelphia, 1760-1780, with arched and serpentine crest above a Gothic pierced splat.
(Christie's) $10,925

The Governor Dummer Chippendale carved mahogany sidechair, Massachusetts, circa 1755-1760, the serpentine crest above a pierced splat with scrolled and carved volutes.
(Christie's) $11,500

A pair of Chippendale carved mahogany side chairs, attributed to the Shop of John Goddard, Newport, Rhode Island, 1760–1775.
(Christie's) $96,000

A Chippendale carved mahogany sidechair, New York, 1760-1780, the serpentine crest with carved acanthus scrolled ears and central carved arch above a pierced Gothic splat.
(Christie's) $2,990

CHIPPENDALE

Chippendale mahogany carved side chair, probably Delaware, late 18th century, refinished. (Skinner Inc.) **$3,250**

Pair of Chippendale ladder-back mahogany carved side chairs, Boston, Massachusetts, circa 1775, 37in. high. (Skinner) **$1,870**

Chippendale mahogany carved side chair, Boston or Salem area, Massachusetts, 1760–80. (Skinner) **$3,300**

A Chippendale carved mahogany side-chair, Philadelphia, 1765–1785, with bead-molded shaped crestrail centering a carved pendent leaf flanked by carved scrolled ears above a pierced and scroll-carved splat over a trapezoidal slip seat, 38in. high. (Christie's) **$7,750**

A pair of Chippendale carved walnut sidechairs, New England, 1750–1770, each with serpentine crestrail continuing to molded scrolling ears above a strap work splat, 38in. high. (Christie's) **$4,600**

A fine Chippendale carved walnut side chair, Philadelphia, circa 1760, with a serpentine crest-rail centered by a shell flanked by foliate boughs and shell-carved ears over fluted stiles, 41³/₄in. high. (Christie's) **$115,000**

A fine and rare Chippendale carved mahogany side chair, Philadelphia, circa 1770, on acanthus- and flowerhead-carved cabriole legs ending in claw-and-ball feet. (Sotheby's) **$175,000**

A fine and rare pair of Chippendale carved walnut side chairs, Philadelphia, circa 1765, each having a shell- and volute-carved crest. (Sotheby's) **$31,050**

A Chippendale carved walnut side chair, Philadelphia, 1760–1780, the serpentine crestrail centered by a lobed shell, on cabriole legs with ball-and-claw feet, 39¹/₂in. high. (Christie's) **$1,210**

CHIPPENDALE

A Chippendale carved and figured walnut side chair, Pennsylvania, circa 1760, the serpentine crest with a shell, ruffle and scroll-carved device.
(Sotheby's) $2,587

One of a pair of Chippendale carved mahogany side chairs, Massachusetts, circa 1790, refinished.
(Skinner Inc.) $625

Antique American country Chippendale side chair, in cherry with fan-carved crest and voluted ears.
(Eldred's) $495

A rare Chippendale mahogany side chair, Portsmouth, New Hampshire, attributed to Robert Harrold, circa 1780, the serpentine crest above a strapwork splat.
(Sotheby's) $5,750

A Chippendale mahogany ladder-back side chair, Philadelphia, circa 1780, the pierced strap-work crest above three similarly shaped back slats.
(Sotheby's) $2,070

Chippendale carved mahogany side chair, Philadelphia 1755–80, the acanthus-carved crest with a seven-lobed central shell above a tassel-carved splat, on cabriole legs.
(Skinner) $45,100

A Chippendale carved mahogany side chair, Philadelphia, 1760–1780, on cabriole legs with ball-and-claw feet, 37¾in. high.
(Christie's) $11,500

A Chippendale carved mahogany side chair, Philadelphia, circa 1770, on cabriole legs ending on claw-and-ball feet.
(Sotheby's) $2,000

A Chippendale carved walnut slipper chair, Philadelphia 1740-1760, on short cabriole legs with trifid feet, 37¾in. high. (Christie's New York) $5,500

CHIPPENDALE

Chippendale mahogany side chair, Western Massachusetts, 18th century, with shaped crest ending in scroll-back terminals.
(Skinner) $1,265

American Country Chippendale ladderback side chair, in mahogany, needlework upholstery, possibly original.
(Eldred's) $220

Chippendale carved mahogany side chair, Philadelphia, 1750–90, old refinish, 39½ in. high.
(Skinner Inc.) $143,000

A Chippendale mahogany side-chair, Newport, Rhode Island, 1765–1785, the serpentine crest with central carving flanked by molded scrolled ears over a pierced interscrolling vase-shaped splat, 38in. high.
(Christie's) $8,500

Chippendale mahogany carved side chair, Boston or Salem, Massachusetts, 1750–80, the shaped crest ends in molded terminals above a pierced splat.
(Skinner) $21,850

A Chippendale mahogany side chair, probably Massachusetts, circa 1770-1800, the serpentine crest with raked molded terminals.
(Skinner) $450

A cherry, Country Chippendale, upholstered side chair, Upper Connecticut River Valley, circa 1790, 38in. high.
(Skinner) $600

A Chippendale mahogany side chair, Philadelphia, 1765–1785, with foliate carved crestrail centering a C-scroll, 36¼in. high.
(Christie's) $43,700

Chippendale mahogany carved side chair, Pennsylvania or Delaware River Valley, 1745–60, 38¾ in. high.
(Skinner Inc.) $2,350

CHIPPENDALE

American Country Chippendale side chair, in maple with tiger maple crestrail, pierced splat, box stretcher, and rush seat.
(Eldred's) $440

A pair of Chippendale carved walnut side chairs, Philadelphia, 1760–80, the serpentine crest with incised edge and ears above a pierced vasiform splat.
(Christie's) $9,200

Chippendale mahogany carved side chair, Massachusetts, 1775–85, needlepoint slip seat, 38in. high.
(Skinner Inc.) $3,050

A Chippendale mahogany ladder-back side chair, Philadelphia, Pennsylvania, circa 1785, the molded serpentine crest continuing to molded stiles.
(Sotheby's) $4,887

A good pair of early Chippendale carved walnut side chairs, Philadelphia, circa 1760, each with a serpentine line-incised and shell-decorated crest.
(Sotheby's) $35,650

A very fine Chippendale carved mahogany side chair, Philadelphia, circa 1770, the molded seat rail on acanthus carved cabriole legs ending in claw-and-ball feet.
(Sotheby's) $65,000

A Transitional Chippendale carved and figured walnut side chair, Pennsylvania, circa 1770, the shell- and volute-carved serpentine crest with reverse-scrolling ears.
(Sotheby's) $5,175

Pair of Chippendale mahogany carved side chairs, Philadelphia, 1755–85, the shaped crests with beaded edges, scrolled terminals and central carved shells.
(Skinner) $35,650

A fine and rare Chippendale carved mahogany side chair, Philadelphia, circa 1770, the shaped volute- and leaf-carved crest above lozenge-carved stiles.
(Sotheby's) $29,900

CHIPPENDALE

Chippendale walnut carved side chair, Pennsylvania, circa 1780, old refinish, 38in. high. (Skinner) $4,887

A pair of Chippendale carved mahogany side chairs, Boston, 1760–80, each with bowed shaped crestrail above a pierced gothic splat. (Christie's) $25,300

A Chippendale cherrywood side chair with a square slip seat, Mass,, 1780-1800, 38in. high. (Christie's) $900

A Chippendale mahogany side-chair, Newport, 1760–1780, the serpentine crestrail centered by diapering flanked by molded scrolling ears over a scrolling, pierced vase-shaped splat, 37¼in. high. (Christie's) $5,500

An extremely fine and rare pair of early Chippendale carved walnut side chairs, Philadelphia, circa 1750, each with a serpentine rope and tassle-molded crest. (Sotheby's) $189,500

A Chippendale walnut side-chair, Philadelphia or Pennsylvania, 1740–1760, the incised serpentine crest flanked by shaped ears above a solid vase-shaped splat over a trapezoidal slip-seat, 39½in. high. (Christie's) $5,250

A good Chippendale carved mahogany side chair, Boston, Massachusetts, circa 1760, the serpentine ruffle and C-scroll carved crest ending in molded ears. (Sotheby's) $1,610

A pair of Chippendale carved mahogany side chairs, Boston, 1760–80, each with serpentine crestrail with molded ears above a pierced interlaced splat. (Christie's) $13,800

An extremely fine and rare Chippendale carved mahogany side chair, Philadelphia, circa 1770, the shaped leaf-carved crest centering a stop-fluted volute- and leaf-carved shell. (Sotheby's) $217,000

FEDERAL

A set of six Federal mahogany side chairs, Philadelphia, 1790–1810, each with bowed crestrail flanked by shaped ears and centering a carved 'pretzel' above three conforming slats flanked by molded stiles.   (Christie's) $19,550

A rare pair of Federal painted and polychrome-decorated birchwood cane-seat side chairs, attributed to John Seymoor, Boston, Massachusetts, circa 1800, each with a horizontal crest above an urn-form splat flanked by square stiles, the trapezoidal seat below on square tapering legs joined by an H-form stretcher; painted allover in tones of green, yellow and red on a black and red field simulating tortoiseshell.   (Sotheby's) $31,050

FEDERAL

Federal mahogany carved side chair, probably New York, circa 1810, old finish, 35in. high.
(Skinner) **$862**

Pair of Federal painted and decorated oval-back side chairs, probably Salem, Massachusetts, circa 1796, made for Elias Hasket Derby.
(Skinner) **$178,500**

A Federal carved mahogany shield-back side chair, Salem, Massachusetts, circa 1795, on square tapering legs, the rear legs flaring inward.
(Sotheby's) **$1,955**

One of a set of six late Federal parcel-gilt and grain-painted sidechairs, circa 1820, the rectangular crest with gilt-banded inset border above a similarly shaped splat.
(Butterfield & Butterfield)
(Six) **$920**

Pair of Federal mahogany shield back side chairs, Massachusetts, circa 1800, the molded arched crest above five molded splats flanked by molded down curving stiles.
(Butterfield & Butterfield) **$1,495**

A fine Federal carved and figured mahogany sidechair, New York, circa 1795, the serpentine molded crest centering a pierced splat adorned with swags, flowerheads, and plumage.
(Sotheby's) **$4,312**

A Federal paint and stencil-decorated plank seat side chair, Lehigh County, Pennsylvania, circa 1810, the horizontal crest flanked by projecting stiles.
(Sotheby's) **$632**

A fine pair of Federal paint-decorated side chairs, New England, circa 1805, each having an oval back centering uprights.
(Sotheby's) **$9,775**

A Federal grain-painted and stencil-decorated rush seat side chair, Philadelphia, circa 1810, the horizontal reverse-scrolling crest above a shaped stay rail.
(Sotheby's) **$2,070**

NEW ENGLAND

Pair of maple side chairs, New England, circa 1780, old refinish.
(Skinner) $1,610

Mahogany balloon-seat side chair, New England, circa 1750, 40¹/₂in. high.
(Skinner) $2,185

A pair of black-painted and turned maple bannister-back rush-seat side chairs, Northern New England, 1740–60.
(Sotheby's) $1,955

A rare turned and carved maple and ash rush seat armchair, New England, 1700–50, the shaped arched crest carved on the reverse *IS*.
(Sotheby's) $1,840

A rare pair of paint decorated pine open armchairs, New England, early 19th century, painted white with floral decoration on the crest rail, slats, seat and front legs.
(Sotheby's) $5,175

Transitional maple side chair, New England, 1760–80, with raked and molded crest terminals above a pierced splat.
(Skinner) $748

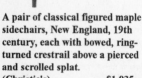

A pair of classical figured maple sidechairs, New England, 19th century, each with bowed, ring-turned crestrail above a pierced and scrolled splat.
(Christie's) $1,035

An unusual paint decorated and gilt stenciled pine tall-back rush-seat hall chair, New England, early 19th century.
(Sotheby's) $805

Pair of fan-back ash, pine and maple side chairs, New England, circa 1780, the serpentine crest rails above seven spindles.
(Skinner) $1,380

NEW YORK

One of a set of four classical mahogany veneer side chairs, Boston or New York, 1830–50, with red velvet slip seat.
(Skinner)　(Four)　**$748**

Two similar rare black-painted maple rush-seat side chairs, attributed to the Dominy family, East Hampton, Long Island, New York, 1740–1800.
(Sotheby's)　**$3,737**

One of a set of six stenciled green-painted side chairs, probably New York, circa 1820, 33¼in. high.
(Christie's)　**$3,500**

One of a set of twelve Federal maple side-chairs, New York, 1790–1810, each with a scrolling concave crestrail over a conforming slat and caned trapezoidal seat, 33½in. high.
(Christie's)　(Twelve)　**$5,500**

Two of a set of six classical mahogany gondola chairs, Duncan Phyfe, New York, circa 1833, each with an arched crest rail, on cabriole legs, 18½in. wide.
(Christie's)　(Six)　**$23,000**

A classical carved mahogany side chair, attributed to Duncan Phyfe, New York, 1805–1815, the scrolled swag tablet crest with sheafs of wheat and ribbon, 33in. high.
(Christie's)　**$5,175**

A Federal mahogany side-chair, New York, 1790–1810, the molded serpentine crestrail above a shield-shaped back, 37¾in. high.
(Christie's)　**$3,300**

Pair of fancy side chairs, New York City, 1805–15, with original faux tiger maple ground accented with dark painted striping and stenciled grape clusters.
(Skinner)　**$1,725**

A Federal mahogany klismos chair, New York, 1790–1810, the carved tablet crest centering intertwined cornucopiae over a lyre splat flanked by scrolled and reeded stiles, 23½in. high.
(Christie's)　**$6,250**

NEW YORK

Joseph P. McHugh and Co. oak side chair, New York, early 20th century, shaped lower leg, 36in. high.
(Skinner Inc.) $450

Two of a set of seven Federal stenciled and paint-decorated rush seat side chairs, American, probably New York, circa 1815.
(Sotheby's)
(Seven) $1,150

A Federal carved curly maple side chair, New York, early 19th century, on saber legs ending in carved paw feet.
(Sotheby's) $3,000

One of a set of twelve Federal maple side-chairs, New York, 1790–1810, each with a scrolling concave crestrail over a conforming slat and caned trapezoidal seat, 33½in. high.
(Christie's) (Twelve) $6,800

Two of a set of six classical mahogany chairs, attributed to Charles-Honore Lannuier, New York, 1810-1819, on paneled klismos legs with carved animal paw feet.
(Christie's)
(Six) $57,500

One of a fine set of six antique American Federal mahogany scrollback dining chairs in the manner of Duncan Phyfe, on reeded splayed legs, probably New York, circa 1810.
(Selkirk's) (Six) $6,400

A classical carved mahogany sidechair, attributed to Duncan Phyfe, New York, 1815-1825, the paneled scrolled tablet crest above a vine-carved lyre support.
(Christie's) $7,475

A rare pair of Federal inlaid mahogany shield-back side chairs, New York, circa 1800, each with a horizontal line and bellflower-inlaid crest.
(Sotheby's) $1,610

A red-painted, turned maple and woven-seat side chair, attributed to the Dominy family, East Hampton, Long Island, New York, 1740–1800.
(Sotheby's) $575

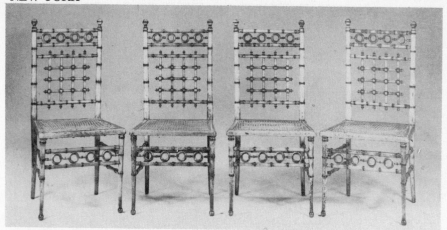

A set of four bamboo-turned figured maple sidechairs, attributed to R.J. Horner & Company, New York City, 1870–85, each with bamboo-turned ring-set tablet crest flanked by turned ball finials.
(Christie's)

$10,925

A fine and rare set of four carved mahogany caned seat saber-leg side chairs, attributed to Duncan Phyfe, New York, circa 1815, each with a horizontal, paneled reverse-scrolling crest carved with inter-locking cornucopiae, wheat, flowers, and ribbons, the flowerhead-carved curule-form backrest within reeded stiles and stayrails, continuing to a trapezoidal cane seat with reeded front rail above acanthus leaf-and hair-carved saber legs ending in paw feet.
(Sotheby's)

$79,500

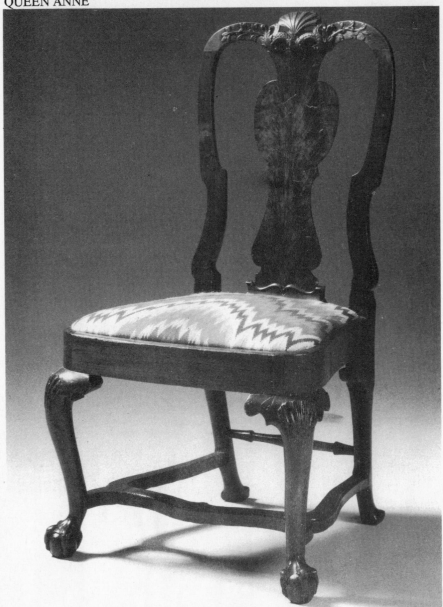

An important Charles Apthorp Queen Anne figured and carved walnut compass-seat side chair, carving attributed to John Welch, Boston, Massachusetts, circa 1735, the shaped crest centering a carved and pierced shell flanked by fish-scale-carved strapwork flanked by carved leafage, the crotch-figured veneered splat below, the compass-shaped stiles and with Cupid's-bow shoe below, the compass-shaped seat enclosing a slip seat cushion on shell-carved cabriole legs joined by molded stretchers ending in frontal claw-and-ball feet.

(Sotheby's) $321,500

QUEEN ANNE

A good Queen Anne walnut side chair, Boston, Massachusetts, 1740–60, the yoke-form crest above a vasiform splat. (Sotheby's) $3,737

A fine and rare pair of Queen Anne walnut sidechairs, Pennsylvania, circa 1750, each with a solid vase-form splat. (Sotheby's) $8,625

Queen Anne walnut side chair, Massachusetts, circa 1780, the serpentine crest rail with scrolled ears, 37¾ in. high. (Skinner Inc.) $2,750

A Queen Anne carved walnut side chair, Philadelphia, Pennsylvania, circa 1730, the serpentine volute- and shell-carved crest above a vase-form splat. (Sotheby's) $85,000

A very fine pair of Queen Anne carved walnut balloon-seat side chairs, Newport, Rhode Island, circa 1755, on shell volute and bellflower-carved cabriole legs. (Sotheby's) $80,000

A Queen Anne walnut sidechair, attributed to William Savery, 1721–1728, Philadelphia, the serpentine incised crestrail with shaped ears above a solid vasiform splat, on cabriole legs with pad feet. (Christie's) $2,990

Queen Anne side chair, New Hampshire, circa 1800, original stained surface with later varnish, replaced splint seat, 43½ in. high. (Skinner Inc.) $3,375

A fine pair of Queen Anne carved and figured walnut side chairs, Pennsylvania, circa 1760, each with a serpentine crest with reverse-scrolling ears. (Sotheby's) $9,775

One of two black-painted Queen Anne side-chairs, New York, late 18th century, each with yoked crestrail over a vase-shaped splat, 41½ in. high. (Christie's) (Two) $2,200

QUEEN ANNE

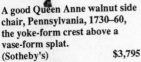

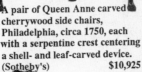

A good Queen Anne walnut side chair, Pennsylvania, 1730–60, the yoke-form crest above a vase-form splat. (Sotheby's) **$3,795**

A pair of Queen Anne carved cherrywood side chairs, Philadelphia, circa 1750, each with a serpentine crest centering a shell- and leaf-carved device. (Sotheby's) **$10,925**

Queen Anne walnut carved side chair, Newport, Rhode Island, or Boston, 1740–50, the shaped crestrail centering a carved shell. (Skinner) **$34,500**

A Queen Anne maple side chair, Massachusetts, 1730-1750, with carved yoke crest above a solid vase shaped splat, 42in. high. (Christie's New York) **$4,300**

A fine and rare pair of Queen Anne carved mahogany sidechairs, Newport, Rhode Island, 1750–1770, each with shaped crest centering a carved shell above a vase-shaped splat flanked by tapering stiles over a balloon seat, 38³/₄in. high. (Christie's) **$100,000**

A Queen Anne carved walnut sidechair, Rhode Island, 1740–1760, the shaped crestrail centering a carved shell above a solid vasiform splat. (Christie's) **$14,375**

A Queen Anne walnut sidechair, Southeastern Pennsylvania, late 18th/early 19th century, the arched crestrail above a solid vase-shaped splat, 37¹/₂in. high. (Christie's) **$863**

An assembled pair of Queen Anne sidechairs, Massachusetts, 1740-1760, each with yoke crest above a vase-shaped splat over a rounded slip-seat. (Christie's) **$14,950**

A rare Queen Anne stained maple side chair, Connecticut, 1740-1760, on cabriole legs with squared knees and pad feet, 43in. high. (Christie's New York) **$48,000**

QUEEN ANNE

Queen Anne walnut carved side chair, Newport, Rhode Island, circa 1760, refinished, 38in. high.
(Skinner Inc.) $8,900

Pair of Queen Anne walnut side chairs, Boston area, 1730–60, with balloon seats.
(Skinner) $13,800

A Queen Anne mahogany sidechair, Pennsylvania, 1750-1760, the arched and serpentine crest with shaped ears above a solid shaped splat.
(Christie's) $4,025

Painted Queen Anne side chair, New England, 18th century, with block and ring turnings, Spanish feet.
(Skinner) $1,100

A fine pair of Queen Anne carved maple rush-seat side chairs, New England, 1725–60, each with a shaped molded crest and stiles.
(Sotheby's) $2,012

The James Bartram Queen Anne carved walnut balloon-seat side chair, Philadelphia, circa 1740, the shaped shell-carved crest above line-incised stiles centering a vase-form splat.
(Sotheby's) $27,600

Antique American Queen Anne side chair in maple, vase shaped back splat, rush seat, turned legs ending in Spanish feet, 42½in. high.
(Eldred's) $350

Two similar Queen Anne mahogany side chairs, Massachusetts, 1740–60, each with a yoke-form crest, and vasiform splat.
(Sotheby's) $5,462

A Queen Anne carved mahogany side chair, Newport, Rhode Island, 1740-1770, the shaped crest with central shell carving, 38½in. high.
(Skinner) $62,700

QUEEN ANNE

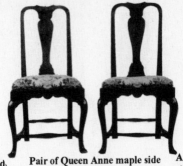

Stained Queen Anne maple side chair, New England, 18th century, with old rush seat and early surface.
(Skinner) $1,150

Pair of Queen Anne maple side chairs, Boston, Massachusetts, 1735-60, with scooped crests, flattened, tapered stiles, 40½in. high. (Skinner) $9,775

A Queen Anne carved walnut side chair, Philadelphia, 1740-60, the bowed crestrail centering a carved shell flanked by double scrolled volutes.
(Christie's) $101,500

Queen Anne crooked-back painted side chair, Massachusetts, circa 1760, the yoked carved crest rail above a vasiform splat and raked molded stiles.
(Skinner) $3,737

A pair of Queen Anne maple side chairs, attributed to William Savery, Philadelphia, 1730–1750, on creased cabriole front legs with trifid feet, 45in. high.
(Christie's) $35,000

Queen Anne carved walnut upholstered side chair, Rhode Island, circa 1750, refinished, worn old leather upholstery.
(Skinner Inc.) $10,600

A Queen Anne carved cherrywood and maple side chair, Boston, Massachusetts, circa 1730, the yoke-form crest above a baluster splat.
(Sotheby's) $3,162

Two similar Queen Anne carved maple side chairs, Massachusetts, 1730–50, each with a carved yoke-form crest above a vasiform splat.
(Sotheby's) $3,737

A Queen Anne dark green-painted maple side chair, Boston, Massachusetts, 1730–50, the yoke-form crest above a vasiform splat.
(Sotheby's) $1,610

A very fine and rare Queen Anne carved and figured walnut compass-seat side chair, Philadelphia, circa 1750, the serpentine shell- and volute-carved crest above a pierced acanthus- and volute-carved vasiform splat flanked by rounded stiles, the slip seat below within a conformingly-shaped frame, on ruffle-, shell- and leaf-carved cabriole legs ending in paneled trifid feet. (Sotheby's) $134,500

SHAKER

Shaker tilter side chair, New Lebanon or Watervliet, New York, circa 1850, with three arched slats, replaced rush seat. (Skinner) $546

Shaker maple side chair, Harvard, Massachusetts, circa 1860, with shaped pommels, tapering stiles, arched slats, cane seat. (Skinner) $1,092

Shaker maple tilter side chair, New Lebanon or Watervliet, New York, circa 1825-50, with old replaced rush seat. (Skinner) $460

One of a pair of Shaker maple and cherry tilter side chairs, Mt. Lebanon, New York, circa 1830, each with three arched slats. (Skinner)
          (Two) $1,495

A pair of Shaker chrome yellow stained tilter side chairs, probably Watervliet, New York, circa 1840, with three arched slats. (Skinner) $9,775

A Shaker maple diminutive slat-back chair, early 20th century, with rounded button finials above swelled cylindrical stiles above a trapezoidal cloth-tape woven seat. (Christie's) $1,610

Shaker cherry and maple tilter side chair, Mt. Lebanon, New York, circa 1830, with three arched slats and old splint seat. (Skinner) $402

Shaker stained tilting side chair, New Lebanon or Watervliet, New York, circa 1850, shaped pommels, tapering back posts and graduated three slats. (Skinner) $1,000

Shaker maple and birch side chair, Harvard, Massachusetts, circa 1860, old refinished surface and replaced rush seat. (Skinner) $862

STICKLEY

One of a fine and rare set of eight Gustav Stickley dining chairs, no. 353, three vertical slats, arched apron.
(Skinner) (Eight) $6,325

Two of a set of six Stickley Bros. dining chairs, including one armchair, circa 1908.
(Skinner)   (Six) $1,500

Gustav Stickley inlaid oak side chair. $2,500

Two of six L. & J.G. Stickley chairs, circa 1912, comprised of one armchair, no. 802, and five side chairs, no. 800, 36½in. high.
(Skinner Inc.)(Six) $1,700

Two Gustav Stickley ladderback chairs, original finish and leatherette seat, Gustav red mark.
(Skinner) $345

Two of a set of five Gustav Stickley dining chairs with rush seats, circa 1907, 37in. high.
(Skinner)   (Five) $2,500

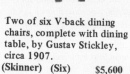

A leather upholstered dining chair, no. 355, by Gustav Stickley, circa 1910, 33¼in. high.
(Skinner) $1,250

Two of six V-back dining chairs, complete with dining table, by Gustav Stickley, circa 1907.
(Skinner) (Six) $5,600

One of six Gustav Stickley dining chairs, circa 1907, three horizontal slats, new seats in cream colored leather, 37½in. high.
(Skinner Inc.) (Six) $3,500

WILLIAM & MARY

A rare William and Mary turned maple upholstered-back side chair, Boston, Massachusetts, 1722–35. (Sotheby's) $2,300

A fine pair of William and Mary black-painted and turned maple ladder-back rush-seat side chairs, Delaware River Valley, 1750–80. (Sotheby's) $6,900

A rare William and Mary black-painted carved maple cane-seat side chair, Boston, Massachusetts, 1717–30. (Sotheby's) $14,950

A William and Mary maple side chair, Boston, Massachusetts, circa 1710, the carved, molded crest rail over molded square stiles, 45½in. high. (Skinner) $12,500

Two nearly identical William and Mary carved cherrywood rush-seat side chairs, New England, 1740-1760, each with a carved yoke-form crest. (Sotheby's) $1,150

A William and Mary red-stained and carved birchwood bannister-back splint-seat side chair, New England, 1730–50. (Sotheby's) $1,610

A fine William and Mary paint-decorated rush seat side chair, New Hampshire, circa 1740, the arched yoke-shaped crest above a vase-form splat. (Sotheby's) $7,475

A pair of William and Mary turned maple rush-seat bannister-back side chairs, Massachusetts, 1730–50, each with a shaped swan's-neck crest above four split balusters. (Sotheby's) $4,312

A rare William and Mary turned and joined walnut wainscot side chair, Southeastern Pennsylvania, 1700–30. (Sotheby's) $27,500

Set of six painted birdcage Windsor side chairs, New England, 1800–20, with curving crests, incised spindles and seats.
(Skinner) $6,325

A good set of six turned brown-painted bow-back Windsor side chairs, Connecticut, circa 1825, each with an arched molded crest above seven flaring spindles and a shaped plank seat.
(Sotheby's) $8,050

WINDSOR

A set of six rod-back mahogany Windsor side chairs, each with triple-rod back above seven spindles flanked by bamboo-turned stiles over a plank seat, 38¹/₂in. high.
(Christie's) $3,450

Assembled set of four fan-back Windsor side chairs, possibly Beriah Green, Preston, Connecticut, 1793–95, the serpentine crestrail above six spindles and vase and ring-turned stiles on shaped saddle seats.
(Skinner) $4,312

Assembled set of eight Windsor fan-back side chairs, New England, circa 1790, the chairs with serpentine crest rails, with bamboo or vase and ring turnings.
(Skinner)   (Eight) $4,887

WINDSOR

Painted fan-back Windsor side chair, probably New England, circa 1780, the serpentine chest rail above six spindles and vase and ring-turned stiles.
(Skinner) $2,070

Pair of bow-back braced Windsor side chairs, probably Connecticut, circa 1780, with seven spindles, shaped saddle seats.
(Skinner) $11,500

Painted fan-back Windsor side chair, New England, 1780–1800, black paint, 35³/₄in. high.
(Skinner Inc.) $425

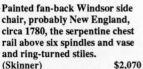

Painted braced fan-back Windsor side chair, possibly Connecticut, circa 1780 the serpentine crest rail above seven spindles.
(Skinner) $2,990

A good pair of black-painted and turned bow-back brace-back Windsor sidechairs, American, circa 1785, each with an arched molded crest and stiles centering ten flaring spindles.
(Sotheby's) $7,475

Braced fan-back maple and ash Windsor side chair, New England, late 18th century, shaped crest with vase and ring turned legs and stretchers, 37¹/₂in. high.
(Skinner) $1,320

One of a fine and rare set of six Federal paint decorated step down Windsor side chairs, Daniel Stewart, Farmington, Maine, circa 1820 .
(Sotheby's)(Six) $32,200

A pair of green-painted and turned Windsor fan-back side chairs, branded Joseph Henzey, Philadelphia, Pennsylvania, 1760–1806.
(Sotheby's) $37,950

A paint decorated Windsor side chair, New England, circa 1830, on turned legs joined by turned stretchers ending in tapered feet.
(Sotheby's) $1,380

WINDSOR

A good green and gray painted bow back brace-back turned Windsor side chair, New England, circa 1780.
(Sotheby's) $1,150

One of a set of six paint decorated Windsor side chairs, probably Pennsylvania, circa 1820.
(Sotheby's) (Six) $14,950

A fan-back Windsor sidechair, Philadelphia, 1765-1780, painted green with a layer of rust and ocher underneath.
(Christie's) $1,380

Painted decorated child's bowback Windsor side chair, New England, 1790–1810, gold striping on light blue ground, 24³/₄in. high.
(Skinner Inc.) $2,250

A paint decorated maple Windsor armchair and side chair, New England, mid 19th century, the chairs with turned crestings and medial splats.
(Sotheby's) $805

A painted Windsor fan-back side-chair, New England, 1780–1800, the serpentine bowed crestrail with shaped ears above seven spindles flanked by baluster-turned stiles, 37¼in. high.
(Christie's) $1,150

One of a set of six painted and decorated Windsor chairs, Pennsylvania, circa 1835, original light green paint, 33⁵/₈in. high.
(Skinner Inc.)   (Six) $2,350

Grained Windsor chair for stand-up desk, New England, early 19th century, original red and black graining, 46in. high
(Skinner Inc.) $650

A brace-back Windsor side back, branded *M.BLOOM/ N.YORK*, 1787–93, the hooped and molded crestrail centering nine swelled spindles.
(Christie's) $2,760

A set of six turned Windsor bow-back side chairs, each with an arched line incised crest centering nine faux bamboo spindles, American, circa 1820.
(Sotheby's) $7,475

Four similar paint-decorated bow-back Windsor side chairs, American, 18th/19th century, each with an arched molded crest inset with turned flaring spindles.
(Sotheby's) $920

A Chippendale walnut easy chair, North Shore, Massachusetts, 1765-1775, the arched, canted and upholstered back flanked by shaped wings continuing to outward scrolled arms and arm supports, above an upholstered seat, on cabriole legs joined by swelled and blocked H-stretchers and pad-and-disk feet, 43in. high.
(Christie's) $20,700

Natural finish wicker side chair, late 19th century, 45in. high.
(Skinner) $403

A longhorn armchair, attributed to Wenzel Friedrich, San Antonio, Texas, circa 1889.
(Christie's) $5,175

Circular mahogany easy chair, Middle Atlantic States, 1800–15.
(Skinner) $2,860

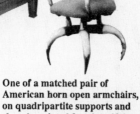

An American polychrome corner chair, late 19th century, the back in the form of a winged Indian figure and with downswept padded arms.
(Christie's) $6,370

Pair of walnut and upholstered cube chairs, New York, circa 1920, reupholstered spring cushion seat with upholstered back, brass mounted feet, unsigned.
(Skinner) $3,163

One of a matched pair of American horn open armchairs, on quadripartite supports and sharply pointed feet, late 19th century.
(Christie's) (Two) $4,200

Aesthetic Movement ebony inlaid maple slipper chair, circa 1870–80, attributed to Herter Brothers, New York, with India Rubber Co., casters.
(Skinner) $690

A painted and gilded cabriole armchair, Philadelphia, 1790–1810, the arched crest above an upholstered tablet back.
(Christie's) $81,700

William and Mary style walnut wing chair, late 19th century, with 18th century petit point upholstery.
(Skinner) $3,850

Lifetime Morris chair, pegged construction, through tenons on arms, four vertical side slats, quartersawn oak.
(Skinner)   **$2,875**

Two Renaissance Revival walnut, marquetry and part-ebonized slipper chairs, circa 1875–85, 36in. high.
(Skinner)   **$2,645**

An adjustable back armchair, attributed to J. Young & Co., circa 1910, 31½in. wide.
(Skinner)   **$1,150**

A Federal mahogany bergère, Massachusetts, 1790–1810, the arched crestrail above a padded back and sides continuing down to arm supports.
(Christie's)   **$3,680**

Pair of Art Deco black lacquer club chairs, circa 1930, each rectangular angled upholstered back flanked by sloped rounded armrests.
(Butterfield & Butterfield)
                                   $517

A William and Mary birchwood upholstered open armchair, American or Canadian, circa 1700, on vase-and-block-turned legs joined by an arched and scrolled frontal stretcher.
(Sotheby's)   **$4,025**

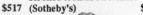

A tufted Turkish Revival upholstered armchair, American, 19th century, the rounded stuffed and shirred crestrail above a tufted and reclining barrel back.
(Christie's)   **$2,070**

Two of a set of four Eastlake Victorian parlor chairs in walnut, one gentleman's chair and three lady's chairs, all with arms.
(Eldred's)   (Four)   **$1,000**

A carved oak armchair, attributed to Bembe and Kimmel, New York, circa 1857, the horizontal molded crestrail centering a carved shield above a padded back, on vase shaped lotus carved legs.
(Christie's)   **$6,325**

Limbert slant arm Morris chair, original medium brown finish with slight overcoat.
(Skinner) **$2,530**

Modern walnut and upholstered lounger, America, black corduroy upholstery on walnut frame, 51½in. long.
(Skinner) **$748**

An American Arts & Crafts oak reclining chair with reclining mechanism, in the manner of A. H. Davenport of Boston. (Phillips) **$375**

Important Warren McArthur upholstered aluminium tilting swivel armchair, Rome, New York, circa 1935, original blue leather upholstery on spun aluminium frame with four casters.
(Skinner) **$6,325**

Charles and Ray Eames Lounge 670 and ottoman, designed 1956, for Herman Miller, Zeeland, Michigan, rosewood veneer on laminated wood shell with original black upholstery, 32½in. wide.
(Skinner) **$1,840**

Rococo Revival rosewood laminated side chair, attributed to J. H. Belter, circa 1860, on carved seat rail and cabriole legs, 33¾in. high. (Skinner Inc.) **$525**

Art Deco bird's-eye maple club chair, circa 1930, the rectangular upholstered back with rounded corners and sides.
(Butterfield & Butterfield) **$1,150**

American iron campaign folding arm chair, 19th century, with pale gray buttoned leather upholstery.
(Butterfield & Butterfield) **$675**

American 19th century style spoon back armchair, on squat cabriole legs and scrolled feet, upholstered in red and ivory fabric. (County Group) **$725**

A Plail Bros. barrel-back armchair, Wayland, N.Y., circa 1910, 33in. high. (Skinner) **$1,375**

An upholstered oak armchair with cut out sides, circa 1905, 28¾in. wide. (Skinner) **$1,750**

A laminated mahogany armchair, circa 1900, 45in. high. (Skinner) **$870**

One of a fine and large pair of American modern gothic walnut and oak parlor chairs, attributed to Daniel Pabst, the design attributed to Frank Furness, circa 1877. (Butterfield & Butterfield) (Two) **$2,350**

A pair of Aesthetic carved and ebonised side chairs, attributed to Herter Brothers, New York City, 1870–90. (Christie's) **$3,680**

A classical mahogany upholstered armchair en gondole, Duncan Phyfe, New York, circa 1833, the arched back and curled arms that begin as carved scrolls, 25in wide. (Christie's) **$99,300**

American Aesthetic Movement rosewood, inlay and parcel-gilt slipper chair, attributed to Herter Brothers, New York City, circa 1880, 30¼in. high. (Skinner) **$3,450**

Stainless steel and leather lounge chair, with head roll, supported by leather buckled straps on X-shape stainless steel frame, 29½in. high. (Skinner Inc. **$675**

Fancy wicker armchair, by Heywood Bros. & Co., Mass., 39in. high. (Skinner) **$2,000**

L. & J. G. Stickley slat-sided armchair, circa 1912, style no. 408, 26½in. diam. (Skinner) $2,100

A Gustav Stickley adjustable back drop armchair, no. 369, circa 1907, signed with red decal, 38in. high. (Skinner) $6,350

A slat sided armchair with cushion seat, by L. & J. G. Stickley, circa 1912. $2,100

Gustav Stickley fixed back armchair, circa 1907, no. 324, flat arm over six vertical slats, 39in. high. (Skinner) $1,250

A Gustav Stickley bird's-eye maple wide slat cube chair, circa 1903-04, no. 328. (Skinner) $3,750

Gustav Stickley Morris chair, circa 1910, no. 332, adjustable back, five vertical slats, straight seat rail, unsigned, 40in. high. (Skinner Inc.) $5,000

A Gustav Stickley bow armchair, no. 335, circa 1905, signed with small red decal, 37½in. high. (Skinner) $8,800

A Gustav Stickley willow armchair, circa 1907, 39in. high, 31in. wide. (Skinner) $750

A Gustav Stickley bent arm spindle Morris chair, circa 1907, with spring cushion seat. (Skinner) $18,750

STICKLEY

Gustav Stickley mahogany bow armchair, circa 1907, no. 336, 36in. high. (Skinner) $2,800

Rare leather sling seat arm chair, Toby Furniture Co., Chicago, circa 1900, design attributed to Gustav Stickley, unsigned, 33in. wide. (Skinner Inc.) $4,300

An L. & J. G. Stickley adjust-able back flat armchair, no. 412, circa 1909, 35in. wide. (Skinner)

          $3,800

L. & J.G. Stickley adjustable back armchair, Fayetteville, New York, c. 1909, no. 470, flat arm with arched support, 27$^{1}/_{2}$in. wide. (Skinner Inc) $1,250

A Gustav Stickley slat-sided cube chair, no. 331, circa 1910, 25¼in. wide. (Skinner) $7,500

A bent arm spindle Morris chair, no. 369, by Gustav Stickley, with adjustable back, 24in. high. (Skinner) $18,750

A Gustav Stickley willow arm-chair, circa 1910, the tall back with square cut-outs centered by flat arms, unsigned, 42¾in. high. (Skinner) $5,000

Early Gustav Stickley oak Morris chair, No. 2341, circa 1901, adjustable back, flat shaped arm over two vertical slats and interior arched corbels. (Skinner) $2,875

L. & J. G. Stickley fixed back armchair, circa 1912, with up-holstered spring cushion seat with back cushion, unsigned, 32in. high. (Skinner) $6,500

A Classical Revival ebonized and rosewood veneer chair, attributed to Herter Brothers, New York City, 1870–85.
(Christie's) $7,475

American ladderback armchair, in an old reddish-brown finish, turned stiles, finials, and front stretcher, rush seat.
(Eldred's) $440

Norman Cherner laminated and bentwood armchair, circa 1958, for Plycraft, Lawrence, Massachusetts, unsigned.
(Skinner) $575

A carved and stained chair, American, 20th century, the rectangular carved and pierced splat of a face with swirling carved hair, 37¼in. high.
(Christie's) $345

Mission oak slat-sided cube chair, 1914, seven vertical back slats, six vertical slats under each arm, inscribed *Made by John Derwallis – 1914.*
(Skinner) $575

A diminutive slat-back armchair, Delaware Valley, late 18th/early 19th century, the three graduated shaped slats flanked by cylindrical stiles, 25in. high.
(Christie's) $805

One of a pair of American hickory open armchairs, on simple turned legs, stamped 'Old Hickory, Artinsvill, Indiana'.
(Bearne's)   (Two) $1,000

Painted ladder-back armchair, Long Island or New Jersey, 1730–1800, old black paint with gold accents, old painted splint seat.
(Skinner) $1,610

Painted maple slat back arm-chair, New Jersey or Hudson River Valley, 1725-1775, 40in. high.
(Skinner) $1,630

115

A black-stained turned oak
Pilgrim century great chair,
with turned finials centering
flaring backrests.
(Sotheby's) $4,600

Arts and Crafts armchair,
quartersawn oak, nine vertical
back spindles, dark original
finish.
(Skinner) $633

Painted crown great chair,
Connecticut, last half 18th
century, the heart-pierced
shaped crest above four
molded balusters.
(Skinner) $6,900

Painted and turned maple
ladder-back armchair, probably
Portsmouth, New Hampshire,
18th century.
(Skinner) $5,750

Twig armchair, 20th century,
shaped arms and back
comprised of Southern woods,
49in. high.
(Skinner Inc.) $500

Plail Co. barrel back armchair,
Wayland, New York, circa
1910, spring cushion seat
over wide front seat rail, 40in.
high. (Skinner Inc.) $1,380

Harden & Co. armchair, circa
1910, wide straight crest rail
over three vertical back slats,
flat arms over three wide
vertical slats.
(Skinner) $400

Painted ladderback armchair,
England or America, 18th
century, (significant paint loss
and restoration), 48^{1}/2in. high.
(Skinner Inc.) $225

Handcraft Furniture slant back
Morris chair, circa 1910, No.
497, stationary back with wide
arms over five vertical slats,
41in. high.
(Skinner Inc.) $2,800

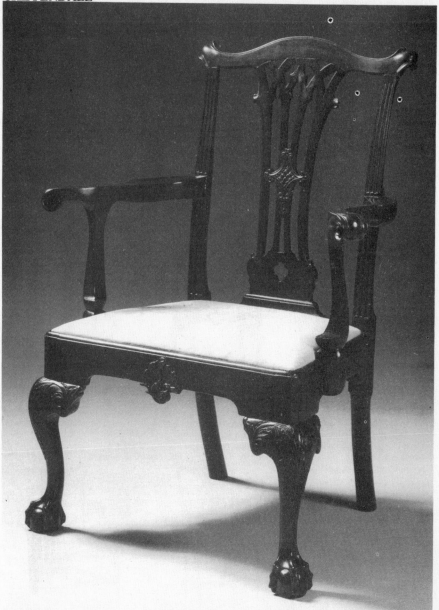

An important Chippendale carved mahogany gothic back armchair, Philadelphia, circa 1760, the arched serpentine crest with scrolled ears above a pierced beaker-form splat centering a diamond and flowerhead carved lunette, fluted stiles flanking, the shaped arms ending in scrolled handholds above incurvate arm supports and a trapezoidal seat, the front seat rail carved with an asymmetrical acanthus-leaf device, acanthus-leaf and strap-work-carved cabriole legs ending in claw-and-ball feet.
(Sotheby's) $508,500

CHIPPENDALE

An extremely rare Chippendale carved walnut armchair, Philadelphia, 1760–1780, on cabriole legs with stocking trifid feet, appears to be original leather-upholstered seat, 39¾in. high. (Christie's) $60,000

A Chippendale walnut open armchair, probably Philadelphia, circa 1780, the shaped crest and pierced splat above a slip-seat. (Sotheby's) $750

Fine and rare Chippendale carved mahogany open armchair, Philadelphia, circa 1760.
(Sotheby's) $134,500

A Chippendale walnut armchair, Pennsylvania, 1750–1780, the serpentine crestrail with scrolling ears centering a shell above a spurred vase-shaped splat and serpentine, scrolling arms, 41½ in. high. (Christie's) $30,250

An important Chippendale carved mahogany Gothic-back armchair, Philadelphia, circa 1760, the arched serpentine crest with scrolled ears above a pierced beaker-form splat. (Sotheby's) $508,500

A Chippendale carved walnut armchair, Philadelphia, 1760–1780, the serpentine crestrail centering a foliate and petal carved cartouche above a pierced vase-shaped splat, on cabriole legs with ball-and-claw feet.
(Christie's) $20,700

A Chippendale carved walnut armchair, Philadelphia, 1760–80, the serpentine crestrail centering a carved shell motif flanked by molded outward scrolling ears, 40½in. high. (Christie's) $18,400

A Chippendale carved mahogany armchair, Portsmouth, New Hampshire, 1765-1775, the serpentine molded crestrail above an interlaced pierced splat. (Christie's) $34,500

A Chippendale carved mahogany armchair, attributed to Daniel Trotter, Philadelphia, 1780-1790, the pierced double-bowed crestrail with rosette-reserved ears. (Christie's) $14,950

FEDERAL

A Federal carved mahogany armchair, with scrolling molded tablet crestrail flanked by reeded stiles over X-shaped molded ribs, 35in. high. (Christie's) $3,000

A pair of Federal carved mahogany armchairs, New York, circa 1800, each with a serpentine crest above a pierced splat.
(Sotheby's) $1,840

The Timothy Edwards Federal carved mahogany armchair, Rhode Island, 1790–1810. (Christie's) $460

A Federal white-painted and parcel-gilt armchair, Philadelphia, circa 1790, the arching molded crestrail decorated with acorns amid oak leaves over a padded tapering back flanked by reeded baluster-turned stiles, 36in. high.(Christie's) $58,750

Two late Federal carved mahogany chairs, New York, 1810-1815, each with tablet crest rail above a carved lyre, 32½in. high. (Christie's New York) $26,600

A Federal carved and inlaid mahogany armchair, attributed to Thomas Howard, Jr., Providence, Rhode Island, 1790-1810, the truncated shield-back inlaid with double lines and bellflowers, 35¼in. high. (Christie's) $3,220

A Federal mahogany arm chair, Salem, Massachusetts, 1790-1810, the rectangular back with reeded crest, stiles and three vertical bars,32¼in. high. (Christie's New York) $2,700

Two of a set of ten Federal carved mahogany chairs, Philadelphia or Baltimore, circa 1800–1810, on square tapering legs joined by H-stretchers. (Butterfield & Butterfield)
(Ten) $11,000

A Federal carved mahogany armchair, attributed to Duncan Phyfe or one of his contemporaries, the horizontal reverse scrolling crest carved with bow knots and wheat sheaves.
(Sotheby's) $5,462

MASSACHUSETTS

Turned maple and ash great chair, probably Massachusetts, circa 1700.
(Skinner) **$9,200**

Joined carved oak great chair, England or southern Massachusetts, 17th century.
(Skinner) **$1,150**

American Boston rocker, with tiger maple toprail.
(Eldred's) **$357**

Maple and ash turned armchair, coastal Massachusetts, mid 18th century, old mustard brown paint.
(Skinner) **$3,335**

A carved oak wainscot armchair, Essex County, Massachusetts, circa 1640–1700, the stepped crestrail carved with double arcades, 36¼in. high.
(Christie's) **$211,500**

A turned maple great-chair, Massachusetts, late 17th/early 18th century, with spool-turned crest rail above a further turned crest rail over three turned vertical splats, 40in. high.
(Christie's) **$5,750**

Federal mahogany lolling chair, Massachusetts, circa 1800, beaded serpentine arms, on molded tapering legs.
(Skinner) **$33,000**

Joined and turned oak great chair, Massachusetts, 17th century.
(Skinner) **$5,175**

A Chippendale mahogany lolling chair, Massachusetts, circa 1780, on square legs joined by stretchers.
(Sotheby's) **$3,500**

NEW ENGLAND

Painted maple and ash armchair, New England, early 18th century, the four arched slats joining turned stiles with ball finials.
(Skinner)   **$5,175**

Turned great chair, New England, all-over dark red stain, worn leather upholstered seat, 44¹/₂in. high.
(Skinner Inc.)   **$4,050**

Painted turned armchair, New England, last half 18th century, the rolled crest rail above a vasiform splat.
(Skinner)   **$1,840**

A Queen Anne turned-maple rush-seat armchair, New England, 1730–60, the shaped crest above a vasiform splat.
(Sotheby's)   **$3,162**

A painted and turned maple double-back conversation 'Courting' chair, New England, 1780–1810, painted brown with yellow highlights, length 43in.
(Sotheby's)   **$10,000**

A black-painted turned maple bannister-back rush-seat armchair, New England, 1740–70, the arched molded crest flanked by vase- and ring-turned finials.
(Sotheby's)   **$2,012**

Maple and ash slat-back armchair, probably New England, 18th century, the turned stiles joining three arched slats.
(Skinner)   **$2,415**

Painted turned slat back arm- chair, New England, last quarter 17th century, rush seat, 42in. high overall.
(Skinner Inc.)   **$15,000**

A paint-decorated maple rush- seat 'Spanish foot' armchair, New England, 1750–80, the arched volute-carved crest above a vase-form splat.
(Sotheby's)   **$4,887**

QUEEN ANNE

Queen Anne maple carved arm chair, Connecticut River Valley, 18th century, 36in. high.
(Skinner Inc.) $6,200

A Queen Anne mahogany armchair, Mass., circa 1750, 42in. high.
(Skinner) $66,000

Kittinger Queen Anne style mahogany armchair, spoon form back with scrolled arm terminals, gold japanned figures and leaves.
(Du Mouchelles) $500

A very fine Queen Anne walnut armchair, Philadelphia, 1740–60, with removable slip seat enclosing a pewter basin, the basin probably Philadelphia, 18th century.
(Sotheby's) $20,000

Queen Anne maple armchair, probably Massachusetts, mid 18th century, the shaped yoked crest rail above a chamfered vasiform splat.
(Skinner) $2,760

A Queen Anne walnut armchair, Pennsylvania, 1740–1760, the scrolling arms with incurved supports above a trapezoidal slip seat concealing the support for a chamber pot, 42^1/2in. high.
(Christie's) $3,850

Antique American Queen Anne armchair, in walnut with vase-shaped splat, outswept scrolled arms.
(Eldred's) $2,420

A Queen Anne carved walnut open armchair, Pennsylvania, circa 1750, the serpentine shell-carved crest above a vase-form splat.
(Sotheby's) $10,350

A Queen Anne figured maple armchair, Philadelphia, 1740–60, the serpentine crestrail with molded ears above a solid vasiform splat, 45^1/2in. high.
(Christie's) $134,500

QUEEN ANNE

The Jacob Meyers fine and rare Queen Anne carved and figured walnut open armchair, Philadelphia, Pennsylvania, circa 1750.
(Sotheby's) $519,500

Antique American Queen Anne spoon-back armchair, in maple with shaped crest rail, finely bent arms with scrolled ends.
(Eldred's) $770

A good Queen Anne carved maple armchair, Philadelphia, 1730-50, the yoke-form molded crest above a baluster splat.
(Sotheby's) $23,000

A Queen Anne maple child's armchair, American, 1740-60, the yoked crestrail above a solid vasiform splat, flanked by ring and baluster turned stiles, 23in.
(Christie's) $1,150

A rare Queen Anne maple armchair, probably Rhode Island, 1740-1760, on lambrequin scrolled cabriole legs with pad feet, 39½in. high.
(Christie's New York) $12,400

A Queen Anne stained and figured maple open armchair, Northeastern New England, probably coastal New Hampshire or Boston area, 1720-50. (Sotheby's) $14,950

A Country Queen Anne transitional tiger maple armchair, New England, mid 18th century, the yoked crest above vasiform splat, 41¼in. high.
(Skinner) $5,625

Queen Anne walnut armchair, Rhode Island, mid 18th century, the yoked crest above a vasiform splat, 39½in. high.
(Skinner Inc.) $50,000

A fine and rare Queen Anne turned walnut open armchair, Boston, Massachusetts, circa 1740, the yoke-form crest above a vasiform splat.
(Sotheby's) $60,250

STICKLEY

Fine Gustav Stickley armchair, five slats under arms, four horizontal back slats, original finish, Gustav Stickley red mark.
(Skinner) $1,900

A Gustav Stickley spindle-sided cube chair, no. 391, circa 1907, 26in. wide.
(Skinner) $22,000

Rare Gustav Stickley oak Eastwood chair, circa 1902-1904, signed with a red decal in a box, 36in. wide. (Skinner Inc.) $25,000

A Gustav Stickley oak 'East-wood' chair with original rope support for seat, circa 1902.
(Skinner) $35,000

Rare and early Gustav Stickley bow arm Morris chair, No. 336, original deep chocolate finish, original pegs and washers, original seat cushion and rope seat foundation.
(Skinner) $16,100

L. & J.G. Stickley fixed back armchair, Fayetteville, New York, circa 1910, no. 438, four horizontal back slats, 24¹/₂in. high.
(Skinner Inc.) $950

L. & J. G. Stickley tall back armchair, with spring cushion seat, no. 837, circa 1907, 44in. high.
(Skinner) $950

Gustav Stickley slant arm Morris chair, no. 369, circa 1904, adjustable back with five horizontal back slats, held with round pegs.
(Skinner) $5,500

One of a set of six Gustav Stickley dining chairs, including 'one armchair, circa 1907, 18in. wide.
(Skinner)   (Six) $5,600

STICKLEY

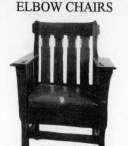

One of a pair of Gustav Stickley armchairs, No. 360, original finish with good quarter-sawn oak, Gustav red decal on both.
(Skinner) (Two) $3,450

Arts and Crafts armchair, attributed to Charles Stickley, large tenons with extended corbels.
(Skinner) $978

Gustav Stickley 'rabbit ear' armchair, 1901-02, signed, 41½in. high.
(Skinner) $1,000

A tall spindle-back armchair, no. 386, by Gustav Stickley, 49½in. high.
(Skinner) $15,000

A leather upholstered dining armchair, by Gustav Stickley, circa 1910, no. 355A, 36¼in.
(Skinner) $2,500

Gustav Stickley armchair, no. 366, circa 1907, straight crest rail over three vertical slats, flat arms with front corbels, 26in. wide.
(Skinner) $350

Gustav Stickley revolving office chair, no. 361, circa 1904, signed with decal in a box, 28in. wide.
(Skinner) $2,180

Stickley Brothers-style inlaid armchair, arched apron, pegged construction.
(Skinner) $1,495

L. & J. G. Stickley oak Morris chair, No. 830, circa 1912, spring cushion seat, 'The Work of...' decal.
(Skinner) $1,265

WILLIAM & MARY

A William and Mary black-painted splint-seat bannister-back armchair, New England or Long Island, 1720–50.
(Sotheby's) **$1,725**

A William and Mary turned poplar great chair, Massachusetts, 1660-1690, the turned double crestrail with urn-and-flame finials.
(Christie's) **$10,925**

A William and Mary black and painted and carved maple bannister-back armchair, New England, probably Connecticut, 1730–50, the arched crest with scrolled ends.
(Sotheby's) **$8,912**

A William and Mary banister-back crown great-chair possibly by Nathaniel Street, Norwalk area, 1725–1745, with scrolled crown and quadruple heart-pierced crest, 48^7/$_8$in. high.
(Christie's) **$22,500**

A William and Mary carved and turned red-stained maple rush-seat open armchair, New England, 1730–50, the yoke-form crest above a vasiform splat.
(Sotheby's) **$2,875**

A William and Mary crown great-chair attributed to the shop of Thomas Salmon, Stratford, Connecticut, 1725–1735, on turned legs joined by double turned stretchers, 43in. high.
(Christie's) **$8,500**

A William and Mary painted bannister back armchair, probably Massachusetts, circa 1750, the cut out splat above five split bannister spindles, 46in. high.
(Skinner) **$1,880**

A William and Mary red-painted great chair, Connecticut, 1735–1745, with scrolled and heart-pierced crown crest above four vertical molded bannisters over a rushed seat, 46^1/$_2$in. high.
(Christie's) **$2,760**

A William and Mary carved and turned maple bannister-back rush-seat armchair, Boston, Massachusetts, 1730–50, the pierced crest comprising C-scrolls and stylized leaves.
(Sotheby's) **$21,850**

WINDSOR

Sack-back Windsor chair, Rhode Island or Massachusetts, 1770–90, old dark green paint, 36in. high.
(Skinner)   **$5,175**

Antique American plank seat Windsor armchair with bamboo turnings.
(Eldred's)   **$130**

Windsor comb-back armchair, Pennsylvania, 1765–80, refinished.
(Skinner)   **$4,312**

A fan-back Windsor sidechair, Woodbury, Connecticut, 1780-1810, the arched crest with rounded ears above six swelled spindles.
(Christie's)   **$1,035**

Windsor maple, ash, and poplar low-back armchair, with vase and ring turnings and saddle seat.
(Skinner)   **$1,265**

A blue-painted Windsor sack-back armchair, New England, late 18th century, the arching crestrail above seven spindles and shaped arms over baluster-turned supports and a shaped plank seat, retains 19th century paint, 43^{1}/₂in. high.
(Christie's)   **$13,000**

Hickory ash and chestnut comb-back Windsor armchair, Philadelphia area, 1760–80, with scrolled and carved crest terminals.
(Skinner)   **$5,462**

Windsor comb-back applied armchair, New England, circa 1810, with carved mahogany scrolled arms and bamboo turnings.
(Skinner)   **$747**

Windsor ash and maple comb-back armchair, Pennsylvania, 18th century.
(Skinner)   **$6,600**

WINDSOR

A painted and turned Windsor bow-back armchair, American, circa 1795, on turned legs joined by turned stretchers.
(Sotheby's) $1,495

Painted low back Windsor armchair, Philadelphia area, 1765–80, dark green later paint, 28in. high.
(Skinner Inc.) $925

Child's painted sack-back Windsor chair, New England, late 18th century, painted black, 25in. high.
(Skinner Inc.) $500

A comb back Windsor arm-chair, Pennsylvania, late 18th century, on flaring baluster turned and cylindrical legs with ball feet, 42in. high.
(Christie's New York) $5,500

A pair of black-painted, parcel-gilt and turned maple continuous-arm Windsor chairs, Rhode Island, circa 1760.
(Sotheby's) $37,950

A good carved and turned Windsor comb-back armchair, Philadelphia, Pennsylvania, circa 1760–80, the serpentine arched crest terminating in volute-carved terminals.
(Sotheby's) $7,475

A very fine painted and turned Windsor brace-back armchair, Rhode Island, circa 1780, the incised bowed crest above nine baluster-turned and tapered spindles. (Sotheby's) $10,000

A rare green-painted low-back Windsor armchair, Philadelphia, circa 1765, the concave line-incised arms with outscrolled terminals.
(Sotheby's) $2,875

A turned and carved Windsor comb-back armchair, Pennsylvania, circa 1760–80, the shaped crest with volute-carved ears.
(Sotheby's) $5,462

WINDSOR

Painted sack-back Windsor armchair, New England, circa 1780, the bowed crest rail above seven spindles.
(Skinner) $3,335

Maple and ash comb-back Windsor armchair, Connecticut, 1780–1800, with shaped curving crest above a shaped incised seat.
(Skinner) $1,610

Antique American sack-back Windsor armchair, Rhode Island, 18th century, in pine, maple and other woods.
(Eldred's) $575

A black-painted sack-back Windsor armchair, Lancaster County, Pennsylvania, late 18th/early 19th century, the arched crestrail above seven turned-cylindrical spindles.
(Christie's) $19,550

A pair of black-painted turned and carved bow-back Windsor armchairs, New England, probably Rhode Island, early 19th century.
(Sotheby's) $5,462

A carved sack-back Windsor armchair, Rhode Island, 1780–1800, the arched crest above seven spindles over a continuous armrail with scrolled knuckle hand grips.
(Christie's) $5,520

Grain painted and stencil decorated Windsor commode chair, Connecticut, early 19th century, the crest with floral stenciled decoration.
(Skinner) $1,725

Painted writing arm Windsor chair, Connecticut, 1780-1800, with baluster and ring turned splayed legs. (Skinner Inc.) $8,750

A fine black, green and red-painted carved comb-back Windsor armchair, Pennsylvania, circa 1785, on vase- and ring-turned legs.
(Sotheby's) $13,225

Natural finish child's table chair with shelf by Heywood Brothers, late 19th century.
(Skinner) $250

A William and Mary turned maple and hickory splayed-leg child's chair, New England or Long Island, New York, 1720–60.
(Sotheby's) $920

Late 19th/20th century natural finish wicker child's highchair by Heywood Brothers.
(Skinner) $200

A birchwood and ash rush-seat ladder-back weaver's chair, American, 1800–1820, the back with three slats, the arms and rush-seat below on turned legs joined by stretchers.
(Sotheby's) $1,955

Rare painted Windsor highchair, possibly southeastern Massachusetts, circa 1780, the serpentine crest rail with circular terminals above five spindles and vase and ring turned stiles.
(Skinner) $28,750

A slat-back high chair, Delaware Valley, late 18th/early 19th century, centering four shaped and graduated slats flanked by cylindrical stiles, 37¼in. high.
(Christie's) $3,910

Slat back maple child's high chair, Philadelphia or the Delaware River Valley, 1720-1760, old color, old twisted hemp seat, 39in. high.
(Skinner Inc.) $7,500

A rare William and Mary turned maple splayed-leg high chair, New England, 1690–1720, with turned finials above ring-and-sausage-turned stiles.
(Sotheby's) $5,175

A fine and rare black painted high chair, Delaware River Valley, 1730-1760, with four graduated and arched slats, on turned front feet, 38in. high.
(Christie's) $7,550

HIGH CHAIRS

Maple and ash turned high chair, Delaware River Valley, late 18th century, 40³/₄in. high. (Skinner) $920

Painted Windsor rod-back highchair, New England, early 19th century, *TH* carved on underside of seat.
(Skinner) $1,150

Bow-back Windsor high chair, New England, circa 1790, original black paint, 33in. high. (Skinner) $19,550

A black-painted banister-back child's high-chair, New England, 19th century, the ring and baluster-turned stiles framing a scalloped crestrail above three bannisters over a rush seat, 36¹/₂in. high. (Christie's) $2,250

Chippendale birch high chair, probably Massachusetts, circa 1780, the shaped crest rail above vase splat, 36½in. high. (Skinner) $3,600

A very fine and rare green- and yellow-painted and turned Windsor sack-back child's highchair, New York, circa 1760–80, the arched crest above seven spindles.
(Sotheby's) $51,750

Painted turned child's high chair, Bergen County, New Jersey, late 18th century, worn old green paint, replaced rush seat.
(Skinner Inc.) $880

A green-painted and turned cherrywood bow-back Windsor highchair, New England, possibly Rhode Island, early 19th century. (Sotheby's) $1,035

Painted ash and maple child's ladderback highchair, New England, 18th century, original black paint (missing foot rest), 38½in. high. (Skinner Inc.) $4,050

A Federal mahogany lolling chair, Massachusetts, 1790–1800, the serpentine crest above a raked upholstered back over shaped arms above molded downswept arms above an over-upholstered trapezoidal seat, on ring turned legs and tapered feet.
(Christie's) $5,175

Federal mahogany inlaid lolling chair, probably Massachusetts, circa 1790, the rectangular back with serpentine crest.
(Skinner) $3,737

Federal mahogany inlaid lolling chair, New England, circa 1800.
(Skinner) $1,540

A Federal mahogany lolling chair, New England, circa 1790, the shaped crest with peaked ears above a padded back.
(Sotheby's) $19,550

A Federal inlaid mahogany lolling chair, Massachusetts, 1790-1810, the serpentine crest above an upholstered back, flanked by outward scrolling arms.
(Christie's) $8,625

The Joseph Wharton Chippendale carved mahogany upholstered open armchair, Philadelphia, Pennsylvania, circa 1770, raised on frontal square molded legs.
(Sotheby's) $585,500

A Chippendale carved mahogany lolling chair, Portsmouth area, New Hampshire, circa 1785, the upholstered back with serpentine-shaped crest.
(Sotheby's) $35,650

A Federal mahogany lolling chair, Massachusetts, 1790-1810, the serpentine crestrail above a canted upholstered back, 41in. high.
(Christie's) $18,400

A Federal mahogany lolling chair, coastal Massachusetts or New Hampshire, circa 1810, the serpentine crest flanked by shaped arms.
(Christie's) $10,925

Federal mahogany lolling chair, New England, circa 1800, with molded arms and legs, old surface, 42in. high.
(Skinner Inc.) $6,375

Federal mahogany lolling chair, probably Massachusetts, circa 1790, 45½in. high.
(Skinner) **$1,495**

A Chippendale mahogany lolling chair, Massachusetts, circa 1780, the serpentine crest above a padded back.
(Sotheby's) **$2,070**

A Federal mahogany lolling chair, Mass., circa 1815, 44in. high.
(Skinner) **$6,800**

A fine and rare Federal inlaid mahogany lolling chair, Northeastern Massachusetts, circa 1815, on ring-turned bulbous tapered reeded legs and turned tapering feet.
(Sotheby's) **$25,875**

One of a pair of Chippendale mahogany upholstered arm-chairs, Charlestown, New Hampshire, circa 1795, attributed to Bliss and Horswill.
(Skinner) (Two) **$30,800**

A Federal inlaid mahogany lolling-chair, Massachusetts, 1790–1810, with downswept line-inlaid supports above a padded trapezoidal seat, 46in. high.
(Christie's) **$11,500**

A Federal stained maple lolling chair, Massachusetts or New Hampshire, circa 1800, the slightly arched crest above a padded back.
(Sotheby's) **$1,610**

A Federal mahogany lolling chair, Massachusetts, circa 1790, the serpentine crest flanked by shaped arms on molded downswept supports.
(Sotheby's) **$4,600**

A Federal carved mahogany lolling chair, possibly Lemuel Churchill, Boston, circa 1810, bowed front seatrail, on square tapering molded legs.
(Christie's) **$9,775**

A Federal carved mahogany lolling chair, Salem, Massachusetts, 1780–1790, the serpentine crest above molded and rosette-carved shaped arms over downswept molded arm supports, on square tapering molded front legs joined by rectangular stretchers, 42in. high. (Christie's)
$51,750

A child's spindle back arm rocker, unsigned, circa 1915, 24¼in. high.
(Skinner) $500

Early 20th century wicker arm rocker, 31in. wide.
(Skinner) $275

Limbert rocking Morris chair, original light brown finish with overcoat.
(Skinner) $4,025

An American Arts & Crafts stained oak rocking chair, in the manner of David Kendal for Phoenix Furniture.
(Phillips) $225

Pair of late 19th century American rocking chairs, stained hardwood frames with turned decoration.
(Peter Wilson) $577

Hand forged steel rocker, 20th century, bent steel, with tufted upholstered suede back and seat, 45in. high.
(Skinner Inc.) $300

Harden oak slat-sided rocker, Camden, New York, dome tack leather back upholstery and spring cushion seat, Harden paper label.
(Skinner) $805

Limbert open-arm adjustable back rocker, circa 1910, no. 518, flat-arm over elongated corbels, original upholstered spring cushion seat, branded mark, 36¾in. high.
(Skinner) $1,500

Harden Co. oak arm rocker, Camden, New York, circa 1910, leather upholstered spring cushion, five pierced vertical back slats, four-bowed side slats.
(Skinner) $863

Painted and decorated ladder-back rocking armchair, Providence, Rhode Island, early 19th century.
(Skinner) $747

Rococo Revival laminated rosewood side chair, probably John Henry Belter, New York, mid 19th century , with later rockers, 33in. high.
(Skinner) $633

Adirondack rocking chair, bentwood oak slats with natural timber supports.
(Skinner) $1,840

Paint decorated arrow-back rocking chair, possibly Maine, circa 1830, three graduated horizontal slats above four arrow spindles.
(Skinner) $575

A pair of painted bentwood rockers, Pennsylvania, early 20th century, each in unusual sculptural form having curled branch-form sides.
(Sotheby's) $1,380

A red-painted ladderback rocking armchair, coastal New Hampshire or Southern Maine, 1750–1800, the horizontal slats flanked by cylindrical stiles.
(Christie's) $690

Wakefield Rattan Co. natural finish wicker rocking chair, late 19th/20th century, bearing a paper label, 35in. high.
(Skinner) $633

Plail Bros. barrel-back rocker, with spring cushion seat, N.Y., circa 1910, 31½in. high.
(Skinner) $875

Painted and decorated Salem rocking chair, by J. D. Pratt, Lunenburg, Massachusetts (minor paint loss), 43½in. high. (Skinner Inc.) $1,750

SHAKER

Shaker tiger maple and cherry armed rocking chair, New Lebanon, circa 1840, the four arched slats joining turned tapering stiles.
(Skinner) $4,312

Shaker maple armed rocker, New Lebanon, New York, circa 1850, old splint seat over-upholstered, 44³/₄in. high.
(Skinner Inc.) $13,000

Shaker production maple #4 slat-back chair with rockers, Mount Lebanon, New York, 1880–1920, with dark stain, identifying Shaker label.
(Skinner) $632

A brown Shaker No. 7 rocking arm-chair, Mt. Lebanon, New York with shawl bar over four arched vertical slats, with woven seat on cylindrical tapering legs joined by double stretchers with rockers, 40³/₄in. high.
(Christie's) $1,980

Shaker child's cherry armless production rocking chair, marked #1, Mount Lebanon, New York, circa 1875, with early cherry finish and an old splint seat.
(Skinner) $1,092

A Shaker rocking armchair, Mt. Lebanon, New York, 19th century, the acorn finials above cylindrical stiles centering a woven back.
(Christie's) $1,380

A fine Shaker turned curly maple rocker, New Lebanon Community, New York, first half 19th century, the back comprised of four slats.
(Sotheby's) $6,900

Shaker production cherry armless #3 web-back chair with rockers, Mount Lebanon, New York, 1880–1920, with identifying label.
(Skinner) $460

Shaker child's maple rocking chair, Mt. Lebanon, New York, circa 1870, the horizontal shawl bar over three arched slats, 27½in. high.
(Skinner Inc.) $2,250

STICKLEY

Fine L. & J.G. Stickley high-back rocker, V-sided arms and back over six vertical slats, drop in spring cushion.
(Skinner) **$977**

A Gustav Stickley child's arm rocker, no. 345, signed with small red decal and paper label, circa 1904-06.
(Skinner) **$750**

L. & J.G. Stickley rocker, circa 1910, no. 837, concave crest rail over four vertical slats, spring cushion seat, 39in. high.
(Skinner Inc.) **$630**

L. & J.G. Stickley high-back rocker, six vertical back slats, arched apron, original medium brown finish, conjoined Stickley label.
(Skinner) **$920**

A tall back, slat sided rocker with leather spring cushion by Gustav Stickley, 41½in. high. **$1,100**

L. & J.G. Stickley rocker, inverted V-back over five vertical slats, original finish, branded mark.
(Skinner) **$460**

WINDSOR

A painted bow back Windsor rocking chair, probably New England, circa 1830, the bowed crest rail above seven tapering incised spindles.
(Skinner) **$880**

A late Windsor bamboo-turned grain-painted and stenciled child's rocker, American, circa 1820–1829, the crest rail stenciled with flowers and leaves.
(Sotheby's) **$1,150**

A painted, stenciled and decorated pine and maple Windsor arrowback rocking armchair, New England, circa 1820.
(Sotheby's) **$1,725**

A Chippendale carved mahogany wing armchair, New York, circa 1770, the serpentine crest flanked by ogival wings continuing to outscrolled supports centering a loose-fitted cushion and overupholstered bowfronted seat on cabriole legs ending in claw-and-ball feet. (Sotheby's) $13,800

CHIPPENDALE

Chippendale mahogany and walnut easy chair, Southern New England, 1760–90, 45in. high.
(Skinner Inc.) $15,025

A Chippendale mahogany easy chair, Massachusetts, 1750–1780, the canted back with serpentine crest.
(Christie's) $32,200

Chippendale mahogany easy chair, New England, 18th century, with molded legs and stretchers.
(Skinner) $5,175

A fine and rare Chippendale carved mahogany wing armchair, New York, circa 1770, the serpentine crest flanked by ogival-shaped wings.
(Sotheby's) $29,900

Chippendale mahogany easy chair, Newport, Rhode Island, 1770–1790, with stop fluted front legs, and old dark surface, upholstered in pale green silk damask.
(Skinner) $9,775

A Chippendale mahogany easy chair, New England, circa 1780, the serpentine crest flanked by ogival wings and outscrolled arms.
(Sotheby's) $4,025

A Chippendale mahogany wing chair, Philadelphia, circa 1780, the serpentine crest flanked by ogival wings with outscrolled arms.
(Sotheby's) $6,325

An important Chippendale carved mahogany wing armchair, Philadelphia, circa 1770, the arched upholstered back flanked by ogival wings.
(Sotheby's) $350,000

A Chippendale carved mahogany wing armchair, Boston, Massachusetts, circa 1755, the arched crest flanked by ogival wings.
(Sotheby's) $17,250

CHIPPENDALE

A Chippendale upholstered wing chair, New England, circa 1810, 45¾in. high. (Skinner) $2,250

A Chippendale mahogany wing armchair, New England, circa 1785, the arched crest flanked by ogival wings. (Sotheby's) $5,462

A fine Chippendale mahogany wing chair, New England, circa 1780, on square molded legs joined by stretchers. (Sotheby's) $7,475

A Chippendale mahogany easy chair, Salem, Massachusetts, 1770-1790, on square corner molded legs joined by a molded H-stretcher, 33in. wide. (Christie's New York) $10,300

Fine antique American Chippendale wing chair with mahogany frame, chamfered straight legs with stretchers, red brocade damask upholstery, 44in. high. (Eldred's) $4,250

A Chippendale carved mahogany easy chair, New York, 1760–1780, on cabriole legs with foliate carved knees and ball-and-claw feet, 44¼in. high. (Christie's) $4,250

A Chippendale cherrywood wing armchair, New England, circa 1800, the serpentine crest flanked by ogival wings. (Sotheby's) $3,450

A Chippendale mahogany wing armchair, New England or New York, circa 1785, the arched crest flanked by ogival wings and outscrolled arms. (Sotheby's) $6,037

A Chippendale mahogany easy chair, New England, circa 1780, the arched crest flanked by ogival wings. (Sotheby's) $2,300

A fine and rare Chippendale carved and figured-mahogany easy chair, Philadelphia, circa 1770, the arched crest flanked by ogival wings and downswept arms on C-scrolled supports centering a loose-fitted cushion and overupholstered seat on cabriole legs ending in claw-and-ball feet. (Sotheby's) $310,500

A good Chippendale carved mahogany easy chair, New York, circa 1770, the arched crest flanked by ogival wings and outscrolled arms on downswept supports centering a loose-fitted cushion and overupholstered seat on cabriole legs ending in claw-and-ball feet.
(Sotheby's) $32,200

FEDERAL

An American Federal mahogany easy chair, 1795-1815. $6,500

Federal mahogany upholstered easy chair, New England, circa 1790, 46in. high. (Skinner) $2,750

An American Federal inlaid mahogany easy chair, 1790-1810. $3,500

A Federal mahogany wing chair with serpentine crest, New York, 1790-1810, 47in. high. (Christie's) $1,500

A Federal mahogany wing armchair, American, probably New York, circa 1800, the arched back flanked by ogival wings and scrolled arms. (Sothebys) $4,312

A Country Federal child's mahogany wing chair, New England, circa 1770, 30¼in. high. (Skinner) $6,800

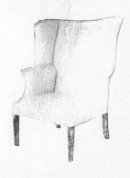

A Federal mahogany easy chair, on square tapering legs joined by a box stretcher, New England, 1790-1800. (Christie's) $3,500

A good Federal turned mahogany wing chair, northern coast of New England, circa 1810. (Sothebys) $23,000

Federal mahogany upholstered easy chair, probably New England, circa 1800, upholstered in white damask. (Skinner) $1,265

FEDERAL

A Federal mahogany easy chair, New England, circa 1810, on ring-turned tapering legs, ending in peg feet. (Sotheby's) $8,625

A Federal mahogany easy chair with serpentine crest, 35in. wide. $6,000

Federal mahogany easy chair, New England, circa 1790, the tapering molded legs with stretchers, 47in. high. (Skinner Inc.) $5,600

A Federal carved mahogany easy chair, New York, 1790-1810, the arched back flanked by shaped wings continuing to outward scrolled arms. (Christie's) $4,600

A Federal mahogany easy chair, American, 1790-1810, with arched crest flanked by shaped wings, 45¾in. high. (Christie's New York) $2,070

A Federal mahogany barrel-back easy chair, Massachusetts, 1790–1810, the arched bowed crestrail above an upholstered back and shaped wings, 45in. high. (Christie's) $3,680

A Federal inlaid mahogany wing chair, New York or New England, circa 1800, the serpentine crest with peaked ears flanked by ogival wings. (Sotheby's) $4,887

A Federal mahogany barrel back easy chair, Philadelphia, 1800-1815, with curving wings above scrolled arms, 47½in. high. (Christie's New York) $6,850

A Federal mahogany wing chair, New York or New England, circa 1800, the serpentine crest flanked by ogival wings and outscrolled arms. (Sotheby's) $3,162

QUEEN ANNE

A Queen Anne walnut and maple wing armchair, Boston, Massachusetts, 1740–60, the upholstered back with arched crest.
(Sotheby's) $34,500

Queen Anne wing chair, 18th century, in mahogany with red upholstery.
(Eldred's) $1,760

A Queen Anne turned walnut easy chair, New England, circa 1730, the arched crest flanked by ogival wings on conical supports.
(Sotheby's) $12,650

Queen Anne painted upholstered easy chair, probably New England, 1740, with arched crest and shaped arms ending in scrolled terminals.
(Skinner) $6,900

A Queen Anne walnut wing armchair, Boston, Massachusetts, 1735–50, on cabriole legs ending in pad feet joined by block- and vase-turned stretchers.
(Sotheby's) $85,000

A fine Queen Anne carved walnut wing armchair, Newport, Rhode Island, circa 1765, the arched upholstered back flanked by ogival wings.
(Sotheby's) $35,000

A Queen Anne walnut wing armchair with padded back, outscrolled arms, bowed seat and squab cushion covered in gros-point needlework.
(Christie's) $15,000

A Queen Anne walnut easy chair on cabriole legs with pointed slipper feet, N.Y., 1735-55. (Christie's) $24,200

A Queen Anne walnut wing armchair covered in later yellow and purple patterned needlework on cabriole legs joined by a turned H-shaped stretcher.
(Christie's) $3,250

QUEEN ANNE

A Queen Anne walnut wing armchair, Massachusetts, circa 1750, the back with arched crest and shaped wings.
(Sotheby's) $22,500

Queen Anne walnut easy chair, Massachusetts or Rhode Island, 1730–1750, refinished, 45in. high.
(Skinner) $26,400

A Queen Anne walnut and maple easy chair, probably Massachusetts, circa 1760, on cabriole legs ending in pad feet.
(Skinner Inc.) $40,000

A walnut wing armchair of Queen Anne design, scrolling arms and seat upholstered in figured brocade, on cabriole legs with pad feet.
(Christie's S. Ken) $3,000

Queen Anne walnut and maple wing armchair, Massachusetts, circa 1750, the upholstered arched crest flanked by ogival wings above outscrolled arms, on cabriole legs joined by stretchers.
(Butterfield & Butterfield) $11,500

A Queen Anne walnut easy-chair, Massachusetts, 1735–1755, the arched crest flanked by downswept shaped wings above vertically scrolled arms above an upholstered seat over cabriole legs.
(Christie's) $17,250

Queen Anne walnut carved easy chair, Pennsylvania, circa 1740–60, shell-carved knees and pad feet with carving, 20th century upholstery, 41in. high.
(Skinner Inc.) $58,900

A Queen Anne style easy chair, upholstered in a red, white and blue bargello patterned fabric. $3,000

A fine Queen Anne leather-upholstered turned walnut and maple wing armchair, Boston, Massachusetts, circa 1760.
(Sotheby's) $75,000

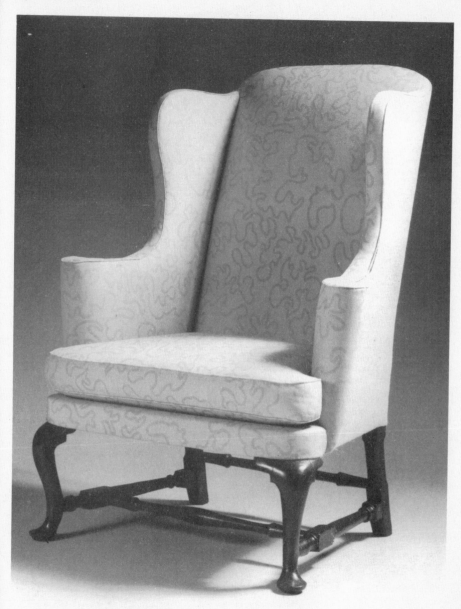

A fine Queen Anne carved and turned walnut easy chair, Boston, Massachusetts, 1740–1760, the arched crest flanked by ogival wings continuing to conical supports, centering a loose-fitted cushion and overupholstered bow fronted seat, on cabriole legs joined by turned block-and-vase-form stretchers and ending in pad feet.
(Sotheby's)

$79,500

Oak chest, designed by George Washington Maher, circa 1912, green colored oak, cedar lined, brass handles, ends with fielded panels incorporating the motif of *Rockledge*, 60in. wide.
(Skinner Inc.) $2,500

A cherrywood and pine dough box on stand, Pennsylvania, first half 19th century, the rectangular removable top above a well, length 48in.
(Sotheby's) $1,250

A paint-decorated pine blanket chest, signed John Selzer, Dauphin County, now Lebanon County, Pennsylvania, dated *1793*, 52in. wide.
(Sotheby's) $12,650

An Afro-American painted and decorated yellow pine slave's trunk, Southern, 19th century, the rectangular hinged lid opening to a divided well, 24in. wide.
(Sotheby's) $2,250

Painted and carved sea chest, New England, early 19th century, the rectangular lift top opens to reveal a polychrome portrait of the ship 'Molo', 34³/₄in. wide.
(Skinner) $6,325

Rare William and Mary grain painted spice chest, Massachusetts, early 18th century, 18³/₄in. wide.
(Skinner) $12,500

Painted twig chest, Adirondack area, New York, early 20th century, the hinged top opens to a cavity, 33³/₄in. wide.
(Skinner) $633

A painted trunk, probably Pennsylvania, late 18th/early 19th century, the hinged rectangular top with thumbmolded edge lifting to an open compartment lined with portions of Claypoole's Advertiser, 1793 (Philadelphia), 38¹/₄in. wide.
(Christie's) $1,000

A carved and painted white-pine trinket chest, Jacob Weber, Fivepointville, Lancaster County, Pennsylvania, 1840-1850, 6in. long.
(Sotheby's) $6,900

CHESTS

Early Gustav Stickley oak cedar lined chest, circa 1901, original dark finish and black finished iron hardware, unsigned, 40in. long.
(Skinner) $7,475

Paint decorated dome top trunk, lined with southeastern Massachusetts newspaper dated *1814*, 21³/₄in. wide.
(Skinner) $1,495

A 17th century American pine chest attributed to Essex County MA, the rising plank top enclosing a lidded till, 50in. wide.
(Boardmans) $7,904

A fine and rare William and Mary paneled pine and turned maple valuables chest, Massachusetts, 1700–40, 19³/₄in. wide.
(Sotheby's) $20,700

An experimental Gustav Stickley cedar-lined chest, circa 1901-02, 27¾in. wide. $12,500

Painted pine, oak and maple paneled joined chest, probably Hampshire County, Massachusetts, circa 1720, 30in. wide.
(Skinner Inc.) $8,000

A cedar chest-on-frame, Bermuda, 1750–70, the rectangular molded hinged top opening into a single compartment fitted with a till, 52in. wide.
(Christie's) $5,175

Walnut sugar chest, Southeastern United States, circa 1820, replaced brasses, 35in. wide.
(Skinner) $1,092

A pine and turned poplar dough box, Pennsylvania, 19th century, the rectangular removeable top opening to a tapering well, 38in.
(Sotheby's) $402

DOWER

Rare Roycroft bridal chest, mortise and tenons on sides, cast iron hardware, orb mark on front, 39¼in. wide.
(Skinner) $17,250

Chippendale walnut inlaid dower chest, Pennsylvania, circa 1774, 49in. wide.
(Skinner) $2,000

Paint decorated dower chest, Pennsylvania, late 18th century, the overhanging top with molded edge (feet added; repainted), 54in. wide overall. (Skinner Inc.) $1,000

Federal walnut inlaid dower chest, Pennsylvania, circa 1800, the rectangular molded top opens to an interior with till, 49in. wide.
(Skinner) $1,495

A Roycroft oak bridal chest, East Aurora, New York, circa 1912, with extended serpentine sides, 36½in. wide.
(Skinner) $9,300

Painted dower chest, Pennsylvania, late 18th century, all-over blue-green paint, some original brasses, 50½in. wide.
(Skinner Inc.) $1,500

A painted and decorated chest, Pennsylvania, dated 1824, the rectangular top with red-painted flower-decorated teal oval reserves on a bird's-eye maple faux-grained ground, 52¾in. wide.
(Christie's) $29,900

A fine paint decorated pine three-drawer dower chest, Pennsylvania, early 19th century, 43in. wide.
(Sotheby's) $6,900

A painted and decorated dower chest, Pennsylvania, circa 1787, the hinged rectangular top with applied molded trim decorated with three painted floral panels, 48¾in. wide.
(Christie's) $8,000

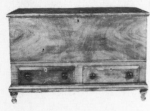

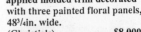

Grain painted pine dower chest, Pennsylvania, early 19th century, with lidded till, two drawers, original red and yellow graining, 47.25in. wide.
(Skinner) $690

Dower chest, Pennsylvania, early 19th century, the rectangular molded top over a dovetailed case with painted decorations, on molded base, 51in. wide.
(Skinner) $1,850

Painted dower chest, probably Pennsylvania, early 19th century, original worn green paint, old replaced brasses and hinges, 45¼in. wide.
(Skinner Inc.) $1,750

SIX BOARD

Grain painted poplar six board chest, Pennsylvania, 1830–40, with molded top and lidded till, early graining simulates tiger maple, 42in. wide.
(Skinner) $805

Shaker orange painted six board chest, a Maine, New Hampshire, or Massachusetts community, mid 19th century, 44¼ in. wide.
(Skinner) $1,725

Putty decorated ocher and mustard pine six-board blanket box, New England, circa 1820, 42in. wide.
(Skinner) $3,190

Grain painted and decorated six-board chest, New England, late 18th century, with lidded till, with a black central painted motif, outlined in yellow with *M.A.Y.* in yellow, 40in. wide.
(Skinner) $1,870

Grain painted six-board chest, New England, early 19th century, the yellow ocher and burnt umber fanciful graining in imitation of mahogany, 38½in. wide.
(Skinner Inc.) $1,050

Small grained pine six-board chest, New England, 19th century, the hinged lid opens to an interior with lidded till, 37½in. wide.
(Skinner) $1,495

A painted and punch decorated six-board pine chest, New London, Connecticut, 1700–1730, with rectangular hinged lid above a case with two rows of intersecting punchwork semi-circles, 31½in. wide.
(Christie's) $15,000

Grain painted pine six-board chest, probably Connecticut, 1825–40, original mustard and burnt sienna paint to resemble mahogany, 35½in. wide.
(Skinner) $1,035

Painted and decorated poplar six board chest, Soap Hollow, Somerset County, Pennsylvania, 1875, probably by John Sala, Sr., (1810-1882) 46in. wide. (Skinner Inc.)
$4,000

Early 19th century grain painted pine six board chest with hinged lid, probably New England, 47¾in. wide.
$2,250

Grain painted six-board chest, New England or New York State, early 19th century, red and yellow graining to simulate mahogany, 36in. wide.
(Skinner Inc.) $450

Grain painted and paint decorated poplar six-board chest, Schoharie County, New York, first quarter 19th century, 37¾in. wide.
(Skinner) $1,265

An unusual paint decorated pine chest with drawers, attributed to Thomas Matteson, South Shaftsbury, Vermont, circa 1830, 39¹/₄in. wide.
(Sotheby's) $20,700

Child's whalebone and exotic woods inlaid mahogany chest of drawers, America, 19th century, 27¹/₂in. wide.
(Skinner Inc.) $6,100

Grain painted chest of drawers, Maine, circa 1830, the top overhangs a case of drawers on a base with front and side shaping, 40in. wide.
(Skinner) $4,600

A rare paint-decorated pine and birchwood chest of drawers, probably Guilford area, Connecticut, circa 1720, decorated with stylised tulips and pansies in polychrome, 38in. wide.
(Sotheby's) $4,600

A rare William and Mary walnut chest of drawers, Eastern Pennsylvania, probably Chester County, early 18th century, the molded base continuing to ball feet, 41³/₄in. wide.
(Sotheby's) $10,000

A William and Mary red-painted chestnut and pine chest-of-drawers, Eastern Connecticut, 1725–1735, the rectangular top with molded edge, on turned feet, 39¹/₂in. wide.
(Christie's) $12,100

Roycroft oak chiffonier, East Aurora, New York, circa 1907, signed with *Roycroft* across front, 42in. wide.
(Skinner Inc.) $9,300

Grain painted chest over drawers, Massachusetts, 1825-35, with burnt sienna and mustard putty paint and green sponging, 40in. wide.
(Skinner) $31,050

Fine American Renaissance inlaid maple and rosewood tall chest of drawers by Herter Brothers, New York, circa 1872, 37in. wide.
(Butterfield & Butterfield) $23,000

Grain painted chest of drawers, probably Maine, 1835–45, with ocher and red graining simulating mahogany, 41⅝in. wide.
(Skinner) $575

Antique American Hepplewhite bowfront chest in cherry, cock beaded drawer fronts, French feet, brass knobs, 41in. wide.
(Eldred's) $1,925

William and Mary poplar and oak chest of drawers, probably Connecticut, first quarter 18th century, 40in. wide.
(Skinner) $7,475

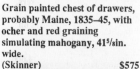

A grain-painted seed chest, possibly John Boyer, Pennsylvania, 19th century, the rectangular hinged slant-lid opening to a fitted interior with three compartments, 18¾in. wide.
(Christie's) $23,000

Antique American Sheraton four-drawer chest in cherry, scrolled splashguard, turned and ribbed legs, brass knobs, 43in. wide.
(Eldred's) $1,210

A rare Pilgrim century oak, pine and birchwood chest of drawers, Massachusetts, 1660–1700, case fitted with three long drawers, each drawer front with geometric moldings, 37in. wide.
(Sotheby's) $13,225

A William and Mary maple bun foot chest, Massachusetts, circa 1700–1720, the case fitted with four graduated long drawers, 37¾in. wide.
(Christie's) $40,250

Painted pine tall chest of drawers, Connecticut River Valley, mid 18th century, replaced brasses, old red paint, 38¼in. wide.
(Skinner) $3,220

Maple, cherry and tiger maple veneer chest of drawers, inscribed *Made by Asa Loomis in the year 1816*, Shaftsbury, Vermont, 42½in. wide.
(Skinner) $6,325

CHIPPENDALE

A Chippendale curly maple chest-of-drawers, probably New Hampshire, 1775-1810, 39in. wide. (Christie's) $8,200

Chippendale walnut chest of drawers, probably Virginia, late 18th century, the rectangular top with applied molded edge, 39in. wide. (Skinner) $1,380

A Chippendale walnut tall chest of drawers, Pennsylvania, circa 1780, the rectangular cove molding above an arrangement of three short over two short drawers, 41in. wide. (Sotheby's) $6,325

A Chippendale walnut chest-of-drawers, mid-Atlantic, 1760-1780, the rectangular molded top above a conforming case fitted with four graduated thumbmolded drawers, 40in. wide. (Christie's) $3,680

A Chippendale mahogany chest-of-drawers, Mid-Atlantic States, 1760–1790, the rectangular top with line inlaid edge above a case fitted with four graduated long drawers, on straight bracket feet, 37in. wide. (Christie's) $2,990

A Chippendale walnut chest-of-drawers, labeled Joseph Newlin, Wilmington, Delaware, 1770–1790, the case fitted with two short drawers and three graduated long drawers, on ogee bracket feet, 40in. wide. (Christie's) $17,250

A Chippendale birchwood reverse serpentine-front chest of drawers, North Coastal New England, possibly New Hampshire, circa 1780, 45in. wide. (Sotheby's) $14,950

A Chippendale carved and figured mahogany highboy base, Philadelphia, circa 1765, now fitted with a rectangular molded top with flowerhead-carved edge, 43¹/₂in. wide. (Sotheby's) $9,775

Chippendale mahogany veneer serpentine chest of drawers, Philadelphia, circa 1789, probably the work of Jonathan Gostelowe (1744–1795), 48in. wide. (Skinner Inc.) $25,000

CHIPPENDALE

A Chippendale cherrywood reverse serpentine-front diminutive chest-of-drawers, on ogee backet feet, 33in. wide. (Christie's) **$3,220**

Chippendale maple tall chest of drawers, probably Rhode Island, circa 1780, 36in. wide. (Skinner) **$3,300**

Chippendale maple chest of drawers, New Hampshire, mid 18th century, 37$\frac{1}{2}$in. wide. (Skinner) **$2,415**

A Chippendale inlaid mahogany chest of drawers, American, circa 1780, the rectangular molded top above four cockbeaded drawers, 42$\frac{1}{4}$in. wide. (Sotheby's) **$2,185**

Chippendale tiger maple chest of drawers, Rhode Island, late 18th century, the rectangular molded edge top above four thumb-molded edge-graduated long drawers, 38in. wide. (Butterfield & Butterfield) **$9,000**

Chippendale mahogany chest of drawers, on molded bracket base, brasses are old replacements, old refinish, 38$\frac{1}{2}$in. wide. (Skinner Inc.) **$18,700**

American Chippendale oxbow-front chest, in mahogany with molded top and bottom edge, four graduated drawers with brass escutcheons, 45$\frac{1}{2}$in. wide. (Eldred's) **$2,860**

A Chippendale inlaid and figured mahogany serpentine-front chest of drawers, probably Portsmouth, New Hampshire, circa 1790, 40in. wide. (Sotheby's) **$10,350**

A Chippendale mahogany bow-front chest-of-drawers, case fitted with four graduated cockbeaded long drawers over a molded base, 41$\frac{1}{2}$in, wide. (Christie's) **$1,035**

Chippendale mahogany chest of drawers, Norwich, Connecticut area, 18th century, 38in. wide. (Skinner) $8,050

Chippendale mahogany oxbow bureau, Connecticut, circa 1790, cockbeaded drawers, replaced brasses, 35in. wide. (Skinner Inc.) $8,250

A Chippendale birch reverse-serpentine chest-of-drawers, Upper Connecticut River Valley or Northern Massachusetts, 1760–80, 45in. wide. (Christie's) $4,600

A Chippendale carved cherrywood serpentine chest-of-drawers, probably Lyme, Connecticut, 1780–1800, with serpentine front and molded edges, on ogee bracket feet with elaborately double-scrolled brackets, 39¹/₄in. wide. (Christie's) $31,000

A Chippendale cherrywood high chest-of-drawers, probably New London County, Connecticut, 1760–1780, in two sections, on cabriole legs with pad feet, 82¹/₄in. high, 38³/₄in. wide. (Christie's) $85,000

A Chippendale cherrywood reverse serpentine chest of drawers, signed by George Belden, Hartford, Connecticut, circa 1790, the molded rectangular top with an oxbow front edge, 34³/₄in. wide. (Christie's New York) $23,000

Chippendale cherry oxbow chest of drawers, Connecticut, circa 1780, with three reverse serpentine graduated drawers, 44in. wide. (Skinner Inc.) $1,875

A Chippendale maple chest-of-drawers, Southern Connecticut or Rhode Island, 1770–1800, the case with four graduated thumbmolded drawers, on shaped bracket feet, 34in. wide. (Christie's) $2,990

A fine Chippendale cherrywood reverse serpentine chest of drawers, Connecticut, 1760-1780, the rectangular top with serpentine molded edge, 38³/₄in. wide. (Christie's New York) $78,000

CHIPPENDALE, CONNECTICUT

Chippendale cherry carved base to chest on chest, probably Colchester, Connecticut, late 18th century, 41in. wide. (Skinner) $2,300

Chippendale cherry chest of drawers, probably New London County, Connecticut, last quarter 18th century, 38½in. wide. (Skinner) $4,025

Chippendale cherry chest of drawers, Connecticut, 18th century, the molded two-board top above a case of drawers, 43in. wide overall. (Skinner) $3,737

A Chippendale cherrywood block-front chest-of-drawers, Connecticut, circa 1775, with blocked front edge above a conforming case fitted with four graduated long drawers above a molded base, on ogee bracket feet, 37½in. wide. (Christie's) $12,300

An important Chippendale block- and shell-carved cherrywood chest of drawers, Colchester-Norwich area, Connecticut, circa 1770, 40in. wide. (Sotheby's) $398,500

Chippendale cherry chest of drawers, Connecticut River Valley, late 18th century, with molded top, engaged quarter columns and cock beaded drawers, 38in. wide. (Skinner) $7,475

Cherry Chippendale chest of drawers, Connecticut, 18th century, molded top overhangs a case of thumbmolded drawers, 37½in. wide. (Skinner) $3,335

Painted poplar chest over drawers, Connecticut River Valley, late 18th century, the hinged top opens to a well above two working drawers, 41in. wide. (Skinner) $432

Chippendale cherry carved chest of drawers, Connecticut, mid to late 18th century, with dentil molding on the cornice, 38in. wide. (Skinner) $2,070

A Chippendale carved mahogany bombé chest-of-drawers, Boston or Salem, 1770–1785, the molded rectangular top with cusped corners above a bombé case fitted with four conforming and graduated thumbmolded long drawers over a rectangular molded base centered by a shaped pendant drop, on ogee bracket feet, 37in. wide.
(Christie's) $827,500

CHIPPENDALE, MASSACHUSETTS

Small Chippendale mahogany chest of drawers, Massachusetts late 18th century, the four graduated drawers with cockbeaded surrounds, 36in. wide overall. (Skinner Inc.) $19,800

A very fine and rare Chippendale mahogany serpentine-front chest of drawers, Boston, Massachusetts, circa 1780, 36in. wide. (Sotheby's) $82,250

A fine Chippendale figured mahogany serpentine-front chest of drawers, Boston-area, Massachusetts, circa 1780, 39in. wide. (Sotheby's) $25,300

A Chippendale mahogany serpentine chest-of-drawers, Massachusetts, 1760–1780, on short bracketed cabriole legs with ball-and-claw feet, appears to retain original brasses, 38in. wide. (Christie's) $34,000

A Chippendale mahogany block-front chest-of-drawers, Boston, Massachusetts, 1760–1780, the molded rectangular top with blocked and shaped front above a conforming case, on bracket feet, appears to retain original brasses, 36in. wide. (Christie's) $60,500

A Chippendale mahogany reverse serpentine chest-of-drawers, Boston, 1765–1775, with a leather lined writing slide over four graduated long drawers each with cockbeaded surrounds, 41in. wide. (Christie's) $19,550

A Chippendale mahogany block-front chest of drawers, Massachusetts, circa 1760, the oblong molded top with recessed center section, 36in. wide. (Sotheby's) $14,950

Chippendale mahogany carved veneer serpentine chest of drawers, Boston or Salem, Massachusetts, 18th century, with molded top with canted corners, 41¹/₂in. wide overall. (Skinner) $74,000

Chippendale cherry serpentine chest of drawers, Massachusetts, circa 1780, the overhanging molded top above a conforming shaped cockbeaded case, 34¹/₄in. wide. (Skinner) $9,775

Chippendale mahogany reverse serpentine chest of drawers, Massachusetts, 1760–80, drawers with cockbeaded surrounds, 39¼in. wide. (Skinner Inc.) $16,200

A Chippendale figured maple serpentine-front chest of drawers, New England, probably Massachusetts, circa 1790, the oblong top with thumbmolded edge, width of top 38¼in. (Sotheby's) $8,050

Chippendale mahogany block-front bureau, Boston, Massachusetts, 1760–90, refinished, brasses appear original, 34¾in. wide. (Skinner Inc.) $39,900

A Chippendale carved mahogany reverse-serpentine chest of drawers, Massachusetts, 1775–1790, with molded edge reverse-serpentine front above a conforming case, 41in. wide. (Christie's) $10,000

A Chippendale figured mahogany bow-front chest of drawers, Massachusetts, 1800, the shaped thumbmolded top above four graduated long drawers, on bracket feet, case 36½in. wide. (Sotheby's) $9,775

A Chippendale mahogany block-front chest-of-drawers, Massachusetts, 1760-1780, fitted with four graduated drawers over a molded conforming base with central drop, 33¼in. wide. (Christie's) $79,500

A good Chippendale carved and figured mahogany serpentine-front chest of drawers, Massachusetts, circa 1770, the oblong molded top with shaped front, width of top 40in. (Sotheby's) $20,000

Chippendale mahogany oxbow serpentine chest of drawers, Massachusetts, last quarter 18th century, 34in. wide. (Skinner) $17,250

A Chippendale figured cherrywood chest of drawers, New England, probably Connecticut, circa 1780, rectangular thumbmolded top, width of top 33½in. (Sotheby's) $8,625

Chippendale mahogany serpentine chest of drawers, eastern Massachusetts, 1760–80, with a molded and blocked top overhanging a conforming case of graduated drawers, 36in. wide overall.
(Skinner) $24,150

A Chippendale birch reverse serpentine chest of drawers, Massachusetts, circa 1780, on claw and ball feet, 41in. wide. $11,750

Rare Chippendale mahogany serpentine-front chest of drawers, Boston, 1760–80, four graduated drawers surrounded by cockbeading on a molded base, 33¼in. wide.
(Skinner) $178,500

A fine Chippendale carved and figured walnut reverse-serpentine block-front chest of drawers, Massachusetts, circa 1780, the shaped molded top with four graduated long drawers, 37in. wide.
(Sotheby's) $35,650

A Chippendale cherrywood reverse-serpentine chest-of-drawers, Massachusetts, 1760–1780, the rectangular thumbmolded top with reverse serpentine front above a conforming case, 36¾in. wide.
(Christie's) $40,250

A good Chippendale walnut serpentine-front chest of drawers, Massachusetts, circa 1785, the oblong thumb-molded top with reverse serpentine front edge, 39½in. wide.
(Sotheby's) $9,200

A fine and rare Chippendale carved and figured mahogany serpentine front chest of drawers, Boston area, Massachusetts, circa 1770, width of top 39¾in.
(Sotheby's) $60,250

Chippendale wavy birch bow-front chest of drawers, Massachusetts, circa 1780, the rectangular top with bow front and beaded edge, 35in. high.
(Skinner) $12,100

Chippendale cherry chest of drawers, Massachusetts, late 18th century, with scratch beaded overhanging top above four thumb-molded drawers, 37in. wide.
(Skinner) $2,760

CHIPPENDALE, MASSACHUSETTS

A Chippendale fruitwood reverse serpentine chest of drawers, Mass., circa 1780, 38in. wide. $22,000

A Chippendale mahogany serpentine-front bombé chest-of-drawers, Boston, 1760–80, 36in. wide.
(Christie's) $27,600

A Chippendale applewood serpentine-front chest of drawers, Massachusetts, circa 1785, the oblong top with incised edge, 39in. wide.
(Sotheby's) $4,950

A Chippendale mahogany veneer chest-of-drawers, Salem, Massachusetts, 1760–1780, the molded serpentine top over a conforming case fitted with four cockbeaded graduated long drawers, on ogee bracket feet, 42in. wide.
(Christie's) $12,200

A fine Chippendale mahogany reverse serpentine chest of drawers, Massachusetts, 1760–1780, with four graduated long drawers with cockbead surrounds over a conforming base molding, on ogee bracket feet, 37in. wide.
(Christie's) $12,900

A fine Chippendale carved mahogany block front chest of drawers, Massachusetts, 1760–1780, with four graduated long drawers over conforming base molding above a shell-carved pendant, on ogee bracket feet, 37³/₈in. wide.
(Christie's) $25,000

A good Chippendale mahogany serpentine-front chest of drawers, Massachusetts, circa 1780, the molded base continuing to ball and claw feet, 38³/₄in. wide.
(Sotheby's) $12,500

A Chippendale mahogany serpentine-front chest of drawers, Massachusetts, circa 1770, on ogee bracket feet, 40¹/₂in. wide.
(Sotheby's) $6,050

A Chippendale birchwood reverse-serpentine chest of drawers, Massachusetts, circa 1780, the oblong molded top with reverse serpentine front, 39¹/₂in. wide.
(Sotheby's) $6,900

A Chippendale mahogany reverse-serpentine chest-of-drawers, North Shore, Massachusetts, 1760–1780, the rectangular top with reverse-serpentine front and molded edge above a conforming case fitted with four graduated long drawers with cockbeaded surrounds over a molded base centering a fan-carved pendant, on short cabriole legs with ball-and-claw feet, 38in. wide. (Christie's) $34,500

A rare Chippendale carved mahogany blockfront chest-of-drawers, Boston or Salem, 1760–1780, the molded rectangular top with rounded blocking above a conforming case fitted with four cockbeaded and graduated long drawers, all similarly blocked, over a conforming molded base above a central shaped pendant drop, on cabriole legs with hairy ball-and-claw feet, the sides with brass bale handles, appears to retain original brasses, 36in. wide. (Christie's) $607,500

CHIPPENDALE, NEW ENGLAND

A Chippendale mahogany serpentine-front chest-of-drawers, New England, 1760–80, the rectangular top with serpentine front, 42in. wide. (Christie's) $5,520

Chippendale cherry chest of drawers, New England, 18th century, case 38½in. wide. (Skinner) $1,610

Country Chippendale tiger maple chest of drawers, Southern New England, circa 1780, 35in. wide. (Skinner) $4,840

Chippendale pine chest of drawers, New England, late 18th century, flat molded cornice above a case of five graduated thumbmolded drawers, 35½in. wide. (Skinner) $4,312

A Chippendale maple chest-of-drawers, New England, 1760–1780, the molded rectangular top above a conforming case fitted with four thumbmolded graduated long drawers, 38½in. wide. (Christie's) $1,650

A Chippendale tiger maple chest-of-drawers, New England, 1760–1790, the rectangular top over a conforming case fitted with two short drawers over four graduated long drawers, on bracket feet, 36¾in. wide. (Christie's) $2,200

A Chippendale stained birchwood chest of drawers, New England, circa 1780, the rectangular thumbmolded top with four graduated long drawers, 38¼in. wide. (Sotheby's) $2,587

Chippendale red painted cherry chest of drawers, New England, late 18th century, the rectangular overhanging top above case of four graduated drawers, 40¼in. wide. (Skinner) $1,265

Chippendale maple and birch chest of drawers, New England, circa 1790, the rectangular molded top above a cock beaded case, 37¾in. wide. (Skinner) $2,990

CHIPPENDALE, NEW ENGLAND

A Chippendale birchwood chest of drawers, New England, circa 1780, the rectangular top above four long drawers, 38³/₄in. wide. (Sotheby's) **$1,495**

Painted Chippendale chest of drawers, New England, mid 18th century, document drawer, old red paint, 37³/₄in. wide. (Skinner Inc.) **$3,250**

A Chippendale curly maple five-drawer chest, New England, circa 1780, 37¼in. wide. (Skinner) **$2,500**

CHIPPENDALE, PENNSYLVANIA

A Chippendale carved walnut chest of drawers, Pennsylvania, circa 1780, with four graduated molded long drawers, quarter-columns flanking, on ogee bracket feet, 35in. wide. (Sotheby's) **$12,500**

Chippendale walnut chest of drawers, Pennsylvania, circa 1770, the rectangular molded edge top above four graduated long drawers on ogee bracket feet, width of case 36³/₄in. (Butterfield & Butterfield) **$2,588**

A Chippendale walnut chest of drawers, Lancaster County, Pennsylvania, circa 1785, the rectangular thumbmolded top above three short and three long graduated molded drawers, 42in. wide. (Sotheby's) **$4,125**

A Chippendale figured walnut chest of drawers, Pennsylvania, circa 1770, the rectangular molded top above four graduated thumbmolded long drawers, 36in. wide. (Sotheby's) **$4,025**

Cherry Chippendale chest of drawers, Pennsylvania, 18th century, with molded top above thumbmolded graduated drawers, 38in. wide. (Skinner) **$4,312**

A Chippendale mahogany chest-of-drawers, Penn., circa 1780, 38in. wide. (Skinner) **$4,375**

FEDERAL

Federal cherry chest of drawers, 39³/₄in. wide.
(Skinner) $1,210

Federal cherry inlaid chest of drawers, coastal southern United States, circa 1800, with stringing outlining the cockbeaded drawers, 38in. wide.
(Skinner) $1,495

Federal applewood inlaid chest of drawers, Haddam, Connecticut, early 19th century, with inlaid canted corners, 39¹/₂in. wide.
(Skinner) $4,400

A Federal mahogany bow-front chest-of-drawers, Philadelphia, 1780–1790, the rectangular thumbmolded top with bowed front above four cockbeaded graduated long drawers flanked by fluted quarter columns, 43in. wide.
(Christie's) $12,650

A late Federal mahogany veneer chest-of-drawers, New York, 1810–1820, the rectangular top above a conforming case fitted with a crossbanded long drawer veneered in imitation of three short drawers, 46¹/₂in. wide.
(Christie's) $2,750

A Federal mahogany bow-front chest-of-drawers, Eastern Connecticut, 1790–1810, the rectangular top with bowed front over a conforming case, on French feet, 43¹/₂in. wide.
(Christie's) $3,300

A Federal cherrywood reverse-serpentine chest-of-drawers, Connecticut, 1790-1810, the molded overhanging reverse-serpentine top above a conforming case, 42⁵/₈in. wide.
(Christie's) $8,050

A Federal inlaid walnut serpentine-front chest of drawers, Maryland, circa 1800, with four beaded and graduated long drawers outlined with stringing, 41¹/₂in. wide.
(Sotheby's) $9,350

A Federal inlaid mahogany chest-of-drawers, New York, 1790–1810, on flaring bracket feet, appears to retain original brasses, 45¹/₄in. wide.
(Christie's) $3,250

FEDERAL

Federal cherry inlaid chest of drawers, probably Connecticut, circa 1790, the rectangular overhanging top with molded edge, 38¾in. wide.
(Skinner) $6,900

A Federal inlaid mahogany bowfront dressing bureau, the top drawer fitted with a mirror, 38in. wide. $6,250

Federal mahogany veneer and cherry chest of drawers, Connecticut River Valley, circa 1800, brasses replaced, 41in. wide.
(Skinner Inc.) $2,900

A Federal inlaid and figured walnut chest of drawers, Pennsylvania, circa 1810, the rectangular top with projecting cornice above four graduated molded long drawers, 42in. wide.
(Sotheby's) $2,070

Federal flame birch and mahogany veneer chest of drawers, Eastern Massachusetts, or Southern New Hampshire, circa 1810, with carved and turned flanking columns, 40½in. wide.
(Skinner) $1,610

A late Federal paint-decorated birchwood chest of drawers, Parish Hill, Maine, 1825–45, the rectangular top surmounted by a shaped scrolling splashboard, 41½in. wide.
(Sotheby's) $4,600

Federal cherry inlaid chest of drawers, possibly Pennsylvania, circa 1800, the projecting molded top above row of inlaid diamonds, 43¾in. high.
(Skinner Inc.) $1,375

A Federal inlaid and figured mahogany chest of drawers, New York, circa 1815, the rectangular top above a crossbanded frieze, 46½in. wide.
(Sotheby's) $1,840

A Federal inlaid walnut child's chest of drawers, Pennsylvania, circa 1820, with four graduated cockbeaded line-inlaid drawers, 18½in. wide.
(Sotheby's) $6,325

A Federal mahogany and figured maple veneered chest-of-drawers, Boston, Massachusetts, 1790–1810, on bracketed turned tapering feet, 42in. wide. (Christie's) $6,875

A Federal carved mahogany chest of drawers, Salem, Massachusetts, 1810-1820, with four cockbead molded long drawers flanked by spiral turned columns, 44in. wide. (Christie's New York) $4,400

A fine Federal inlaid mahogany bowfront chest of drawers, Massachusetts, 1790-1810, the bowfront top edged with lozenge pattern inlay, 41¾in. wide. (Christie's) $10,000

Federal mahogany carved and mahogany veneer chest of drawers, probably Salem, Massachusetts, circa 1820, the rectangular top with ovolo corners and bead carved edge, 40¾in. wide. (Skinner) $1,150

A Federal mahogany bow-front chest-of-drawers, Massachusetts, circa 1780–1800, the bowed top with thumbmolded edge above a conforming case fitted with four graduated and cockbeaded drawers, 44in. wide. (Christie's) $5,750

A Federal inlaid mahogany bow-front chest-of-drawers, Newburyport, Massachusetts, 1800–1810, four graduated long drawers each cockbeaded with diamond and bellflower inlaid escutcheons surrounded by stringing, 41⅝in. wide. (Christie's) $9,775

A fine Federal inlaid mahogany chest of drawers, Boston area, Massachusetts, circa 1805, the shaped skirt continuing to reeded legs, on brass casters, 41in. wide. (Sotheby's) $10,500

Federal cherry inlaid bowfront chest of drawers, Massachusetts, early 19th century, the bowfront top outlined in stringing above a conforming case of cockbeaded drawers, 38in. wide. (Skinner) $2,300

A Federal mahogany and bird's eye maple chest of drawers, Salem, Massachusetts, 1800-1815, the rectangular top with reeded edge and outset rounded corners, 42in. wide. (Christie's New York) $4,400

FEDERAL, MASSACHUSETTS

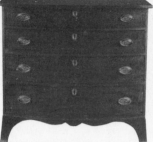

Federal mahogany inlaid
bowfront chest of drawers,
probably Massachusetts, circa
1800, 38in. wide.
(Skinner) $4,887

Federal inlaid mahogany bow-
front chest of drawers,
Massachusetts, circa 1790–1810,
on flaring French feet, 39in.
wide.
(Butterfield & Butterfield)
                             $3,500

A Federal carved mahogany
bow-front chest-of-drawers,
North Shore, Massachusetts,
1790–1810, 44³/₄in. wide.
(Christie's) $6,900

FEDERAL, MID-ATLANTIC STATES

A Federal inlaid mahogany bow-
front chest of drawers, Mid-
Atlantic States, circa 1800, the
oblong top above four
cockbeaded graduated drawers,
36in. wide.
(Sotheby's) $2,587

A Federal inlaid mahogany
chest-of-drawers, Mid-Atlantic,
1790–1810, the bowfront top
with line inlay surrounding four
graduated cockbead and line-
inlaid drawers, on French feet,
41in. wide.
(Christie's) $2,640

A good Federal inlaid mahogany
bow-front chest of drawers,
Mid-Atlantic States, circa 1800,
the oblong crossbanded top
above four graduated line-inlaid
long drawers, 39in. wide.
(Sotheby's) $3,737

Federal mahogany inlaid
bureau, Middle Atlantic States,
1795–1810, old surface, replaced
brasses, 44¹/₂in. wide.
(Skinner Inc.) $5,300

A fine Federal inlaid and figured
cherrywood bow-front chest of
drawers, Mid Atlantic States,
probably Philadelphia, circa
1800, 42¹/₂in. wide.
(Sotheby's) $2,587

Federal mahogany inlaid
butler's desk, probably Middle
Atlantic States, circa 1800,
refinished, brasses replaced,
42in. wide.
(Skinner Inc.) $2,125

FEDERAL, NEW ENGLAND

A Federal inlaid mahogany bow front chest of drawers, New England, 1790-1810, on flared French feet, 42in. wide. (Christie's) **$3,250**

Federal mahogany veneer carved chest of drawers, New England, early 19th century, 37¼in. wide. (Skinner) **$575**

A Federal inlaid cherrywood bow front chest of drawers, New England, 1790-1810, the bowed top with inlaid cross-banding, on French feet, 40¾in. wide. (Christie's New York) **$4,400**

A Federal cherrywood chest-of-drawers, New England, 1790–1810, the case fitted with four graduated long drawers flanked by reeded columns continuing to ring-turned and cylindrical tapering legs, 44½in. wide. (Christie's) **$1,610**

A rare and important Federal carved and paint decorated pine tall chest with drawers, signed *Elijah Royce*, dated 1788, Northern New England, 37½ in. wide. (Sotheby's) **$28,750**

A good Federal satinwood-inlaid mahogany bow-front chest of drawers, New England, circa 1800, with four cock-beaded and graduated long drawers, 40in. wide. (Sotheby's) **$3,575**

A Federal figured maple-inlaid cherrywood chest of drawers, New England, circa 1810, the rectangular top with crossbanded edge above four long drawers, 42½in. wide. (Sotheby's) **$6,325**

A Federal curly maple-inlaid birchwood chest of drawers, New England, circa 1820, the rectangular top above four cockbeaded graduated drawers, width 41in. (Sotheby's) **$3,500**

A Federal inlaid and figured birchwood chest of drawers, New England, circa 1815, the rectangular top above four crossbanded graduated long drawers, 42¾in. wide. (Sotheby's) **$5,175**

FEDERAL, NEW ENGLAND

Federal birch and pine chest of drawers, New England, circa 1800, 36in. wide.
(Skinner) **$2,530**

A Federal inlaid and veneered mahogany bow-front chest-of-drawers, New England, 1790–1810, 40¼in. wide.
(Christie's) **$7,475**

Federal grain painted chest of drawers, New England, circa 1820s, the scrolled back board above the two tiered bureau, 39in. wide. (Skinner Inc.) **$4,400**

Federal mahogany bow-front chest of drawers, New England, circa 1800, the molded edge bow-front top above a conforming case with four graduated long drawers above a shaped apron on French feet, width 39¼in.
(Butterfield & Butterfield) **$690**

A Federal grain-painted birchwood chest of drawers, Northern New England, possibly Maine or New Hampshire, circa 1820, the rectangular top surmounted by a recessed superstructure, 42in. wide.
(Sotheby's) **$2,070**

Federal birch mahogany and bird's-eye maple chest of drawers, New England, circa 1820, rectangular overhanging top above a case of four cockbeaded graduated drawers, 39in. wide.
(Skinner) **$1,610**

Federal cherry inlaid chest of drawers, Northern New England, circa 1820, with bone inlaid escutcheons, old glass pulls, 40in. wide.
(Skinner) **$1,955**

Federal wavy birch chest of drawers, New England, late 18th century, the rectangular overhanging top above a cockbeaded case, 38½in. wide.
(Skinner) **$2,070**

Federal cherry and tiger maple chest of drawers, New England, the cherry top above tiger maple drawer fronts, 43in. wide.
(Skinner) **$1,380**

Federal maple with bird's-eye maple and mahogany veneer chest of drawers, New Hampshire, circa 1800, brasses probably original, 42¼in. wide. (Skinner Inc.) **$1,250**

Federal mahogany veneer and cherry bowfront chest of drawers, New Hampshire, early 19th century, 41¾in. wide. (Skinner) **$2,185**

Federal birch inlaid bowfront chest of drawers, attributed to Joseph Clark, Portsmouth or Greenland, New Hampshire, 1810–14, 39¼in. wide. (Skinner) **$8,050**

A Federal inlaid and flame birch veneered mahogany chest of drawers, Portsmouth, New Hampshire, 1790–1810, the rectangular top with bowed front edged with crossbanding and stringing, on French feet, 40in. wide. (Christie's) **$30,000**

Federal cherry bird's-eye maple and mahogany chest of drawers, probably New Hampshire, 1820–30, the cockbeaded drawers outlined in stringing, 38⅝in. wide. (Skinner) **$4,025**

Federal birchwood bow front chest of drawers, New Hampshire, circa 1810, the rectangular bow front top above four graduated long drawers on shaped bracket feet, length of case 39in. (Butterfield & Butterfield) **$1,955**

A very fine Federal flame birch and ivory-inlaid mahogany bow-front chest of drawers, Portsmouth, New Hampshire, circa 1805, 41¼in. wide. (Sotheby's) **$35,000**

A Federal inlaid mahogany and flame-birch veneered chest-of-drawers, Portsmouth, New Hampshire, 1805–15, 41¼in. wide. (Christie's) **$18,400**

A Federal inlaid mahogany and birchwood bow-front chest of drawers, Portsmouth, New Hampshire, circa 1810, 41in. wide. (Sotheby's) **$189,500**

NEW ENGLAND

Joined oak and pine paneled chest of drawers, New England, 17th century, with pine thumb molded top above four drawers, 39in. wide.
(Skinner) **$20,700**

A rare and unusual paint decorated apothecary chest, New England, early 19th century, 35in wide.
(Sotheby's) **$25,300**

Pine and poplar small multi-drawer chest, New England, circa 1840, original graining on top with mahogany staining on the drawers, 23.5in. wide.
(Skinner) **$1,380**

Fine pine grained and bird's-eye maple painted apothecary chest, New England, 19th century, with rectangular gallery above thirty-two small graduated drawers, 6ft. $^{1}/_{2}$in. high.
(Butterfield & Butterfield) **$30,000**

An American golden maple chest of drawers, in mid 18th century New England style, two long and three short drawers with engraved lacquered brass plate handles, 3ft. 6in.
(Woolley & Wallis) **$4,032**

Grain painted pine chest, New England, 1843, inscribed on reverse *Elihu Nye May 10, 1843* with scrolled splash board above graduated drawers, 30$^{3}/_{4}$in. wide.
(Skinner) **$1,495**

Grain painted chest, New England, early 19th century, faux mahogany with simulated indistinct stringing, 41$^{3}/_{4}$in. wide.
(Skinner Inc.) **$1,250**

Red painted pine spice chest, probably New England, last quarter 19th century, the case of eleven drawers with incised borders in a chamfered case, 25in. wide.
(Skinner) **$805**

Classical grained and veneered chest, northern New England, 1835–45, the original orange and yellow graining in simulation of tiger maple, 41in. wide.
(Skinner) **$287**

NEW ENGLAND

Birch chest of drawers, New England, circa 1800, refinished, original brass pulls, 36in. wide. (Skinner Inc.) $2,500

American chest of drawers, in cherry with four graduated drawers, ogee bracket base, 46in. wide. (Eldred's) $880

Birch chest of four drawers, New England, circa 1780, replaced brasses, 37in. wide. (Skinner) $1,840

An Empire carved and painted pine chest with drawers, New England, circa 1830, the shaped apron continuing to turned legs ending in ball feet, 41¾in. wide. (Sotheby's) $9,775

A Chippendale cherrywood serpentine-front chest of drawers, New England, probably Connecticut, circa 1795, the oblong top with beaded edge, width of top 38⅜in. (Sotheby's) $8,000

Grain painted pine open cupboard, New England, circa 1820, retains original simulated burnt sienna mahogany and mustard graining, 61in. wide. (Skinner) $3,850

A grain painted pine five-drawer chest, New England, circa 1780, 37¾in. wide. (Skinner) $7,500

Small painted pine storage chest, New England, early 19th century, the rectangular top with applied beaded edge, 18½in. wide. (Skinner) $690

Painted birch chest of drawers, Northern New England, circa 1800, drawers beaded, all over original red paint, 43¾in. wide. (Skinner Inc.) $4,700

QUEEN ANNE

Queen Anne cherry base to highboy, Connecticut, circa 1770, old refinish, old brasses, 39in. wide.
(Skinner) $1,380

Queen Anne maple base to high chest of drawers, Dunlap School, New Hampshire, circa 1780.
(Skinner) $2,200

Queen Anne maple base to high chest, Connecticut or Rhode Island, circa 1770, old red stain, original brasses, 37¹/₂in. wide.
(Skinner) $2,185

A fine Queen Anne mahogany block-front chest of drawers, Boston, Massachusetts, circa 1765, the molded base with shaped pendant continuing to bracket feet, width 35¹/₂in.
(Sotheby's) $75,000

A mahogany chest of American Queen Anne Boston style with molded waved rectangular top, the block front with four graduated long drawers, on cabriole legs and claw-and-ball feet, 32¹/₂in. wide.
(Christie's) $6,650

A Queen Anne figured mahogany block-front chest of drawers, Boston, Massachusetts, circa 1750–70, the oblong top with thumbmolded edge, 36in. wide.
(Sotheby's) $145,500

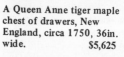

A Queen Anne tiger maple chest of drawers, New England, circa 1750, 36in. wide. $5,625

Queen Anne grain-painted base to high chest of drawers, New England, late 18th century, on four cabriole legs ending in pad feet joined by valanced skirt, 39in. wide.
(Skinner) $3,737

A Queen Anne carved mahogany block-front chest of drawers, Boston, circa 1750, the oblong, thumb-molded top with blocked front, 36in. wide.
(Sotheby's) $321,500

SHAKER

Shaker cherry five drawer chest of drawers, New Lebanon, 36in. wide.
(Skinner) $1,092

Shaker cherry and tiger maple chest over two drawers, *Built by W. D. Shimnway 1835 when he was 18 years old*, 42in. wide.
(Skinner) $1,265

Shaker pine chest of drawers, probably New Lebanon, New York, mid 19th century, with five graduated drawers, 34in. wide.   (Skinner) $690

Butternut Shaker chest of drawers, Mt. Lebanon, circa 1880, the rectangular top above the case of five graduated quarter-round molded drawers, 40in. wide.
(Skinner) $14,950

A fine Shaker maple cupboard with chest of drawers, Mount Lebanon, New York, mid-19th century, the molded top above a paneled cupboard door opening to a single shelf, 94in. high. (Christie's) $24,000

Shaker pine chest of drawers, Harvard, Massachusetts, 1830-40, the rectangular top with rounded edge above a case of four graduated thumbmolded drawers on bracket feet, 39in. wide. (Skinner) $17,250

Shaker yellow painted pine and basswood chest of drawers, New Lebanon, New York, 1825-40, the case of four graduated molded drawers, 44in. wide.
(Skinner) $5,175

A Shaker red stained tall chest, New Lebanon, New York, 1820-40, the rectangular top with breadboard ends above a conforming case, 42in. wide.
(Christie's) $27,600

Shaker cherry case of three drawers, Mt. Lebanon, New York, 1830-40, signed *Made by Andrew Fortier Feb'ry 6th1881*, 39in. wide.
(Skinner) $1,265

STICKLEY

A Gustav Stickley three-drawer bedside stand, style no. 842, copper hardware with loop handles, circa 1907, 29½in. high.　**$1,800**

Stickley Bros. set of drawers with swinging mirror, circa 1910, 38in. wide.　**$1,000**

Gustav Stickley chest of drawers, circa 1907, two half drawers over three long drawers, 37in. wide. (Skinner)　**$2,800**

A Gustav Stickley chest-of-drawers, no. 901, with wooden pulls, circa 1907, 37in. wide. (Skinner)　**$1,800**

Early Gustav Stickley six-drawer chest, circa 1902-04, no. 902, reverse V splashboard, two half-drawers over four graduated drawers with square wooden pulls, 40in. wide. (Skinner)　**$5,600**

A Gustav Stickley nine-drawer tall chest, no. 913, circa 1907, 36in. wide, 50in. high. (Skinner)　**$6,250**

A nine-drawer tall chest with cast bronze faceted pulls, by Gustav Stickley, circa 1904-06, 36in. wide. (Skinner)　**$9,300**

Stickley Brothers chest of drawers, circa 1912, rectangular swivel mirror, two short drawers over three long drawers, 44in. wide. (Skinner Inc.)　**$500**

Gustav Stickley six-drawer chest, circa 1907, no. 902, reverse V splashboard, two half-drawers over four graduated drawers, signed with red decal, 52½in. high. (Skinner Inc.) **$5,600**

A Chippendale mahogany chest-on-chest, New York City, 1760–1780, in two sections; the upper case with molded cornice with canted corners above a conforming case fitted with three thumb molded short drawers over three thumb molded and graduated long drawers, all flanked by fluted canted corners; the lower case with applied mid-molding with canted cormers above a conforming case fitted with a thumbmolded writing slide over three thumbmolded and graduated long drawers, on a conforming molded base with straight bracket feet, 45½in. wide.
(Christie's) $27,600

Chippendale walnut carved chest on chest, Massachusetts or New Hampshire, late 18th century, some original brass, 41in. wide.
(Skinner) $13,800

A fine Chippendale inlaid and carved cherrywood bonnet-top chest-on-chest, Connecticut, circa 1790, in two parts, 41in. wide.
(Sotheby's) $17,250

A fine Chippendale carved mahogany block-front bonnet-top chest-on-chest, Boston, Massachusetts, circa 1770, 42in. wide.
(Sotheby's) $60,000

George III mahogany chest-on-chest, circa 1800, the thumb-molded denticulated top above two short and two long drawers flanked by canted and fluted stiles, 40in. wide.
(Butterfield & Butterfield) $4,400

An important Federal carved and figured mahogany serpentine-front chest-on-chest, the carving attributed to Samuel McIntire, Salem, Massachusetts, circa 1795, 45¼in. wide.
(Sotheby's) $350,000

A Chippendale figured maple chest-on-chest, New Hampshire, 1760–1790, carved with a fan centered by a pair of short drawers over four long drawers, the lower section with four long drawers, 34¼in. wide.
(Christie's) $19,350

Chippendale birch chest on chest, New Hampshire, circa 1780, old refinish, brasses and escutcheons replacements, 38in. wide. (Skinner Inc.) $10,000

The Samuel Morris Chippendale carved mahogany chest-on-chest, Philadelphia, 1760–1780, in three sections, on ogee bracket feet, 95½in. high, 43½in. wide.
(Christie's) $74,800

A Chippendale maple chest-on-chest, Mass., circa 1780, 38in. wide. $10,900

Chippendale cherry chest on chest, New England, circa 1800, early red stained surface, original brass, 38¼in. wide. (Skinner) $4,600

A Chippendale maple chest-on-chest, in two parts, probably New Hampshire, 1760-90, 38½in. wide. $20,000

A Chippendale carved mahogany chest-on-chest, possibly by Thomas Potts, Philadelphia or vicinity, circa 1774, 43in. wide. (Christie's) $13,800

A Chippendale figured and carved scroll-top mahogany chest-on-chest, Philadelphia, Pennsylvania, circa 1780, in three parts, on a molded base and ogee bracket feet, 47in. wide. (Sotheby's) $11,500

A Queen Anne carved and figured walnut bonnet-top chest-on-chest, Goddard Townsend School, Newport, Rhode Island, circa 1775, 42½in. wide. (Sotheby's) $85,000

A fine Chippendale carved mahogany scroll-top chest-on-chest, Philadelphia, circa 1770, in three parts, on a molded base and ogee bracket feet, 47in. wide. (Sotheby's) $16,500

Chippendale mahogany carved chest on chest, New London County, Connecticut, 1760–80, on a serpentine lower case, 44¼in. wide. (Skinner Inc.) $34,000

American mahogany chest-on-chest, broken arch top with three flame finials, upper section with three over four drawers, 40in. wide. (Eldred's) $6,600

Carved Chippendale cherry chest on chest, Connecticut, 1760–90, with pin-wheel carved drawer, old replaced brass, 39in. wide. (Skinner) $12,650

A very fine and rare Queen Anne highly figured walnut chest-on-chest, Philadelphia, Pennsylvania, 1750–1770, in two parts; the upper section with a rectangular overhanging cornice with chamfered corners above five short and three long graduated thumbmolded drawers; the lower section fitted with a mid-molding above two short and two graduated thumbmolded long drawers, width of cornice 45in.
(Sotheby's)

$40,250

An important Derby family Federal carved and figured mahogany serpentine-front chest-on-chest, the carving attributed to Samuel McIntire and/or Samuel Field McIntire, Salem, Massachusetts, circa 1795, in two parts; the upper section with a pitch-molded and dentil-carved pediment centering a giltwood wing-spread American eagle, the serpentine lower section with four graduated serpentine cockbeaded long drawers, 45¼in. wide.   (Sotheby's) $178,500

Chippendale cherry bonnet top chest-on-chest, probably Connecticut, circa 1770, 38½in. wide.
(Skinner) $6,600

Chippendale maple carved chest on chest, New England, circa 1780, old refinish, some original brass, 38¾in. wide.
(Skinner Inc.) $14,000

Chippendale style cherry chest on chest, America, circa 1900, 88½in. high.
(Skinner Inc.) $6,250

A fine and rare Queen Anne carved and grain-painted maple chest-on-chest-on-frame, attributed to the Dunlap family, Bedford, New Hampshire, 1777–1792, 36½in. wide.
(Sotheby's) $310,500

Chippendale carved cherrywood and birch bonnet-top chest on chest, New England, late 18th century, on ball-and-claw feet centering a foliate-carved pendant, 38in. wide.
(Butterfield & Butterfield)
                                        $5,150

A Chippendale mahogany chest-on-chest, Philadelphia, 1760-1790, the upper section with molded overhanging cornice above three small drawers over two short drawers above three long graduated drawers, 43¼in. wide. (Christie's) $6,900

The John Mills family Chippendale cherrywood chest-on-chest, by Major Dunlap, New Hampshire, circa 1780, 41½in. wide. (Christie's) $70,000

A Chippendale carved cherrywood chest-on-chest on frame, Connecticut, probably Woodbury, circa 1770, on C-scroll carved frontal cabriole legs, 39¾in. wide.
(Sotheby's) $12,500

A Queen Anne maple chest-on-chest, in two sections, New Hampshire, 1740-70, 41in. wide. (Christie's)
                                      $15,700

An oak and poplar chest with drawer, probably Conn., 1690-1710, 48½in. wide.
(Christie's) $23,000

A sulphur inlaid sycamore blanket chest-over-drawers, Lancaster County, Pennsylvania, dated *1781*, the rectangular top with applied molding, 55¾in. wide.
(Christie's) $46,000

Painted and decorated pine chest over drawer, Taunton, Massachusetts area, early 18th century, with thumbmolded, cleated top opening to a cavity above a drawer, 44in. wide overall.
(Skinner) $31,050

Painted pine and poplar chest over drawer, New England, early 18th century, the molded lift top above a half-round molded case, 36in. wide.
(Skinner) $4,600

Grain painted chest over drawer, New England, early 19th century, with, molded hinged top and a base with side shaping, 42¹⁄₈in. wide.
(Skinner) $20,700

Grain painted pine chest over drawers, northern New England, second quarter 19th century, the top lifts above a cavity with molded lidded till, 36⁷⁄₈in. wide.
(Skinner) $1,150

Oak and pine joined chest with drawer, Massachusetts, circa 1650–1700, old finish, 42³⁄₄in. wide.
(Skinner) $4,600

Oak and pine carved and paneled chest over drawers, Hadley area, Massachusetts, 1690–1710, 49¹⁄₂in. wide.
(Skinner Inc.) $11,500

Red painted poplar chest over drawer, Connecticut, mid 18th century, molded lift top above a double arch molded case, 36in. wide. (Skinner) $4,600

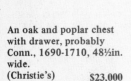

A red painted child's blanket chest-over-drawers, Schaefferstown, Pennsylvania, circa 1838, the rectangular hinged top with applied molding, 31¼in. wide.
(Christie's) **$5,520**

Blue painted chest over drawers, New England, early 19th century, the old blue is over an earlier blue-green paint, 38in. wide.
(Skinner) **$6,900**

Smoke grained child's chest over drawer, New England, 1830s, with recessed panel sides, original surface and wooden pulls, 31in. wide.
(Skinner) **$1,380**

A carved and painted oak Hadley chest-over-drawers, Hampshire County, Connecticut, 1680–1730, the case with three carved panels, 46in. wide.
(Christie's) **$206,000**

Grain painted chest over drawers, Massachusetts, late 18th century, the hinged molded lift top opens to a well, 46in. high, 35¼in. wide.
(Skinner) **$4,485**

Oak and pine paneled chest over drawers, New England, dated *1691* and initials *H.C.S.*, 41³/₈in. wide.
(Skinner) **$13,200**

Vinegar putty painted chest over drawers, Southeastern New England, circa 1835, the molded hinged top above a deep well, 40in. wide.
(Skinner) **$6,325**

Joined and paneled pine chest with drawer, Hampshire County, Massachusetts, 1710–30, paneled sides, drawer on channel runner, 38in. wide.
(Skinner) **$5,175**

Red painted pine chest over drawers, Milton, New Hampshire, area, circa 1830, with molded hinged top above a cavity, 38in. wide.
(Skinner) **$3,450**

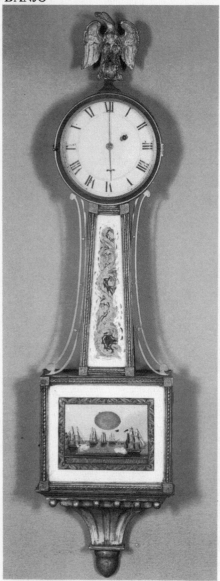

A Federal giltwood and églomisé banjo clock, dial signed by David Williams (1769-1823), Newport, 1815-1820, the central carved giltwood spreadwinged eagle above a circular glazed door above an églomisé decorated throat enclosed by rope-carved frame, above a rectangular base with églomisé decorated panel depicting a ship battle and inscribed 'The Constitution's Escape', 42in. long.
(Christie's) $57,500

A Federal giltwood and églomisé banjo clock, possibly Aaron Willard (1783-1864), Boston, circa 1810, the circular glazed dial door with brass bezel enclosing a white-painted dial with Roman numeral chapter ring above a tapering throat with conforming mint-green, white, black and gilt-decorated églomisé panel decorated with pendant floral vine with a border, 34¾in. high.
(Christie's) $32,200

BANJO

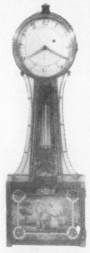

Classical gilt and mahogany lyre-form banjo timepiece, probably Mass., circa 1820, 40in. high. (Skinner) $3,500

Mid 19th century banjo timepiece with alarm, signed A. Willard, Jnr., Boston, 33½in. high. $25,000

A Federal mahogany giltwood and églomisé banjo clock, Mass., 1815-25, 40in. high. $3,500

A federal giltwood mahogany banjo timepiece, by Lemuel Curtis, Mass., circa 1820, 32in. high. $12,000

An unusual mid 19th century American rosewood hanging wall timepiece, the 7in. circular white painted dial signed *E. Howard & Co. BOSTON*, 28½in. high. (Christie's) $1,000

Presentation banjo timepiece, Waltham Clock Co., Waltham, Mass., 20th century, eagle finial, brass bezel, 43in. (Skinner) $2,500

A Federal mahogany giltwood and églomisé banjo clock, Samuel Whiting, Concord, Mass., circa 1815, surmounted by a giltwood acorn finial, 34in. high. (Sotheby's) $4,025

A Federal banjo clock, Oliver Gerrish, Portland, Maine, circa 1820, with an eglomisé tablet depicting buildings and a river, 40in. high. (Christie's) $51,750

BANJO

A Federal gilt and églomisé lyre-shaped wall clock, dial signed *Aaron Willard, Boston,* early 19th century, 40½in. high.
(Christie's) $3,500

A fine Federal mahogany and églomisé panel banjo clock, Lemuel Curtis, Mass., circa 1815, 33in. high.
(Christie's) $22,500

A Federal presentation mahogany banjo time-piece, by A. Willard, circa 1820, 40½in. high.
          $4,750

Antique American banjo clock in mahogany, by A. Willard, Boston, 33½in. high.
(Eldred's) $3,500

Walnut banjo timepiece, dial: *E. Howard and Co., Boston,* circa 1840, 44in. high.
(Skinner) $2,500

Fine custom-made banjo clock by Foster S. Compos of Pembroke, Mass., inlaid mahogany case with presentation bracket, 41½in. high.
(Eldred's) $2,000

A Federal mahogany giltwood and églomisé banjo clock, Lemuel Curtis, Concord, Mass., circa 1825, 30in. high.
(Sothebys) $3,450

A Classical mahogany and parcel-gilt girandole clock, probably Lemuel Curtis, Concord, Mass., circa 1820, 47in. high.
(Sothebys) $10,925

BANJO

An early 19th century American mahogany cased wall clock, 30in. high. $2,000

A Federal mahogany lyre timepiece, Henry Allen Hinckley, Mass., circa 1825, 38in. high. $4,500

A Federal giltwood and églomisé banjo clock, New England, circa 1825, 32in. high. (Sothebys) $3,910

Federal banjo mahogany timepiece, probably New Hampshire, circa 1820, 34in. high. (Skinner) $1,610

Antique American banjo clock in mahogany, with gilt and reverse-painted throat and lower tablet, 37in. high. (Eldred's) $495

A fine and rare Federal giltwood églomisé and mahogany banjo clock, David Williams, Newport, Rhode Island, circa 1815, 40in. high. (Sotheby's) $3,450

A Classical mahogany and églomisé banjo clock with alarm mechanism, labeled *Jonathan Billings, Acton, Massachusetts, 1839,* 41in. high. (Sothebys) $4,500

A Federal églomisé and brass-mounted mahogany banjo clock, Aaron Willard, Jr., Boston, Mass., circa 1815, 32in. high. (Sothebys) $6,325

MIRROR CLOCKS

Classical mahogany carved looking glass clock, Munger and Benedict, Auburn, New York, circa 1825, 39¹/₂in. high.
(Skinner) **$1,870**

Giltwood mirror wall timepiece, A. Chandler, Concord, New Hampshire, circa 1830, 30in. high.
(Skinner) **$1,500**

Classical Revival mahogany mirror clock by Marsh, Gilbert & Co., Connecticut, circa 1830, 36½in. high. **$1,000**

Mirror timepiece, James Collins, Goffstown, New Hampshire, circa 1830, with eight-day weight driven movement, painted iron dial, 30in. height.
(Skinner) **$2,185**

Classical mahogany triple decker mirror clock, C. & L. C. Ives, Bristol, Connecticut, circa 1831, with eight-day brass wagon spring driven movement, 36¹/₂in. high.
(Skinner) **$3,680**

Federal gilt gesso and mahogany veneer mirror timepiece, Joshua Wilder, Hingham, Massachusetts, circa 1815, the molded cornice with applied spherules, 16in. wide.
(Skinner) **$25,300**

A Federal mahogany mirror clock, by Asa Munger, Auburn, New York, circa 1830, 39in. high. $3,000

An Empire carved mahogany and veneer mirror clock, by Hotchkiss & Benedict, N.Y., circa 1825, 39in. high.
$1,750

Empire carved mahogany mirror clock by Munger & Benedict, New York, circa 1830, 39½in. high.
$3,000

PILLAR & SCROLL

Antique American pillar and
scroll shelf clock in mahogany
with brass finials, painted dial,
31in. high.
(Eldred's)   **$600**

A Federal mahogany pillar
and scroll clock, by E.
Terry & Sons, Conn., circa
1820, 29in. high.   **$2,250**

Federal mahogany pillar
and scroll clock, by Ephraim
Downs for G. Mitchell, Conn.,
circa 1820, 31in. high. **$1,350**

A Federal curly maple-inlaid
mahogany pillar-and-scroll shelf
clock, labeled *Eli Terry,
Plymouth, Connecticut,* circa
1830, 30¹/₂in. high.
(Sotheby's)   **$1,725**

A Federal mahogany shelf
clock, labeled *Seth Thomas,
Plymouth, Connecticut,* first
quarter 19th century, the
swan neck pediment above
a rectangular case with double
glazed door, 29in. high.
(Christie's)   **$1,500**

Federal mahogany pillar and
scroll clock, E. Terry and Sons,
Plymouth, Connecticut, circa
1825, the painted wooden dial
above an eglomise tablet, 16¹/₂in.
wide.
(Skinner)   **$978**

Federal mahogany pillar
and scroll clock, by Eli
& Samuel Terry, Conn.,
circa 1825, 28½in. high.
                          $1,250

A Federal mahogany pillar-and-
scroll shelf clock, by Eli Terry &
Sons, Plymouth, Connecticut,
1815–1825, on bracket feet, 31in.
high.
(Christie's)   **$1,850**

A Federal mahogany and
églomisé pillar-and-scroll shelf
clock, labeled *Eli Terry & Sons,
Plymouth, Connecticut,* circa
1830, 31in. high.
(Sotheby's)   **$1,500**

PILLAR & SCROLL

Federal mahogany pillar and scroll clock, Riley Whiting, Winchester, Connecticut, circa 1820, 30in. high.
(Skinner Inc.) $800

A Federal pillar and scroll mahogany shelf clock, by Jeromes & Darrow, Bristol, Connecticut, first quarter 19th century, 29¹/₂in. high.
(Christie's) $1,150

Federal mahogany pillar and scroll clock, Bishop and Bradley, Waterbury, Connecticut, circa 1825.
(Skinner Inc.) $1,750

A late Federal pillar-and-scroll mahogany shelf clock, labeled by Seth Thomas, Eli Terry Patent, Plymouth, Connecticut, circa 1820, eglomisé panel with a central medallion and village scene, 29in. high.
(Christie's) $1,725

Pillar and scroll mahogany and églomisé shelf clock, Eli Terry, Plymouth, Connecticut, 1820, parcel-gilt decorated and white painted wooden dial with églomise landscape, trees and Greek Revival house, height 31in.
(Butterfield & Butterfield)
                      $1,610

Federal mahogany and mahogany veneer pillar and scroll shelf clock, Seth Thomas, Plymouth, Connecticut, circa 1818, with thirty-hour strap wood movement, 30¹/₄in. high.
(Skinner) $3,105

A Federal mahogany pillar-and-scroll shelf clock, by Eli Terry & Sons, Plymouth, Connecticut, 1815–1825, on bracket feet, 31in. high.
(Christie's) $1,750

Federal mahogany pillar and scroll clock, Eli Terry and Sons, Plymouth, Connecticut, circa 1820, 30-hour wooden movement, 32in. high.
(Skinner Inc.) $1,250

A Federal mahogany eglomise shelf clock, by Eli Terry and Sons, Plymouth, Connecticut, circa 1820, with swan neck pediment, 30½in. high.
(Christie's New York) $3,500

PILLAR & SCROLL

A Federal mahogany pillar and scroll clock, by E. Terry & Sons, circa 1835, 31in. high. **$1,500**

Federal mahogany pillar and scroll clock, E. Terry & Sons, Conn., circa 1825, 31in. high. **$1,000**

Federal mahogany pillar and scroll clock, by Ephraim Downes, Conn., circa 1825, 31in. high. **$1,250**

Mahogany and mahogany veneer pillar and scroll shelf clock, Erastus Hodges, Torrington Hollow, Connecticut, circa 1830, with thirty-hour wooden weight driven movement, 29in. high. (Skinner) **$3,220**

A late Federal mahogany pillar and scroll shelf clock, Seth Thomas, Plymouth, Connecticut, circa 1820, with a glazed cupboard door flanked by colonettes and enclosing a white dial with Arabic chapter ring, 31in. high. (Christie's) **$1,350**

A Federal pillar and scroll shelf clock by Seth Thomas, Plymouth, Connecticut, circa 1805, the swan's-neck pediment centering three brass urn finials, 31in. high. (Christie's) **$3,500**

Federal mahogany pillar and scroll clock, Seth Thomas, Plymouth, Connecticut, circa 1818, rare off center strap wood movement, 29in. high. (Skinner) **$4,125**

Federal mahogany pillar and scroll clock, Riley Whiting, Winchester, Connecticut, circa 1825, thirty-hour wooden movement, 30in. high. (Skinner Inc.) **$1,000**

Federal mahogany and mahogany veneer pillar and scroll clock, Seth Thomas, Plymouth, Connecticut, circa 1820, old refinish, 31in. high. (Skinner) **$1,265**

A rare Federal inlaid rosewood and eglomisé 'Acorn' shelf clock, Connecticut, circa 1825, attributed to The Forrestville Connecticut Clock Manufactory, the hinged eglomisé door with arched and peaked upper section opening to a white-painted dial, supported between two serpentine uprights with acorn finials, on a stepped base, 25in. high.
(Sotheby's) $12,650

SHELF

A walnut double dial calendar shelf clock, by Seth Thomas Clock Co., 32in. high. **$2,750**

Gothic mahogany shelf clock, Brewster and Ingrahams, Bristol, Ct., circa 1840, 19³/₄in. high.
(Skinner) **$935**

Federal mahogany and tiger maple shelf timepiece, by Aaron Willard, Boston, circa 1815, 35½in. high. **$20,000**

Mahogany double steeple shelf clock, Birge and Fuller, Bristol, Connecticut, circa 1845, with eight-day brass wagon spring movement, 27in. high.
(Skinner) **$862**

Rosewood shelf timepiece, probably Atkins Clock Mfg. Co., Bristol, Connecticut, circa 1855, 30-day wagon spring movement, 17½in. high.
(Skinner Inc.) **$1,450**

Classical mahogany carved mantel clock, E. Terry and Sons, Plymouth, Connecticut, circa 1820–24, with eight-day weight driven wooden movement, 37in. high.
(Skinner) **$575**

Empire mahogany carved shelf clock, by Eli Terry & Son, Conn., circa 1825, 31in. high. **$1,350**

A hammered copper shelf clock, by Tiffany & Co., New York, early 20th century, on rectangular brass platform base, 11in. high.
(Skinner Inc.) **$1,000**

Empire triple decker shelf clock, by Birge, Mallory & Co., circa 1840, 36in. high. **$1,000**

SHELF

A Federal inlaid mahogany
shelf clock, by David Wood,
Mass., circa 1800, 33¾in.
high.   **$75,000**

Victorian 'ginger bread'
framed shelf clock with an
Ansonia Clock Co. striking
movement.   **$200**

A Federal mahogany shelf
clock, by Reuben Tower,
Massa., 1836, 34½in. high.
                        $12,750

Classical mahogany carved
mantel clock, Sylvester Clark,
Straitsville, Connecticut, for Hill
Wells & Co., circa 1830, with
brass eight-day Salem bridge-
type movement, 31½in. high.
(Skinner)   **$3,565**

A Victorian carved walnut shelf-
clock by Seth Thomas
Company, Thomaston,
Connecticut, circa 1890, of violin
form carved with foliage
centering a glazed cupboard door
painted in gilding with musical
motifs, 29in. high.
(Christie's)   **$3,500**

L. & J. G. Stickley mantel
clock, Fayetteville, New York,
circa 1910, designed by Peter
Heinrich Hansen, signed with
Handcraft decal, 22in. high.
(Skinner Inc.)   **$7,000**

A Federal stained maple shelf-
clock, O. Brackett, Vassalboro,
Maine, 1815-1825, with molded cornice above a square
glazed door with floral painted
corners, 29¼in. high.
(Christie's)   **$25,000**

Mahogany and stencil decorated
miniature timepiece with alarm,
Silas Hoadley, Plymouth,
Connecticut, the black painted
scroll with stenciled eagle and
shield, 12in. wide.
(Skinner)   **$2,070**

A Federal walnut shelf timepiece, possibly rural Massachusetts, circa 1820, the hood with
molded cornice above a glazed
kidney door, 32in. high.
(Skinner Inc.)   **$3,750**

SHELF

A Federal mahogany inlaid shelf timepiece, by A. Whitcombe, Massa., circa 1790, 13½in. high. **$25,000**

Empire mahogany hollow column clock, Connecticut, circa 1835, 31in. high. **$750**

Massachusetts mahogany shelf timepiece, John Bailey, Lynn, Massachusetts, circa 1808, flaring French feet, 36in. high. (Skinner Inc.) **$4,000**

Round gothic mahogany veneer shelf clock, Brewster and Ingrahams, circa 1845, with eight day brass spring movement, 19¾in. high. (Skinner Inc.) **$550**

Mahogany and églomisé shelf clock, circa 1830, the white painted wood dial inscribed *Joseph Ives, New York* above a box base with an églomisé paneled hinged door depicting a landscape, height 28¼in. (Butterfield & Butterfield) **$11,500**

Rare Silas Hoadley mantel clock, in mahogany veneers with painted dial, stenciled pilasters and reverse-painted lower tablet, upside down works and alarm, 26in. high. (Eldred's) **$2,200**

Rare Federal mahogany inlaid shelf timepiece, John Gains, Portsmouth, New Hampshire, circa 1800, eight-day weight driven brass movement, 41in. high. (Skinner) **$20,000**

An Empire paint-decorated and etched glass shelf clock, J.B. Mills & Co., New York, circa 1840, the rectangular cove molding on columnar supports, 22¼in. high. (Sotheby's) **$805**

Rare acorn shelf clock, Forestville Manufacturing Co., with fuse movement, Bristol, Connecticut, circa 1850, 24in. high. (Skinner) **$4,125**

SHELF

Gothic mahogany steeple clock with fusée, Smith and Goodrich, Bristol, Ct., circa 1840, 19½in. high.
(Skinner) $302

Colonial Revival mahogany inlaid shelf clock, America, late 19th/20th century, with spring driven movements, 16in. high.
(Skinner) $920

Double steeple mahogany wagon spring shelf clock, by Birge & Fuller, Conn., circa 1846, 26in. high.
                          $3,000

A Gustav Stickley oak mantel clock, early 20th century, the door with faceted cut-out framing brass dial, Seth Thomas movement, 13¾in. high.
(Skinner Inc.) $2,500

Classical mahogany shelf clock, E. and G.W. Bartholomew, Bristol, Connecticut, circa 1830, the flat molded cornice above a glazed door, 29¾in. wide.
(Skinner) $690

Gustav Stickley mantel clock, circa 1902, overhanging top above single door with copper hardware, Seth Thomas works, 21in. high
(Skinner) $6,500

An Empire carved mahogany shelf clock, by M. Leavenworth & Son, Conn., 30in. high. $2,250

A rosewood shelf clock, attributed to Atkins Clock Mfg. Co., Conn., circa 1855, 18¾in. high. $2,500

An Empire carved mahogany shelf clock, by Riley Whiting, Conn., circa 1825, 29½in. high. $600

A fine and rare Federal inlaid and brass-mounted mahogany mantle clock, Silas W. Howell, Albany, circa 1810, the inlaid domed pediment surmounted by brass urn-form finials with bookend and oval inlaid dies below, on brass-mounted fluted quarter-columns centering a glazed line-inlaid arched door opening to an engraved brass dial, with a female figure in the arched and floral spandrels centering the inscription *Silas W. Howell, Albany,* the oval inlaid case below on a flaring plinth. Eight-day brass and steel, spring powered, movement, 19½in. high.
(Sotheby's) $18,400

TALL CASE

A pine polychrome decorated tall case clock, Connecticut, circa 1830, 85in. high. $10,000

A Gustav Stickley oak tall case clock, circa 1902-04, 71in. high. $12,500

A Federal pine grain painted tall case clock, by S. Hoadley, Conn., circa 1830, 86in. high. $20,000

A Federal mahogany inlaid tall case clock, by Samuel Foster, New Hampshire, 1798, 86in. high. $15,000

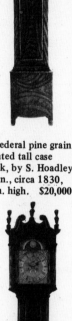

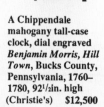

A Federal inlaid mahogany and flame birch tall-case clock, works by Aaron Willard, case attributed to John or Thomas Seymour, Boston, circa 1800, 103³/₄in. high. (Christie's) $65,000

A Chippendale carved mahogany tallcase clock, dial signed by Samuel Rockwell, Providence, Rhode Island, 1760-1770. (Christie's) $52,900

A Chippendale mahogany tall-case clock, dial engraved *Benjamin Morris, Hill Town*, Bucks County, Pennsylvania, 1760–1780, 92¹/₂in. high (Christie's) $12,500

Chippendale mahogany tall case clock, Pennsylvania, late 18th century, inscribed *Geo Lively, Baltimore*, 7ft. 7in. high. (Butterfield & Butterfield) $2,500

TALL CASE

A Federal inlaid mahogany tallcase clock, dial signed by Aaron Willard, circa 1805-10, 94½in. high. $22,500

Cherry tall case clock, Isaac Brokaw, New Jersey, circa 1780, 88in. high.
(Skinner) $3,300

Gustav Stickley tall case clock, c. 1902, with copper numerals within tall slightly flared case, 70³/₄in. high
(Skinner Inc) $7,500

A Chippendale carved walnut tall case clock, Pennsylvania, circa 1770, 8ft. 1¹/₄in. high.
(Sotheby's) $4,500

A grained and stenciled tallcase clock by Riley Whiting, Winchester, Connecticut, circa 1820, 86³/₄in. high.
(Christie's) $7,500

A Federal mahogany tall-case clock, by Benjamin Willard, Roxbury, Massachusetts, circa 1775, 93in. high.
(Christie's) $7,688

A fine paint decorated clock, attributed to Riley Whiting, Winchester, Connecticut, circa 1820, 82in. high.
(Sotheby's) $26,450

A Federal inlaid mahogany tall-case clock, Aaron Willard, Roxbury, Massachusetts, circa 1805, the hood with three brass ball-and-spire finials, 91in. high.
(Christie's) $22,500

TALL CASE

Tiger maple tall case clock, dial inscribed *William Stillman in Hopkinton 1786*, 83in. high. (Skinner)
$7,475

An American carved walnut longcase regulator, signed *Howard & Davis, Makers -* Boston, circa 1851, 8ft.0½in. high. $30,000

Antique American pine long case clock, painted wooden dial signed, *Edwards, Ashby 505*, 80in. high. (Eldred's)
$1,210

A Federal inlaid mahogany tallcase clock, dial signed by Aaron Willard, 1805-10, 88½in. high.
$30,000

A Federal ivory-inlaid mahogany bow-front tall case clock, John Esterlie, Maytown, Pennsylvania, circa 1815, 8ft. 4¼in. high. (Sotheby's) $10,000

Arts and Crafts oak tall case clock, circa 1910, brass numerals and dial over leaded glass cabinet door, 75½in. high. (Skinner Inc.) $1,250

Mahogany tall case clock, William Claggett (1695–1749), Newport, Rhode Island, (1725–40), 88¼in. high. (Skinner Inc.) $20,000

Pine tall case clock, Nathaniel Haneye, Bridgewater, Massachusetts, 18th century, with wooden movement, 82in. high. (Skinner) $3,025

TALL CASE

A Federal inlaid mahogany tallcase clock, dial signed Alex. J. Willard, early 19th century, 86¾in. high. $4,500

Federal cherry inlaid tall case clock, Asahel Cheney, Northfield, Connecticut, circa 1800, 84in. high. (Skinner) $5,225

A Chippendale cherrywood tall case clock, dial signed by Thos. Harland, Conn., circa 1775, 95in. high. $20,000

Federal mahogany veneer tall case clock, Simon Willard, Roxbury, Massachusetts, circa 1800, 98¼in. high. (Skinner Inc.) $25,000

Federal walnut inlaid tallcase clock, Pennsylvania, circa 1770–1810, 7ft. 11in. high. (Butterfield & Butterfield) $4,500

A mahogany longcase sidereal regulator with break circuit work, signed *Wm. Bond & Sons, Boston,* circa 1858, 64½in. high. $30,000

A Chippendale carved walnut tall case clock, Pennsylvania, 1870–1890, the hood with carved swan's neck pediment, 92in. high. (Christie's) $4,750

Tall case clock, circa 1800, in mahogany with wooden works, bonnet top, reeded quarter columns, turned feet, 93in. high. (Eldred's) $1,500

TALL CASE

Federal cherry inlaid tall case clock, Nicholas Goddard, Rutland, Vermont, 89¼in. high. (Skinner) $5,175

Painted pine tall case clock , Riley Whiting, Winchester, Connecticut, circa 1830, 83in. high. (Skinner) $4,888

Federal mahogany inlaid tall case clock, Southeastern US, circa 1790, 104.5in. high. (Skinner) $9,200

Federal cherry tall case clock, possibly Massachusetts, circa 1810, 85in. high. (Skinner) $6,900

A Federal carved maple tallcase clock, dial signed *Abner Rogers, Berwick, Maine,*1800-1820, 99½in. high. (Christie's) $8,050

A Chippendale grain-painted flat-top thirty-hour tall-case clock, Henry Hahn, Reading, Pennsylvania, dated 1784. (Sotheby's) $23,000

Bird's eye maple, tiger maple and maple tall case clock, Silas Hoadley, Plymouth, Connecticut, circa 1825, 85in. high. (Skinner) $2,875

A Federal mahogany dwarf tall-case clock, by Reuben Tower, Hingham, Massachusetts, 1816, 50in. high. (Christie's) $211,500

Small Federal cherry inlaid tall-case clock, probably Massachusetts, circa 1810, 85in. high. (Skinner)

$4,312

Grain painted tall case clock, Silas Hoadley, Plymouth, Connecticut, circa 1830, 89in. high. (Skinner)

$3,737

Pine dwarf clock, Rubin Tower, Kingston, Massachusetts, 1810–30, 48in. high. (Skinner)

$13,800

Grain painted tall case clock, Riley Whiting, Winchester, Connecticut, 1813–30, 91in. high. (Skinner)

$2,760

A Federal inlaid mahogany tall-case clock by William Cummens, Massachusetts, circa 1802–1810, 90in. high. (Christie's)

$25,300

A Federal transitional yellow and red grain-painted thirty-hour tall-case clock, Oley Township, Berks County, Pennsylvania, circa 1825.(Sotheby's)

$74,000

Federal mahogany inlaid tall case clock, by Levi Hutchins Concord, New Hampshire, circa 1810, 100in. high. (Skinner)

$5,750

A Federal mahogany dwarf tall-case clock, Massachusetts, 1790–1810, white circular dial above a blue painted ground with a swagged floral garland, 54^{1}/2in. high. (Christie's)

$10,925

CLOCKS

Jolly Tar wall timepiece, manufactured by Baird Clock Co., New York, 30½in. high. **$2,500**

Rosewood octagon wall timepiece, Joseph Ives, New York, circa 1830, with thirty day wagon-spring movement, 25½in. high.
(Skinner) **$1,380**

Rosewood veneer wall regulator, by Seth Thomas, Conn., circa 1860, 31¼in. long. **$1,250**

Rosewood octagon wall timepiece, probably Atkins Whiting & Co., Bristol, Connecticut, mid 19th century, with thirty-day wagon spring movement, 25½in. high.
(Skinner) **$690**

An Ever Ready Safety Razor advertising clock, made of wood with American 8 day movement, the price of 12 blades on the pendulum.
(Auction Team Köln) **$2,000**

A mahogany and eglomise gallery clock, Crosby & Vosburgh, New York, circa 1850, the octagonal surround centering a glazed door, 25ft. ½in high.
(Sotheby's) **$1,750**

A walnut regulator wall clock, by E. Howard & Co., Boston, circa 1875, 43in. high. **$6,000**

Boston Beer Co. wall timepiece, manufactured by the New Haven Clock Co., circa 1900, 14in. diam. **$1,250**

Late 19th century walnut regulator timepiece, by the Chelsea Clock Co., Mass., 35in. high. **$1,750**

Walnut regulator timepiece,
Seth Thomas, Thomaston,
Connecticut, 1860, 31¹/₂in. high.
(Skinner) $715

Late 19th century pressed
wood advertising timepiece,
by Baird Adv. Clock Co.,
31in. long. $2,750

A walnut calendar time-
piece, by New Haven Clock
Co., circa 1900, 32in. long.
                        $1,000

Mahogany and mahogany
veneer wall timepiece, Aaron
Willard, Boston, early 19th
century, the molded wooden
bezel enclosing a white painted
dial, 30in. high.
(Skinner) $2,990

A Coca Cola neon advertising
clock with second hand and
surrounding neon tube with
typical Coca Cola Stop Sign
symbol, in green hammered
casing, 40 x 39cm, 1942.
(Auction Team Köln) $500

A classical carved mahogany
and eglomisé eight-day wall
clock, labeled *Eli Terry, Jr.,*
Connecticut, circa 1835, height
36in.
(Sotheby's) $2,000

A cherry wall regulator timepiece, by Seth Thomas Clock
Co., Conn., circa 1880, 36in.
long. $1,500

Handpainted opal glass hanging
clock, Wavecrest-type circular
frame housing, Welch
Company, Forestville,
Connecticut, 6in. high.
(Skinner Inc.) $350

Waterbury oak long drop
regulator school house
clock with hexagonal
face, 32¼in. high. $700

A Federal cherrywood corner cupboard, Pennsylvania, circa 1810, in two sections; the upper case with a triangular molded cornice with canted corners above a conforming cased fitted with two doors, each embellished with a square raised panel over a rectangular raised panel; the lower section with conforming applied mid-molding above a conforming case fitted with two doors, each embellished with a rectangular raised panel, over a shaped skirt, on French feet, 48in. wide. (Christie's) $5,175

American corner cupboard, in pine with twelve-light door above two paneled doors, 89in. high.
(Eldred's) $1,100

Country Chippendale walnut corner cabinet, Pennsylvania, circa 1780, the shaped back-board joining three-quarter round shelves, 24in. wide.
(Skinner Inc.) $8,800

Pine corner cupboard, probably New York State, 18th century, 57in. wide.
(Skinner) $3,680

A paint-decorated poplar corner cupboard, Pennsylvania, circa 1785, the upper section with molded dentil-carved cornice, 46in. wide.
(Sotheby's) $6,900

American corner cupboard in pine with molded cornice two doors enclosing three shelves, painted blue with yellow interior, New York State, 19th century, 54in. wide.
(Eldred's) $1,760

An important paint-decorated poplar bonnet-top corner cupboard, Pennsylvania, dated 1817, the upper section with molded swan's-neck crest, 43in. wide.
(Sotheby's) $96,000

An important Queen Anne carved and blue- and red-painted pine corner cupboard, New York, probably Long Island, circa 1760, 43in. wide.
(Sotheby's) $18,400

A paneled yellow pine hanging corner wall cupboard, Pennsylvania, 1750–70, the molded cornice above a double-paneled hinged door opening to shelves, 34in. wide.
(Sotheby's) $39,100

Grain painted pine and poplar corner cupboard, possibly Pennsylvania, circa 1830, 83in. high, 55½in. wide.
                            $5,000

Classical carved walnut veneered glazed corner cabinet, Ohio, 1830–40, refinished, brass replaced, 55in. wide.
(Skinner Inc.) $5,150

Cherry corner cupboard, Ohio, circa 1840, glazed doors open to a two-shelved interior above a single drawer, 56in. wide.
(Skinner Inc.) $2,000

A 'mahoganised' poplar corner cupboard, Southern, possibly South Carolina, 1800–30, in one piece, 46in. wide.
(Sotheby's) $5,750

American one-piece corner cupboard, in cherry, molded cornice with dentil decoration, two eight-light doors above two paneled doors, 82in. high.
(Eldred's) $3,740

Pair of Kentucky corner cupboards, one early 19th century and the other a turn-of-the-century copy, each in cherry with broken-arch top, 37in. wide.
(Eldred's) $1,540

George III oak corner cupboard, second half 18th century, with a reeded frieze above two sets of paneled doors flanked by reeded angles, 4ft. 3in. wide.
(Butterfield & Butterfield) $3,400

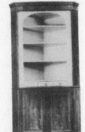

American two-part mahogany corner cupboard with molded cornice, the fitted interior in upper section painted blue, 33in. wide, 91in. high.
(Eldred's) $1,760

Renaissance style walnut corner cabinet, late 19th century, carved throughout with scrolling acanthus leaves and masks, 59½in. wide.
(Skinner) $1,280

An American 'Aesthetic Movement' polychromed ebonized corner cabinet, circa 1865, possibly by Kimbal and Cabus, 39¼in. wide.
(Christie's) $16,445

CHIPPENDALE

Chippendale pine paneled corner cupboard, New England, 18th century, 45in. wide. (Skinner) $4,600

A Chippendale cherrywood corner cupboard, Pennsylvania, circa 1790, in two parts, the upper with molded cornice above glazed doors, 52in. wide. (Sotheby's) $7,475

Chippendale-style pine corner cupboard, New England, 20th century, 38in. wide. (Skinner) $1,430

A fine Chippendale carved walnut corner cupboard, probably Lancaster County, Pennsylvania, 1760-1780, the upper part with molded swan neck pediment, 91½in. high. (Christie's New York) $11,000

A Chippendale painted poplar corner cupboard, mid-Atlantic States, 1760–1780, the upper part with a molded cornice with canted corners above a pair of arched glazed cupboard doors, 82in. high. (Christie's) $3,300

A Chippendale mahogany corner-cupboard, Philadelphia, 1760–1780, the upper section with broken pitched pediment with molded dentiled cornice filled with lattice-work, on ogee bracket feet, 54½in. wide. (Christie's) $36,000

A Chippendale carved poplar scroll-top corner cupboard, Pennsylvania, late 18th century, the overhanging cove molding with canted corners surmounted by a swan's-neck pediment, 4ft. wide. (Sotheby's) $7,475

A Chippendale painted and carved pine corner cupboard, New Jersey, 1750–1770, the elaborately molded cornice above two fielded panels, 51in. wide. (Christie's) $7,000

A Chippendale pine corner cupboard, Pennsylvania, 1760–1800, in two parts, the reverse-breakfronted overhanging cornice with canted corners, 4ft. 5in. wide. (Sotheby's) $3,162

FEDERAL

Late Federal two-part cherry corner cupboard, probably North Carolina, circa 1800, 46in. high.
(Skinner) **$6,000**

American architectural corner cupboard, late 18th/early 19th century, in yellow pine with molded surround, probably Mid-Atlantic States, 87in. high.
(Eldred's) **$880**

Poplar glazed corner cupboard, probably Pennsylvania, circa 1810, 43in. wide.
(Skinner) **$2,645**

A rare paint-decorated pine corner cupboard, Pennsylvania, 1790-1820, in two parts, the molded and rope carved cornice above an arched glazed door, 4ft. ½in. wide.
(Sotheby's) **$13,800**

A good Federal pine corner cupboard, American, probably Delaware River Valley, first quarter 19th century, 52¼in. wide.
(Sotheby's) **$6,500**

A paint-decorated pine corner cupboard, Pennsylvania, first half 19th century, the molded cornice above a hinged glazed door, 44in. wide.
(Sotheby's) **$2,875**

A painted pine Federal corner cupboard, America or England, circa 1800, 49in. wide.
(Skinner) **$3,750**

Late Federal carved birch corner cupboard, early 19th century, with swan's neck cresting centering three urn-shaped finials, 45in. wide.
(Butterfield & Butterfield) **$4,200**

Federal cherry glazed corner cupboard, probably Fairfield County, Ohio, circa 1820–35, the lower case with a single shelf, replaced brasses, 41½in. wide.
(Skinner Inc.) **$5,500**

Cherry glazed corner cupboard, Middle Atlantic States, circa 1830, old refinish, replaced brasses, 46½in. wide. (Skinner) $3,450

Glazed pine paneled corner cupboard, Middle Atlantic States, 19th century, glazed doors open to a three-shelved interior, 48½in. wide. (Skinner) $2,415

A grain painted corner cupboard, mid-Atlantic States, mid-19th century, with coved cornice above an egg-and-dart molding, 87in. high. (Christie's) $3,550

A Federal walnut corner cupboard, Pennsylvania or Middle Atlantic States, circa 1810, the molded and reeded cornice above a pair of glazed hinged doors, 51¾in. wide. (Sotheby's) $6,000

A Federal carved mahogany corner cupboard, mid-Atlantic States, 1800-1810, with over-hanging broken molded cornice above two paneled cupboard doors, 80½in. high. (Christie's New York) $4,125

Federal cherrywood corner cupboard, mid-Atlantic States, early 19th century, the two hinged glazed doors opening to three shelves above a molded waist, 4ft. 3in. wide. (Butterfield & Butterfield) $3,400

A rare yellow-painted pine 'turkey-breast' corner cupboard, Middle Atlantic States, circa 1780, on a molded and dentil-carved base, 56in. wide. (Sotheby's) $10,500

Federal carved pine corner cupboard, mid-Atlantic States, early 19th century, the lower molded panel doors opening to one shelf over a molded base, 46½in. wide. (Butterfield & Butterfield) $3,050

Cherry and tiger maple inlaid paneled corner cupboard, Middle Atlantic States, 19th century, the three shaped shelves above a recessed panel door, 41½in. wide. (Skinner) $1,610

Cherry corner cupboard, New England, circa 1810, old refinish, 42in. wide. (Skinner) $2,530

Painted corner cupboard, New England, circa 1790, the flat molded cornice above four cupboard doors, 49in. wide. (Skinner) $4,025

A Federal pine corner cupboard, New England, mid-19th century, with molded cornice, 90in. high. (Christie's) $4,375

A Federal grain-painted corner cupboard, New England, early 19th century, the upper section with a molded cornice above a case fitted with two six-lighted doors, 54¹/₂in. wide. (Christie's) $3,450

A Federal red-painted corner-cupboard, Northern New England, early 19th century, the upper section bowed with molded cornice hung with spherules over a frieze, 56¹/₂in. (Christie's) $13,500

A Federal painted pine corner cupboard, New England, 19th century, in two parts, on bracket feet, painted in an overall mustard ground with green detailing, 39¹/₂in. wide. (Christie's) $85,000

A Federal cherrywood corner cupboard, American, probably New England, first quarter 19th century, the shaped skirt continuing to bracket feet, 42¹/₂in. wide. (Sotheby's) $8,000

Federal pine corner cupboard, New England, early 19th century, the hinged paneled doors opening to shelves, on bracket feet, 47in. wide. (Butterfield & Butterfield) $3,100

Pine glazed corner cupboard, probably New England, late 18th century, flat cove molded cornice above a glazed door, 45in. wide. (Skinner) $2,415

FEDERAL, PENNSYLVANIA

Federal pine glazed corner cupboard, Pennsylvania, circa 1810, 50in. wide.
(Skinner) $2,415

A Country Federal cherry corner cupboard, Penn., circa 1820, 56½in. wide.
                        $2,250

Walnut glazed corner cupboard, probably Pennsylvania, circa 1820, 48in. wide.
(Skinner) $1,840

A late Federal maple-inlaid cherrywood corner cupboard, probably Pennsylvania, circa 1820, in two parts, the upper section with molded cornice, 53in. wide.
(Sotheby's) $9,200

Country Federal poplar corner cupboard, possibly Pennsylvania, circa 1825, in two sections, the projecting molded cornice above cockbeaded glazed door, 45in. wide.
(Skinner) $2,800

A Federal paneled cherrywood corner cupboard, Lebanon County, Pennsylvania, circa 1830, in two parts, the cove molding above two glazed and mullioned doors, 4ft. 3¾in. wide.
(Sotheby's) $1,610

A Federal walnut corner cupboard, Pennsylvania, circa 1820, overhanging cove molding and field paneled cupboard doors below, 4ft. wide.
(Sotheby's) $2,185

A Federal grain-painted corner cupboard, Pennsylvania, early 19th century, with scalloped cornice above a glazed cupboard door, 84in. high.
(Christie's) $8,250

Federal cherry glazed inlaid corner cupboard, probably Pennsylvania, early 19th century, refinished, 47in. wide.
(Skinner Inc.) $4,100

A heart-decorated walnut cradle, Pennsylvania, circa 1800, the scrolled heart-pierced headboard and footboard flanked by canted reeded sides, 40in. long, (Sotheby's) $1,610

Painted Windsor cradle, New England, circa 1810, retains old brown paint over blue green, 38in. long. (Skinner) $2,300

A carved and joined walnut cradle, Pennsylvania, late 18th century, the arched headboard with heart-pierced crest flanked by rectangular posts, 30³/₄in. wide. (Christie's) $2,300

A rare heart-decorated chestnut and cherrywood child's cradle on stand, Pennsylvania, 1780–1800, on an arched base joined by a double medial transverse, length 39in. (Sotheby's) $5,750

A Gothic Revival carved walnut crib, New York, 1840–1860, the pointed pillar cornerposts joined by slatted sides forming pointed arches, on square legs, 43in. long. (Christie's) $1,495

A Chippendale cherrywood cradle, American, probably mid-Atlantic states, circa 1770, with two shaped flaring stiles mounted with brass carrying handles, 42in. long. (Sotheby's) $1,495

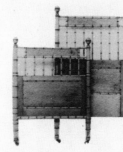

A 19th century mahogany half-tester child's bed, with canopy and spindles to all sides, 49in. long. (Boardmans) $730

American Victorian maple and bird's-eye maple veneer bamboo crib, circa 1870, 53½in. long. $1,000

A late Federal mahogany child's crib with tester, American, first half 19th century, with a serpentine tester, width 48½in. (Sotheby's) $2,990

218

American Renaissance Revival rosewood and marquetry credenza, third quarter 19th century, 75in. wide.
(Skinner) $3,520

Stow & Davis, Georgian style mahogany credenza, mid 20th century, a rectangular top with beveled edge, 58in. wide.
(Du Mouchelles) $400

Renaissance Revival burl veneer and ebonised wood sideboard cabinet, America, circa 1865, 53in. wide.
     $2,000

American Renaissance Revival walnut, parquetry and part ebonized credenza, third quarter 19th century, the back stenciled *Manufactured by Edward Hixon & Co.*, 60 in. long
(Skinner) $4,025

American Rococo Revival walnut and burl walnut credenza and overmantel mirror, third-quarter 19th century, raised on a plinth base, 59$^{1}/_{2}$in. wide.
(Skinner Inc.) $2,880

Renaissance Revival rosewood and marquetry credenza, third quarter 19th century, the shaped rectangular top above a central cabinet door enclosing three shelves, 46in. wide.
(Skinner) $2,200

American Renaissance Revival gilt bronze mounted rosewood and marquetry credenza, probably New York, circa 1865–1875, with incised, ebonized and painted highlights, 74in. wide.
(Skinner) $11,500

Stickley Arts and Crafts style oak credenza-hutch, circa 1994, upper hutch open center area with shelves, flanked by double cabinets, 91in. long.
(Du Mouchelles) $2,000

An American 'Aesthetic Movement' copper-mounted parcel-gilt and lacquered ebonized credenza, circa 1865, by Herter Brothers, 66$^{1}/_{2}$in. wide.
(Christie's) $14,576

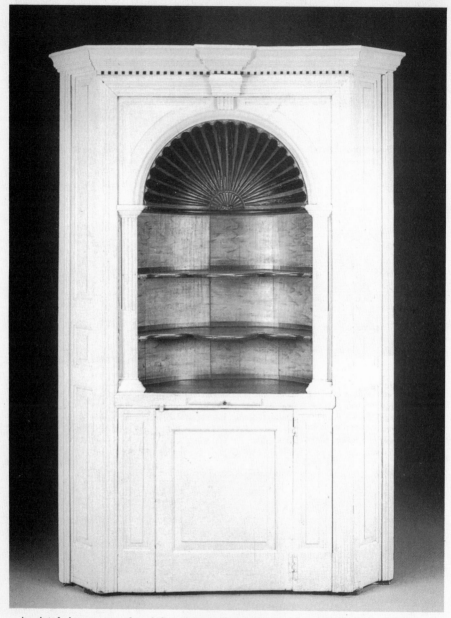

A painted pine corner cupboard, Connecticut, circa 1760–1780, painted light green with canted sides and a molded cornice centering a central keystone and a triglyph over a large open arch with paneled spandrels above a recessed storage compartment with a black painted shell with cyma edge, above two shaped shelves with a faux-grained backdrop flanked by projecting columns, the lower section paneled, with a central hinged door; together with five similarly molded architectural panels, door, and mantle, 56½in. high, 72½in. wide. 7¼in. deep. (Christie's)

$21,850

Four-door cupboard, circa 1860, butternut and pine, wooden pulls, iron hinges, shellac or varnish finish, 49in. wide. (Skinner) $2,760

A fine and rare paneled pine trastero, Rio Abajo Region, New Mexico, circa 1800, of tall rectangular form, fitted with two cupboard doors, 4ft. 3in. wide. (Sotheby's) $68,500

Tall two-door cupboard, circa 1800, pine, door over door, applied bracket base with arched cut-outs, 49¼in. wide. (Skinner) $17,250

An ocher-painted pine cupboard, American, probably New York State, 1730–80, the dramatically stepped overhanging cornice above a cupboard door, 39in. wide. (Sotheby's) $4,025

Cupboard (top section of secretary), circa 1860, chestnut, pine, porcelain knobs, brass hinges, two paneled doors, interior containing numerous pigeonholes, 42½in. wide. (Skinner) $747

Country Federal cherry two-part cupboard, possibly Pennsylvania, circa 1820, on shaped bracket feet (refinished, replaced pulls, restoration), 46in. wide. (Skinner Inc.) $1,800

Double cupboard over case of drawers, probably Groveland, New York, circa 1840, pine, built in two sections with removable cupboard top, 36½in. wide. (Skinner) $27,600

Pine slant back cupboard, New England, 18th century, four thumb molded shelves, old stain and varnish, 75in. high. (Skinner Inc.) $6,800

Painted pine stepback cupboard, New England, early 19th century, old wooden pulls and catches, old red paint with later varnish, 73¼in. high. (Skinner Inc.) $4,700

A red- and brown-painted pine
and poplar two-part cupboard,
first half 19th century, in two
parts, 4ft. 4in. wide.
(Sotheby's)   **$3,450**

American cupboard, in pine
with single door, shaped bracket
feet, 38½in. wide.
(Eldred's)   **$550**

Classical Revival mahogany
veneer commode, Eastern
America, mid 19th century,
brasses replaced, 25½in. wide.
(Skinner Inc.)   **$1,100**

A cupboard with drawer and
doors, Cambridge,
Massachusetts, 1680–1700, in
two parts, the upper section with
projecting cornice and dentil
frieze mounted with corbels,
48⅞in. wide.
(Christie's)   **$100,000**

A pine trastero with grainero,
Penasco, New Mexico, circa
1870, the scrolling rectangular
pediment above two reeded
cupboard doors, 4ft 4in. wide.
(Sotheby's)   **$5,000**

Grain painted pine cupboard,
Maine, mid 19th century, with
early red and black graining
simulating rosewood, two
recessed panel doors, 37¼in.
wide.
(Skinner)   **$488**

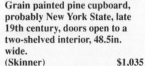

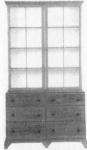

A red-painted poplar two-part
pewter or 'Dutch' cupboard,
Pennsylvania, circa 1840, the
overhanging cornice above two
glazed doors.
(Sotheby's)   **$16,100**

Grain painted pine cupboard,
probably New York State, late
19th century, doors open to a
two-shelved interior, 48.5in.
wide.
(Skinner)   **$1,035**

Shaker pine burned orange
glazed cupboard over drawers,
Harvard Massachusetts
Community, inscribed *Ziba
Winchester 1836,* 51in. wide.
(Skinner)   **$46,000**

Shaker painted pine cupboard over case of drawers, Mt. Lebanon, New York, circa 1830, with quarter-round cornice molding, 36in. wide.
(Skinner) $79,500

Tool cupboard, Harvard, Massachusetts, circa 1875, pine, walnut drawer fronts, gray paint, later iron hardware, 38¾in. wide.
(Skinner) $1,955

A Federal tiger maple cupboard with two glazed doors, 1800-10, 54½in. wide. $6,250

Fine Elizabethan Revival oak two-part cupboard, upper section with two carved paneled doors flanked by supporting columns, on bun feet, probably early 20th century, 43in. wide.
(Eldred's) $1,540

Pair of American marquetry small cupboards, designed and executed by T. F. Adelhelm, 1938, with glazed doors enclosing shelves over a frieze drawer, 21in. wide.
(Butterfield & Butterfield) $3,737

A fine and rare paint decorated pine apothecary chest and cupboard, Massachusetts, 1770–90, the lower section fitted with forty-two small molded drawers, painted allover in blue-green, 41½in. wide
(Sotheby's) $151,000

A rare diminutive spindle-door pine trastero, New Mexico, 1780–1800, with a shaped removable cornice, flanked by stiles with stepped finials, 31in. wide.
(Sotheby's) $60,250

A walnut punched-tin-inset food safe, Pennsylvania, first half 19th century, the rectangular top above two short drawers and two cupboard doors, 41in. wide.
(Sotheby's) $2,587

A red-painted pine cupboard, Texas, mid-19th century, the rectangular projecting cornice above a pair of recessed paneled cupboard doors, 50in. wide.
(Christie's) $2,300

A Federal blue-painted cupboard with two glazed doors, possibly N. Jersey, 1775-1810, 50in. wide. (Christie's) **$9,000**

Pine paneled cupboard, North America, first half 19th century, the two doors on rat-tail hinges, 46in. wide. (Skinner Inc.) **$3,850**

Early 19th century Shaker pine commode with hinged slant lid opening to reveal a shelf interior, 18in. wide. **$6,000**

Painted paneled and carved pine cupboard, New Jersey area, early 19th century, with molded overhanging top above a cupboard with applied moldings, 40½in. wide. (Skinner) **$3,450**

Cupboard, purchased at Canterbury, New Hampshire, circa 1870, pine, original bright yellow stain, replacement iron latch, 25½in. wide. (Skinner) **$1,955**

A rare Chippendale red-painted pine pewter cupboard, Pennsylvania, circa 1770, the rectangular overhanging cornice above three shelves, 4ft. 4in. wide. (Sotheby's) **$6,325**

A salmon-painted pine cupboard, American, 19th century, the recessed upper section with hinged cupboard doors, 37¼in. wide. (Sotheby's) **$4,600**

Joined, paneled and painted oak court cupboard, probably Massachusetts, 17th century, refinished, 50in. wide. (Skinner Inc.) **$13,500**

Painted pine two door cupboard, New England, mid 19th century, old green paint, shaped sides opens to four shelf interior, 28½in. wide. (Skinner) **$2,415**

Country Federal glazed tiger maple cupboard, Western Pennsylvania or Ohio, 19th century, 45¼ in. wide. (Skinner Inc.) $4,400

Painted glazed cupboard, New England, first quarter 19th century, black paint, cream interior, brasses replaced, 56¼ in. wide. (Skinner Inc.) $3,400

A painted and grained pine Empire cupboard, New England, circa 1830, 18¼ in. deep. (Skinner) $2,000

A good punch-decorated tinware and painted poplar pie safe, Pennsylvania, early 19th century, two cupboard doors each depicting a star- and heart-decorated pot, 43½ in. wide. (Sotheby's) $7,475

One-door cupboard, believed to have come from Sabbathday Lake, Maine, circa 1790, pine, case pegged together, single board overhanging top, 36½ in. wide (at base) (Skinner) $17,250

A red and gray painted paneled pine cupboard probably New York, 1730–60, the projecting molding above two large raised panel doors, 4ft. 6in. wide. (Sotheby's) $2,645

Painted cupboard, probably Georgia, mid 19th century, opens to a two-shelved interior, all over original red paint and pulls, 59½ in. wide. (Skinner Inc.) $6,150

Carved pine buffet, Canadian Provinces, 18th century, the rectangular top above two molded   single drawers and two carved diamond point cupboard doors, 58¾ in. wide. (Skinner Inc.) $4,800

Grained pine cupboard, Maine, mid-19th century, the molded top above a paneled door on four turned ball feet, 41½ in. wide. (Skinner) $2,300

HUTCH

A figured maple and birchwood hutch cupboard, New England, early 19th century, in two parts, the overhanging cornice above glazed doors, 5ft. wide.
(Sotheby's)   **$9,200**

Carved and paint decorated wood watch hutch, New England, early 19th century, 12¹/₂in. high.
(Skinner)   **$1,840**

American hutch cupboard, early 19th century, in pine with molded cornice and three shelves above two paneled doors, 52in. wide.
(Eldred's)   **$1,100**

A carved pine hutch, Mid-Atlantic States, probably New Jersey, 1750–1800, the upper section with a reverse break-fronted cornice with dentil molding, 4ft. 4in. wide.
(Sotheby's)   **$4,600**

A Chippendale blue-painted pine hutch cupboard, Pennsylvania, circa 1780, in two parts, the projecting lower section with three short drawers and two field-paneled cupboard doors, 5ft. 1in. wide.
(Sotheby's)   **$33,350**

A Chippendale walnut hutch cupboard, Pennsylvania, circa 1790, the molded and dentil-carved cornice above open shelves, 53¹/₂in. wide.
(Sotheby's)   **$3,737**

SCHRANK

A walnut Schrank, Lancaster County, Pennsylvania, 1755–1765, the rectangular flaring molded cornice above a conforming channel molding, 75¹/₂in. wide.
(Christie's)   **$14,950**

A paint-decorated poplar Schrank, Pennsylvania, dated *1769*, in several parts, decorated allover in green, red and orange, 6ft. 6in. wide.
(Sotheby's)   **$40,250**

A carved walnut Schrank, attributed to Peter Holl III, Pennsylvania, late 18th century, the repeating outset cyma-molded cornice above a conforming case, 71¹/₂in. wide.
(Christie's)   **$12,650**

Pine wall cupboard, New England, 18th century, 25in. wide.
(Skinner) $4,025

A Chippendale pine hanging corner cupboard, Penn., 1760-85, 46in. high, 26½in. wide. $2,750

Mid/late 18th century Chippendale poplar hanging cupboard, Penn., 36½in. high, 27in. wide.
(Christie's) $1,300

A fine and rare paneled walnut hanging wall cupboard with drawer, Pennsylvania, circa 1760, the molded cornice above a paneled molded door, 29in. wide.
(Sotheby's) $28,750

A walnut hanging cupboard, Pennsylvania, possibly Lebanon or Montgomery Counties, mid-late 18th century, flaring molded rectangular cornice above a conforming case, 23¼in. wide.
(Christie's) $12,650

A good painted and decorated pine hanging wall cupboard, Pennsylvania, circa 1780, the molded cornice above a hinge glazed door opening to shelves, width 31in.
(Sotheby's) $7,500

Hanging cupboard, from The Tailor's Shop building in Shaker Village, Harvard, Massachusetts, pine, old red paint, brass knob, 19in. wide.
(Skinner) $977

A poplar hanging cupboard, Ephrata, Penn., 1743-60, 18½in. wide, 24½in. high.
(Christie's) $1,200

Walnut inlaid wall cabinet, Chester County area, Pennsylvania, 1720–60, tulip and berry line inlay on drawer front, 24¾in. high.
(Skinner Inc.) $7,500

A classical mahogany writing table, New York, 1820-1840, the hinged rectangular top with canted corners and crossbanded edges, 23in wide.
(Christie's) $1,150

Gustav Stickley oak and wrought iron secretary, designed by Harvey Ellis, circa 1904, 56in. wide.
(Skinner) $21,500

A classic American school desk with chair, both height adjustable, circa 1920, desk 76 x 61 x 89 cm.
(Auction Team Köln) $250

Tiger maple fall-front desk, New England, early 19th century, the fall front reveals an interior of seven valanced compartments and twelve drawers, 20³/₄in. wide.
(Skinner) $3,450

An American 'Aesthetic Movement' parcel-ebonized walnut and marquetry secretary bookcase, third quarter 19th century, by Herter Brothers, with a reeded rectangular top above a fall-front door, 57¹/₂in. wide.
(Christie's) $18,400

A walnut patent desk, inset with a decorated cast iron letter box inscribed *Manufactured By Wooton Desk Manufacturing Company, Indianapolis, W S Wooton's Patent October 6th 1874*, 3ft. 7in. wide.
(Spencer's) $4,500

An American walnut roll-top desk, with a D-shaped tambour top enclosing a fitted interior with three frieze drawers below.
(Christie's S. Ken)
                               $2,800

Heywood Wakefield painted wicker desk, late 19th century, shelved superstructure above a rectangular writing surface, 37in. wide.
(Skinner Inc.) $1,000

An inlaid oak secretary, designed by Harvey Ellis for Gustav Stickley, circa 1903-04, 42in. wide.
(Skinner) $120,000

A lady's oak desk with fall-front, circa 1890, 28½in. wide.
(Skinner) $800

A Victorian mahogany veneered chair-desk, attributed to Stephen Hedges, New York City, circa 1854, 35in. wide.
(Christie's) $29,900

A mid 19th century American Wooton Desk Co. burr-walnut paneled office desk. (Locke & England) $15,000

A fine and rare Federal mahogany lift-top writing table with drawer, labeled *John T. Dolan*, New York, circa 1805, on reeded tapering legs ending in vase-form feet on brass casters, width 33in.
(Sotheby's) $20,000

Arts and Crafts drop front desk, Paine Furniture retail tag, brass stamp hinges and pulls with copper patina, 36in. wide.
(Skinner) $747

Rare Charles Rohlfs carved drop front desk with swivel base, Buffalo, New York, 1900, Gothic style, signed with logo, 25½in. wide.
(Skinner Inc.) $13,200

American Country two-tier writing desk, 19th century, one drawer in base, modern grain-painted decoration, 27¹/₂in. wide.
(Eldred's) $250

American butler's secretary, circa 1830–1840, walnut, upper drawer with paneled front pulling down to reveal a fitted interior, 39¹/₂in. wide.
(Eldred's) $358

Painted pine stand-up desk, western Massachusetts, early 19th century, original red wash with grained pull-out writing surface, 31.25in. wide.
(Skinner) $1,380

A Chippendale pine standing desk, New England, 1780-1810, 30½in. wide. $2,000

Quaint Furniture oak desk, circa 1910, single drawer flanked by side bookshelves over two vertical side slats, 40in. wide.
(Skinner) $325

Painted stand up desk, New England, with scrolled back splash above a hinged top, 26³/₈in. wide.
(Skinner) $862

An Arts and Crafts oak writing cabinet, the shaped rectangular top with curved three-quarter gallery above open recess, fall flap and short drawers, 94cm. wide. (Christie's) $950

Shop-O'-The-Crafters slant front desk, Ohio, circa 1906, style no. 279, signed with paper label, 42in. wide.
(Skinner) $750

A fine and rare walnut schoolmaster's desk, Pennsylvania, circa 1780, the rectangular hinged slant lid with molded paper stop, 29¾in. wide.
(Sotheby's) $10,000

Charles Rohlfs dropfront oak desk, Buffalo, New York, circa 1907, shaped gallery top above slant front, 25½in. wide.
(Skinner) $3,800

Roycroft oak writing desk, No. 91, East Aurora, New York, circa 1906, original copper hardware, interior fitted with letter slots and short central drawer, 18¾in. wide.
(Skinner) $2,760

American schoolmaster's desk, in pine under original blue-green paint, upper section with slant lid and applied molding rail, 31½in. wide.
(Eldred's) $1,265

FEDERAL

A Federal inlaid mahogany butler's desk and cabinet, New York, circa 1820, the rectangular top above a pull-out writing section, 47in. wide. (Sotheby's) $2,070

A Federal mahogany inlaid tambour fall desk, probably Massachusetts, circa 1810, refinished, replaced brasses, 37³/₄in. wide. (Skinner) $3,680

Federal cherry inlaid sideboard with desk drawer, probably Massachusetts, circa 1810, old refinish, 40¹/₂in. wide. (Skinner) $2,990

A Federal mahogany butler's-desk, New York, early 19th century, fitted with a pair of cockbeaded short drawers above a crossbanded secretary drawer, on turned tapering reeded legs and brass ball feet, 51¹/₂in. wide. (Christie's) $4,800

A late Federal mahogany lady's writing desk, attributed to John or Thomas Seymour, Boston, 1800–1820, the rectangular top with hinged out-folding writing slab, 29in. wide. (Christie's) $4,000

Federal cherry inlaid half sideboard/desk, Rutland, Vermont area, circa 1825, the rectangular top with ovolo corners and inlaid edge, 46¹/₈in. wide. (Skinner) $4,025

Federal mahogany veneer lady's desk, New England, early 19th century, the doors open to an interior of small drawers and valanced compartments, 39¹/₄in. wide. (Skinner) $1,725

A late Federal carved mahogany butler's desk, New York, 1810–1825, with cockbeaded long drawer over a hinged drawer opening to reveal a fitted interior, 43in. wide. (Christie's) $4,600

Federal mahogany veneer lady's desk, New England, circa 1810, old refinish, pulls replaced, 38¹/₄in. wide. (Skinner Inc.) $1,050

An American mahogany roll-top desk by A Cutler & Son, Buffalo, the lower part with two pillars of four drawers flanking center frieze drawer, circa 1880, 153 cm. (Auction Team Köln) $2,000

Roll-top desk, early 20th century, in oak with fitted interior, six drawers, paneled ends, 41in. wide. (Eldred's) $500

A Queen Anne style block-and – shell carved mahogany kneehole desk, in the Goddard-Townsend tradition, Wallace Nutting Reproductions, 20th century, 38in. wide. (Sotheby's) $12,650

A Chippendale carved mahogany block-front bureau-table, Newport, Rhode Island, 1750–1770, the rectangular thumbmolded top above a blocked case fitted with one long drawer, 39in. wide. (Christie's) $156,500

A golden roll top desk with cherrywood inlay, the ends embellished with carved leaf decoration, by Schrenk & Co., Connecticut, bearing patent date 1888, 60in. wide. (Schrager Auction Galleries) $7,000

A Chippendale carved mahogany block-front and shell-carved bureau-table, Goddard or Townsend Workshops, Newport, Rhode Island, 1750–1760, with a coved frieze and long blocked drawer carved with three shells above a recessed kneehole, 36³/₄in. wide. (Christie's) $125,000

A rare Queen Anne japanned kneehole bureau, probably Boston area, 1730-1750, with a central recessed bank of five graduated drawers, 34¼in. wide. (Christie's) $290,000

A Queen Anne mahogany block-front bureau-table, Boston, 1740–1760, the rectangular top with rounded blockfront above a conforming case, on straight bracket feet, 22in. wide. (Christie's) $32,200

Queen Anne carved mahogany block front kneehole dressing table, Boston, circa 1750, the thumb-molded top with blocked front above a conforming case, 36in. wide. (Skinner) $20,700

A Chippendale mahogany blockfront kneehole desk, Massachusetts, 1760-1780, the molded rectangular top with blocked edge, 33in. wide. (Christie's) $51,750

A late Victorian Chippendale Revival carved mahogany kidney-shaped knee-hole desk, the leather-lined top above three frieze drawers, on C-scroll carved bracket feet, 51in. wide. (Christie's) $6,815

A Queen Anne japanned kneehole bureau, Boston, 1720–1740, the case fitted with one long drawer over an arched valanced drawer, 34in. wide. (Christie's) $96,000

The Samuel Whitehorne Queen Anne block-and-shell-carved mahogany kneehole desk, attributed to Edmund Townsend, Newport, Rhode Island, circa 1780, 36¼in. wide. (Sotheby's) $3,632,500

A Chippendale block-front kneehole-desk, Massachusetts, 1760–1780, the rectangular top with molded edge and blocked front over a conforming case fitted with a long drawer over a short scalloped valance drawer and recessed kneehole backed by a fan-carved door, 35in. wide. (Christie's) $40,000

A Chippendale mahogany block-front kneehole-bureau, Boston, 1760–1780, the rectangular top with blocked front and molded edge over a conforming case fitted with a long drawer over a short scalloped valance drawer and recessed kneehole, 36½in. wide. (Christie's) $100,000

A rare Chippendale figured mahogany kneehole desk, Philadelphia, circa 1775, the oblong molded top with notched corners above one long drawer, 39½in. wide. (Sotheby's) $9,775

A fine and rare Queen Anne mahogany block-front kneehole dressing table, Boston, Massachusetts, circa 1760, on scroll-cut bracket feet, width 36in. (Sotheby's) $100,000

A Queen Anne carved and figured mahogany block-front kneehole dressing table, Boston, Massachusetts, circa 1750, 34in. wide. (Sotheby's) $255,500

Stained pine carved fall front lady's desk, probably New England, circa 1900, with two exterior short drawers above the fall front, 24in. wide.
(Skinner) $863

American slant-lid desk, 18th century, in cherry, stepped interior with nine pigeonholes and fourteen drawers, 40½in. wide.
(Eldred's) $2,640

Grain painted standing desk, probably Pennsylvania, circa 1825–40, original yellow ocher and burnt umber feather graining, 32in. wide.
(Skinner Inc.) $1,500

Paine Furniture Co. drop front desk, two over two drawers with pyramid wooden pulls, three interior drawers and twelve pigeonholes, 38in. wide.
(Skinner) $460

A painted Country birch slant top desk, probably Western Massachusetts, circa 1780, the fall front reveals a stepped interior of valanced compartments, 38in. wide.
(Skinner) $15,400

Maple grained desk, Southern New England, circa 1800, the interior with valanced compartments and recessed panel prospect door, old refinish, 38½in. wide. (Skinner Inc.)
    $6,250

Painted maple slant lid desk, New England, late 18th century, with stepped valanced multi-drawer interior, 35.75in. wide.
(Skinner) $7,475

American serpentine-front desk, 18th century, in mahogany with four drawers, molded apron and claw and ball feet, 41½in. wide.
(Eldred's) $14,850

American slant-lid desk, in maple with turned legs, fitted interior with seven drawers and eight pigeonholes, 41½in. wide.
(Eldred's) $935

CHIPPENDALE

Chippendale mahogany block front desk, late 18th century, base restoration including four repaired feet, 36½in. wide. (Skinner Inc.) $3,500

American Chippendale four-drawer slant-lid desk, in tiger maple, ogee bracket base, 38¾in. wide. (Eldred's) $12,650

Chippendale walnut slant lid desk, Maine, 18th century, the lid opens to a stepped interior of valanced compartments and small drawers, 33¼in. wide. (Skinner) $6,900

Antique American Chippendale slant lid desk in tiger maple, fitted interior with six drawers and seven pigeon holes, four drawers with molded fronts, 40in. wide. (Eldred's) $7,300

A fine and rare Chippendale carved walnut and cherrywood serpentine-front slant front desk, signed by John Shearer, Martinsburg, Virginia, dated 1805, 39in. wide. (Sotheby's) $28,750

Antique American Chippendale slant lid desk in mahogany, seashell, herringbone and line inlay, four graduated drawers, fitted interior with an inlaid prospect door and four small drawers, 37in. wide. (Eldred's) $1,500

A Chippendale maple slant top desk, the fall-front opening to reveal a fitted interior, circa 1790, 36in. wide. (Skinner) $2,000

A Chippendale walnut desk, the hinged lid with molded bookrest opening to a fitted interior, probably Virginia, 1760-80, 36in. wide. (Christie's) $7,500

Chippendale tiger maple slant lid desk, possibly New Jersey, last quarter 18th century, interior retains old black paint, 35¾in. wide. (Skinner) $5,462

Chippendale cherry slant lid desk, Connecticut, circa 1780, refinished replaced brasses, 38in. wide. (Skinner) **$3,737**

Chippendale maple slant lid desk, Connecticut, late 18th century, replaced brass, old refinish, 36in. wide. (Skinner) **$2,300**

Chippendale cherry slant top desk, Norwich-Colchester, Connecticut area, 1760–1800, replaced brasses, 41¼in. wide. (Skinner Inc.) **$3,500**

A Chippendale cherrywood slant-front desk, Eastern Connecticut, 1760–1780, the slant lid enclosing an interior fitted with a shell-carved small drawer over two shaped small drawers flanked by fluted pilasters, 40¾in. wide. (Christie's) **$15,700**

A diminutive Chippendale carved cherrywood slant-front desk, Woodbury, Connecticut, 1760–1780, the rectangular top above a thumbmolded slant lid opening to a fitted interior with fan-curved and fluted prospect door flanked by document drawers, 39in. wide. (Christie's) **$84,000**

A Chippendale carved cherrywood slant-front desk, Connecticut, 1760–80, the rectangular thumbmolded slant-lid opening to an interior fitted with a pinwheel carved prospect door, 40¾in. wide. (Christie's) **$1,840**

Chippendale cherry slant lid fall front desk, probably Connecticut, circa 1790, fall front reveals fitted interior, 40in. wide. (Skinner) **$3,220**

Chippendale cherry and tiger maple slant lid desk, Connecticut, late 18th century, the two-tiered interior with a fan-carved central drawer, 36in. wide. (Skinner) **$3,850**

A Chippendale figured maple slant front desk, Eastern Connecticut or Rhode Island, circa 1780, the molded base on ogee bracket feet, 36in. wide. (Sotheby's) **$3,162**

A Chippendale mahogany block-front slant top desk with fitted interior, Salem, Mass., 1760-90, 43½in. wide. (Christie's) $24,200

Chippendale mahogany carved block front desk, North Shore, Massachusetts, 1770–90, old refinish, replaced brasses, 40¾in. wide. (Skinner Inc.) $15,400

A fine and rare Chippendale carved mahogany block-front slant-front desk, Boston, Massachusetts, circa 1770, 42in. wide. (Sotheby's) $60,250

A Chippendale carved cherry-wood reverse serpentine desk, Massachusetts, 1780-1800, with thumb molded slant lid enclosing a compartmented interior, 44¼in. wide. (Christie's New York) $13,000

Chippendale cherry and tiger maple slant lid desk, possibly Massachusetts, last half 18th century, case of four thumb molded graduated drawers, 35⅝in. wide. (Skinner) $4,312

A very fine and rare Chippendale carved and figured mahogany slant-front desk with blocked lid, Salem, Massachusetts, circa 1765, 41½in. wide. (Sotheby's) $101,500

A fine Chippendale carved mahogany block-front desk, Boston, 1760-1780, the case with four graduated and blocked long drawers, 43in. wide. (Christie's) $78,000

Chippendale painted maple fall front desk, probably Massachusetts, circa 1750, on bracket feet centering a carved fan pendant, 38in. wide. (Skinner) $4,312

Chippendale mahogany slant lid fall front desk, Massachusetts, late 18th century, the fall front above case of four incised beaded graduated drawers, 40¾in. wide. (Skinner) $4,025

A Chippendale birch reverse-serpentine front desk, Mass., 1765-85, 42½in. wide. (Christie's) $12,500

A Chippendale mahogany reverse serpentine slant-front desk, Massachusetts, 1760–1780, on short cabriole legs with ball-and-claw feet, 43³/₄in. wide. (Christie's) $6,170

A Chippendale mahogany slant top desk, the fall-front reveals a fitted interior, Mass., circa 1780, 40in. wide. (Skinner) $6,800

A Chippendale mahogany reverse-serpentine slant-front desk, Eastern Massachusetts, 1760–1780, the rectangular hinged lid opening to reveal a fitted interior with central fan-carved drawer, 42¹/₄in. wide. (Christie's) $10,925

A Chippendale mahogany reverse-serpentine slant-front desk, North Shore, Massachusetts, 1760–1780, thumbmolded hinged lid opening to a stepped interior, 39⁵/₈in. wide. (Christie's) $9,200

A Chippendale carved mahogany serpentine slant-front desk, Massachusetts, circa 1770, the **rectangular** hinged lid carved with a concave fan flanked by two convex fans, 40in. wide. (Sotheby's) $8,000

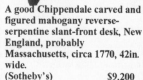

A Chippendale mahogany slant front desk, Massachusetts, circa 1780, with shaped bracket feet and remnants of central drop, 40in. wide. (Skinner) $13,200

A good Chippendale carved and figured mahogany reverse-serpentine slant-front desk, New England, probably Massachusetts, circa 1770, 42in. wide. (Sotheby's) $9,200

A Chippendale carved mahogany slant front desk, signed *Joseph Davis,* Newbury-port, Massachusetts, circa 1775, on ball and claw feet, 40in. wide. (Christie's New York) $9,600

A fine Chippendale carved and figured mahogany slant front desk, Boston or Salem, Massachusetts, circa 1770, the hinged lid opening to an interior with two stacks of three blocked short drawers, the uppermost drawer fan-carved centering four valanced pigeonholes with short drawers below, and document drawers centering a blocked and fan-carved prospect door, opening to reveal a shaped valance and blocked drawer, the entire removable center section with three secret drawers behind, the molded shell with three thumbmolded drawers below, the conformingly shaped case with four graduated long drawers within beaded surrounds, 40in. wide. (Sotheby's) $44,850

Chippendale maple slant lid desk, probably Massachusetts, circa 1780, 38¾in. wide. (Skinner) $2,415

A Chippendale mahogany slant lid serpentine desk, Mass., circa 1780, 41½in. wide. (Skinner) $8,500

Chippendale mahogany slant-top desk, Massachusetts, circa 1790, brasses appear to be original, old refinish, 40in. wide. (Skinner) $4,400

Chippendale carved serpentine mahogany slant lid desk, North Shore Massachusetts, 1785–1800, the prospect door with mirror and fan carving, 42in. wide. (Skinner Inc.) $15,000

Chippendale mahogany oxbow serpentine fall-front desk, North Shore, Massachusetts, circa 1780, on ogee bracket feet, 43in. wide. (Skinner) $5,462

Chippendale mahogany veneered slant lid desk, probably Massachusetts, circa 1800, on molded bracket base, replaced pulls, 39¾in. high. (Skinner Inc.) $4,370

Chippendale mahogany carved slant lid desk, Massachusetts, 18th century, refinished, old brasses, 41¾in. wide. (Skinner Inc.) $5,900

A very fine and rare Chippendale carved and figured mahogany block-front slant-front desk with blocked lid, Boston, Massachusetts, circa 1770, 41¼in. wide. (Sotheby's) $85,000

Chippendale mahogany oxbow slant lid desk, probably Massachusetts, circa 1780, replaced brasses, 42in. wide. (Skinner) $5,175

Chippendale sycamore slant lid desk, New England, late 18th century, a stepped interior of small drawers, 36in. wide. (Skinner Inc.) **$3,850**

A Chippendale figured maple and walnut slant-front desk, New England, probably Massachusetts, circa 1780, 37in. wide. (Sotheby's) **$4,600**

Chippendale birch slant lid desk, New England, circa 1800, the interior of small drawers and valanced compartments, 41½in. wide. (Skinner Inc.) **$2,000**

Chippendale maple slant lid desk, Southeastern New England, circa 1780, the fall front above case of four thumbmolded graduated drawers, 40in. wide. (Skinner) **$3,335**

A Chippendale tiger maple slant lid desk, the fall-front reveals a stepped interior, New England, circa 1780, 36in. wide. (Skinner) **$5,600**

Chippendale tiger maple slant lid desk, northern New England, late 18th century, the interior with small drawers and valanced compartments, 40in. wide. (Skinner) **$5,175**

Chippendale tiger maple slant lid desk, New England, circa 1800, the interior has small drawers and open valanced compartments, 40½in. wide. (Skinner Inc.) **$6,880**

Chippendale tiger maple slant lid desk, New England, late 18th century, the interior with open valanced compartments and small drawers, 40in. wide. (Skinner) **$2,760**

Chippendale birch child's desk, southeastern New England, late 18th century, the fall front above a cockbeaded case of four graduated drawers, 15in. wide. (Skinner) **$4,312**

CHIPPENDALE, NEW ENGLAND

Chippendale maple desk, New England, late 18th century, replaced hardware, 35¼in. wide. (Skinner Inc.) $4,400

A Chippendale carved birchwood slant-front desk, New England, circa 1780, the rectangular top with hinged slant front lid, 38½in. wide. (Sotheby's) $3,450

Chippendale maple slant-lid desk, New England, 18th century, with two-tier interior of valanced compartments and small drawers, 37¼in. wide. (Skinner) $3,105

Chippendale tiger maple slant front desk, New England, late 18th century, the lid with thumb-molded-edge, opening to a compartmentalised interior with six valanced pigeonholes, 37in. wide. (Butterfield & Butterfield) $5,500

Chippendale maple and cherrywood slant front desk, New England, late 18th century, the thumb-molded edge slant lid enclosing a compartment interior with six valanced pigeonholes centering two document drawers, 40¼in. wide. (Butterfield & Butterfield) $3,770

A Chippendale mahogany slant-front desk, New England, 1760–1790, the thumbmolded slant lid opening to a fitted interior of short drawers over valanced pigeonholes, 41in. wide. (Christie's) $4,250

Chippendale maple and tiger maple slant lid desk, New England, late 18th century, the fall front opens to an interior of valanced compartments and drawers, 37in. wide. (Skinner) $2,415

A Chippendale figured maple slant front desk, New England, 1760-1780, with thumb molded slant lid opening to a fitted interior with six valanced pigeonholes, 93.7cm. (Christie's New York) $13,300

Chippendale maple slant lid desk, New England, late 18th century, with a stepped interior of small compartments, flanking a prospect door, 36½in. wide. (Skinner) $4,600

A Chippendale carved walnut slant-front desk, Chester County, Pennsylvania, 1760–1780, the rectangular slant-lid with molded edge opening to a fitted interior with central prospect door, blocked short document drawers and valanced pigeonholes all over a case fitted with two thumbmolded short drawers above three thumbmolded long drawers flanked by fluted quarter columns, appears to retain original brasses, 41in. wide.
(Christie's) $29,900

CHIPPENDALE, NEW HAMPSHIRE

Chippendale carved tiger maple slant lid desk, New Hampshire, late 18th century, stepped interior of small drawers and valanced compartments, 37½in. wide. (Skinner Inc.) $12,375

A Country Chippendale cherry slant front desk, probably Charlestown, New Hampshire, 1760-1780, 36in. wide. $24,200

Chippendale wavy birch oxbow slant lid desk, New Hampshire, late 18th century, with an interior of small drawers and valanced compartments, 41in. wide. (Skinner) $5,175

PENNSYLVANIA

A Chippendale figured walnut slant-front desk, Pennsylvania, circa 1780, the case with four graduated thumbmolded long drawers, 40in. wide. (Sotheby's) $4,887

A Chippendale walnut slant-front desk, Pennsylvania, 1760–1780, the rectangular hinged lid opening to a fitted interior above a case fitted with thumb-molded graduated long drawers, on ogee bracket feet, 41½in. wide. (Christie's) $7,150

A Chippendale figured maple slant-front desk, Pennsylvania, 1770–1780, the rectangular top above a molded slant-lid enclosing an elaborately fitted interior, on ogee bracket feet, 41in. wide. (Christie's) $20,500

PHILADELPHIA

A Chippendale carved walnut slant-front desk, Philadelphia, 1760–80, the rectangular hinged thumbmolded slant-lid opening to a fitted interior, 39¼in. wide. (Christie's) $5,750

A Chippendale carved walnut slant-front desk, Philadelphia, 1769-80, the thumbmolded slant lid opening to a compartmented interior, 42in. wide. (Christie's) $29,900

A Chippendale carved mahogany slant-front desk, Philadelphia, 1760-1780, the rectangular top above a conforming slant-lid opening to reveal a fitted interior, 41¼in. wide. (Christie's) $7,475

CHIPPENDALE, RHODE ISLAND

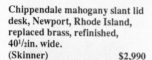

Chippendale mahogany slant lid desk, Newport, Rhode Island, replaced brass, refinished, 40½in. wide.
(Skinner) $2,990

Chippendale maple slant-lid desk, Rhode Island, 18th century, original brass, 35½in. wide.
(Skinner) $4,887

Chippendale maple and tiger maple slant lid desk, probably Rhode Island, late 18th century, replaced brasses.
(Skinner) $4,888

Chippendale maple slant lid desk, Rhode Island, 18th century, the interior with scrolled and valanced compartments above two tiers of small drawers, 36¾in. wide.
(Skinner) $6,325

A Chippendale tiger maple slant lid desk, Rhode Island, circa 1780, the slant lid opens to reveal an interior of valanced compartments and small end-blocked drawers, 38in. wide.
(Skinner) $19,000

A Chippendale mahogany slant-front desk, Rhode Island, 1760–1780, the rectangular top above a thumbmolded slant lid, 37½in. wide.
(Christie's) $25,300

A Chippendale carved figured maple slant front desk, Rhode Island, 1760-80, 38in. wide.
(Christie's) $14,000

Chippendale mahogany carved fall front desk, probably Newport, Rhode Island, circa 1750, the fall front above a case of four thumbmolded graduated drawers, 37in. wide.
(Skinner) $29,900

A good Chippendale carved and figured mahogany slant-front desk, Newport, Rhode Island, 1770–80, 39¼in. wide.
(Sotheby's) $8,050

FEDERAL

A rare Federal carved and paint decorated pine slant front desk, New England, early 19th century, 36in. wide. (Sotheby's) $34,500

Federal cherry inlaid slant lid desk, New England, circa 1800, the interior of small drawers and valanced compartments, 40in. wide. (Skinner Inc.) $2,750

An antique Federal period mahogany slantfront desk of desirable small size, decorated with line inlay, the flap enclosing a fitted interior, 34in. wide. (Selkirk's) $3,700

A Federal inlaid and figured mahogany slant-front desk, Baltimore, Maryland, circa 1805, the molded hinged rectangular lid inlaid with a central oval reserve, 39$\frac{1}{2}$in. wide. (Sotheby's) $3,737

Federal walnut inlaid slant-front desk, Pennsylvania, early 19th century, the thumb-molded edge top with string quarter fan-inlay opening to a compartmentalised interior, 42in. wide. (Butterfield & Butterfield) $3,200

A Federal inlaid cherrywood slant-front desk, Maryland or Pennsylvania, circa 1790, the rectangular top above a slant lid with line inlay centering an inlaid patera opening to a fitted interior with a corner fan-inlaid prospect door, 38in. wide. (Christie's) $12,100

A Federal cherrywood slant-front desk, Mid-Atlantic States, circa 1800, the rectangular top with hinged slant-front lid opening to a shell-carved prospect door, 45in. wide. (Sotheby's) $4,025

Federal birch and butternut slant lid desk, probably Massachusetts, circa 1810, the interior with ten valanced compartments flanked by three drawers, 39.75in. wide. (Skinner) $2,185

Federal mahogany and mahogany veneer inlaid slant lid desk, probably Massachusetts, circa 1800, the fall front above a case of four cockbeaded graduated drawers, 41$\frac{1}{2}$in. wide. (Skinner) $3,105

246

Queen Anne walnut inlaid slant lid desk, Massachusetts, 1730–50, the hinged lid with two inlaid stellate devices, 38in. wide. (Skinner) $5,463

Queen Anne maple child's desk on frame, probably southeastern New England, last half 18th century, 23½in. wide. (Skinner) $4,312

A Queen Anne cherrywood desk-on-frame, Connecticut, 1740–60, on short cabriole legs and pad feet, 34¼in. wide. (Sotheby's) $4,025

A Queen Anne cherrywood desk-on-frame, probably New Hampshire, 1760–1780, the upper section with thumbmolded slant-lid opening to a fitted interior with five valanced pigeonholes, on short cabriole legs, 41in. wide. (Christie's) $10,300

Queen Anne tiger maple and cherry slant lid desk, possibly Vermont, circa 1750, the interior with central fan-carved drawer and two valanced compartments, 36in. wide. (Skinner) $5,175

A Queen Anne maple inlaid slant top desk, New England, 18th and 19th century, the slant lid with burl panels centering a sun motif, 34¾in. wide. $18,700

A fine Queen Anne tiger maple slant lid desk, Massachusetts, circa 1750, on scrolled cabriole legs ending in pad feet, 37½in. wide. (Skinner) $58,000

Queen Anne cherry slant lid desk on frame, Norwich, Connecticut, circa 1750, 34¾in. wide. (Skinner) $5,462

Fine Queen Anne tiger maple slant lid desk, New Hampshire, circa 1750, the slant lid opens to a double tier stepped interior, old finish, 37½in. wide. (Skinner Inc.) $60,500

WILLIAM & MARY

A William and Mary red-painted walnut slant-front desk, New England, early 18th century, the base molding on ball feet, 36in. wide.
(Sotheby's) $10,637

A William and Mary walnut veneered slant-front desk, Boston, 1700-1725, the rectangular veneered top with herringbone surround, 35³/8in. wide. (Christie's) $10,350

A William and Mary desk-on-frame, Massachusetts, circa 1710–1730, in two parts, the upper section opening to a fitted interior, 27¹/4in. wide.
(Christie's) $27,600

A William and Mary walnut slant-front desk, Philadelphia, 1730–50, the rectangular top with molded hinged slant-front opening to a fitted interior, 36in. wide.
(Sotheby's) $9,775

A rare William and Mary mahogany slant-front desk, Philadelphia, 1730–50, the rectangular top with molded gallery above a slant-front, 39in. wide.
(Sotheby's) $49,450

A William and Mary red-stained figured maple and birchwood diminutive slant-front desk-on-frame, New England, circa 1730, in two parts, 27¹/2in. wide.
(Sotheby's) $27,600

A William and Mary burl walnut veneered slant-front desk Boston, 1710-1725, the rectangular top centering a veneered rectangular panel, 35¾in. wide.
(Christie's) $74,000

A walnut and feather-banded bureau with rectangular top and hinged slope above a fitted interior with three graduated drawers below, on later bun feet, early 18th century, 39in. wide.
(Christie's) $6,500

William & Mary walnut inlaid and maple slant lid desk, Boston, early 18th century, slant lid and drawers inlaid with two panels of contrasting stringing, 34in. wide.
(Skinner) $4,888

A Classical mahogany veneered and brass-mounted secrétaire à abattant, School of Duncan Phyfe, New York City, 1815–1830, the rectangular top above a veneered frieze concealing a drawer over a conforming case fitted with a brass-mounted fall-front and felt lined door opening to eight pigeonholes above a short drawer flanked on each side by two short drawers over a long drawer, all above two cupboard doors, the whole flanked by outset veneered columns with brass capitals and bases, 38½in. wide.

(Christie's) $13,800

An oak drop-front desk, by Gustav Stickley, circa 1912, 32in. wide.
(Skinner) $1,880

Gateleg dropfront desk, circa 1912, arched gallery top and flat sides, branded *The Work of L. & J. G. Stickley,* 31½in. wide. $1,250

Gustav Stickley drop front desk, original dark brown finish, ink stain to front, Gustav Stickley red mark, 29in. wide.
(Skinner) $6,900

A Gustav Stickley drop-front desk, the doors opening to reveal a fitted interior, circa 1906, 38in. wide.
(Skinner) $3,750

L. & J. G. Stickley writing desk and chair, circa 1912, desk no. 610, chair no. 913, lower shelf with kneehole; chair with curved crest rail, both branded *"The Work of L. & G. Stickley"*. $800

An early Gustav Stickley chalet desk, circa 1901-2, the arched gallery top with pierced corner cut-outs and keyed tenon sides, 45¾in. high.
(Skinner) $2,500

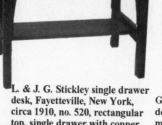

Gustav Stickley slant lid desk, Eastwood, New York, circa 1907, gallery top, slant lid front over single drawer with brass v-pulls, 30in. wide.
(Skinner Inc.) $1,250

L. & J. G. Stickley single drawer desk, Fayetteville, New York, circa 1910, no. 520, rectangular top, single drawer with copper pulls, lower median shelf through-tenon, 36in. wide.
(Skinner) $1,100

Gustav Stickley oak fall-front desk, No. 729, circa 1912, medium finish, fitted interior in chestnut, Craftsman paper label, 36½in. wide.
(Skinner) $1,955

STICKLEY

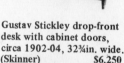

Gustav Stickley table desk, similar to no. 430, circa 1903, central drawer flanked by small stacked double side drawers, 36in. wide.
(Skinner) **$700**

An inlaid oak drop-front desk, designed by Harvey Ellis for Gustav Stickley, 1903-04, style no. 706, 30in. wide.
$25,000

Fine and rare Gustav Stickley nine-drawer desk, original leather top and tacks, chamfered sides with large keys and tenons, large wooden pulls, 53½in. wide.
(Skinner) **$5,462**

An L. & J. G. Stickley drop-front writing desk, no. 613, writing surface with fitted interior, circa 1910, 32in. wide.
(Skinner) **$1,000**

L. & J. G. Stickley desk and chair, no. 611 and 1313, circa 1910, flat top desk with central letter compartments flanked by single small drawers.
(Skinner) **$1,250**

Gustav Stickley drop-front desk with cabinet doors, circa 1902-04, 32¾in. wide.
(Skinner) **$6,250**

A Gustav Stickley desk, no. 721, circa 1912, 29in. high.
$630

Gustav Stickley desk, circa 1912, letter file with two small drawers on rectangular top over two half drawers, 22¾in. wide.
(Skinner Inc.) **$950**

Early Gustav Stickley drop front desk, 1902-04, step-down gallery, chamfered drop front with copper strap hinges over two open shelves, 52in. high.
(Skinner) **$8,100**

Rare and fine Shop of the Crafters china cabinet, no. 326, finely inlaid wood, some overcoat to original color, 63¼in. high x 42in. wide x 15⅝in. deep. (Skinner) $3,450

American oak china cabinet, circa 1880, leaded and curved glass, raised on carved claw feet, 50in. wide.
(Du Mouchelles) $800

Fine L. & J.G. Stickley two-door china cabinet, original dark brown finish, 48in. wide.
(Skinner) $4,312

Pine architectural glazed cupboard, Connecticut, 1750, traces of old color, 65in. wide.
(Skinner) $5,750

A Limbert single door china cabinet, no. 1347, Grand Rapids, Michigan, circa 1907, 34¼in. wide.
(Skinner) $2,500

One of a pair of grained glazed cabinets, Massachusetts, mid-19th century, the glazed doors open to a four-shelf interior, 70³/₄in. wide, open.
(Skinner)
(Two) $5,175

Rare L. & J.G. Stickley china cabinet, No. 746, chamfered backboards, interior original finish, exterior overcoated with good color, 44in. wide.
(Skinner) $5,175

Gustav Stickley one door china closet, circa 1907, no. 820, 36in. wide. $2,500

Classical mahogany and mahogany veneer vitrine cabinet, Middle Atlantic States, 1815–25, the rectangular top with cockbeaded pedimented backboard, 28³/₄in. wide.
(Skinner) $1,840

Mission oak two-door china closet, no. 2017, circa 1910, 46½in. wide.
(Skinner) $630

A pair of brass andirons, attributed to Daniel King, Philadelphia, 1760–1770, each with spiral flame and diamond finial, 24in. high.
(Christie's) $46,000

Late 18th century wrought iron broiler, probably Pennsylvania, 20in. long. $600

A pair of molded cast-iron owl andirons, American, 20th century, in the half-round, with cut-out round eyes, height 14in.
(Sotheby's) $4,888

A pair of Chippendale brass and iron firetools attributed to Daniel King, Philadelphia, circa 1760, the tongs with penny grips, 28in. high.
(Christie's) $2,860

Pair of large patinated bronze figural andirons of American Indians by Louis Potter, first quarter 20th century, Roman Bronze Works, New York, 22in. high.
(Butterfield & Butterfield) $4,950

A cast-iron Egyptian Revival parlor stove, N. Pratt & Company, Albany, New York, circa 1837–1844, 58½in. high.
(Christie's) $2,300

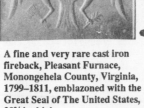

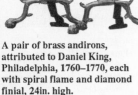

A pair of cast-iron and molded copper andirons, probably American, late 19th/early 20th century, molded with serpents in relief, 23½in. high.
(Sotheby's) $2,875

A fine and very rare cast iron fireback, Pleasant Furnace, Monongehela County, Virginia, 1799–1811, emblazoned with the Great Seal of The United States, 29¾in. high.
(Sotheby's) $31,050

A pair of molded and painted cast-iron figural andirons, American, 20th century, cast with the figure of a man, his hands on his knees, 17in. high.
(Sotheby's) $690

A rare painted pine leather and wrought-iron fireplace bellows, probably Mahantongo Valley, Pennsylvania, dated *1847*, 18in. long.
(Sotheby's) $11,500

Aesthetic Movement ebonised walnut and ivory inlaid brass mounted coal scuttle and shovel, circa 1870, with incised brass strapwork and geometric inlaid panels, 12in. high.
(Skinner) $2,070

A brass and wrought-iron fireplace trivet, American, probably Maryland or Virginia, first quarter 19th century, 17^{1}/$_{2}$in. long extended.
(Sotheby's) $747

A pair of painted cast-iron andirons, American, early 20th century, relief-cast in the form of George Washington dressed in Continental Army uniform, 20^{3}/$_{4}$in. high.
(Christie's) $575

Cast iron stove plate, Pennsylvania, c. 1750, 'Dance of Death', pattern, the inscription translated 'Here fights with me the bitter death/And brings me in death's stress' 22in. x 24in.
(Skinner Inc.) $500

A pair of wrought-iron heart andirons, New England, early 19th century, each with arched supports ending in penny feet, 16^{3}/$_{8}$in. high.
(Sotheby's) $2,530

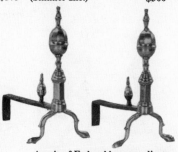

Four piece wrought iron fireplace set, attributed to Gustav Stickley, circa 1905, with strapwork log holder, unsigned, 33^{1}/$_{2}$in. high.
(Skinner Inc.) $6,000

A pair of Federal brass andirons with matching firetools, by John Molineux, Boston, Massachusetts, 1800–1810, each with bell finial above a faceted octagonal turning above a hexagonal plinth with spurred arched legs, 19^{1}/$_{2}$in. high.
(Christie's) $6,820

A pair of cast-iron dachshund andirons, American, 20th century, each cast in the half-round with a dachshund seated on its haunches, 13^{1}/$_{4}$in. high.
(Sotheby's) $2,587

Pair of signed brass andirons, America, early 19th century, 22in. high.
(Skinner Inc.) $2,000

Stove, cast iron, wooden knob, canted sides, rare three-leg form with penny foot, hinged door with latch, 17½in. high.
(Skinner) $805

A pair of Federal late 18th/ early 19th century bell metal andirons, 24in. high.
                                  $1,600

A set of three steel fire irons, with engraved urn finials, knopped shafts, and shaped pierced shovel, late 18th century.
(Christie's) $1,540

A cast iron stove plate, probably by Mary Ann Furnace, York County, Pennsylvania, circa 1761, depicting two tulip and heart decorations, 24½in. high.
(Christie's) $990

A pair of cast-iron Columbia-on-shell andirons, American, 20th century, each cast in the half-round with the figure of Columbia holding a flaming torch, 17½in. high.
(Sotheby's) $402

A rare copper tea kettle, Benjamin and/or Joseph Harbeson, Philadelphia, circa 1800, with a hinged strap handle, 11in. high.
(Sotheby's) $1,955

A pair of brass andirons, probably New York, 1790–1810, each with steeple-top above a ball with mid-band over a faceted hexagonal plinth, 22in. high.
(Christie's) $1,320

A wrought copper large pot, Pennsylvania, 19th century, the tapering cylindrical form with flat bottom and rolled brim, 22in. diameter.
(Christie's) $403

256

A wrought iron trivet, stamped **J.W.**, Pennsylvania, early 19th century, the rounded open triangular form with star-punch decoration.
(Christie's) **$173**

A pair of Federal steeple top faceted plinth brass andirons with matching shovel and tongs, New York, 1790-1810.
(Christie's New York) **$9,680**

A carved walnut bellows, attributed to Samuel McIntire, Salem, Massachusetts, circa 1800, 20in. long.
(Christie's) **$23,000**

A pair of cast iron sun-face andirons, stamped *B & H*, late 19th/early 20th century, the circular fluted finial centering an articulated face, 16³/₄in. high.
(Christie's) **$1,380**

Elihu Vedder wrought iron fireback, New York, 1882, The Sun God, cast with the face of a man surrounded by flowing hair, 27¾in. wide.
(Skinner Inc.) **$3,100**

A pair of brass andirons, attributed to William or Richard Wittingham, New York, circa 1791–1821, the ball-and-ring shaped finial above a reeded sphere over a tapering and flaring cylindrical support, 19¹/₂in. high.
(Christie's) **$9,200**

A pair of Chippendale brass andirons, American, late 18th century, each with a ball-and-flame finial over a baluster and ring-turned support, 21¹/₂in. high.
(Christie's) **$9,350**

A pair of cast-iron satyr andirons, American, 20th century, each cast in the half-round with the head of a satyr with pierced eyes and mouth, 11³/₈in. high.
(Sotheby's) **$1,035**

A rare decorated cast-iron fireback, Virginia, circa 1730, of arched oblong form the crest centering a shell flanked by leafage, 30¹/₄in. high.
(Sotheby's) **$72,900**

Aesthetic period fireplace surround, with Trent tiles, surround 62½in. wide.
(Skinner) $1,150

Federal carved mantel, possibly Salem, Massachusetts, circa 1800, 73½in. wide.
(Skinner) $1,320

A Federal white-painted pine fireplace surround, American, circa 1810, the reverse breakfronted mantel above a conformingly-shaped and paneled frieze, 6ft. 9in. wide.
(Sotheby's) $690

An important Neoclassical sculpted white marble fireplace surround, circa 1798, with an overhanging guilloche-carved mantel on figural stiles, 6ft. wide.
(Sothebys) $222,500

A fine Federal carved and gessoed pine fireplace mantel, attributed to Robert Wellford, Philadelphia, circa 1805, painted white, overall width 6ft. 11in.
(Sotheby's) $4,025

American oak mantel, late 19th– early 20th century, 60in. wide, egg molding above a beveled glass mirror flanked by two sets of Doric columns.
(Du Mouchelles) $1,000

Federal painted fireplace mantel, probably New England, circa 1810, 78³/₄in. wide.
(Skinner) $770

Cast bronze fireplace surround, Murdoch Foundry, Boston, in the manner of Elihu Vedder, 30½in. wide.
(Skinner) $2,530

A white painted pine and shell-decorated fireplace mantle, American, possibly New York, 1800–30, the reverse-breakfronted overhanging mantel above a recessed frieze, 5ft. 6in. wide.
(Sotheby's) $10,925

A carved and painted pine mantel, possibly New York, circa 1830, the rectangular molded shelf above a cove-molded edge, 51in. high.
(Christie's) $805

Dixon & Sons cast iron fireplace surround, scroll design, impressed *Dixon & Sons, Philadelphia*, 34in. wide.
(Skinner) $1,380

American School, 19th/20th century, Owls and Ivy, a fireplace surround, unsigned, oil on three panels, assembled dimensions, 37 x 43in.
(Skinner) $3,575

A fine Queen Anne carved and figured cherrywood bonnet-top high chest of drawers, Connecticut, 1740–1770, in two parts; with a swan's neck pediment surmounted by three stylized urn-and-spire finials above three short drawers, the center one fan-carved with undulating rays, and four graduated thumbmolded long drawers; the lower section with a mid-molding and two thumbmolded long drawers above a shaped apron on cabriole legs and pad feet, width of pediment 40in.   (Sotheby's) $48,875

Queen Anne maple bonnet-top high chest of drawers, probably Massachusetts, 1780, old brasses, 38³/₄in. wide.
(Skinner) $41,400

A Queen Anne carved and figured walnut chest-on-frame, Pennsylvania, circa 1755, in two parts, 42in. wide.
(Sotheby's) $21,850

A Queen Anne carved cherrywood high chest-of-drawers, in two sections, on cabriole legs with pad feet, 39in. wide.
(Christie's) $8,625

Maple high chest on frame, Goffstown, Bedford or Henniker, New Hampshire, probably by Major John or Lieutenant Samuel Dunlap, late 18th century, 77¹/₂in. high.
(Skinner Inc.) $20,000

The Mifflin family matching Chippendale carved mahogany high chest-of-drawers and dressing table, Philadelphia, 1750–55, chest 44¹/₄in. wide; dressing table 34in. wide.
(Christie's) $717,500

A Queen Anne tiger maple high chest-of-drawers, New Hampshire, Dunlap School, 1740–1770, the upper case with molded cornice above three thumbmolded short drawers 40¹/₄in. wide.
(Christie's) $24,200

Queen Anne walnut high chest of drawers, Boston or Salem, Massachusetts, circa 1750, on four cabriole legs ending in pad feet on platforms, 37³/₄in. wide.
(Skinner) $29,900

A Queen Anne tiger maple high chest of drawers, North Shore, Massachusetts, 1740–1760, in two sections, on cabriole legs with pad feet, 38in. wide.
(Christie's) $10,000

William and Mary birch and maple high chest of drawers, probably Massachusetts, circa 1730, old refinish, replaced brasses, 36in. wide.
(Skinner) $5,462

William and Mary walnut and walnut veneer and pine tall chest of drawers, New England, 18th century, refinished, 35½in. wide.
(Skinner) $5,175

A Queen Anne tiger maple high chest of drawers, Salem, Massachusetts, 1730-1760, the center fan carved above a scalloped skirt, 38¼in. wide.
(Christie's) $30,000

Queen Anne tiger maple high chest of drawers, Newburyport, Massachusetts, circa 1760, the top section with flat molded cornice, 38⅜in. wide.
(Skinner) $20,700

Queen Anne tiger maple high chest of drawers, Massachusetts, circa 1760, the top section with flat molded cornice above case of four thumbmolded graduated drawers, 37¾in. wide.
(Skinner) $28,750

A Queen Anne carved mahogany high chest-of-drawers, Connecticut or New York, 1760-1780, the upper section with bonnet top and molded broken scroll pediment, 42½in. wide.
(Christie's) $85,000

A William and Mary black-painted high chest-of-drawers, Pennsylvania, 1720–1740, the upper section with rectangular molded cornice over two short drawers and three graduated long drawers, 39in. wide.
(Christie's) $10,000

Queen Anne maple carved high chest of drawers, Salem or Newburyport, Massachusetts, circa 1760, the top section with flat molded cornice, 36¼in. wide. (Skinner) $24,150

A Queen Anne walnut high chest of drawers, Massachusetts, 1740-1760, on cabriole legs with pad feet, the rear legs of maple, 41½in. wide.
(Christie's New York) $12,500

Queen Anne painted pine high chest of drawers, probably Hartford, Connecticut area, circa 1740, the top sections with flat molded cornice, 37in. wide.
(Skinner) $35,650

A Queen Anne birchwood flat-top high chest of drawers, New England, probably New Hampshire, 1740-1770, in two parts; the upper section with a rectangular overhanging cornice above two short drawers and three graduated thumbmolded long drawers; the lower section with a mid-molding, three short drawers with a shell-carved shaped apron on cabriole legs ending in pad feet, width of mid-molding 39in.
(Sotheby's) $8,625

A William and Mary burl-maple veneered high chest-of-drawers, Boston, 1710–1725, in two parts; the upper with a cove-molded veneered cornice above a case fitted with a veneered pulvinated long drawer all over two short drawers and three graduated long drawers each with crossbanded and veneered drawer fronts, above a mid-molding; the lower section with mid-molding over a case fitted with three short drawers above a shaped skirt, 38½in. wide. (Christie's) $18,400

Queen Anne cherry high chest of drawers, Rhode Island or Connecticut, 1750–70, brasses appear original, 46in. wide. (Skinner Inc.) **$8,500**

Queen Anne cherry bonnet top high chest of drawers, Concord, Massachusetts, last quarter 18th century, 38in. wide. (Skinner) **$17,250**

Queen Anne maple high chest of drawers, Oyster Bay, Long Island, New York, circa 1760, 39¹/₂in. wide. (Skinner) **$7,150**

A Queen Anne walnut high chest of drawers, Pennsylvania, 1740–1760, the upper section with coved cornice above three short and three long thumb-molded drawers, 41¹/₂in. wide. (Christie's) **$20,625**

The important Gilbert family matching Queen Anne walnut high chest of drawers and dressing table, Salem, Massachusetts, 1750–1770, on cabriole legs with pad feet, 38in. wide. (Christie's) **$180,000**

Queen Anne walnut chest on frame, Pennsylvania, circa 1760–80, the top section with flat molded cornice above a case of three thumbmolded short drawers, 38in. wide. (Skinner) **$26,450**

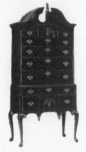

A Chippendale carved walnut high chest-of-drawers, Salem, Massachusetts, 1760–1780, on cabriole legs with pad-and-disk feet, 84in. high, 40in. wide. (Christie's) **$65,000**

Queen Anne maple high chest of drawers, Salem, Massachusetts, 1740-1760, on cut out skirt joining four cabriole legs, 37³/₄in. wide. (Skinner Inc.) **$20,000**

Queen Anne carved walnut high chest, Hingham, Massachusetts area, 1740–60, with thumb molded drawers, one of which is fan carved, 39¹/₄in. wide. (Skinner) **$34,500**

The Stevenson-Phillips Family Chippendale carved mahogany high chest-of-drawers, Philadelphia, 1765–1775, in two sections; the upper with molded broken swan's neck pediment terminating in carved rosettes above a tympanum with applied scroll-carved decoration over a case fitted with three short thumbmolded drawers above two similar drawers over three graduated and thumbmolded long drawers all, flanked by fluted quarter-columns; the lower section with applied mid-molding above a conforming case fitted with one thumbmolded long drawer over three similar short drawers, 44¼in. wide.
(Christie's) $376,500

Queen Anne maple highboy,
New England, mid 18th century,
36in. wide.
(Skinner) $7,700

A fine Queen Anne carved
cherrywood bonnet-top highboy,
Connecticut, circa 1760, on
cabriole legs ending in pad feet,
40in. wide.
(Sotheby's) $31,050

William and Mary walnut and
burl walnut highboy, 40in. wide.
(Skinner) $1,380

Queen Anne carved cherrywood
flat top highboy, Connecticut,
circa 1750, the upper section
with dentil molded cornice
above three thumbmolded
edge short drawers centering a
stylised shell, width 40in.
(Butterfield & Butterfield)
                             $5,175

Queen Anne tiger maple bonnet
top highboy, probably
Connecticut, circa 1740–1760, in
two parts, the upper section with
molded swan's neck cornice
flanked by three baluster-turned
finials, width 40in.
(Butterfield & Butterfield)
                            $16,100

Queen Anne walnut and maple
flat top highboy, New England,
1740–1760, the upper section
with a molded cornice above
two short and three long thumbmolded edge drawers, on
cabriole legs ending in pad feet,
width 38¼in.
(Butterfield & Butterfield)
                             $8,625

A Queen Anne burl maple-
veneered diminutive flat-top
highboy, Boston, Massachusetts,
1720–50, in two parts, the
shaped beaded skirt hung with
turned pendants, 37in. wide.
(Sotheby's) $65,750

A William and Mary burl-
veneered walnut and maple
highboy, Boston-Ipswich area,
Massachusetts, 1700–1720, on
trumpet- and vase-turned legs,
39in. wide.
(Sotheby's) $167,500

A fine and rare Queen Anne
carved and figured maple
highboy, attributed to Powder
Major John Demeritt,
Portsmouth or Dover, New
Hampshire, 1740–60, 45in. wide.
(Sotheby's) $18,400

American Queen Anne highboy, 18th century, in walnut, on cabriole legs and duck feet, 36½in. wide.
(Eldred's) $5,500

A Queen Anne figured maple flat-top highboy, New England, 1750–70, on cabriole legs centering a shaped apron, lower case 28in. wide.
(Sotheby's) $13,800

A Queen Anne cherry highboy on four cabriole legs, Conn., circa 1770, 37¼in. wide.
(Skinner) $14,500

A very fine Queen Anne burl-walnut veneered and maple diminutive flat-top highboy, Boston, Massachusetts, circa 1740, 37½in. wide.
(Sotheby's) $37,500

A very good Queen Anne maple bonnet-top highboy, Rhode Island, circa 1765, the shaped skirt continuing to removable cabriole legs, 38½in. wide.
(Sotheby's) $8,500

A good Queen Anne carved maple flat-top highboy, New England, probably Eastern Connecticut, circa 1750, in two parts, 39¼in. wide.
(Sotheby's) $26,450

A Queen Anne maple flat-top highboy, probably Oyster Bay, Long Island, New York, circa 1750, in two parts, 39½in. wide.
(Sotheby's) $18,400

A fine and rare Chippendale carved and figured walnut bonnet-top highboy, Salem, Massachusetts, circa 1765, in two parts, 38½in. wide.
(Sotheby's) $90,500

A fine and rare Queen Anne richly figured maple flat top highboy, Delaware River Valley, 1740–60, in two parts, 42in. wide.
(Sotheby's) $68,500

A Queen Anne carved and figured maple bonnet-top diminutive highboy, Connecticut, circa 1750, in two parts; the upper section with a broken swan's neck pediment centering an urn-and-flame finial, the case fitted with three short drawers, the center one pinwheel-carved above four graduated long drawers; the lower section with a mid molding, one long drawer and three short drawers, the center one fan-carved above a shaped skirt on peaked cabriole legs ending in pad feet, 37in. wide. (Sotheby's) $34,500

A Queen Anne inlaid and veneered walnut high chest-of-drawers, Boston, 1740–1760, in two
sections; the upper case with broken swan's neck pediment above a rectangular case with a string-
inlaid and eight-pointed star over three string-inlaid thumbmolded short drawers, above four
similarly embellished long drawers; the lower case rectangular with applied molding over two
string-inlaid and thumbmolded short drawers, the central one with recessed and inlaid fan, over a
string-inlaid and shaped skirt with central recess, on cabriole legs with padded disk feet, 41¼in.
wide.
(Christie's) $134,500

A Queen Anne cherrywood highboy, probably Wethersfield, Conn., circa 1740-65, 37½in. wide. $25,000

Queen Anne maple bonnet top highboy, New England, circa 1760, 38in. wide. $7,500

A Queen Anne figured and carved maple flat-top highboy, Pennsylvania, circa 1750, in two parts, 41½in. wide. (Sotheby's) $21,850

A good Queen Anne figured walnut flat-top highboy, Pennsylvania, circa 1760, in two parts, the upper section with molded cornice above five short and three long molded graduated drawers, 44½in. wide. (Sotheby's) $50,000

A Queen Anne curly maple bonnet top highboy, New England, circa 1770, 36¾in. wide. (Skinner) $4,375

Provincial George I oak and walnut highboy, first half 18th century, the flat rectangular cornice above two short and three full cock beaded and molded drawers, upon a conforming base, 39in. wide. (William Doyle Galleries) $3,335

A Chippendale carved and figured walnut highboy, Pennsylvania, circa 1780, in two parts, on shell-carved cabriole legs ending in claw-and-ball feet, 44½in. wide. (Sotheby's) $6,900

A Queen Anne carved mahogany bonnet-top highboy, Goddard-Townsend School, Newport, Rhode Island, circa 1765, 38½in. wide. (Sotheby's) $398,500

A Queen Anne carved and figured cherrywood flat-top highboy, Massachusetts, circa 1750, in two parts, on cabriole legs ending in pad feet, 39½in. wide. (Sotheby's) $9,775

A William and Mary gumwood kas in two sections, New York, 1725-55, 54in. wide. $7,500

An 18th century Chippendale poplar kas, Hudson Valley, New York, 56in. wide. $3,500

An 18th century gumwood kas, in three sections, Long Island, N.Y., 74½in. wide. $10,000

A William and Mary gumwood kas, New York, 1725–1755, the upper part with an elaborately molded bold cornice above two fielded panel double cupboard doors enclosing two shelves, 65½in. wide.
(Christie's) $6,200

A William and Mary paneled sycamore kas, Hudson River Valley, New York, circa 1730–60, the rectangular molded overhanging cornice above two raised paneled cupboard doors, 5ft. 11in. wide.
(Sotheby's) $6,900

A William and Mary carved cherrywood kas, Hudson River Valley, early 18th century, on turned feet, 6ft. 1in. wide.
(Sotheby's) $8,000

A maple and walnut kas, in two sections, N.Y., or N. Jersey, 1750-1800, 72in. wide. (Christie's) $5,500

A William and Mary paneled gumwood kas, New York or New Jersey, 1730–80, in three parts, 6ft. 4½in. wide.
(Sotheby's) $4,600

Cherry kas, Hudson River Valley, 18th century, the heavy cornice molding above paneled doors, 62in. wide.
(Skinner) $2,415

A Federal mahogany linen press, signed by I. Bailey, New Jersey, 1807, 48in. wide. $13,500

A Federal inlaid mahogany linen press, in two sections, probably New York, circa 1785-1805, 45in. wide. $12,000

A Chippendale mahogany and mahogany veneer linen press, circa 1780, 48in. wide. $25,000

Chippendale cherry linen press, Eastern America, circa 1780, the molded cornice above two paneled doors, 42in. wide. (Skinner Inc.) $4,650

A Chippendale figured maple linen-press, Pennsylvania, 1760–1780, the upper section with elaborately molded cornice about two arched paneled cupboard doors fitted with three shelves, on bracket feet, 48in. wide. (Christie's) $17,000

A Queen Anne maple linen press, Westchester County, New York, 1750–1785, in two sections, the upper with a molded over-hanging cornice, 42¼in. wide. (Christie's) $66,300

A yellow pine linen press, Texas, mid-19th century, the rectangular molded cornice above a paneled fireze, 60in. wide. (Christie's) $2,300

A Chippendale red gum linen press, New York State, 1750-1800, on a molded base with bracket feet, 51½in. wide. (Christie's) $5,250

A Federal mahogany linen press, New York, circa 1820, the removable projecting cornice above a pair of hinged paneled doors, 54in. wide. (Sotheby's) $5,000

A rare Queen Anne inlaid birchwood lowboy, Boston area, Massachusetts, circa 1740, the rectangular top inlaid with a central mariner's compass star with line-inlaid edge above a case with one long and three short line-inlaid drawers, the center drawer inlaid with a fan, the shaped skirt hung with pendants continuing to cabriole legs ending in pad feet. Appears to retain its original rare bright cut-decorated brass handles and escutcheon plate, some restoration to feet and possibly restoration to some inlays. Patches to case. Height 29⅛in, width of top 34½in, width of case 29¾in., depth of top 22⅛in., depth of case 18in.
(Sotheby's)

$43,125

A Queen Anne cherrywood lowboy, Connecticut, circa 1760, the shaped skirt continuing to cabriole legs, 34in. wide.
(Sotheby's) $7,475

A good Queen Anne carved cherrywood lowboy, Connecticut, 1760–80, the oblong molded top with notched corners, 34½in. wide.
(Sotheby's) $25,300

A fine Queen Anne carved and figured walnut lowboy, Philadelphia, circa 1750, on volute-carved cabriole legs, case 31in. wide.
(Sotheby's) $107,000

Antique American walnut Queen Anne lowboy, first half 18th century, three drawers with engraved brasses, one marked on sides with Masonic square and compass, 29½in. wide.
(Eldred's) $1,100

A rare Queen Anne walnut veneered lowboy, Boston Massachusetts, circa 1740, on cabriole legs ending in pad feet, adorned with gilt-shell decoration, width of top 32in.
(Sotheby's) $45,000

A fine and rare Chippendale carved and figured walnut lowboy, Philadelphia, circa 1780, the rectangular thumbmolded top above one long and three short drawers, 38in. wide.
(Sotheby's) $60,250

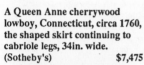

An American cherrywood lowboy, 19th century, with molded rectangular top above three long drawers, the lowest centered by a sunburst motif, 42in. wide.
(Christie's) $4,579

A fine Queen Anne walnut lowboy, New York, 1730–60, the incised cyma-shaped skirt continuing to faceted cabriole legs, width 36¼in.
(Sotheby's) $25,000

A Chippendale carved walnut lowboy, Pennsylvania, circa 1770, having shell-carved cabriole legs ending in claw-and-ball feet.
(Sotheby's) $15,000

A Queen Anne japanned, carved walnut and pine lowboy, Massachusetts, circa 1765, the japanning first quarter 19th century, 34in. wide. (Sotheby's) $7,250

A Chippendale carved mahogany lowboy, signed *Wallace Nutting*, early 20th century, in the Philadelphia manner, width 36½in. (Sotheby's) $4,000

A Queen Anne maple dressing table, Connecticut, 1740–60, the rectangular molded top above a conforming case, 38½in. wide. (Christie's) $4,830

A Queen Anne carved and figured cherrywood lowboy, Massachusetts, 1750–70, the rectangular thumbmolded top above one long drawer and three short drawers, case 30½in. wide. (Sotheby's) $8,050

A very fine Chippendale carved mahogany lowboy, Philadelphia, circa 1770, the shaped skirt continuing to shell-carved cabriole legs ending in claw-and-ball feet, 36⅞in. wide. (Sotheby's) $100,000

A Queen Anne burl-veneered walnut lowboy, Boston, Massachusetts, 1730–60, the shaped cockbeaded skirt continuing to cabriole legs, width of top 34¼in. (Sotheby's) $9,775

A fine Queen Anne carved cherrywood lowboy, Connecticut, circa 1760, the triple arched skirt below with a turned pendant finial, top 36in. wide. (Sotheby's) $25,300

A good Queen Anne walnut lowboy, New England, probably Massachusetts, circa 1740, the rectangular thumbmolded top with notched corners, 35in. wide. (Sotheby's) $20,700

A William and Mary carved and turned walnut lowboy, Boston, Massachusetts, 1720–50, the molded and crossbanded-top above three herringbone-inlaid drawers, 34in. wide. (Sotheby's) $6,325

A William and Mary black-painted maple and walnut lowboy, Massachusetts, 1720–50, the rectangular top with molded edge, 33in. wide.
(Sotheby's) $63,000

A Queen Anne carved walnut lowboy, Pennsylvania, circa 1750, the rectangular thumb-molded top with notched corners, 34¼in. wide.
(Sotheby's) $37,950

A fine and rare William and Mary walnut veneered, inlaid and turned oak or ash lowboy, New England, circa 1730, 32½in. wide.
(Sotheby's) $18,400

A fine and rare Queen Anne carved cherrywood scalloped top lowboy, Connecticut, circa 1770, the oblong top with scalloped sides above a case with one long and three short drawers, 36in.
(Sotheby's) $387,500

A Chippendale walnut lowboy, Pennsylvania, circa 1765, the rectangular molded top with notched front corners above four molded drawers, width 36¾in.
(Sotheby's) $16,500

A Chippendale carved and figured walnut lowboy, the carving attributed to Bernard and Jugiez, Philadelphia, Pennsylvania, circa 1765, 34½in. wide.
(Sotheby's) $29,900

The Rodman family Queen Anne figured cherrywood lowboy, Rhode Island, circa 1750, the rectangular molded top with notched corners, top 37¾in. wide.
(Sotheby's) $35,650

A fine Chippendale mahogany lowboy, Pennsylvania or New Jersey, circa 1765, the shaped skirt continuing to cabriole legs, 34¼in. wide.
(Sotheby's) $35,000

A fine Chippendale carved mahogany lowboy, Philadelphia, circa 1770, the rectangular molded top above a case with one long and three short molded drawers, 35¼in. wide.
(Sotheby's) $32,200

An important Chippendale carved and figured mahogany scroll-top spice chest, Philadelphia, Pennsylvania, circa 1765, of high chest of drawers form, in two parts; the upper section with scrolled swan's-neck crest ending in flowerhead-carved terminals centering a cabochon-carved pierced cartouche flanked by urn-and-flame finials, the tympanum carved with a pierced shell flanked by acanthus leaves, 22in. wide.
(Sotheby's) $123,500

Early 19th century miniature Federal mahogany tilt-top tea table, American, 9in. high. (Christie's) **$1,500**

A fine paint decorated miniature pine foot stool, Landis Valley, Pennsylvania, early 19th century, 8in. long. (Sotheby's) **$2,300**

Bird's-eye maple cannon ball doll's bed, America, circa 1830, the turned base on ball posts, 8¾in. high. (Skinner) **$500**

Miniature painted Chippendale tall chest, made by Jabez Rice, Massachusetts, early 19th century, painted brown, 15³/₈in. high. (Skinner Inc.) **$8,800**

Miniature country Chippendale bureau, America, late 18th century, raised on a molded bracket base (refinished, minor repairs), 14in. high. (Skinner Inc.) **$400**

A miniature slat-back chair, American, 19th century, the two arched slats painted with flowers centered by leaves, 10in. wide. (Christie's) **$437**

Miniature engraved whalebone and baleen inlaid exotic wood stool, 19th century, with compass star and heart motif, 4³/₄in. high. (Skinner) **$1,150**

An American, 19th century, miniature Federal mahogany four-post bedstead with canopy, 15½in. high. (Christie's) **$500**

Miniature paint decorated Windsor armchair, America, last half of 19th century, the black ground painted with floral decoration, 8¼in. high. (Skinner Inc.) **$850**

A miniature Federal painted and decorated pine blanket chest, Penn., circa 1810/30, 26½in. wide.
(Christie's) $25,000

19th century miniature painted tin piano and stool, with hinged keyboard cover, 3¼ x 3½in.
$175

A 19th century miniature green painted pine blanket chest, American, 9½in. high.
(Christie's) $600

A classical miniature carved mahogany chest-of-drawers, New York, 1830–1840, on carved lion's-paw feet, 23³/₄in. wide.
(Christie's) $1,980

An American, 18th century, miniature Queen Anne maple and pine slant-front desk, with a cherrywood mirror, the desk 11in. high.
(Christie's) $5,500

A miniature painted blanket box, signed Edward Cornell and dated December 24, 1809, 13½in. high. (Robt. W. Skinner Inc.) $2,600

A 19th century miniature grain painted bowfront chest-of-drawers, American or English, 12in. high.
(Christie's) $1,750

A 19th century, American, miniature classical maple fiddleback chair, 10¾in. high, 8¼in. wide. (Christie's)
$900

19th century tin miniature fireplace and tongs, 4in. long. $150

A Federal mahogany
miniature chest of
drawers, 1790-1810,
14½in. wide. $1,500

A 19th century miniature
tilt-top tea table, 13in. high.
(Skinner) $450

A 19th century miniature,
Empire mahogany veneer
chest-of-drawers, New
England, 15in. wide.
(Skinner) $850

An American late Fede-
ral mahogany miniature
chest of drawers, 10in.
wide. $2,000

An Empire mahogany minia-
ture sofa, American, circa
1840, 19in. wide.
(Christie's) $2,500

A 19th century miniature
Federal mahogany picture
mirror, American, 9½in.
high. (Christie's) $1,500

A 19th century miniature,
Empire mahogany and pain-
ted chest-of-drawers, American,
19½in. wide. $1,500

19th century miniature
painted side chair, American,
9¾in. high.
(Christie's) $500

A painted miniature pine blanket chest, attributed to Joseph
Long Lehn, Pennsylvania, circa 1890, decorated with floral
decals and landscapes, 8½in.
wide. (Christie's) $1,500

An American, 19th century, miniature painted bannister-back armchair, 9½in. high. (Christie's) $800

Late 19th century miniature Chippendale walnut slant-front desk, American, 7¼in. high. (Christie's) $2,500

A 19th century painted miniature ladder-back armchair, American. $400

A fine miniature roll-top desk, early 20th century in neoclassical style, opening to reveal seven drawers, some inlaid with satinwood obelisques and ebony fences, 25in. high. (Sotheby's) $2,743

Paint decorated child's chest of drawers, America, circa 1840, top surfaces painted with compôte of fruit, wreathed landscape reserves and floral sprays, 20in. wide. (Skinner) $862

A Federal cherrywood and curly maple miniature one-drawer side table, New England, circa 1825, on ring-and-spirally-turned legs, 10¼in. wide. (Sotheby's) $575

A miniature Chippendale mahogany desk and bookcase, Rhode Island, 1760-80, 16in. high. (Christie's) $3,200

A miniature William and Mary dower-chest, New England, 1710–1725, on four ball and baluster-turned feet, 12¼in. wide. (Christie's) $4,620

A miniature Federal secretary, America, circa 1830, 13½in. wide. $4,000

A Federal carved giltwood looking glass, New York, 1785–1800, the giltwood foliate carved urn flanked by scrolled swags with bowed corners and hanging swags above a molded rectangular frame, with gadrooned edge enclosing a glass plate over a foliate and leaf carved pendant base, 52 x 23½in.
(Christie's) $14,950

Giltwood carved girandole mirror, England or America, 19th century, with eagle, diaper patterned plinth and leafage, 40in. high.
(Skinner) $920

American Chippendale mirror, with scrolled pediment, apron and ears, 18¹/₂ × 12in.
(Eldred's) $605

American Sheraton two-part mirror, in mahogany with carved crest and reeded and ribbed columns, 44 × 22in.
(Eldred's) $357

A Chippendale parcel-gilt mahogany looking glass, labeled by John Elliott, Philadelphia, Pennsylvania, 1753-1761, the rectangular frame with serpentine gilded and carved border, 56in high.
(Christie's) $7,475

A Federal carved ebonised mahogany dressing glass with drawers, Boston, Massachusetts, circa 1820, the mirror plate pivoting between reeded and scrolled uprights, 20³/₄in. wide.
(Sotheby's) $1,100

A Chippendale mahogany looking glass, American 1760-1780, the rectangular frame with gilt and carved mirror edge surmounted by an arched top, 45¹/₄in. high.
(Christie's) $1,610

A fine Federal inlaid and parcel gilt mahogany wall mirror, New York, circa 1795, surmounted by an urn with spray of flowers and wheat ears, height 53¹/₄in.
(Sotheby's) $24,150

A rare red-painted carved pine wall mirror, New England, 1740–80, the shaped crest decorated with incised stylised leaves above a molded slip, 18in. high.
(Sotheby's) $6,325

A Federal mahogany and giltwood mirror, New York, 1780–1800, the molded and gilded swan's-neck pediment with rosettes centering a lobed urn with flowers, 57¹/₂in high.
(Christie's) $3,680

A Chippendale figured mahogany mirror, American, second half 18th century, the arched scrolling crest flanked by shaped ears, 12½in. wide. (Sotheby's) **$1,380**

A Neo-Grec giltwood console mirror, New York City, 1870–90, the broken pediment centering a bust-carved cartouche, 88in. high. (Christie's) **$5,175**

Painted Chippendale mirror, New England, mid 18th century, the shaped crest over molded and incised frame, 19¾in. high. (Skinner Inc.) **$6,000**

A good classical giltwood and part-ebonised convex four-light girandole, New York, circa 1825, surmounted by a spreadwing eagle finial, 48in. high. (Sotheby's) **$10,350**

An Empire ebonized, giltwood and eglomisé mirror, American, late 19th century, the steamship 'Citizen' above a rectangular glass plate, 29 x 13½in. (Christie's) **$2,875**

A classical giltwood convex mirror, American, early 19th century, the black-painted and carved spreadwing eagle perched on a plinth above a circular reeded frame, 45in. high. (Christie's) **$7,150**

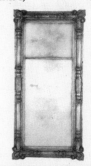

Classical giltwood looking glass, Continental, early 19th century, the projecting molded cornice hung with spherules, 48½in. high. (Skinner Inc.) **$1,100**

A Tramp Art mirror, Forked River, New Jersey, late 19th/early 20th century, the cyma-curved and shaped top centering an applied sawtooth boss, 56in. high. (Christie's) **$2,300**

A classical giltwood pier mirror, American, 1810–20, the rectangular frame headed at each corner with applied fleurs-de-lys, 61½in. high. (Christie's) **$1,955**

Mahogany inlaid and gilt gesso looking glass, probably New England, circa 1790, old surface, 37.5in. high.
(Skinner) $1,150

A 19th century Federal gilt-wood girandole mirror, 54½in. high, 40in. wide.
(Christie's) $8,000

Federal gilt gesso looking glass, labeled *E. Lothrop, Boston,* circa 1820, original condition, 14¼in. wide.
(Skinner) $632

Classical giltwood mirror, America, second quarter, 19th century, the projecting molded cornice hung with acorn spherules above a tablet, 55in. high.
(Skinner Inc.) $3,750

A rare Chippendale carved mahogany dressing mirror, Boston, 1765–1775, with molded and gilt frame between two canted double-bead molded supports, 16³/₈in. high.
(Christie's) $6,250

A Chippendale mahogany and giltwood mirror, labeled by James Musgrove, Philadelphia, circa 1780, the pierced and scrolled pediment centering a carved phoenix, 30in. high.
(Christie's) $3,500

New Hampshire mirror timepiece, Abiel Chandler, Concord, New Hampshire, circa 1830, ebonized and gold painted split baluster case with eight-day weight driven brass movement.
(Skinner) $11,500

A fine Federal inlaid maple and mahogany dressing mirror, Philadelphia, 1800-1810, on ogee bracket feet, 22½in. wide.
(Christie's) $1,600

Federal gilt gesso looking glass, probably Massachusetts, circa 1815, standing figure of America, flanked by eglomisé tablet of urns of flowers, 16in. wide.
(Skinner) $9,775

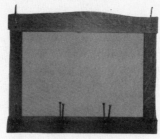

A Federal giltwood and verre eglomisé mirror, Boston, Massachusetts, 1790–1810, a large rectangular verre eglomisé panel painted with a romantic landscape, 48½in.
(Christie's) $4,500

A Gustav Stickley hall mirror, style no. 66, circa 1905-06, 28in. high, 36in. wide. (Skinner Inc.) $2,000

Federal gilt gesso looking glass, cornice with spheres above the reverse painted tablet of two children dancing, 13½in. wide.
(Skinner) $1,150

A painted and carved Federal courting mirror, painted in old red and black with yellow ocher, circa 1820, 12in. high.
(Skinner) $5,000

A classical carved pine giltwood convex mirror, possibly New York, circa 1825, the spreadwing eagle above a spherule-mounted circular frame, 4ft. 4in. high.
(Sotheby's) $3,162

A red-painted mirror, Pennsylvania, early 19th century, rectangular, with split-baluster and cornerblocks enclosing a conforming looking glass, 11⅝ x 9½in.
(Christie's) $978

A very rare red-japanned pine small wall mirror, England or Boston, Massachusetts, circa 1735, the shaped crest centering an exotic bird, 17½in. high.
(Sotheby's) $10,350

A red-painted pine wall mirror, American, 18th century, the arched and peaked crest above a rectangular mirror plate, 15in. high.
(Sotheby's) $4,887

Chippendale mahogany looking glass, labeled Peter Grinnell & Son, Providence, Rhode Island, early 19th century, 39in. high.
(Skinner Inc.) $700

A Federal mahogany veneered looking glass, American, 1800–1815, the broken swan's neck
pediment above a veneered and string-inlaid tympanum centered by an inlaid acorn, flanked by
inlaid plinths surmounted by brass urn finials, over a rectangular mirror flanked by freestanding
colonettes on an inlaid base, 21½in. high, 14in. wide.
(Christie's) $6,325

Mahogany dressing glass, America or England, circa 1790, the scrolled crest above a molded frame and mirror plate on tapering stiles, 13¹/₄in. wide. (Skinner)   **$518**

A Federal gilt three-part overmantel looking glass, English, 1800–1810, of Palladian triptych form divided by two clustered columns, 55¹/₂in. wide. (Christie's)   **$2,300**

A classical mahogany pier mirror, New York, 1825-1830, the cove molded pediment with outset corners, 17⁷/₈in. wide. (Christie's)   **$4,025**

A Federal gilt looking glass, American or English, 1800–1810, with carved ebonized crossed ferns tied with rope and tassels surmounted by a star, flanked by ebonized figures, 20in. wide. (Christie's)   **$2,300**

A classical gold and silver parcelgilt carved dolphin looking glass, New York, 1815–1825, with articulated vert antique scales and gilt cornucopia scrolled tails, 31in. wide. (Christie's)   **$23,000**

A Federal gilt and eglomise panel looking glass, Providence, Rhode Island, 1800–1810, centering an eglomise panel decorated with swags of flowers and leaves centering an eagle medallion over a beveled glass, 15⁵/₈in. wide. (Christie's)   **$7,475**

A fine classical carved and gilded pine cornucopia mirror, American, probably New England, early 19th century, 36in. high. (Sotheby's)   **$19,550**

A late Federal painted and stenciled pine frame with mirror, American, mid 19th century, 17in. high. (Sotheby's)   **$690**

A Federal gilt and carved girandole looking glass, American or English, 1810-1815, the concave frame surmounted by a carved eagle, 53in. high. (Christie's)   **$16,100**

Giltwood looking glass, America, second quarter 19th century, 52in. high.
(Skinner Inc.) $1,750

A table top mirror on shoe foot base, by Gustav Stickley, circa 1910, 21¼in. high.
(Skinner) $1,250

Federal giltwood and eglomisé looking glass, America, early 19th century, 58¾in. high.
(Skinner Inc.) $1,500

Federal carved giltwood and eglomisé looking glass, Baltimore, circa 1801, the molded cornice with gilt spherules above white reverse painted on glass panels, 42½in. high.
(Skinner) $18,400

A Federal carved giltwood convex mirror, American, early 19th century, with carved spreadwing eagle perched on a rocky plinth flanked by scrolled leafage above a cylindrical molded frame, 34in. high.
(Christie's) $5,000

A Federal eglomisé and figured maple looking glass, New England, 19th century, the rectangular frame with outset squared corners above an eglomisé panel, 33¾ x 19in.
(Christie's) $1,840

A Federal eglomisé looking glass, Pennsylvania, 19th century, the rectangular frame enclosing a rectangular eglomisé panel depicting a landscape.
(Christie's) $690

A late Federal mahogany shaving mirror, William Fisk, Boston, Massachusetts, 1810–1825, swiveling between baluster and ring-turned supports with ball finials above a rectangular case, 24in high.
(Christie's) $1,250

Federal gilt gesso looking glass, possibly Massachusetts, circa 1810, cornice with applied spiral molding and foliate banding, 45in. high.
(Skinner) $2,415

Federal giltwood looking glass, America, first quarter 19th century, with eglomisé tablet of "Harmony", 46in. high.
(Skinner Inc.) $3,750

Shop-O'-The Crafters mahogany wall mirror, Ohio, 1910, 27½in. high, 30½in. wide.
(Skinner) $1,500

Federal giltwood looking glass, America, early 19th century, projecting molded cornice hung with spherules, 45in. high.
(Skinner Inc.) $600

A classical giltwood mirror, probably Boston, 1805–1830, the broken molded cornice hung with acorns over a frieze centered by a fruiting grape vine flanked by ogee-arched niches, 67¹/₂in. high.
(Christie's) $6,500

Federal mahogany carved and mahogany veneer dressing stand, Boston or Salem, Massachusetts, 1800–15, with flanking C-scrolled brackets with brass mounts and reeding, 21in. wide.
(Skinner) $2,415

A Federal giltwood verre eglomisé mirror, probably Boston, 1810–1820, with broken molded cornice above a frieze with vines and berries flanked by flowerheads over an eglomisé panel depicting a naval hero, 21in. wide.
(Christie's) $2,250

A gilt pier mirror, probably American, 1815-1825, the broken rectangular cornice hung with acorn pendants, 58in. high.
(Christie's) $2,750

Giltwood mirror, probably Philadelphia, circa 1830, half round colonnettes ornamented with raised floral baskets, 32½ x 22in.
(Skinner) $750

Labeled Federal giltwood and eglomisé mirror, Cermenati & Monfrino, Boston, circa 1806, tablet with naval engagement, 32¹/₄ x 17in.
(Skinner Inc.) $800

Classical giltwood looking glass, America, circa 1830, 39¹/₂in. high.
(Skinner) $660

Limbert hall mirror, no. 22, circa 1910, oak frame with slats at each side of mirror, seven copper hooks, branded mark, 23¹/₂in. high.
(Skinner) $990

Federal mahogany veneered inlaid and parcel gilt looking glass, England/America, late 18th century, 57in. high.
(Skinner Inc.) $27,500

A Federal gilt looking glass with eglomisé panel, American, 1800-1810, the rectangular frame with overhanging cornice above an eglomisé panel, 39in. high.
(Christie's) $3,220

A gilt girandole mirror, American, 1820–1830, surmounted by an ebonised eagle on a rocky plinth flanked by acanthus leaves, the coved mirror frame hung with spherules, 30¹/₄in. high.
(Christie's) $15,400

A classical carved giltwood verre églomisé mirror, New York, 1815–1825, the broken molded pediment above a verre églomisé panel depicting a tropical island and a ship, 47in. high.
(Christie's) $1,650

A classical diminutive gilt and carved girandole looking glass, American or English, 1810–1820, the circular frame punctuated with gilt spheres, 27¹/₂in. high.
(Christie's) $6,325

A late Federal stenciled pine frame with mirror, American, mid 19th century, with gilt stencil stylized floral and fruit motifs, 17in. x 13in.
(Sotheby's) $690

A Federal carved and gilt girandole looking glass, American, or English, 1810-1815, the concave frame decorated with spheres and reeded ebony rim, 35in high.
(Christie's) $2,990

A Queen Anne walnut looking glass, American or English, 1750–1770, the upward scrolling pediment centering a hollow reserve with giltwood phoenix flanked by scrolled ears over a cove-molded rectangular frame centering a rectangular plate with narrow gilt surround, on a shaped pendant base, 27½in. high, 16¼in. wide.
(Christie's)

$2,300

Peloupet, Pelton & Company Victorian rosewood melodian, 19th century, 54in. long, rectangular with rounded corners, lift top.
(Du Mouchelles) $350

Classical rosewood veneer and stenciled pianoforte, Philadelphia, 1825-37, with gilded tablet inscribed *Loud Brother–Philadelphia*, 70in. wide.
(Skinner) $2,070

A classical carved mahogany and rosewood pianoforte, signed *Daniel Thomas Warrented: 87 New York*, 1815–1825, the rectangular inlaid top with rounded corners, above a conforming rosewood case with mahogany panels, 68in. wide.
(Christie's) $3,680

Chickering mahogany baby grand piano, circa 1926, 64in. long, having Ampico mechanism, Hepplewhite style case, with bench.
(Du Mouchelles) $3,000

Starck, Art Deco style mahogany spinet piano, circa 1950, 58in. wide.
(Du Mouchelles) $500

Cable Midget spinet of Chicago, rosewood piano, circa 1950, raised on square pillar supports.
(Du Mouchelles) $500

American Victorian rosewood spinet piano, mid 19th century, 46in. wide, by Geo. A. Prince & Co. of Buffalo, New York.
(Du Mouchelles) $500

Baldwin mahogany spinet piano, circa 1970, 40½in. high, 58in. wide, 25in. deep, having tapered fluted legs with matching bench.
(Du Mouchelles) $1,000

Weber-Aeolian walnut reproducer grand piano, 1929, French case with curved cabriole legs with floral carvings.
(Du Mouchelles) $3,000

Marshall and Wendell mahogany baby grand Ampico player piano, 1925, Hepplewhite style case, serial #104032, 56in. wide, 60in. long.
(Du Mouchelles) $2,500

Classical mahogany inlaid square pianoforte, by Alpheus Babcock, Boston, circa 1820, with rosewood and stamped brass inlays, 66in. wide.
(Skinner) $4,140

A classical inlaid mahogany and brass-inlaid pianoforte, Gibson and Davis, New York, active 1810–1820, the base attributed to Duncan Phyfe, 71¼in. wide.
(Christie's) $16,100

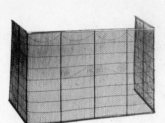

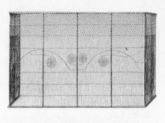

A Federal brass-mounted iron and wirework folding fire screen, probably New York, circa 1810, the hinged tripartite screen surmounted by a domed brass cap, width closed 38¼in. (Sotheby's) $3,162

A Chippendale carved and figured mahogany adjustable firescreen, New England, circa 1770, on peaked downswept legs ending in slipper feet, diameter 22in. (Sotheby's) $4,600

A good Federal brass and wirework folding firescreen, probably New York, circa 1800, of rectangular form with hinged wings beneath convex brass cap, 36in. wide. (Sotheby's) $2,587

Arts and Crafts fireplace screen, circa 1910, triptych design comprised of three repousse copper panels decorated with stylized fish and naturalistic motifs, in hammered copper and riveted frame, 38in. wide. (Skinner Inc.) $650

A pair of classical parcel-gilt firescreens, possibly New York, 19th century, each with an urn finial over a cylindrical shaft, 59⅜in. high. (Christie's) $5,750

Paint decorated three- paneled folding screen, America, 19th century, each section decorated with rocaille and a laden compote within scrolled border, 5ft. high. (Skinner Inc.) $420

A fine and rare Chippendale inlaid and parcel-gilt carved mahogany firescreen, Salem, Massachusetts, circa 1780, width of screen 19½in. (Sotheby's) $2,875

A hammered copper and wire pictorial firescreen, attributed to Thomas Molesworth, Shoshone Furniture Company, Cody, Wyoming, circa 1935, 42¼in. wide. (Sotheby's) $3,737

Federal style mahogany pole screen, circa 1940, with 19th century needlework, needlepoint panel depicting shepherdess with sheep. (Du Mouchelles) $300

Painted three panel floor screen, depicting an elephant family moving through the jungle, signed *Ernest Brierly*, 8ft. wide. (Skinner Inc.) $3,130

A Federal mahogany fire screen, New England, circa 1800, the ball finial above a flaring shaft fitted with an adjustable shield-form screen, 4ft. 6in. high. (Sotheby's) $1,495

Painted pine fireboard, possibly Central Massachusetts, circa 1815, depicting fruit and flowering boughs in a vase, 37½in. wide. (Skinner Inc.) $32,500

A three-sectioned oak screen, by Gustav Stickley, circa 1913, each panel 21½in. wide, 66in. high. (Skinner) $12,500

A late Federal rosewood firescreen, probably Boston, mid-19th century, with three hinged rectangular panels over trestle supports with hipped downswept legs, 40½in. high. (Christie's) $1,650

An inlaid oak three-paneled screen, designed by Harvey Ellis for Gustav Stickley, circa 1903-04, 66¾in. high, each panel 20in. wide. (Skinner) $30,000

An early Gustav Stickley leather fire-screen, 1902, 35in. high, 31in. wide. (Skinner) $3,100

Classical rosewood carved and rosewood grained parcel-gilt ormolu mounted firescreen, probably New York, circa 1830, 38in. high. (Skinner) $21,850

A wrought-iron and pierced copper fire-screen, circa 1900, 34½in. wide. (Skinner) $400

A Queen Anne carved mahogany desk-and-bookcase, Boston, 1745–1755, in two parts; the upper section with molded swan's neck pediment terminating in carved rosettes centering acanthus-carved and reeded urn-and-flame finials above a tympanum centering an applied shell over two arched fielded paneled cupboard doors opening to an interior with two concave volute-carved shells above rows of valanced pigeonholes and document slots, the lower section with mid-molding over a slant-lid opening to a fitted interior, all over a block-front case fitted with four graduated long drawers with cockbeaded surrounds above a molded base, on shaped bracket feet, with brass side carrying handles, 41½in. wide. (Christie's) $51,750

A Provincial George I carved oak double bonnet-top bureau bookcase, first quarter 18th century, on cabriole legs ending in square pad feet, 36in. wide. (Sotheby's) **$2,530**

Small painted poplar secretary desk, possibly Western New York, circa 1850, 35in. wide. (Skinner) **$2,750**

A paint-decorated secretary bookcase, signed *R. Cahoon*, Santuit, Massachusetts, dated *1947*, in two parts, 42in. wide. (Sotheby's) **$17,250**

An antique American Renaissance Revival figured walnut cylinder desk and bookcase, the top member with architectural pediment, circa 1880, 8ft. 1in. high. (Selkirk's) **$2,500**

A Queen Anne figured mahogany block-front bonnet-top secretary-bookcase, Boston, Massachusetts, 1750–75, in two parts, 40in. wide. (Sotheby's) **$255,500**

The Edward Jackson parcel-gilt inlaid and figured mahogany mirrored bonnet-top secretary bookcase, Boston, Massachusetts, 1738–48, 39¾in. wide. (Sotheby's) **$1,432,500**

A fine Queen Anne figured cherrywood bonnet-top secretary bookcase, New England, probably Connecticut, 1750–70, in two parts, 38in. wide. (Sotheby's) **$31,050**

An Empire carved mahogany secretary bookcase, New York, 1820–1830, the upper section with a pair of Gothic mullioned glazed doors, 46½in. wide. (Christie's) **$6,325**

Cherry slant-front secretary, surmounted by broken arch pediment, bonnet top, carved intaglio sunburst crest, American, 18th century, 39½in. wide. (Schrager) **$2,000**

CHIPPENDALE

Chippendale mahogany carved desk bookcase, Newport, Rhode Island, circa 1760, the top section with molded swan's neck cresting, 39in. wide. (Skinner) $56,350

A Chippendale carved and figured walnut secretary bookcase, Pennsylvania, circa 1770, in two parts, on ogee bracket feet, 39in. wide. (Sotheby's) $24,150

Chippendale mahogany carved desk and bookcase, Boston area, 1770–1800, the scrolled pediment with carved rosettes above cyma curved paneled doors, 40³/₈in. wide. (Skinner) $14,950

A Chippendale carved cherrywood secretary bookcase, New England, probably Connecticut, circa 1780, in two parts, the upper section with shaped cornice, 44in. wide. (Sotheby's) $5,462

A Chippendale mahogany desk and bookcase, possibly Charleston, S. Carolina, 1760-90, 53in. wide, 109in. high. (Christie's) $250,000

A Chippendale mahogany desk-and-bookcase, Massachusetts, 1760–1780, the upper section with a pair of scalloped paneled doors opening to an interior fitted with shelves, 39³/₄in. wide. (Christie's) $21,850

Chippendale cherry desk and bookcase, Connecticut, late 18th century, refinished, replaced brasses, 36¹/₄in. wide. (Skinner Inc.) $3,150

A Chippendale block front desk and bookcase in two sections, Mass., 1760-80, 40½in. wide. $50,000

A Chippendale figured cherrywood secretary bookcase, Connecticut, circa 1780, in two parts, on ogee bracket feet, 38in. wide. (Sotheby's) $4,312

SECRETARIES

Empire two-part secretary, in mahogany veneers, upper section with two glazed cathedral doors, 40in. wide. (Eldred's) **$1,595**

A fine and rare Classical mahogany and bird's eye maple secrétaire à abattant, Philadelphia, 1820-1830, on acanthus carved lion's paw feet, 36½in. wide. **$55,000**

A classical mahogany and satinwood desk-and-bookcase, New York, dated *August 29, 1816*, on beehive reeded baluster feet with brass ferrule castors, 46½in. wide. (Christie's) **$17,250**

American classical mahogany secretary bookcase, New York, circa 1825, in two parts, the upper carcase with a later triangular pediment above cabinet doors with gathered silk panels, width 38¾in. (Butterfield & Butterfield) **$4,025**

A classical carved mahogany writing table-and-bookcase, Anthony H. Jenkins, Baltimore, Maryland, 1837-1840, the upper section with glazed bookcase doors centering anthemion and foliate-carved mullions, 46in wide. (Christie's) **$8,625**

A classical figured maple inlaid and mahogany veneered cherrywood secretary bookcase, American, probably New York or New England, circa 1830, in three parts, on vase and ring-turned feet, 46¼in. wide. (Sotheby's) **$8,050**

A Classical rosewood desk and bookcase, probably Boston 1825-1835, on flaring hex-agonally faceted legs above a shaped medial shelf, 50½in wide. (Christie's New York) **$17,000**

Classical mahogany and mahogany veneer glazed desk/bookcase, New England, circa 1830, the flat molded cornice above two glazed doors, 45½in. wide. (Skinner) **$4,600**

A fine and rare Classical secretaire bookcase, New York, 1822-1838, the double glazed cupboard doors with gothic pattern mahogany and gilt-wood muntins, 58in. wide. (Christie's New York) **$50,000**

301

FEDERAL

Country Federal grain painted secretary desk, second-quarter 19th century, with faux mahogany grained interior, 39½in. wide.
(Skinner Inc.) $8,400

A Federal mahogany secretary with glazed panel doors above a fold-down writing surface, circa 1795, 40in. wide. $12,500

Federal cherry desk and bookcase, Southern New England, early 19th century, two-shelved divided upper interior, 41½in. wide.
(Skinner Inc.) $4,150

Important American Federal secretary, New York State, circa 1800–20, in mahogany, upper section with scrolled and inlaid cornice above two astragal glazed doors, 43in. wide.
(Eldred's) $14,300

An American maple Federal secretaire bookcase, the raised cornice with three urn finials above a pair of arched glazed doors, with hinged baize-lined writing slope below, 19th century, 31in. wide.
(Christie's) $4,500

A fine and rare Federal diminutive satinwood-inlaid mahogany cylinder-front secretary/bookcase, Philadelphia or Baltimore, circa 1805, supported on line-inlaid square tapering legs, 36in. wide.
(Sotheby's) $75,000

A good Federal polychrome-decorated brass-mounted mahogany-lined cherrywood linen press, New York or New Jersey, circa 1795, in two parts, 4ft. wide.
(Sotheby's) $8,740

A fine and rare Federal inlaid and figured mahogany secretary bookcase, attributed to John Shaw, Annapolis, Maryland, circa 1795, in three parts, 42in. wide.
(Sotheby's) $19,550

Federal cherry inlaid desk and bookcase, Middle Atlantic States, circa 1810, the upper case with open sectioned beaded shelves, 40.25in. wide.
(Skinner) $3,105

A Federal inlaid mahogany secretary-desk, attributed to John Seymour and Son, Boston, 1794–1809, in two parts; the upper section with a rectangular top with band inlaid edge above a conforming case fitted with inlaid tambour doors punctuated by inlaid fluted pilasters opening to reveal an interior fitted with arched pigeonholes with ivory line and oval inlay over two short drawers above a short drawer; the lower section with mid-molding and fall-front lined writing surface above a case fitted with three graduated line-inlaid long drawers, 37½in. wide.
(Christie's) $145,500

A Federal mahogany desk-and-bookcase, Massachusetts, 1800–1820, in two sections; the upper
section with a shaped cornice centered by a brass eagle and ball finial flanked by brass urn and
steeple finials above a rectangular molding, over a conforming case fitted with two double-arched
glazed doors opening to a compartmented interior above two short drawers with cockbeaded
surrounds; the lower section with a hinged flip-top writing surface above a rectangular case fitted
with a long drawer with cockbeaded surrounds flanked by lopers, all overhanging two
thumbmolded long drawers, on ring and inverted-baluster turned legs, 37¾in. wide.
(Christie's) $4,600

FEDERAL, NEW ENGLAND

Federal tiger maple desk/
bookcase, New England, circa
1820, 39½in. wide.
(Skinner) $5,000

A good Federal bird's-eye maple
and flame-birch inlaid
mahogany desk and bookcase,
Northeastern Shore, New
England, circa 1815, 41in. wide.
(Sotheby's) $10,350

A good Federal inlaid and
figured mahogany secretary
bookcase, New England, circa
1805, in two parts, 41¼in. wide.
(Sotheby's) $4,025

Federal mahogany veneer
carved and glazed desk
bookcase, New England, 1815–
25, the cornice above glazed
doors opening to movable
shelves.
(Skinner) $1,495

Federal mahogany veneered
glazed secretary, New England,
1830's, interior with four open
compartments above small
drawers, 37½in. wide.
(Skinner Inc.) $2,200

A Federal birch inlaid desk
bookcase, New England, circa
1810, drawer fronts with
mahogany crossbanding,
stringing and bird's eye maple
panels, 38¾in. wide.
(Skinner) $3,737

Federal cherry and flame birch
veneer desk and bookcase, New
England, circa 1815, refinished,
replaced brasses, 40in. wide.
(Skinner Inc.) $4,500

Federal mahogany veneered
glazed secretary, New England,
1830's, interior with four open
compartments above small
drawers, 37½in. wide.
(Skinner Inc.) $2,750

Federal mahogany glazed desk
and bookcase, New England,
circa 1810, refinished, brasses
old replacements, 40½in. wide.
(Skinner Inc.) $2,800

A Federal mahogany veneered inlaid secretary/desk, Mass., circa 1800, 38in. wide. (Skinner) $3,500

Federal mahogany, wavy birch and rosewood inlaid secretary, Massachusetts or New Hampshire, old refinish, brasses appear to be original, 37in. wide. (Skinner) $6,325

A Federal ladies' secretaire, Salem, Massachusetts, 1790–1810, with tambour doors enclosing a compartmented interior, 30½in. wide. (Christie's New York)
$3,300

A Federal inlaid mahogany ladies' writing desk and bookcase, Massachusetts, circa 1805, the lower section with a baize-lined writing flap above a case with three cockbeaded long drawers, on turned tapering legs, 40in. wide. (Sotheby's) $5,175

A Federal inlaid mahogany lady's writing-desk, Boston, 1790–1810, the lower section with applied mid-molding over a hinged felt-lined writing surface above four crossbanded graduated long drawers, on bracket feet, 20in. wide. (Christie's) $11,000

A Federal inlaid mahogany secretary-bookcase, North Shore, Massachusetts, 1790–1810, the shaped cornice flanked by reeded plinths surmounted by two brass urn finials above two glazed cupboard doors with geometric line-inlaid mullions, on French feet, 43in. wide. (Christie's) $15,000

A fine and rare Federal satinwood-inlaid églomisé and ivory-mounted mahogany secretary-bookcase, Boston or North Shore, Massachusetts, circa 1810, 36in. wide. (Sotheby's) $16,100

Federal mahogany and mahogany veneer desk bookcase, Massachusetts, circa 1820, top section with flat molded cornice above two glazed doors, 39in. wide. (Skinner) $2,070

Federal tiger maple and mahogany inlaid desk, Massachusetts, circa 1820, the top section with crossbanded cornice board above two tambour doors, 39¼in. wide. (Skinner) $19,550

FEDERAL, MASSACHUSETTS

A Federal mahogany inlaid desk/bookcase, probably Mass., circa 1800, 37½in. wide. **$6,250**

Federal mahogany inlaid lady's desk, Massachusetts, circa 1790, original brass pulls, 42in. wide. (Skinner) **$4,600**

Federal mahogany veneer glazed desk and bookcase, Massachusetts, 1790–1810, old refinish, 40½in. wide. (Skinner) **$4,600**

A federal flame birchwood-veneered and figured mahogany secretary bookcase, Massachusetts, circa 1800, the lower section with hinged writing flap and four crossbanded graduated long drawers, 40½in. wide. (Sotheby's) **$4,600**

A Federal mahogany and satinwood inlaid secretary bookcase, attributed to the shop of John and Thomas Seymour, Boston, Massachusetts, circa 1800–1815, the top with shaped pediment centering a rectangular panel, 41³/₈in. wide. (Christie's) **$27,600**

Federal mahogany inlaid glazed desk bookcase, probably Massachusetts, circa 1790, shaped gallery with an inlaid central panel above two molded glazed doors, 40in. wide. (Skinner) **$2,990**

A Federal mahogany and mahogany bird's eye maple and wavy birch desk, Massachusetts or New Hampshire, circa 1820, refinished, 41¼in. wide. (Skinner) **$1,725**

A Federal inlaid mahogany and eglomise gentleman's desk-and-bookcase, Salem, Massachusetts, 1790–1810, in two sections, on cylindrical tapering legs, 61¼in. wide. (Christie's) **$6,500**

Federal mahogany veneer glazed desk and bookcase, Massachusetts, circa 1820, the pediment above glazed doors with open to shelves and small drawers, 36¼in. wide. (Skinner) **$1,610**

SHERATON

Antique American Sheraton secretary in pine, molded cornice, two glazed doors, writing surface lifts for storage under. (Eldred's) **$750**

Antique American Sheraton cylinder desk, early 19th century, in mahogany and tiger maple veneers, 41½in. wide. (Eldred's) **$2,750**

American late Sheraton one-piece secretary, in cherry with red paint, molded cornice, two tiger maple-paneled doors above two drawers, 36in. wide. (Eldred's) **$770**

Antique American Sheraton blind-front secretary in mahogany, bonnet top, two paneled doors in upper section, rope-turned legs, 37¹/₂in. wide. (Eldred's) **$1,750**

American Sheraton blind-front secretary, Massachusetts, circa 1810–20, in mahogany and mahogany veneers, upper section opens to reveal shelves, drawers and pigeonholes, 40¹/₂in. wide. (Eldred's) **$1,650**

American Sheraton blind-front secretary, in mahogany, scrolled cornice above two blind-front doors with two drawers below, 39¹/₂in. wide. (Eldred's) **$2,640**

American Sheraton/Empire two-part secretary, in mahogany and mahogany veneers, bonnet top with brass urn finials, 37¹/₂in. wide. (Eldred's) **$1,320**

American Sheraton desk, probably northern New England, early 19th century, in cherry, scrolled backsplash with rosettes above three side-by-side drawers, 38¹/₂in. wide. (Eldred's) **$4,840**

American Sheraton two-part blind-front secretary, in mahogany veneers with satinwood inlaid panels, 40in. wide. (Eldred's) **$1,430**

308

A very rare and early Queen Anne carved and part-ebonized and parcel-gilt figured walnut
bonnet-top secretary bookcase, Boston, Massachusetts, circa 1740, in two parts; the upper section
with molded swan's-neck pediment centering a flame and urn-form finial with arched and
mirrored cupboard doors with gilt-slips below opening to a fitted interior; the lower section with
hinged beaded lid opening to a writing surface and an interior with six valanced pigeonholes and
two blocked short drawers below centering a pull-out removable prospect section, 38½in. wide.
(Sotheby's) $8,000

A Queen Anne walnut daybed, Massachusetts, 1730–1740, the yoked crestrail with outscrolled ears above a solid vasiform splat flanked by a moveable frame over an elongated seat on cabriole legs with padded disk feet joined by arrowhead H-stretchers, 24in. wide.
(Christie's) $19,000

A William and Mary blue-green painted turned maple rush-seat daybed, New England, 1720–1760, the back with arched crest and three molded uprights, adjustable, and flanked by two vase-and reel-turned stiles with ball finials, the rush seat raised on vase and ring-turned legs joined by bulbous turned stretchers; painted blue-green, 6ft. long.
(Sotheby's) $3,162

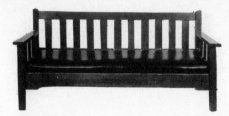

Arts and Crafts settle, with eleven vertical back slats, three slats under arms, 80in. wide. (Skinner) $863

Arts and Crafts settle, circa 1910, crest rail over ten canted vertical back slats, unsigned, 83in. wide. (Skinner) $1,200

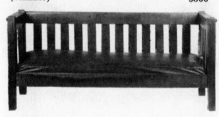

Limbert oak day bed, Michigan, circa 1910, shaped headrest and wide skirt accommodating spring cushions, square raised feet, 79in. long. (Skinner) $800

Lifetime Furniture day bed, Hastings, Michigan, circa 1910, shaped crest rail over nine vertical slats at each end joined by seat and lower rail forming three arches, 77¾in. long. (Skinner) $2,000

Harden oak settle, No. 157, Camden, New York, spring cushion seat, twelve back slats, three side slats under each arm, paper label, 79¾in. long. (Skinner) $1,840

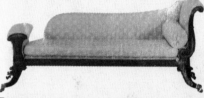

Regency ormolu-mounted grain-painted recamier, circa 1815, the supports mounted with ormolu plumes and foliate scrolls, raised on lobe-carved out-scrolled legs ending in foliate brass feet on casters, 6ft. 4in. wide. (Butterfield & Butterfield) $3,750

A yellow pine daybed, Texas, mid-19th century, rectangular with outwardly flared ends, on square tapering chamfered legs, 77½in. long. (Christie's) $518

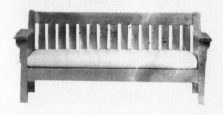

Arts & Crafts oak settle, early 20th century, the rectangular crestrail above fifteen vertical slats over broad arms, 6ft. 6in. long. (Butterfield & Butterfield) $2,875

Rococo Revival rosewood settee, circa 1850–60, 67in. long. (Skinner) **$2,070**

American settee, 19th century, in bird's-eye maple with cane seat and back, 76½in. long. (Eldred's) **$990**

An American Empire carved mahogany sofa, New York, circa 1820, the horizontal bolstered crestrail with foliate-carved terms and upholstered backrest joining outscrolled upholstered armrests, 7ft. 6in. long. (Butterfield & Butterfield) **$2,587**

American Empire mahogany settee, second quarter 19th century, with carved griffin heads, acanthus carved scrolled arms, 60½in. long. (Skinner Inc.) **$1,650**

An antique Baroque Revival walnut chairback settee with three oval padded backrests within carved motifs of scrolls, grapevines, birds and cartouche crestings, 19th century, 68in. wide. (Selkirk's) **$1,250**

Rococo Revival walnut upholstered settee, third-quarter 19th century, grape vine and floral carved serpentine molded crest rail, raised on cabriole legs, 66in. wide. (Skinner Inc.) **$1,380**

Modern velvet upholstered sofa, pale salmon velvet upholstery, stepped, tapering black finished wood feet, unsigned, 84in. long. (Skinner) **$1,500**

Antique American Hepplewhite eight-leg sofa, with line inlay and striped red satin upholstery, 72in. long. (Eldred's) **$1,980**

Late 19th century rococo Revival rosewood settee, N. Schott, America, 65in. wide.
$1,250

Sheraton sofa, in mahogany with scrolled arms and turned legs, 72in. long.
(Eldred's)
$825

American Victorian Renaissance Revival carved rosewood settee, circa 1880, the back in three parts, each elaborate pierced and carved crest set with mother-of-pearl portrait relief, 72in. long.
(William Doyle Galleries)
$1,500

A Victorian rococo laminated rosewood canapé, mid-19th century, by John Henry Belter, with an arched padded back, scrolling padded arms and a serpentine padded seat, 71in. wide.
(Christie's)
$1,725

A William and Mary style couch, York, Maine, with adjustable wings, with two upholstered foot stools, 95in. wide.
(Christie's)
$3,220

An American mahogany scroll end sofa, the back with ribbon-tied laurel-leaf toprail, the scroll end with eagle's head terminals, mid 19th century, possibly Philadelphia, 81in. wide.
(Christie's)
$2,500

American Empire-style sofa, 19th century, in mahogany with allover carved decoration, bowed crestrail, scrolled arms, and paw feet, gold upholstery, 88in. long.
(Eldred's)
$1,045

Renaissance Revival parcel-gilt maple settee and armchair, third quarter 19th century,.
(Skinner)
$6,050

Victorian cast iron garden bench, in vintage design, painted white, 42in. long. (Eldred's) $440

Painted Windsor settle, New England, early 19th century, with early mustard paint and natural arms, 98in. wide. (Skinner) $1,265

A late 19th century Rococo Revival rosewood sofa, impressed *Gentso*?, America, 84in. wide. (Skinner) $800

A rococo Revival laminated rosewood settee, attributed to John Henry Belter, New York, circa 1855, 66in. wide. (Skinner) $12,000

An extremely rare William and Mary turned and joined walnut settle bench, Southeastern Pennsylvania, 1700–1730, the tall square back with molded crest flanked by stiles with shaped tops, 5ft. 8in. long. (Sotheby's) $60,000

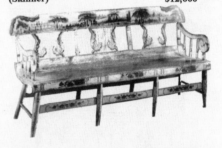

A cream-painted and polychrome-decorated plank-seat settee and four matching side chairs, Pennsylvania, circa 1825, the settee with horizontal crest with shaped ears, 6ft. long. (Sotheby's) $4,025

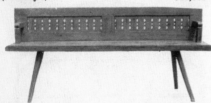

A 19th century veranda settle in the American style with pierced back, jointed arms and stick legs, 73in. wide. (Boardmans) $760

Painted and carved country sofa, probably Pennsylvania, 19th century, original olive green paint, 73¹/₂in. wide. (Skinner Inc.) $2,100

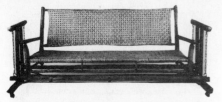

Rare old hickory swing settee, original finish, webbing in excellent condition, 90in. wide.
(Skinner) $6,612

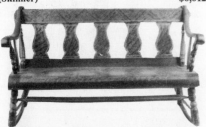

Grain painted rocking settee, New England, 1830–40, burnt orange and black splats outlined in gold striping, natural maple arms, original surface, 50½in. wide.
(Skinner) $9,900

High-backed settle, New England, 1750-1800, the back with tongue and groove boarding, plank seat, 64½in. wide.
(Skinner) $1,840

J. M. Young oak settle, Camden, New York, original medium finish and leather upholstered spring cushion, 78½in. long.
(Skinner) $4,000

Important cast iron garden bench, 19th century, in fern design, pierced shaped back, old lime-green paint, possibly from Cornwall, NY foundry.
(Eldred's) $2,310

J. M. Young oak settle, No. 3701, medium finish, original spring cushion, stenciled model number, 67¾in. long.
(Skinner) $750

Federal carved mahogany triple chairback settee, early 19th century, the triple shield back with carved and pierced urn-shaped splats with outstretched shaped arms, 4ft. 6in. wide.
(Butterfield & Butterfield) $3,800

Roycroft 'Ali Baba' bench, circa 1910, oak slab seat with some exposed bark underneath, plank ends joined by long center stretcher, 42in. long.
(Skinner) $2,060

CHIPPENDALE

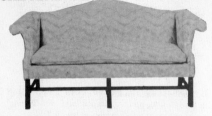

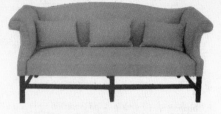

A Chippendale style stained maple sofa on molded Marlborough legs, 76in. long.
$5,000

A Chippendale upholstered sofa, the serpentine back flanked by outward flaring arms, circa 1780, 80in. long.
$7,000

A Chippendale mahogany serpentine-back sofa, Philadelphia, 1765-1785, the canted serpentine peaked camel back flanked by out-scrolling canted arms, 109½in. wide.
(Christie's) **$300,000**

A Chippendale carved mahogany camel-back sofa, late 18th century, on molded square tapering legs joined by a recessed stretcher, 7ft. 6in. wide.
(Sotheby's) **$5,000**

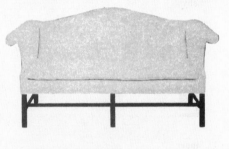

A George III giltwood small sofa in the manner of Thos. Chippendale, the back and seat covered in blue and white floral printed cotton, 58in. wide.
$6,000

A Chippendale style stained maple sofa on molded Marlborough legs, upholstered in ivory striped damask, 76in. long.
(Christie's) **$4,500**

A Chippendale mahogany camel-back sofa, New England, circa 1785, the serpentine upholstered back flanked by downsloping outscrolled arms, on square tapering legs joined by stretchers, 7ft. 6in. long. **(Sotheby's)** **$9,200**

A fine Chippendale mahogany camel-back sofa, Philadelphia, Pennsylvania, circa 1775, on square legs joined by stretchers, 8ft. ½in. long.
(Sotheby's) **$17,250**

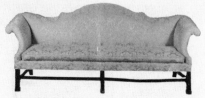

A Chippendale mahogany serpentine-back sofa on Marlborough legs with blocked feet joined by stretchers, Phila., 1765-85, 109½in. wide.
$650,000

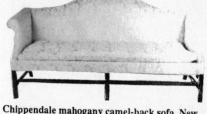

Chippendale mahogany camel-back sofa, New York, 18th century, refinished, 76in. wide. (Skinner Inc.)
$10,300

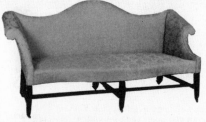

A very fine Chippendale carved mahogany sofa, Philadelphia, circa 1770, having an arched back, flanked by dramatically out-scrolled and sloped arms, 7ft. 6in. wide.
(Sotheby's)
$30,000

A fine Chippendale mahogany sofa, Philadelphia, 1765–1785, with serpentine arched and canted back flanked by downward sloping and outward flaring scrolled arms above a straight seatrail, 98in. wide.
(Christie's)
$22,500

A Chippendale mahogany sofa, Philadelphia, 1770–1790, the canted back with serpentine crest flanked by down-sloping outward scrolling arms above a serpentine seatrail, 85½in. wide.
(Christie's)
$45,000

A Chippendale mahogany camel-back sofa, Philadelphia, Pennsylvania, circa 1770, the upholstered and serpentine back flanked by outscrolled arms, 8ft. 5in. long.
(Sotheby's)
$16,100

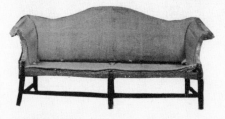

A Chippendale mahogany camel-back sofa, Philadelphia, 1770-1790, the serpentine back with scrolled arms, 89⅝in. wide.
(Christie's)
$32,200

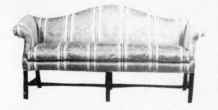

American Chippendale camelback sofa, in mahogany with scrolled arms, molded legs with chamfered inner corners, 84in. long.
(Eldred's)
$5,170

A good Classical carved, figured and stencil-decorated mahogany settee, New York or Boston, circa 1825, the arched tubular crest with acanthus-and volute-carved terminals above a tufted leather upholstered back and seat flanked by cornucopia-form arms, the bolection-molded seatrail below on scrolled, cornucopiae brackets and animal paw feet on casters, stenciled all over with gilt decoration and ebonized highlights, 7ft. 4in. long.
(Sotheby's) $6,325

A good Classical carved and figured mahogany sofa, probably New York or Boston, circa 1825, the horizontal tubular crest with hippocampi terminals, flanked by cornucopia-carved arms centering a semi-overupholstered seat with a bolection molded apron below on fruit-and-flower-carved cornucopia brackets with leaf-carved animal paw feet, 7ft. long.
(Sotheby's) $3,737

CLASSICAL

A Classical carved mahogany and maple veneered sofa, New York, 1815-1825, on carved paw feet, 85½in. wide.
(Christie's)   **$4,000**

A Classical carved and giltwood meridienne, New York, 1825-1835, the scrolling half back carved with a lion's head terminal, 85in. wide. (Christie's New York)   **$6,800**

A fine classical carved mahogany and giltwood récamier, New York, circa 1810, the reeded scrolled arm supports continuing to form a reeded seat rail, on giltwood dolphin feet, 8ft. long.
(Sotheby's)   **$31,050**

A classical carved mahogany sofa, Boston, Massachusetts, circa 1830, the acanthus leaf-carved scrolled and figured crest rail flanked by leaf-carved scrolled arms, 7ft. 4in. long.
(Sotheby's)   **$5,000**

A classical carved mahogany settee, Philadelphia, 1825–1830, the rectangular tablet crest surmounted by a shell and scroll carved cartouche flanked by a cornucopiae-carved serpentine crestrail, 68in. wide.
(Christie's)   **$4,000**

A classical carved mahogany recamier, probably New York, 1825–1835, the scrolled acanthus-carved crest with rosette termini, on cornucopia-carved hairy paw feet fitted with brass castors, 82³/₄in. long.
(Christie's)   **$8,500**

A classical mahogany sofa upholstered in red woven horsehair bordered with brass nails, attributed to Duncan Phyfe, N.Y., circa 1816, 94in. wide. (Christie's)   **$35,000**

A classical upholstered mahogany cylinder arm sofa, circa 1810-30, 72in. long.
(Christie's)   **$1,500**

CLASSICAL

The Salisbury family classical carved mahogany sofa, Isaac Vose & Son, Boston, circa 1820, 88¾in. wide.
(Andrew Hartley) **$25,300**

Classical mahogany and maple veneer sofa, probably Boston, circa 1815, refinished, 80in. wide.
(Skinner Inc.) **$2,250**

A Classical carved mahogany sofa, Boston, 1820-1830, on carved saber legs with leafy feet, 35in. high, 85in. wide (Christie's New York) **$9,500**

Classical mahogany veneered and carved sofa, Boston, circa 1830, embossed green velvet upholstery, old refinish, 72in. wide.
(Skinner Inc.) **$3,500**

Fine small classical carved and parcel gilt mahogany and marble sofa, Philadelphia, circa 1820–1830, on Ionic marble columns with gilt capitals and bases on turned feet, 4ft. 7in. long.
(Butterfield & Butterfield) **$4,800**

A classical carved mahogany sofa, Boston, Massachusetts, circa 1820, the scrolled crest above swan's head-carved arm supports, length 7ft. 1in.
(Sotheby's) **$3,750**

A fine and rare classical brass-inlaid mahogany sofa, attributed to Joseph Barry, Philadelphia, circa 1820, on brass-inlaid saber-legs ending in sleeping lion's head-cast brass caps, length 7ft. 2in.
(Sotheby's) **$25,000**

Classical carved mahogany sofa, New York or Philadelphia, circa 1820, the flaring crest rail continuing to acanthus-carved out-scrolled arms, on cornucopia and wing-carved lion paw feet, length 6ft. 11¼in.
(Butterfield & Butterfield) **$1,955**

CLASSICAL

Classical carved mahogany veneer sofa, North Shore, Massachusetts, 1830–50, upholstered in old stamped velvet, 77in. long.
(Skinner) $1,265

A classical carved mahogany sofa, possibly Boston, 1815–1830, on stylised foliate carved legs with scrolled returns, 86³/₄in. long.
(Christie's) $2,185

Late classical mahogany carved sofa, probably New York, mid 19th century, green and gold silk upholstery, 84in. wide.
(Skinner Inc.) $1,300

Classical Revival carved mahogany veneered upholstered sofa, light green silk watered moreen upholstery, 86¹/₂in. long.
(Skinner Inc.) $1,000

Classical carved mahogany veneer sofa, New York, circa 1820–30, molded veneer crest rail with scrolled arms above leaf carved arm supports, 71¹/₂in. wide.
(Skinner Inc.) $1,900

A fine and rare classical ormolu-mounted carved mahogany sofa, Philadelphia, Pennsylvania, circa 1825, the horizontal reverse-scrolled crest mounted with ormolu masks, 7ft. long.
(Sotheby's) $5,175

Classical carved mahogany sofa, Philadelphia or New York, circa 1815–1820, the foliate carved shaped crest centering a wing spread carved eagle continuing to upholstered out-scrolled arms, length 7ft. 6in.
(Butterfield & Butterfield) $6,325

A classical mahogany sofa, attributed to William King, Jr. (1771–1854), Washington, D.C., the reeded crestrail above a conforming seat flanked by reeded and rosette-carved scrolling arm supports, 90¹/₂in. wide.
(Christie's) $6,325

CLASSICAL

A classical carved mahogany settee, attributed to Duncan Phyfe, 1768–1854, New York, 1820–40, 91½in. long.
(Christie's) $40,250

A classical carved mahogany and mahogany veneer sofa, probably New England, circa 1825, old refinish, 93¼in. wide.
(Skinner) $1,265

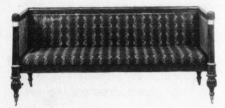

A classical carved mahogany sofa, Boston, 1820–1830, the cylinder crestrail above a quadripartite caned back flanked by caned side with columnar arm supports, 78¾in. wide.
(Christie's) $4,370

A classical carved mahogany sofa, Boston, Massachusetts, circa 1825, the shaped crest with projecting center section with scrolling leaf-carved terminals, 7ft. long.
(Sotheby's) $4,600

Classical carved mahogany veneer small settee, Boston area, third quarter 19th century, with rolled and carved crest, scrolled leaf-carved arms and veneered seat rail, 53½in. wide.
(Skinner) $2,070

A fine classical ormolu-mounted figured mahogany récamier, probably New York, circa 1820, with a reverse-scrolling headrest and shaped, padded backrest, 7ft. 8in. long.
(Sotheby's) $3,450

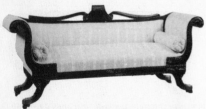

A classical carved mahogany sofa, Baltimore, Maryland, circa 1820, the pierced and reeded crest rail carved with pinwheels and flanked by scrolled arms, 7ft.8in. long.
(Sotheby's) $3,737

An antique American Classical Revival carved mahogany upholstered settee carved with cornucopia and foliate motifs with molded seat rail on paw feet, 7ft. 5in. wide.
(Selkirk's) $2,100

CLASSICAL

Classical mahogany veneer carved sofa, New England, circa 1835, 48in. long.
(Skinner)   **$1,320**

Classical mahogany carved and veneer sofa, possibly Boston, circa 1825, 84in. wide.
(Skinner)   **$2,300**

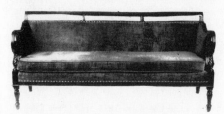

Classical carved mahogany veneer settee, probably Philadelphia, 1810, with scrolled arms and turned legs on castors, 74in. wide.
(Skinner)   **$1,955**

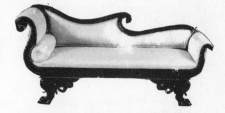

A Classical carved mahogany small recamier, attributed to Quervelle, Philadelphia, circa 1820, on anthemion carved paw feet, 72in. long. (Christie's New York)   **$11,000**

A classical mahogany and parcel-gilt recamier, New York, 1810–1820, with serpentine-molded crestrail terminating in a rosette over a padded back and flaring molded arms carved with rosettes, on gilt foliate bracketed hairy paw legs and casters, 83½in. wide.
(Christie's)   **$4,100**

A fine classical diminutive carved mahogany recamier, probably by Charles White, Philadelphia, circa 1825, on acanthus-carved legs ending in animal paw feet, 65½in. long.
(Sotheby's)   **$4,500**

Classical carved mahogany sofa, Boston, circa 1820–1825, the molded and concave shaped crest terminating in rosette and punchwork scrolls, 6ft. 10in. long.
(Butterfield & Butterfield)   **$1,200**

A classical carved mahogany sofa, New York, circa 1825, the columnar crest with scrolled leaf-carved terminals above scrolled arms, 7ft. 9in. long.
(Sotheby's)   **$2,500**

A Classical carved mahogany sofa, possibly Joseph Meeks and Company (1836–1859), New York City, 1820–1840, the cylindrical downscrolling crest terminating in carved leafage and rosettes above a shaped serpentine upholstered back flanked by upholstered outscrolling arms terminating in carved rosettes over a rectangular seat frame with pulvinated front rail, on cornucopiae carved legs with animal-paw feet, 86⁵/₈in. wide.
(Christie's) $6,325

A fine and rare pair of Classical carved mahogany recamiers, labeled *Charles White, Philadelphia*, circa 1825, each with a scrolled acanthus leaf and roundel-carved crest, the gadrooned seat rail raised on acanthus-carved animal paw feet and brass casters, bearing the label *Charles H. White, Cabinet Warerooms No. 109 Walnut St,* 6ft. long.
(Sotheby's) $11,500

FEDERAL

A Federal carved mahogany sofa, Phila.,
1805-20, 75¾in. long.
(Christie's) **$6,000**

Federal mahogany sofa, New England, circa
1815, 78in. wide.
(Skinner) **$1,500**

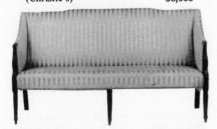

Federal mahogany carved settee, Pennsylvania,
circa 1805, old refinish, blue green striped silk
upholstery, 66in. wide.
(Skinner) **$8,000**

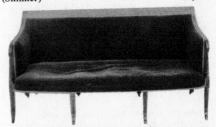

A Federal mahogany sofa on ring turned
reeded legs and brass castors, 75in. long,
circa 1815.
(Skinner) **$8,000**

A Federal mahogany sofa, New England, circa
1825, the arched upholstered back flanked by
reeded baluster-form arm supports, 6ft. 6in.
long.
(Sotheby's) **$5,000**

A rare Federal carved mahogany cane-seat
settee, attributed to Duncan Phyfe or one of his
contemporaries, New York, circa 1815, 6ft. long.
(Sotheby's) **$9,775**

A good Federal mustard-painted and
polychrome-decorated settee, Lehigh County,
Pennsylvania, circa 1820, the shaped tripartite
crest on turned supports, 6ft. 3in.
(Sotheby's) **$1,092**

A Federal mahogany carved sofa, the arched
crest rail with grape and vine decoration,
75in. wide.
(Skinner) **$3,500**

FEDERAL

A Federal mahogany sofa, the padded back with arched crest, 1790-1810, 80¼in. wide.
$8,000

A Federal upholstered mahogany sofa on ring turned and reeded legs, circa 1800-15, 75½in. long.
$10,000

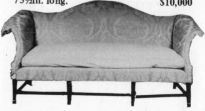

Federal mahogany inlaid sofa, probably Massachusetts, circa 1815, old refinish, 77½in. wide.
(Skinner)
$5,462

A Federal mahogany sofa, New York or Philadelphia, 1785-1810, on square, tapering legs with spade feet, 91in. long. (Christie's New York)
$2,200

A Federal carved mahogany sofa, attributed to Duncan Phyfe or one of his contemporaries, New York, circa 1810, the reversed scrolling horizontal crest carved with a central tablet, 6ft. 2in. long.
(Sotheby's)
$10,350

A late Federal carved mahogany sofa, New York, circa 1825, the upswept crestrail carved with a basket of fruit flanked by griffins and tasseled swags over a padded back, on cornucopia-bracketed paw feet with casters, 86in. wide.
$13,750

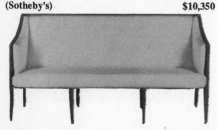

Fine Federal carved mahogany sofa, possibly by Slover and Taylor, New York, circa 1800–1815, on square tapering reeded legs ending in brass and wood wheel casters, 6ft. 6in. long.
(Butterfield & Butterfield)
$17,500

A good Federal carved mahogany sofa, New York, circa 1810, the crest carved with three rectangular reeded panels flanked by reeded downcurving arms, 6ft. 6in. long.
(Sotheby's)
$5,250

FEDERAL

Federal maple inlaid upholstered sofa, probably Maryland, circa 1810, 76in. wide. (Skinner) **$1,540**

Federal mahogany sofa, probably New England, circa 1810, refinished, 80in. long. (Skinner Inc.) **$850**

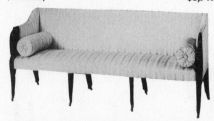

A Federal mahogany sofa, New England, circa 1815, the upholstered back flanked by reeded baluster arm supports, 6ft. 6in. long. (Sotheby's) **$1,840**

A Federal mahogany sofa, the upholstered back and seat with beaded bow front, probably Mass., circa 1810, 73in. wide. **$5,000**

A Federal mahogany sofa, possibly Baltimore, 1790–1810, on square tapering legs with green-painted flower and trailing vine decoration, joined by medial and rear stretchers, 92³/₄in. wide. (Christie's) **$25,000**

A Federal inlaid mahogany sofa-frame, Baltimore, 1790–1810, the serpentine crestrail curving to molded downswept arms above a serpentine seatrail flanked by oval reserves inlaid with shaded foliage over square tapering legs, 78¹/₂in. wide. (Christie's) **$25,000**

A good Federal carved mahogany sofa, Philadelphia, circa 1815, the crest carved with drapery swags, tassels and flowerheads on a punchwork ground, 6ft. 4in. long. (Sotheby's) **$6,000**

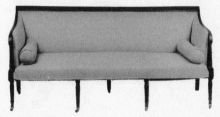

Federal carved mahogany sofa, New York City, circa 1810, with bow knot and sheaves of wheat as well as triglyphs on the crest, reeded arm supports and legs, 78¹/₂in. wide. (Skinner) **$3,450**

FEDERAL

Federal carved mahogany sofa, possibly New England, circa 1800, refinished, 76in. long. (Skinner Inc.) $1,500

A pine upholstered sofa, American, 19th century, the upholstered back and arms raised on tapered block legs, 71in. long. (Sotheby's) $1,265

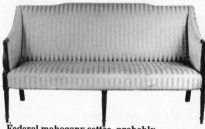

A Feueral mahogany and birchwood settee, New England, probably Massachusetts, early 19th century, on frontal ring-turned tapering legs, 6ft. 4in. long. (Sotheby's) $15,000

Federal mahogany settee, probably Massachusetts, circa 1810, (blue silk upholstery with water stain) 66½in. wide. (Skinner Inc.) $7,100

A Federal carved mahogany sofa, school of Duncan Phyfe, New York, first half 19th century, the crestrail carved with a central panel decorated with a pair of cornucopia, 6ft. 2in. long.
(Sotheby's) $4,600

A Federal carved mahogany sofa, attributed to Slover and Taylor, New York, circa 1795, the horizontal molded crest with projecting fluted tablet, 6ft. 6in. long. (Sotheby's) $9,200

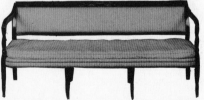

A very fine Federal carved mahogany saber-leg sofa, attributed to Duncan Phyfe, New York, circa 1810, the reeded seat rail on volute-carved and reeded saber legs, 7ft. 6in. long. (Sotheby's) $28,000

A fine Federal carved mahogany sofa, New York or Philadelphia, circa 1810, the paneled crest carved with drapery swags and tassels centering a reserve carved with a bow with arrows, 6ft. 6in. wide. (Sotheby's) $10,500

FEDERAL

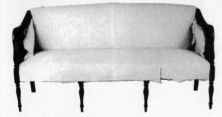

Federal mahogany sofa, New England, early 19th century, old refinish, 74¹/₄in. long. (Skinner Inc.)   **$1,190**

Federal mahogany carved sofa, Salem, Massachusetts, circa 1810, refinished, 75³/₄in. wide. (Skinner Inc.)   **$1,650**

Federal cherry settee, New York, circa 1810, on square tapering legs, with 20th century salmon color stamped moiré, 82in. wide. (Skinner)   **$3,575**

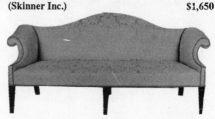

Serpentine upholstered mahogany inlaid sofa, America, 20th century, gold damask upholstery, 84in. wide. (Skinner)   **$19,800**

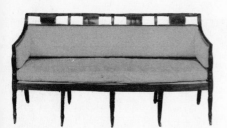

A Federal inlaid mahogany settee, circa 1800, the back with four rectangular crests above an upholstered back rest and arms, 5ft. 11¹/₂in. wide. (Sotheby's)   **$4,500**

Philadelphia camel back sofa, eight legs, circa 1800, with extensive restoration, scroll arms, tight upholstered seat, serpentine front, 76in. long. (Du Mouchelles)   **$3,250**

Federal mahogany inlaid sofa, New Hampshire, circa 1815, attributed to John Gould, Jr., the swelled reeded legs on casters, 79in. wide. (Skinner Inc.)   **$3,400**

A Federal mahogany sofa, New England, 1790–1810, the serpentine crest flanked by downswept outward scrolling arms, with serpentine front seat rail on four rosette-carved and fluted square tapering legs, 91in. wide. (Christie's)   **$4,370**

A Federal figured maple cane-seat settee, New York or New England, circa 1820, the back consisting of two rectangular rails above a caned seat and ring-turned legs joined by stretchers ending in button feet, 6ft. long.
(Sotheby's) $6,900

A Federal inlaid mahogany settee, Philadelphia, 1790–1810, the arched crestrail above an upholstered back flanked by downswept armrests terminating in inlaid handholds over inlaid tapering baluster-turned supports above an upholstered seat with bowed front, on square tapering line and oval inlaid legs, 60in. wide.
(Christie's) $29,900

SPINDLE BACK

Painted Windsor settee, Philadelphia area, 1760–1780, 47in. wide.
(Skinner) $1,540

Maple ash and pine Windsor rod-back settee, stamped *J. Burden, Phila*, early 19th century, 77in. wide.
(Skinner) $3,740

A fine rare green-and red-painted rod-back Windsor settee, probably New Hampshire, 1790-1810, 5ft. 6½in. long.
(Sotheby's) $46,000

Painted and decorated settee, Pennsylvania, early 19th century, the yellow ground with gold and olive-green fruit and floral stencil decoration.
(Skinner) $1,725

Child's painted and decorated settee, America, circa 1840, light green ground with green and yellow pinstriping and pink roses, 24¾in. wide.
(Skinner) $1,620

A turned and painted Windsor knuckle-arm settee, signed by John Wire, Philadelphia, Pennsylvania, 1791–1813, the shaped back above thirty-three tapered spindles, 6ft. 7in. long.
(Sotheby's) $8,050

A turned Windsor settee, American, 1785–1810, the U-shaped back above twenty-nine bulbous spindles, length 6ft. 4¹/₂in.
(Sotheby's) $7,000

Painted and decorated settee, Pennsylvania, early 19th century, all-over light green paint with stencil decoration, 72in. wide.
(Skinner Inc.) $950

SPINDLE BACK

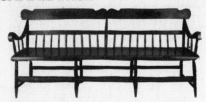

Painted and decorated settee, Pennsylvania, 1830–50, all over old light green paint with stencil decoration and striping, 75¼in. wide. (Skinner Inc.) **$2,200**

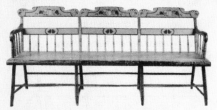

Painted and decorated settee, Pennsylvania, 1830s, with old light green ground paint, accented by gold and green striping, with polychrome fruit stencil decoration, 72in. wide. (Skinner) **$1,955**

A rare turned Windsor sack-back small settee, New England, 1790-1800, the arched crest above thirteen tapered spindles, 42¾in. long. (Sotheby's) **$23,000**

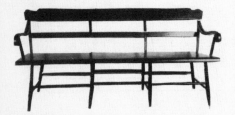

American deacon's bench, Pennsylvania, early 19th century, in brown paint with stenciled decoration, 75in. long. (Eldred's) **$1,430**

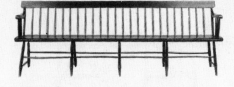

Painted Windsor bench, signed *J.C. Hubbard Boston, J.M. White Boston*, circa 1840, old red stain with black seat, 95in. wide. (Skinner) **$1,955**

Paine Furniture settle, fifteen vertical back spindles, five vertical side spindles, painted black, paper label, 64½in. wide. (Skinner) **$500**

Painted and stencil decorated Windsor day bed, New England, circa 1820's, fold-out hinged sleeping area supported by four wooden pinned legs, allover original yellow paint with gold and black fruit and leaf decoration, fold-out, 49½ x 80⅝in., (Skinner Inc.) **$2,000**

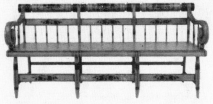

A painted and decorated settee, the rolled crest rail above three slats and twelve spindles, Penn., circa 1825, 76in. long. (Skinner) **$3,400**

A black-painted upholstered Windsor settee, Philadelphia, 1780–1800, the bowed crestrail above twenty nine bamboo-turned spindles over downscrolling arms, each above similarly turned arm supports and four spindles, over an over-upholstered seat, on bamboo-turned legs joined by similar turned H-stretchers, 80in. wide.
(Christie's) $29,900

A Rococo Revival carved rosewood sofa, attributed to John Henry Belter (1804–1863), New York City, 1850–1860, the serpentine crest laminated and pierced with carved C-scrolls, shells, and floral motifs above an upholstered back and continuing to serpentine and molded arms above curved and foliate-carved supports enclosing upholstered sides over an upholstered seat with serpentine front above a conforming frame embellished with relief-carved floral motifs, on similarly carved cabriole legs with scroll feet, 84½in. wide.
(Christie's) $27,600

STICKLEY

L. & J.G. Stickley prairie settle, Fayetteville, New York, circa 1912, no. 220, wide flat arms and crest rail supported by corbels over inset panels, 84½ in. wide.
(Skinner Inc.) $25,000

Rare   L. & J. G. Stickley spindle 'Prairie' settle, circa 1912, no. 234 the broad even sided flat crest rail over spindles, two section seat, unsigned, 86 in. wide.
(Skinner) $110,000

An L. & J. G. Stickley slat-back settle, style no. 281, with spring cushion seat, circa 1912, 76 in. wide.
(Skinner) $3,100

A Gustav Stickley bird's-eye maple wide slat settee, no. 214, circa 1903-04, 50¼ in. wide.
(Skinner) $5,600

Early Gustav Stickley oak settle, circa 1901, original leather upholstery, brass dome top tacks and medium brown finish, 55³/₈ in. wide.
(Skinner) $2,000

An early Gustav Stickley settle with arched slats, 1901-03, 60 in. wide.
(Skinner) $34,300

Gustav Stickley even arm settle, circa 1907, no. 208, straight rail over eight vertical slats on back, three on each end, with Southwestern designs, 76 in. long.
(Skinner Inc.) $11,000

L. & J. G. Stickley oak couch, No. 291, circa 1910, two-part box cushion, five vertical slats at each end, Handcraft Furniture decal, 72 in. long.
(Skinner) $1,265

STICKLEY

Gustav Stickley day bed, circa 1902–03, no. 216, wide crest rail over five vertical slats, with cushion, signed with large red decal, 31in. wide. (Skinner) **$3,000**

A Gustav Stickley paneled settle, no. 189, signed with large red decal with signature in a box, 1901-03, 84in. long. (Skinner) **$9,400**

Gustav Stickley knock-down settee, New York, circa 1907, 12in. wide horizontal back slat, 84in. long. (Skinner Inc.) **$11,000**

A Stickley Bros. slat-back settle, signed with paper label, Quaint, circa 1910, 72in. wide. (Skinner) **$6,250**

L. & J. G. Stickley Onondega Shops settle, circa 1902, molded crest rail over thirteen canted vertical slats, original medium finish, unsigned, 76¼in. wide. (Skinner) **$4,500**

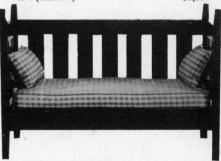

A Gustav Stickley slat-back settle, no. 206, circa 1904-06, 60in. wide. (Skinner) **$21,800**

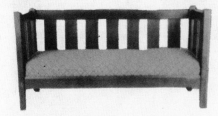

L. & J.G. Stickley settle, circa 1912, no. 216, straight crest rail, seven vertical slats across back, 72in. wide. (Skinner) **$3,100**

An oak hall settle with leather covered spring cushion seat, by Gustav Stickley, 56in. wide. (Skinner) **$4,300**

Grain painted standing shelves, New England, circa 1830, five rectangular graduated shelves, 42¼in. wide.
(Skinner) $1,495

L. & J. G. Stickley magazine and bookcase, circa 1910, 48in. wide. $2,500

Roycroft oak 'Little Journeys' book stand, East Aurora, New York, original medium finish, copper tag, 26⅛in. long.
(Skinner) $604

A scroll-carved chestnut hanging shelf, possibly Northern Chester County, Pennsylvania, 19th century, centering three rectangular shelves with repeating serpentine fronts, 23in. wide.
(Christie's) $2,990

A scrolled five-tier hanging corner shelf, Pennsylvania, 19th century, centering five graduated quarter-fan shelves flanked on each side by scrolling serpentine support, 51in. high.
(Christie's) $2,185

Grain painted bucket bench with drawer, probably New England, early 19th century, painted dark brown to resemble mahogany over an earlier green, 25.75in. wide.
(Skinner) $1,610

Limbert open book rack, Michigan, circa 1910, flat sides centering three open shelves, 28in. high.
(Skinner) $1,000

Oak bookcase, 20th century, gallery top, shelf with double keyed tenon over median shelf with single keyed tenons, 28⅛in. wide. (Skinner Inc.) $350

A Gustav Stickley V-top bookrack, signed with red decal in a box, 1902-04, 31in. wide, 31in. high.
(Skinner Inc.) $2,000

A carved pine bucket bench, Pennsylvania, early 19th century, the arched back with scalloped sides centering three shelves, 46¾in. wide.
(Sotheby's) **$1,495**

Blue painted wall shelf, probably New England, first third 19th century, 20½in. wide.
(Skinnner) **$1,380**

Gustav Stickley open slat-sided bookshelf, circa 1909, 27in. wide.
(Skinner) **$1,300**

Roycroft Little Journeys book stand, circa 1910, rectangular overhanging top over two lower shelves, keyed tenons, 26¼in. wide.
(Skinner) **$930**

A pair of Federal carved giltwood brackets, American, 19th century, each shaped shelf above a carved spread winged eagle support, on a tassel carved pendant, 13in. high.
(Christie's) **$6,900**

Tobey Chalet magazine stand, attributed, dark brown finish, original tacks, arched apron, 43in. high.
(Skinner) **$1,265**

A carved paneled pine trastero, New Mexico, circa 1800, of rectangular form with stiles projecting above the case, 47½in. wide.
(Sotheby's) **$10,350**

A painted and decorated hanging shelf, American, early 19th century, the shaped sides joined by two molded shelves, 18¼in. wide.
(Christie's) **$805**

Roycroft 'Little Journeys' bookrack, circa 1910, rectangular overhanging top, two lower shelves with keyed tenons through vertical side slats, 26¼in. wide.
(Skinner) **$500**

A very rare red-painted and carved pine hanging spoon rack, New England, 1700–1730, the circular finial pierced for hanging above two tiers of spoon supports, 28½in. high. (Sotheby's) $4,600

A brown-painted pine repisa, Las Vegas Area, New Mexico, circa 1850, the pierced scrolling crest flanked by scrolling sides, 21in. wide. (Sotheby's) $1,035

Rococo Revival walnut etagère, mid 19th century, arched mirrored back with a grape cluster scroll carved crest, 50in. wide. (Skinner) $1,840

An Art Deco burr-walnut and mahogany three-tier occasional table, on inswept uprights, on bracket feet, 23½in. wide. (Christie's) $334

A pair of Federal gilt wall brackets, American, circa 1790, each tapered shelf above a tapering gadrooned support and scrolled sides, 13¾in. high. (Christie's) $34,500

A grain painted wall shelf with scalloped sides, New England, circa 1840, 25½in. wide. $2,000

A mid-Victorian mahogany metamorphic three-tier dumb waiter, with standard ends and dual supports with turned feet joined by a stretcher, 44in. wide. (Christie's) $1,489

A pair of figured maple hanging shelves, American, early 19th century, each in the shape of a lyre with a shelf and pierced stars below, 18¼in. high. (Christie's) $4,370

Gustav Stickley bookrack, key and tenons, V-shaped shelf over lower shelf, Gustav Stickley paper label, 30¾in. high, 32in. wide. (Skinner) $1,150

A classical mahogany and mahogany veneer sideboard, Massachusetts, circa 1800, old refinish, old brasses, 47¹/₂in. wide.
(Skinner) $4,370

A Regency ebony-inlaid and figured mahogany bow-front sideboard, first quarter 19th century, the rectangular top with bowed center section, 5ft. wide.
(Sotheby's) $2,300

American Hepplewhite sideboard, in mahogany with three drawers over three cupboard doors, the central one recessed, 53¹/₂in. wide.
(Eldred's) $1,980

Walnut sideboard, circa 1870, backsplash with carved crest above shelves and mirror on a molded white marble top, 82in. high. (Skinner Inc.) $2,150

A Louis XVI style ebonized sideboard with bronze and ormolu mountings, America, 1865-70, approx. 69in. wide. $3,750

Walnut inlaid sideboard, probably North or South Carolina, 1850–75, the top with central rectangular inlay, 44in. wide.
(Skinner) $3,738

A Limbert mirrored oak sideboard, Michigan, circa 1910, 54in. wide.
(Skinner) $1,500

George III style mahogany pedestal sideboard, mid-19th century, serpentine-edged top above three frieze drawers, 6ft. 1in. wide.
(Butterfield & Butterfield) $3,400

Classical mahogany veneer sideboard, Boston, Massachusetts, 1818–1825, with stenciled label *Emmons and Archibald No. 39 Orange Street, Boston*, 74in. wide.
(Skinner) $8,800

Quaint Furniture mirrored
sideboard, circa 1910, gallery
top over mirror flanked by
arched corbels, 48in. wide.
(Skinner)   **$1,200**

Mission rectangular oak
sideboard, circa 1910,
72in. wide.   **$1,875**

Grain painted sideboard,
possibly New England, early
19th century, the rectangular top
with shaped gallery, 40¾in. wide.
(Skinner)   **$1,840**

Harden sideboard, attributed,
original medium brown finish,
quarter-sawn oak, felt lined
center drawer, arched
backsplash, interior shelf,
52¹/₈in. wide.
(Skinner)   **$805**

Renaissance Revival walnut
sideboard, circa 1870, upper
case with carved crest above a
pair of glazed doors, 46½in.
wide. (Skinner Inc.)   **$625**

Lifetime Furniture sideboard,
Grand Rapids, Michigan, circa
1910, mirrored backboard, three
central drawers flanked by
cabinet doors over long lower
drawer, 60¹/₂in. wide.
(Skinner Inc.)   **$750**

Renaissance style oak sideboard, circa 1860, with three
frieze drawers and three
cabinet doors carved throughout, 84½in. wide.
(Skinner)   **$880**

A Renaissance Revival carved
oak sideboard, American, 1860–
1880, the shaped mirrored back
fitted with two shelves
supported by scroll-cut
brackets, 67in. high.
(Christie's)   **$2,875**

Art Deco style burled walnut
buffet, the shaped splashboard
and central-oval top over bowfronted long drawers, 5ft. 7in.
wide.
(Butterfield & Butterfield)
          $3,450

CLASSICAL

Classical mahogany and mahogany veneer sideboard, probably New England, circa 1820, veneered peaked backboard and scrolled gallery, 58in. wide.
(Skinner) $3,105

Classical mahogany veneer carved sideboard, mid-Atlantic States, 1830s, 48in. wide.
(Skinner) $863

A classical figured maple and mahogany sideboard, New York, 1815-1825, the splashboard with volutes and brass rosettes above a rectangular top, 63in. wide.
(Christie's) $6,325

A classical carved mahogany parcel-gilt and ormolu-mounted sideboard, New York, New York, circa 1830, the rectangular top surmounted by a reverse breakfronted black backsplash, 42in. wide.
(Sotheby's) $2,185

A classical mahogany and parcel-gilt sideboard, New York State, first quarter 19th century, the rectangular molded top with upswept scrolling three-quarter splashboard over a conforming case fitted with a pair of bolection-molded short drawers, 49½in. wide.
(Christie's) $3,500

A classical marble-top mahogany pedestal sideboard, branded Wm. Alexander, Pittsburgh, Pennsylvania, circa 1825, on ogee molded plinth and carved paw feet, 1.92m. wide.
(Sotheby's) $9,200

A classical parcel gilt mahogany sideboard, New York, 1820-1830, splashboard with broken pediment, over a pair of crossbanded short drawers, on paw feet, 61¾in. wide.
(Christie's) $3,900

Classical revival mahogany and mahogany and wavy birch veneer inlaid carved sideboard, Massachusetts, circa 1825, 46½in. wide.
(Skinner) $2,000

Classical mahogany and mahogany veneer carved sideboard, New York State, 1830s, with leafage carving flanking a central basket of fruit, 60in. wide.
(Skinner) $2,530

A Federal inlaid mahogany kidney-front sideboard, Philadelphia or Baltimore, circa 1790, the oblong line-inlaid top with crossbanded edge and shaped front above one long drawer with two short cupboard doors centering line-inlaid dies and similarly-inlaid square tapering legs ending in crossbanded cuffs, 6ft.4in. wide.
(Sotheby's) $9,200

A good Federal flame birch-inlaid mahogany bowfront sideboard, North Shore Massachusetts, circa 1810, the bowed oblong top above a conformingly-shaped case fitted with one long drawer opening to a fitted secrétaire interior with pigeonholes, drawers and a baize-lined writing surface above cupboard doors flanked by bottle drawers, further flanked by stacked deep drawers, on ring-turned tapering reeded legs ending in ovoid peg feet, 5ft. 11½in. wide.
(Sotheby's) $4,600

FEDERAL

A good Federal inlaid and figural mahogany sideboard, Baltimore, Maryland, circa 1795, the oblong top with astragal corners, 6ft. 2in. wide. (Sotheby's) $14,950

A Federal inlaid walnut bow-front sideboard, Southern, circa 1800, the oblong top with projecting and bowed center section, 5ft. wide. (Sotheby's) $13,800

A Federal inlaid mahogany serpentine-front sideboard, New York, circa 1800, the oblong top with bowed center section above four frieze drawers, 6ft. 2in. wide. (Sotheby's) $6,900

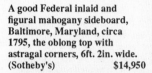

A Federal inlaid mahogany sideboard, Mid-Atlantic States, 1790-1810, serpentine front edge, on square tapering legs with pendant husks and cuff-inlay, 65½in. wide. (Christie's) $11,000

A Federal inlaid mahogany sideboard with serpentine front, Baltimore, 1790-1810, 72in. wide. (Christie's) $50,000

A Federal inlaid mahogany sideboard, Mid-Atlantic States, 1790–1810, the kidney-shaped top edged with lightwood stringing over a conforming case, 72½in. wide. (Christie's) $8,800

Federal cherry inlaid half sideboard, Northern Windsor County, Vermont, 1810–15, the top hinged drawer opens to a desk-like interior, 43¾in. wide. (Skinner) $3,220

A Federal inlaid mahogany sideboard, Pennsylvania, 1790-1810, on square tapering legs, 72in. wide. (Christie's) $20,500

Federal bird's eye maple and cherry sideboard, Vermont, 1815–25, with old pattern glass pulls, refinished, 42in. wide. (Skinner) $2,645

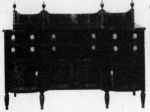

A late Federal mahogany sideboard on tapering leaf carved feet, Mass., 1800-10, 78in. wide.
$950

Federal mahogany inlaid sideboard, probably Massachusetts, circa 1790, the bowfront top flanked by concave ends, 64in. wide.
(Skinner) $7,475

Federal mahogany and maple veneer tiered sideboard, Massachusetts, early 19th century, the two-tiered shaped tops with beaded edges, 69⁵/₈in. wide.
(Skinner) $4,600

A Federal inlaid mahogany sideboard, Massachusetts, 1800–1815, the rectangular top with outset rounded corners and edge inlaid with light and dark wood checkered and chevron banding, on turned feet, 51in. wide.
(Christie's) $5,750

A Federal inlaid mahogany sideboard, the serpentine top edged with line inlay, 72³/₄in. wide. Mass., 1790-1815.
(Christie's) $20,500

A diminutive Federal bird's-eye maple inlaid mahogany sideboard, Salem, Massachusetts or Portsmouth, New Hampshire, 1790-1810, with D-shaped top, the edge with rosewood crossbanding, 60¹/₂in. wide.
(Christie's) $23,000

A Federal mahogany and satinwood inlaid serpentine-front sideboard, Massachusetts, 1790–1810, the shaped top with alternating line inlays above a conforming case, 66¹/₄in. wide.
(Christie's) $21,850

A Federal inlaid mahogany sideboard with bowed serpentine top, Mass., 1790-1810, 72³/₄in. wide.
(Christie's) $8,200

A Federal inlaid mahogany sideboard, Massachusetts, circa 1800, the rectangular top with astragal corners and inlaid edge, 5ft. 11in. wide.
(Sotheby's) $5,175

FEDERAL

A Federal inlaid mahogany sideboard, New York, 1790–1810, the rectangular shaped top with line inlaid edge above a conforming case centering a serpentine bowed long drawer with inlaid surround flanked by inlaid recessed deep cupboard doors, all on six ring and baluster-turned legs with ball feet, 60¼in. wide.
(Christie's) $13,800

A Federal inlaid mahogany sideboard, Rhode Island, 1790–1810, the serpentine top above a conforming case fitted with a central cockbeaded line-inlaid long drawer above a cockbeaded long drawer with line and quarter-fan inlay flanked by cockbeaded cupboard doors with similar inlay all punctuated by star inlay hung by pendant bellflower inlay, on square tapering line-inlaid legs with inlaid cuffs, 69in. wide.
(Christie's) $13,800

FEDERAL

A Federal inlaid mahogany sideboard, Philadelphia or New York, 1790–1810, the rectangular top with swelled center, canted corners and line-inlaid and crossbanded edge above a conforming case fitted with one swelled, line-inlaid and angle-veneered long drawer, flanked by matching concave double-hung sham-drawer doors centering similar cupboard doors on six angled and line inlaid square tapering and cuffed legs, 71in. wide.
(Christie's) $10,925

A Federal inlaid mahogany sideboard, New York City, 1790–1805, the rectangular top with bowed front above a conforming string-inlaid long drawer over double string and quarter-fan inlaid doors flanked by string-inlaid stiles headed by oval reserves and striped inlay, each flanked by a bowed string-inlaid short drawer above a similar door and flanked by embellished stiles, on string-inlaid square legs with pendant-husk inlay and cuffed ankles with tapering feet, 72½in. wide.
(Christie's) $74,000

FEDERAL, NEW ENGLAND

Federal mahogany veneer sideboard, New England, 1790–1810, with stringing outlining drawers, cupboards and legs, cuff inlay, 71in. wide.
(Skinner) $4,888

Small Federal cherry inlaid sideboard, New England, circa 1815, 44in. wide.
$3,150

A Federal inlaid and crossbanded figured mahogany serpentine-front sideboard with slide, New England, circa 1810, on line-inlaid square tapering legs, 1.66m. long.
(Sotheby's) $34,500

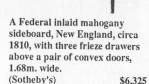

A good Federal bird's eye maple and mahogany inlaid cherrywood small sideboard, New England, probably Connecticut, circa 1815, 46in. wide.
(Sotheby's) $6,250

A Federal inlaid mahogany sideboard, New England, circa 1810, with three frieze drawers above a pair of convex doors, 1.68m. wide.
(Sotheby's) $6,325

A Federal mahogany sideboard, New England, 1790-1810, serpentine top above conforming case fitted with serving slide lined with stenciled leather, on Marlborough legs, 61in. wide.
(Christie's) $75,000

FEDERAL, NEW YORK

Federal mahogany veneer sideboard, New York, circa 1800, three inlaid drawers above a central cupboard flanked by bottle drawers and end cupboards, 67¹/₂in. wide.
(Skinner Inc.) $10,000

Federal carved mahogany sideboard, New York, circa 1815-1820, top with Palladian arched splashboard flanked by reeded columns with acorn finials, 6ft. ¹/₂in. wide.
(Butterfield & Butterfield)$2,050

A Federal inlaid mahogany serpentine-front sideboard, New York, the oblong serpentine top above a conformingly-shaped case, 65¹/₂in. wide.
(Sotheby's) $8,050

FEDERAL, PHILADELPHIA

A fine and rare Federal inlaid mahogany diminutive sideboard, Philadelphia, circa 1800, the oblong top with projecting center section, width 54½in.
(Sotheby's) $35,000

A Federal inlaid and figured mahogany serpentine-front sideboard, Philadelphia or Baltimore, circa 1795, 5ft. 9½in. wide.
(Sotheby's) $9,200

Federal inlaid mahogany sideboard, Philadelphia, circa 1790–1800, the line inlaid serpentine shaped top above a conformingly shaped case, width 6ft. 2¼in.
(Butterfield & Butterfield)
                              $4,888

LIMBERT

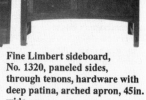

Limbert sideboard, with plate rail, two drawers over two doors and long bottom drawer, original light oak finish, 48in. wide.
(Skinner) $2,185

Unusual Limbert sideboard, Grand Rapids, Michigan, circa 1903, gallery top, three short drawers, three cabinet doors and single long drawer, 59¼in. wide.
(Skinner) $2,100

Fine Limbert sideboard, No. 1320, paneled sides, through tenons, hardware with deep patina, arched apron, 45in. wide.
(Skinner) $2,530

A Limbert sideboard with arched mirrored backboard with corbel detail, Michigan, circa 1910, 47¾in. wide. $1,750

A Limbert mirrored sideboard, no. 1453 3/4, circa 1910, 48in. wide. $1,125

Limbert sideboard, mirrored back over six drawers and two doors, brand mark, original worn finish, 60in. wide.
(Skinner) $4,888

STICKLEY

An oak chest with plate rack by Gustav Stickley, circa 1904, 69½in. wide. $6,800

Rare Gustav Stickley sideboard, circa 1902, the top shelf galleried on three sides, unsigned, 48in. wide.
(Skinner) $7,000

Gustav Stickley oak sideboard, No. 814, circa 1910, original medium finish and hammered iron hardware, 66¼in. wide.
(Skinner) $3,220

An oak sideboard, by Gustav Stickley, 1907, 66in. wide.
(Skinner) $1,800

Gustav Stickley sideboard, circa 1902, no. 967, gallery top over two short drawers and single long drawer, two cabinet doors below, iron hardware, 60in. long.
(Skinner) $7,500

L. & J. G. Stickley oak sideboard, No. 734, circa 1912, original medium finish and hammered iron hardware, 48in. wide.
(Skinner) $1,610

L. & J. G Stickley sideboard, circa 1912, paneled plate rail with corbels, (refinished, some stains and scratches) 54in. wide.
(Skinner) $2,200

L. & J. G. Stickley oak server with open plate rack, circa 1912, no. 750, 48in. wide.
(Skinner) $880

Gustav Stickley sideboard, circa 1907-12, no. 816, plate rack on rectangular top, long drawer over two central drawers, 48in. wide.
(Skinner) $2,500

STICKLEY

An oak sideboard with plate rack and slightly arched apron, by L. & J.G. Stickley, 54in. wide. (Skinner) $1,000

A Stickley Bros. sideboard, Grand Rapids, Michigan, 1912, 60in. wide. (Skinner) $750

Gustav Stickley oak sideboard, circa 1907, 56in. wide. $2,500

Gustav Stickley eight-legged sideboard, circa 1904, no. 817, with plate rack, 70in. wide. (Skinner) $12,500

L. & J.G. Stickley sideboard, circa 1910, no. 738, rectangular plate rack on corresponding top, two long drawers flanked by cabinet doors, 60in. wide. (Skinner) $5,100

Gustav Stickley oak sideboard, No. 804, circa 1907, designed by Harvey Ellis, original medium finish and hammered iron hardware, red decal, $54^{1}/_{4}$in. wide. (Skinner) $7,475

Fine L. & J.G. Stickley sideboard, original hardware with deep patina, plate rail backsplash, original interior, 54in. wide. (Skinner) $4,887

Gustav Stickley oak sideboard, no. 814, circa 1904, open plate rack, three central drawers flanked by two cabinet doors over long drawer, 56in. wide. (Skinner) $3,000

L. &. J. G. Stickley sideboard, circa 1910, no. 738, rectangular plate rack on corresponding top, two long drawers flanked by cabinet doors, 60in. wide. (Skinner) $5,600

Federal birch one-drawer stand, Loudon, New Hampshire, early 19th century, the top overhangs a drawer, 17¾in. wide. (Skinner)   **$747**

A turned wood yarn winder, New Hampshire, late 18th/early 19th century, the cylindrical winding wheel with four painted cross-members, 42¼in. high. (Christie's)   **$2,185**

A William and Mary walnut stand, Penn., 1700-40, 25¼in. wide.   **$3,000**

A Federal carved mahogany two drawer stand, Salem, Massachusetts, 1790–1810, the rectangular top with outset rounded corners decorated with molded roundels over a conforming case fitted with two cockbeaded frieze drawers, 19½in. wide. (Christie's)   **$4,000**

A carved and painted rustic hallstand, Sherman Station, Maine, circa 1870, the shaped, vertical back with carved shield mounted with a carved and painted deer's head with antlers, 83¾in. high. (Christie's)   **$16,100**

Federal cherry and bird's-eye maple stand, Connecticut River Valley, circa 1815-25, cherry top above two drawers with bird's-eye maple facades, dark stained legs, 19in. wide. (Skinner)   **$2,300**

Painted and mahogany veneer stand, Massachusetts or New Hampshire, 1800-15, top and base painted with original red stain, 18in. wide. (Skinner Inc.)   **$6,050**

A Federal mahogany tilt top stand, Salem, Massachusetts, 1790-1810, on tripod cabriole legs with pad feet, 69cm. high. (Christie's New York)   **$1,500**

Painted and grained stand, New England, circa 1825, the top and drawer facade have brown and yellow vinegar painting outlined in black, 18in. wide. (Skinner)   **$4,600**

STANDS

A Federal birch stand, New England, 1790–1810, on reeded and ring-turned legs, 15½in. wide.
(Christie's) $7,475

Tiger maple and cherry stand, Connecticut River Valley, early 19th century, with beaded drawer and skirt, 24in. wide.
(Skinner) $2,760

A Federal figured maple stand, New England, 1805-1815, the rectangular top above a single long drawer, 20³⁄₈in. wide.
(Christie's) $1,610

Extremely rare American Sheraton two-drawer drop-leaf stand, in pine with allover decoupage decoration, 27½in. high.
(Eldred's) $1,760

A Federal mahogany tilt-top stand, New England, circa 1760–1780, the molded square top tilting above a birdcage support over a tapering cylindrical ring-and-urn-turned support, the top 16¾ x 17in.
(Christie's) $5,750

Painted cherry stand, Connecticut River Valley, early 19th century, the scrolled two board top above a base with single beaded drawer, 26in. high.
(Skinner) $4,600

A late Federal figured maple two drawer stand, Pennsylvania, 1810-1820, on tapering baluster and ring turned legs, 17½in. wide.
(Christie's) $3,300

A Federal mahogany stand, Salem, Massachusetts, 1790–1810, on square tapering molded legs joined by X-stretchers, 14¼in. wide.
(Christie's) $2,600

A Federal inlaid birchwood two-drawer stand, New England, circa 1820, each drawer with a compass-star inlaid knob, 16½in. wide.
(Sotheby's) $920

Chippendale walnut tilt-top stand, Pennsylvania, the rimmed top tilts above a stand with suppressed ball on cabriole leg base, 17³/₄in. diameter.
(Skinner) $6,325

A three-tiered muffin stand, by Charles Rohlfs, Buffalo, N.Y., 1907, 34in. high.
(Skinner) $1,750

Stickley Brothers costumer, Grand Rapids, Michigan, circa 1914, no. 187, four iron hooks on post with corbeled cross-stretcher base, 68in. high.
(Skinner Inc.) $300

Shaker cherry and pine tripod stand, probably Mt. Lebanon, New York, circa 1830, the circular top with beveled edge resting on a rectangular cleat, diameter of top18in.
(Skinner) $2,875

Bent plywood tea cart, mid 20th century, top fitted with beverage holder, centering tray, bent wood legs joined by lower median shelf, 20in. wide.
(Skinner Inc.) $300

A black-painted Windsor stand, Pennsylvania, late 18th century/ early 19th century, the circular top above three baluster and ring-turned legs, 21¹/₄in. diam.
(Christie's) $5,175

A Country Federal grain painted maple tray table, possibly New Hampshire, circa 1820, top 17 x 16½in.
(Skinner) $4,050

Painted Tramp art stand with drawers, possibly New York, 1820-40, 17½in. wide.
(Skinner) $200

A Federal bird's-eye maple and cherrywood drop-leaf stand, possibly Robert Dunlap (1779–1865), Bedford, New Hampshire, 1820–40, 30¹/₄in. long (open).
(Christie's) $14,950

Limbert round tall pedestal, circa 1906, no. 267, 32½in. high, 14in. diam.
(Skinner) $10,000

L. & J. G. Stickley dinner gong, Fayetteville, New York, 1912, arched frame supporting circular bronze gong.
(Skinner) $10,000

Federal red stained birch tilt-top stand, Portsmouth, New Hampshire, the octagonal top above a ring-turned pedestal, 23¼in. wide.
(Skinner) $2,300

A Federal inlaid mahogany two-drawer stand, Portsmouth, New Hampshire, 1790–1810, the rectangular top with outset rounded corners over a conforming case fitted with two crossbanded drawers, 18³/₄in. wide.
(Christie's) $33,000

A Chippendale walnut tilt-top stand, Philadelphia, Pennsylvania, circa 1770, the circular dished tilting top with birdcage support above a tapering cylindrical ring-turned support, 22½in. diameter.
(Christie's) $32,200

American Renaissance inlaid maple and rosewood nightstand by Herter Brothers, New York, circa 1872, the later faux marble top within a molded walnut border, 17in. wide.
(Butterfield & Butterfield) $1,250

Bird's eye maple stand, New England, circa 1820, with opalescent glass pulls, 19in. wide.
(Skinner) $747

An oak wastebasket, by Gustav Stickley, 1907, 14in. high, 12in. diam.
(Skinner) $2,500

A Federal figured maple stand, New England, 1800-1810, the rectangular top above a single drawer, 30¼in. high.
(Christie's) $1,495

A Federal birch-veneered and mahogany stand, Portsmouth, New Hampshire, 1790–1815, the rectangular veneered top with band inlaid top and edge above a case fitted with three graduated drawers each with three flame-birch reserves with crossbanded framing, on square tapering legs with veneered panels and socket castors, 16¾in. wide.
(Christie's) $48,300

STANDS

DRINK STANDS

L. & J. G. Stickley square drink stand, Fayetteville, New York, circa 1910, signed with Handcraft decal, 27in. high. (Skinner Inc.) **$900**

Cherry table with drawer, circa 1830, the overhanging top with rounded corners, 18⅝in. wide. (Skinner) **$1,092**

A drink stand, by L. & J. G. Stickley, no. 587, circa 1912, 16in. sq. (Skinner) **$850**

ETAGERES

A Federal mahogany etagère, Boston, 1790–1810, on turned tapering feet with brass cup feet and casters, 53in. high, 17½in. wide. (Christie's) **$4,120**

A grain painted pine and poplar etagere, New England, circa 1820, 35½in. wide. (Skinner) **$560**

Federal mahogany stand, Middle Atlantic States, 1815–25, with four shelves and a single drawer on turned legs with original casters, 21½in. wide. (Skinner) **$920**

LIGHT STANDS

A County Federal tiger maple light stand, New England, circa 1810, the square overhanging top above four square tapering legs, 27¾in. high. (Skinner) **$1,050**

Maple light stand, New England, circa 1800, refinished, replaced pull, 28in. high. (Skinner Inc.) **$810**

Federal birch and bird's eye maple lightstand, New Hampshire, circa 1825, original finish, 27½in. high. (Skinner) **$3,220**

356

MAGAZINE STANDS

An L. & J. G. Stickley magazine rack, no. 45, circa 1912, 44½in. high. (Skinner Inc.) $1,750

A Gustav Stickley slat-sided folio stand, no. 551, 1902-03, 40½in. high, 29½in. wide. (Skinner) $4,300

Early 20th century Mission oak magazine stand with cut out arched sides, 49in. high. (Skinner Inc.) $750

Gustav Stickley Toby magazine stand, circa 1904, square top with corbel supports, unsigned (top reglued), 43in. high. (Skinner Inc.) $1,000

Roycroft magazine pedestal, circa 1906, no. 080, overhanging square top, canted sides with keyed tenons, five shelves, carved oak leaf design, 64in. high. (Skinner) $5,000

An L. & J. G. Stickley slat-sided magazine rack, no. 46, circa 1910, signed with decal, 42in. high. (Skinner Inc.) $2,500

A magazine stand with cut-outs, Michigan, 1910, 20in. wide. (Skinner) $1,000

A Mission oak magazine/wood carrier, circa 1910, 18in. high, 15¼in. wide. (Skinner) $625

Michigan Chair Company magazine stand, No. K125, two vertical slats, keys and tenons, 16½in. wide. (Skinner) $978

MUSIC STANDS

An open-sided music stand, possibly by Stickley, circa 1907, 39in. high. (Skinner) $650

Open-sided music stand, circa 1907, similar to Gustav Stickley no. 670, four tapering posts, centering four shelves with gallery, unsigned, 39in. high. (Skinner Inc.) $1,250

Gustav Stickley inlaid tiger maple open music stand, circa 1904, no. 670, signed with Eastwood label, 39in. high. $12,500

PLANT STANDS

Gustav Stickley oak plant stand, circa 1903, 28in. high. $2,500

A fine and unusual carved and painted pine planter, New England, circa 1835-40, the sides painted with stylised fruit and flower forms, 12in. high. (Sotheby's) $12,650

Limbert octagonal plant stand with cut-outs, Michigan, circa 1910, on box base with double trapezoidal cut-outs, 28½in. high. (Skinner Inc.) $2,500

Octagonal plant stand with cut-outs, Michigan, circa 1910, probably Limbert, with double trapezoidal cut-outs, 28in. high. (Skinner Inc.) $900

A cane-sided plant stand, probably Limbert, circa 1910, 23in. high, the top 16in. sq. (Skinner) $750

Limbert octagonal plant stand, style no. 251, circa 1910, 24¼in. high. $1,750

358

STANDS

SMOKING STANDS

Hanging pipe rack, American, 19th century, in pine, 29in. high. (Eldred's) $220

A marquetry paneled oak smoking rack, possibly Stickley Bros., Michigan, circa 1910, style no. 264-100, 22in. high, 24in. wide. (Skinner) $250

Chrome and bakelite smoking stand, Brooklyn, New York, circa 1930, with chrome topped ashtray and supports, 20¾in. high. (Skinner) $250

UMBRELLA STANDS

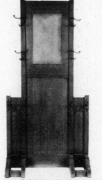

Arts and Crafts wooden umbrella stand, vertical slats with wooden straps, original finish, 17½in. high. (Skinner) $460

Gustav Stickley hall tree, circa 1902–03, with four wrought iron hooks, 74in. high. (Skinner Inc.) $2,800

Gustav Stickley oak slat umbrella stand, No. 100, circa 1907, original medium finish, ten slats riveted to three hammered iron hoops, (missing pan), 24in. high. (Skinner) $1,265

Roycroft oak umbrella stand, East Aurora, New York, circa 1910, signed with logo, (finish partially removed) 29¾in. high. (Skinner) $750

Figural cast iron umbrella stand, 1927 Marcy Foundry Co., in the form of a sailor on a top above a crossed oar and anchor, 27½in. high. (Skinner) $2,760

Arts & Crafts umbrella stand, probably Europe, early 20th century, shaped flat sides with spade trailing to circle cut-out, 22in. wide. (Skinner Inc.) $375

A Chippendale step-back cupboard, Pennsylvania, 1770–1800, the rectangular molded cornice above shaped sides centering two shelves over a rectangular case fitted with three thumbmolded short drawers divided and flanked by rectangular molded reserves above two raised paneled doors centering and flanked by rectangular molded reserves, on a conforming molded base with straight bracket feet, 68¼in. wide.
(Christie's) $25,300

Pine glazed stepback cupboard, Pennsylvania, circa 1840, refinished, replaced pulls, 51in. wide.
(Skinner Inc.) $3,070

An 18th century Chippendale pine step-back cupboard in two sections, Penn., 73½in. wide. (Christie's) $15,000

Antique American two-part step-back kitchen cupboard in pine, molded cornice, glazed and mullioned doors, late 18th century, 50in. wide.
(Eldred's) $3,300

A Chippendale walnut step-back cupboard, Pennsylvania, 1750–1800, the rectangular top with overhanging molded cornice above five vertical beaded tongue-and-groove backboards, 61in. wide.
(Christie's) $20,000

A very fine and rare paint-decorated poplar paneled pewter cupboard, Pennsylvania, 1780-1800, in two parts, the upper section with molded projecting cornice, 5ft.½in. wide.
(Sotheby's) $40,250

A fine grain-painted poplar step-back cupboard, Pennsylvania, 1790–1810, in two parts, the overhanging cove molding above a case with chamfered corners, 5ft. 2in. wide.
(Sotheby's) $44,850

Painted pine paneled step-back cupboard, New England, early 19th century, the cornice molding above two raised panel doors, 36in. wide.
(Skinner) $2,415

Grain painted dresser, Canada or northern New England, circa 1840, open grooved shelves above two raised panel doors which open to a single-shelf interior, 54.5in. wide.
(Skinner) $5,462

Antique American two-part step-back cupboard in pine, upper section with two glazed doors, lower section with two paneled doors, 76in. high.
(Eldred's) $1,400

A Country Federal pine step-back cupboard, circa 1800, 50in. wide.
(Skinner) $1,000

A red-painted pine step-back cupboard, New England, 1740–60, the canted-molded upper section centering two shelves, 35in. wide.
(Sotheby's) $12,650

19th century American pine stepback cupboard, with old red finish, two doors above, each with eight lights, 42in. wide.
(Eldred's) $935

A rare Federal grain painted step-back cupboard, Vermont, early 19th century, the entire surface painted olive with brown sponge painted grain decoration, 63½in. wide.
(Christie's New York) $48,000

Chippendale walnut step back cupboard, possibly Pennsylvania, late 18th/early 19th century, in two parts, the upper section with molded cornice above two glazed doors, 6ft. 8in. wide.
(Butterfield & Butterfield)
          $5,800

An elmwood and pine step-back cupboard, English or Continental, mid-18th century, the rectangular molded cornice above three shelves, 5ft. 4in. wide.
(Sotheby's) $3,737

Pine stepback cupboard, Canadian Provinces, 18th century, the molded cornice above two raised panel cupboard doors, 58in. wide.
(Skinner Inc.) $4,000

A brown- and blue-painted pine step-back cupboard, American, 19th century, the overhanging cornice above three conforming shelves, 5ft. wide.
(Sotheby's) $8,050

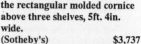

Painted dresser, New York state or New Jersey, 19th century, with three open shelves with plate rails above paneled doors, 72½in. wide.
(Skinner) $5,175

A good gray-painted pine diminutive step-back apothecary cupboard, New England, late 18th/early 19th century, the overhanging rectangular cornice above three molded shelves, the projecting work surface above an arrangement of nineteen drawers over four rows, on a molded base, 38in. wide. (Sotheby's) $19,550

A Federal carved mahogany window seat, attributed to the shop of Duncan Phyfe, N.Y., 1810-20, 40in. wide. (Christie's) **$33,000**

An unusual upholstered hooked rug footstool, New England, circa 1850, on turned maple 'turnip' feet, length 28½in. (Sotheby's) **$1,500**

Classical Revival mahogany stool, possibly New York, circa 1825, 21in. wide. **$650**

A classical mahogany footstool, New York, 1810–1815, on curule legs with raised lozenge at the cross, joined by swelled and ring-turned double medial stretchers, 18in. wide. (Christie's) **$2,990**

Pair of classical mahogany and mahogany veneer window benches, probably Boston, circa 1820, 33½in. wide. (Skinner) **$4,945**

A classical mahogany footstool, Boston, Massachusetts, 1830-1840, on curule legs with scrolled terminus, 16¼in. high. (Christie's) **$1,955**

A Classical mahogany stool, Boston, 1820-1830, on a scrolled curule base joined by a turned stretcher, 20in. wide. (Christie's) **$2,300**

A fancy-painted and decorated footstool, New England, first quarter 19th century, the bowed rectangular top centering a rush seat, on turned cylindrical legs joined by ring and block stretchers, 15¼in. long. (Christie's) **$4,250**

A classical carved mahogany footstool, Boston; Massachusetts, circa 1830, the rectangular seat with a molded and scrolling X-form base, 21in. wide. (Sotheby's) **$1,150**

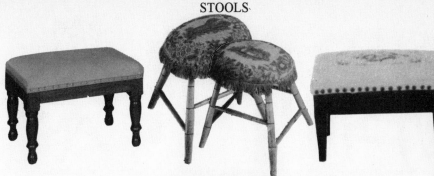

One of a pair of early 19th century late Federal mahogany footstools, 12¾in. long. (Christie's) $9,600

A fine and rare pair of Windsor painted and upholstered pine stools, New England, early 19th century, painted yellow with brown highlights, 15in high. (Sotheby's) $18,400

Roycroft oak upholstered footstool, New York, circa 1910, no. 048, needlepoint cover, 10in. high. (Skinner Inc.) $560

Limbert oak window bench, Grand Rapids, Michigan, 1907, with original leather cushion, branded mark (minor nicks), 24in. wide. (Skinner Inc.) $15,000

Classical mahogany footstool, Boston, 1830s, attributed to Hancock, Holden and Adams, overupholstered rectangular top above double C-scroll base, 16½in. wide. (Skinner) $920

An Arts and Crafts oak stool, the square top with drop-in rush seat, on tapering uprights joined by square stretchers, possibly American. (Christie's) $297

A rare classical paint-decorated and carved mahogany piano stool, Philadelphia, Pennsylvania, circa 1830, on acanthus-carved legs. (Sotheby's) $1,380

A rare pair of green-painted turned birchwood upholstered stools, American, probably New England, 1720–50, each having a rectangular seat on vase- and ring-turned splayed legs. (Sotheby's) $8,050

Gustav Stickley tabouret, no. 603, circa 1907, round top on four square legs, cross stretcher base, 18in. diameter. (Skinner Inc.) $1,000

A rare William and Mary turned maple and birchwood joint stool, New England, 1710–50, the oval chamfered top above a rectangular frieze.
(Sotheby's) **$11,500**

J. M. Young oak and leather upholstered footstool, No. 382, Camden, New York, tacked leather upholstered seat, paper label, 19^1/$_8$in. long.
(Skinner) **$431**

Classical carved mahogany veneer and brass piano stool, New York, 1810–15, the curving veneered crest above a lyre-shaped splat, 32in. high.
(Skinner) **$4,887**

A classical carved mahogany piano stool, Boston, circa 1830, the circular seat revolving above a conforming molded base, legs with ebonized ball turned capitals and feet, 21^1/$_2$in. high.
(Christie's) **$920**

A pair of late Federal mahogany foot-stools, New England, 1800–1820, each with padded rectangular top above a reeded apron with baluster and ring-turned legs, 12in. wide.
(Christie's) **$850**

A Windsor pine stool, Pennsylvania, late 18th/early 19th century, the rounded two-board seat above four splayed cylindrical legs, 25^1/$_4$in. high.
(Christie's) **$575**

A classical rosewood piano stool, American, probably New England, circa 1840, the needlework-covered top above a canted seat frame, 19^1/$_2$in. high.
(Sotheby's) **$402**

A black-painted Windsor foot-stool stamped *J. Stanyan*, Pennsylvania, 1790–1820, on bamboo-turned splayed legs joined by stretchers, 12^3/$_4$in. wide.
(Christie's) **$680**

One of a pair of Windsor stools, New England, 1800-1820, the oval tops on bamboo turned splayed tapering legs, 13in. high.
(Skinner Inc.) **$16,250**

A classical carved mahogany piano stool, attributed to Duncan Phyfe or one of his contemporaries, New York, circa 1810.
(Sotheby's) **$1,725**

An unusual painted pine patriotic footstool, Henry G. Perry, New York, circa 1875, painted with a waving American flag with gilt finial, length 18½in.
(Sotheby's) **$6,000**

A tabouret with cut corners, by L. & J. G. Stickley, no. 560, circa 1912, 16in. wide.
(Skinner) **$1,000**

Classical rosewood piano stool, probably New England, first half 19th century, the circular adjustable molded top on a tapering column, approximately 18in. high.
(Skinner) **$460**

A pair of caned footstools, Duncan Phyfe, New York, 1810–1833, each on four saber reeded legs with ebonised medallions, 13in. wide.
(Christie's) **$4,830**

A Classical mahogany piano stool, New York, 1800-1815, the upholstered circular seat turning above a threaded support, 14in. diam. (Christie's New York) **$1,000**

A William and Mary turned and paint-decorated birchwood joint stool, New England, 1710–40, on vase-turned legs joined by stretchers, 22in. long.
(Sotheby's) **$6,325**

A carved poplar and walnut footstool, American, possibly Hudson River Valley, 1780–1820, the oblong top with concave ends, 12in. wide.
(Sotheby's) **$460**

A classical carved and gilt mahogany piano stool, Baltimore, 1820–1830, on three acanthus-carved and gilt paw feet, 32⅞in. high.
(Christie's) **$3,050**

A Stickley Bros. spindle sided footstool, circa 1907, with stretchers centering seven spindles each side, unsigned, 20½in. wide.
(Skinner) $3,750

A Gustav Stickley footstool with notched feet, style no. 726, circa 1902-04, 12¼in. wide.
(Skinner) $1,000

A Gustav Stickley mahogany footstool, circa 1904-1906, with upholstered seat, arched seat rail and exposed tenons, 20¼in. wide.
(Skinner) $750

L. & J.G. Stickley footstool, Syracuse and Fayetteville, New York, circa 1918, no. 397, signed with decal, 20in. wide.
(Skinner) $650

A leather upholstered footstool, no. 300, by Gustav Stickley, 20in. wide, circa 1905.
(Skinner) $1,250

L. & J. G. Stickley footstool, circa 1918, original spring cushion and upholstery, medium finish, 20in. wide.
(Skinner) $500

Gustav Stickley oak foot stool, No. 300, circa 1904, leather upholstery and black-finished dome tacks, through tenon stretchers, unsigned, 20in. long.
(Skinner) $1,380

A Gustav Stickley upholstered footstool with tacked leather surface, no. 300, circa 1905, 20½in. wide.
(Skinner) $2,500

Gustav Stickley footstool with cross stretcher base, circa 1902, no. 725, arched sides with leather upholstery and tacks, 16½in. wide.
(Skinner) $1,650

Four piece suite of Heywood-Wakefield wicker seat furniture, a settee, armchair and two side chairs, raised on circular legs. (Skinner) $1,250

A Limbert oak dining room set comprising a pedestal table with four boxed leaves, diameter 54in., and a set of four dining chairs, circa 1910. (Skinner) $4,400

Early 20th century Plail & Co., barrel-back settee and matching armchairs, 46¼in. long. (Skinner) $6,800

Art Deco tubular steel salon suite, second quarter 20th century, comprising a settee and two club chairs, each rectangular backrest joined by continuous scrolled armrests continuing to supports, settee 4ft. long.
(Butterfield & Butterfield) $4,312

Renaissance Revival rosewood and marquetry parlor suite, circa 1865-75, comprising two settees, two pairs of armchairs, and two side chairs.
(Skinner) $7,475

A suite of Rococo Revival carved and laminated rosewood seating furniture, attributed to J. and J. W. Meeks, New York City, 1850–1859, the sofa with a serpentine crest headed and centered by a gadrooned broken swan's-neck pediment, the sofa 63½in. wide.
(Christie's) $11,000

A suite of Neo-Grec carved and inlaid seating furniture, comprising two sofas, two parlor arm chairs, two ladies slipper chairs and two side chairs, the sofa 79in. wide. (Christie's)   **$29,900**

Harden three-piece suite, circa 1910, including settee, armchair and rocker, concave crest rail over five vertical slats, bent arm over four vertical slats, spring cushion seat. (Skinner)   **$1,250**

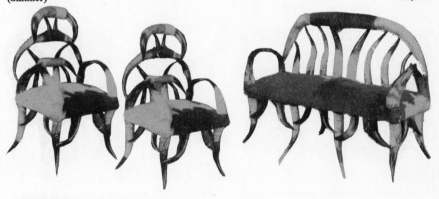

A Texas Steerhorn and hide-upholstered three piece suite comprising a settee and two matching armchairs, the settee 62in. wide. (Christie's)   **$2,020**

Three pieces of Limbert furniture, Grand Rapids, Michigan, circa 1910, open arm rocker, and matching armchair, both with straight crest rail, open-arm settle, with straight crest rail. (Skinner) $1,560

Renaissance Revival rosewood three-piece furniture suite, third quarter 19th century, 42in. high.
(Skinner) $1,725

Seven-piece suite of wicker seating furniture, late 19th/early 20th century, comprising a settee, pair of armchairs, rocking armchair, occasional table, planter, all bearing metal labels for Paine Furniture, Co., Boston.
(Skinner) $4,312

Four-piece suite of Renaissance Revival rosewood, marquetry and gilt-incised seating furniture, third-quarter 19th century, comprising a settee, armchair and two side chairs, settee 64in. long. (Skinner) $1,495

Three-piece Art Deco living room suite, by Collins and Alkman Corporation, circa 1929, wood mohair upholstery with wood veneer accents and feet, couch upholstery in shades of burgundy with gold piping. $2,500

Part of a four-piece Harden & Co. livingroom set, comprising: settee, rocker and two armchairs, settee 54in. wide, circa 1910. (Skinner) $2,800

Tiger maple and cherry breakfast table, New England, circa 1800, refinished, brass replaced, 28¼in. high. (Skinner Inc.) $2,100

A classical carved and inlaid mahogany breakfast table, attributed to Duncan Phyfe, New York, 1805–1815, 49½in. wide open. (Christie's) $7,500

Classical mahogany drop leaf table with drawer, possibly New York, circa 1815, old refinish, 51½in. long (open). (Skinner) $863

Classical mahogany veneer breakfast table, probably Boston, circa 1815, the drop leaves over four curving beaded legs, 42in. wide. (Skinner) $1,120

A Queen Anne figured walnut drop-leaf breakfast table, Boston, Massachusetts, 1740–60, the oblong top with two hinged D-shaped leaves, on cabriole legs ending in pad feet, 27in. long, extended. (Sotheby's) $19,550

A Federal mahogany breakfast table, New York, 1810–1820, the rectangular top with clover-shaped drop leaves above an apron with a frieze drawer on either side, 40¼in. wide (open). (Christie's) $5,175

Federal cherry breakfast table, New England, early 19th century, single drawer with beading and replaced brass, 36in. wide. (Skinner Inc.) $765

Federal mahogany inlaid breakfast table, New York City, circa 1790, with a working and a simulated drawer, 31¼in. wide. (Skinner) $11,500

A classical carved mahogany breakfast table, New York, 1810–1820, the rectangular top with two hinged double elliptical drop leaves, 49½in. wide (open). (Christie's) $11,500

Federal mahogany breakfast table, probably New York area, circa 1815, the rectangular top with shaped leaves above a beaded skirt, 34in. wide. (Skinner) **$1,610**

A classical carved mahogany and tropical wood breakfast table, New York, 1810–1820, the rectangular top with double-elliptical drop leaves, 47³/₄in. wide (open). (Christie's) **$48,300**

Federal cherry breakfast table, New England, circa 1810, refinished, replaced brass pull, 32¹/₂in. wide. (Skinner Inc.) **$1,000**

Classical mahogany veneer table, probably Baltimore, Maryland area, 1815–20, with reeded top, pedestal and four curving legs ending in brass paw feet, 42³/₄in. extended. (Skinner) **$978**

Chippendale mahogany breakfast table, New London County, Connecticut, 18th century, with chamfered legs, shaped stretchers and early brass, 20.75in. wide. (Skinner) **$3,105**

Federal mahogany veneer carved breakfast table, New England, 1810–20, rectangular leaves with rounded corners flank cockbeaded veneered sides, 19³/₄in. wide. (Skinner) **$1,092**

A classical carved mahogany and mahogany veneer breakfast table, New York, circa 1815–1820, with one working and one faux drawer, 37¹/₂in. wide. (Skinner) **$4,312**

Federal cherry breakfast table, New England, circa 1800, serpentine shaped top above shaped skirts flanked by squared tapering molded legs, 17¹/₂in. wide. (Skinner) **$1,035**

Classical mahogany carved breakfast table, probably New York, circa 1825, the top with shaped drop leaves above a cockbeaded inlaid apron, 40in. wide. (Skinner) **$1,150**

A Chippendale mahogany card table, the rectangular hinged top with serpentine molded edges and outset rounded corners above a rectangular frame fitted with an incised long drawer over pierced knee returns, on molded Marlborough legs with block feet, 33¾in. wide.
(Christie's) $27,600

A Classical brass-inlaid and carved mahogany card table, Boston, 1820–1840, the rectangular hinged top with brass Greek-key banding and canted corners above a conforming and coved veneered frame with a brass and ebonized banding over carved molding above a leaf and C-scroll carved lyre pedestal over an octagonal inlaid and brass-mounted base above carved molding, on reeded downswept legs fitted with hairy-paw castors, 36in. wide.
(Christie's) $19,550

Classical mahogany carved card table, New England, early 19th century, 35in. wide. (Skinner Inc.) $530

Reproduction Hepplewhite-style card table, in mahogany with serpentine front and inlaid edge and apron, 36in. long. (Eldred's) $550

Transitional cherry card table, Amesbury, Massachusetts, late 18th century, hinged top, with end pieces running vertically, 36in. wide. (Skinner) $1,150

Late Classical carved mahogany card table, probably New York State, circa 1830, old surface, $36^3/4$in. wide. (Skinner Inc.) $1,400

A good pair of classical stenciled and gilt brass-inlaid rosewood swivel-top card tables, New York, circa 1825, 36in. wide. (Sotheby's) $11,500

Queen Anne mahogany card table, Boston, Massachusetts, 1730–60, with turret-like corners, thumb-molded drawer, cabriole legs and high pad feet, $26^1/4$in. wide. (Skinner) $134,500

American console card table, New England, late 18th/early 19th century, in mahogany, modified 'D'-form, banded inlay to edge, $34^1/2$in. wide. (Eldred's) $3,850

A paint decorated pine tilt-top gaming table, American, probably New York, circa 1840-1860, 28in high. (Sotheby's) $7,475

The Hubbard family Queen Anne mahogany concertina-action gaming table, Boston, 1730–50, 34in. wide. (Christie's) $29,900

CHIPPENDALE

A Chippendale carved mahogany card table, Rhode Island or Massachusetts, 1770-1790, with hinged serpentine top, 32in. wide. (Christie's New York) $3,400

A Chippendale mahogany card table with scalloped front skirt, Mass., circa 1770, 31½in. wide, open.
$10,000

Chippendale cherry inlaid card table, Massachusetts, 1750–80, rectangular top with fluted edge above an undercut inner top, 31¼in. wide.
(Skinner) $5,750

A Chippendale carved mahogany card table, Philadelphia, circa 1770, the rectangular hinged top with thumbmolded edge above conforming apron, 35½in. wide. (Christie's) $8,625

Chippendale mahogany gaming table, probably Massachusetts, late 18th century, on four molded Marlborough legs, 35in. wide. (Skinner) $1,495

A Chippendale carved mahogany card table, Philadelphia, 1760-1780, the rectangular hinged top above a conforming case fitted with a thumbmolded long drawer, 33in. wide.(Christie's) $40,250

A Chippendale carved mahogany card table, Boston-Salem, Massachusetts, circa 1760, the hinged oblong top with squared outset corners, 32in. wide extended.
(Sotheby's) $134,500

A Chippendale carved mahogany card-table, Philadelphia, 1760–1770, the hinged rectangular top on four cabriole legs with ball-and-claw feet, 34⅛in. wide. (Christie's) $35,650

The Van Vechten family Chippendale carved and figured mahogany serpentine-front five-leg card table, New York, circa 1770, top 34¼in. wide. (Sotheby's) $266,500

CHIPPENDALE

A Chippendale carved walnut card table, Philadelphia, 1760–80, on foliate and flowerhead carved cabriole legs, 36in. wide. (Christie's) $8,625

A good Chippendale carved and figured mahogany card table, Philadelphia, circa 1780, on square molded legs, 34in. wide. (Sotheby's) $8,625

A rare Chippendale carved and figured mahogany serpentine-front card table, Philadelphia, circa 1775, top 38in. wide. (Sotheby's) $29,000

A Chippendale carved mahogany five-legged card-table, New York, 1760-1780, the serpentine top with squared outset corners above a conforming skirt, 34in wide. (Christie's) $123,500

A Chippendale figured mahogany diminutive serpentine-front stop-fluted card table, Goddard-Townsend School, Newport, Rhode Island, circa 1780, 32in. wide. (Sotheby's) $41,400

A Chippendale carved mahogany card table, Philadelphia, 1760-1780, the rectangular molded hinged top above a conforming apron, 32¼in. wide. (Sotheby's) $34,500

An extremely fine and rare Chippendale carved mahogany card table, Boston-Salem, Massachusetts, circa 1765, the oblong top with squared outset corners, width 31¼in. (Sotheby's) $150,000

Rare small mahogany serpentine Chippendale card table, probably Rhode Island, circa 1760 (minor imperfections), 24in. wide. (Skinner Inc.) $9,400

A Chippendale carved mahogany card table, New York, 1760–80, the serpentine hinged top with square corners above a conforming apron, 34¼in. wide. (Christie's) $46,000

CLASSICAL

Classical mahogany veneer carved card table, New York, 1820–30, 36¼in. wide. (Skinner) **$632**

Classical mahogany card table, New York or New Jersey, circa 1830, refinished, 36in. wide. (Skinner Inc.) **$2,400**

Classical carved mahogany veneer card table, Mid Atlantic States, 1830, 36in. wide. (Skinner) **$546**

A Classical gilt stenciled mahogany card table, New York, 1825-1835, on four acanthus carved legs with lion's paw feet, 36in. wide. (Christie's New York) **$2,600**

Classical carved mahogany veneer and brass card table, probably New York or New Jersey, 1820s, with swivel top, veneered skirt and leaf carved lyre shaped pedestal, 35¾in. wide. (Skinner) **$2,300**

A classical mahogany carved and inlaid gaming table, New England, circa 1820, with tiger maple crossbanded borders and brass inlaid stringing, 35½in. wide. (Skinner) **$1,955**

A classical mahogany and ormolu card table, New York, 1820–40, the rectangular hinged top with rounded corners and band inlay, 36¼in. wide. (Christie's) **$5,750**

Classical Revival carved mahogany card table, Salem, Massachusetts, circa 1820, the rectangular top with reeded edge, 35½in. wide. (Skinner Inc.) **$3,100**

Classical carved mahogany veneer card table, attributed to Isaac Vose & Son, Boston, Massachusetts, 1820s, 33in. wide. (Skinner) **$1,495**

CLASSICAL

Classical mahogany and rosewood veneer card table, probably Boston, circa 1815, refinished, 36in. wide. (Skinner Inc.) $1,060

Classical mahogany card table, probably Massachusetts, circa 1820, old refinish, 34³/₄in. wide. (Skinner) $1,265

Classical carved mahogany veneer card table, Middle Atlantic States, circa 1830, some refinish, 36in. wide. (Skinner Inc.) $1,250

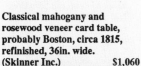

A classical mahogany card table, New York, 1815–1825, the rectangular patera veneered top with canted corners above a foliate carved pedestal and quadripartite base, 35³/₄in. wide. (Christie's) $1,840

Classical mahogany carved and mahogany veneer card table, Massachusetts, circa 1820, the shaped top with beaded edge above a conforming skirt, 35¹/₂in. wide. (Skinner) $1,725

An important classical gilt-metal mounted mahogany and rosewood swivel-top card table, labeled *Charles Honoré Lannuier, New York*, circa 1810, 35³/₄in. wide. (Sotheby's) $310,500

Classical mahogany carved veneered card table, New England, circa 1830, with curving legs ending in brass paw feet, 35¹/₄in. wide. (Skinner) $900

Classical carved veneered brass inlaid table, probably New York, circa 1820s, the green marble top with triple banded edge, 33in. wide. (Skinner) $8,125

A classical eagle-decorated swivel-top mahogany card table, New York, circa 1830, on a circular plinth and downswept legs, 40in. wide. (Sotheby's) $1,725

CLASSICAL

A classical inlaid and carved mahogany serpentine-front card table, Salem, Massachusetts, circa 1820, 39in. wide.
(Sotheby's) $2,875

Classical carved mahogany veneer card table, Boston, circa 1825–35, old refinish, 35½in. wide.
(Skinner) $1,265

Classical mahogany and mahogany veneered with brass inlaid card table, Massachusetts, circa 1825, 37in. wide.
(Skinner) $1,092

A classical mahogany veneer card-table, attributed to Duncan Phyfe, New York, 1820–1830, the crossbanded D-shaped hinged top swiveling above a conforming apron, 35½in. wide.
(Christie's) $4,130

One of a pair of classical mahogany brass-inlaid card-tables, attributed to Charles-Honore Lannuier, New York, 1810–1819, on four waterleaf-carved legs with paw castors, 35¼in. wide.
(Christie's)
(Two) $101,500

Classical carved mahogany and satinwood veneer card table, New York City, 1800–15, the top with canted corners pivots above the satinwood skirt, 37½in. wide.
(Skinner) $6,900

A fine classical carved mahogany and rosewood brass-inlaid swivel-top card table, Philadelphia, Pennsylvania, circa 1825, 38in. wide.
(Sotheby's) $4,025

A classical brass-inlaid carved and figured mahogany games table, North Shore, Massachusetts, circa 1820, 36¾in. wide.
(Sotheby's) $3,737

A fine classical carved mahogany swivel-top card table, labeled *Stephen and Moses Youngs*, New York, circa 1815, 36in. wide.
(Sotheby's) $7,500

CLASSICAL

Classical mahogany carved and veneer gaming table, probably New York, circa 1825, 36in. wide.
(Skinner) $460

Classical carved mahogany and veneer card table, probably Massachusetts, circa 1820, 38¼in. wide.
(Skinner) $1,760

Classical mahogany carved card table, Massachusetts, circa 1820, 36in. wide.
(Skinner) $1,045

A classical mahogany, figured maple and parcel-gilt card-table, stamped *H. Lannuier, New York,* 1815–1819, on four gilded waterleaf-carved animal paw feet with castors, 36½in. wide.
(Christie's) $23,000

A classical ebony and rosewood-inlaid mahogany swivel-top card table, Boston, Massachusetts, circa 1820, 35½in. wide open.
(Sotheby's) $2,185

A classical carved mahogany card-table, attributed to Duncan Phyfe, New York, 1805-1810, the rectangular top over rope-turned columns above a platform base, 35¾in. wide.
(Christie's) $4,600

Classical carved mahogany and mahogany veneer brass inlaid card table, probably Massachusetts, circa 1820, 37in. wide.
(Skinner) $1,320

Classical mahogany carved and mahogany veneer card table, possibly Massachusetts, circa 1825, on a turned and carved post and concave shaped platform, 36in. wide.
(Skinner) $978

A classical mahogany cardtable, New York, 1800–20, the hinged clover-shaped top above a conforming apron on five ring-turned and reeded legs, 35¾in. wide.
(Christie's) $2,300

FEDERAL

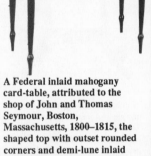

Federal mahogany inlaid card table, probably Massachusetts, circa 1790, the folding top with bowfront square corners, 35¾in. wide. (Skinner) $1,955

A Federal inlaid mahogany card table, Mass., 1800-15, 34in. wide. (Christie's) $1,650

A Federal inlaid mahogany card table with D-shaped top, Mass., 1790-1810, 34in. wide. (Christie's) $5,500

Federal inlaid mahogany card table, Massachusetts, circa 1810, the banded inlaid edge serpentine shaped hinged top above a conformingly shaped frieze on tapering reeded legs, length 35¼in. (Butterfield & Butterfield) $2,070

A late Federal carved mahogany card table, Salem, Massachusetts, 1800–1815, the hinged serpentine top with outset rounded corners over a conforming frieze on rope-turned legs, 37in. wide. (Christie's) $1,540

A Federal inlaid mahogany card-table, attributed to the shop of John and Thomas Seymour, Boston, Massachusetts, 1800–1815, the shaped top with outset rounded corners and demi-lune inlaid edges, 36in. wide. (Christie's) $19,550

A good Federal inlaid mahogany serpentine card table, attributed to Bryant & Loud, Boston, Massachusetts, circa 1815, the shaped top with lunette-inlaid edge, 35¼in. wide. (Sotheby's) $3,250

A fine Federal inlaid mahogany games table, Salem Area, Massachusetts, circa 1795, the rectangular top with astragal corners and cross-banded edge, 35½in. wide. (Sotheby's) $3,500

Federal mahogany and satinwood card table, Massachusetts, circa 1810, the molded edge serpentine shaped hinged top above a conformingly shaped frieze, length 37in. (Butterfield & Butterfield) $1,035

Federal mahogany and birch veneer card table, Massachusetts or New Hampshire, circa 1800, 35³/₄in. wide. (Skinner Inc.) **$8,750**

A fine Federal inlaid mahogany games table, signed *William Marlen, Boston, Massachusetts,* circa 1795, 35³/₄in. wide. (Sotheby's) **$14,950**

A fine Federal inlaid and figured mahogany card table, New York, circa 1805, the oblong top with line-inlaid edge, 34³/₄in. wide. (Sotheby's) **$4,600**

An important Federal satinwood-inlaid and figured mahogany demi-lune games table, labeled *John Seymour & Son, Creek Square, Boston, Massachusetts, 1794-96.* (Sotheby's) **$541,500**

A Federal inlaid mahogany card table, North Shore, Massachusetts, 1790–1810, on square double tapering line-inlaid legs with inlaid cuffs, 36in. wide. (Christie's) **$17,250**

American Federal inlaid card table, Massachusetts, circa 1800, in mahogany with mahogany and satinwood veneers, 36in. wide. (Eldred's) **$4,620**

A Federal inlaid mahogany card table, Massachusetts, 1790–1810, on ring-turned and reeded tapering legs with ball and cylinder feet, 36¹/₂in. wide. (Christie's) **$2,300**

Federal mahogany and flame birch veneer card table, Massachusetts, circa 1800, with an inlaid edge and ovolo corners, 36in. wide. (Skinner) **$1,955**

Federal mahogany veneer carved card table, North Shore, Massachusetts, with shaped top and ovolo corners above legs with leaf carving, 36in. wide. (Skinner) **$5,462**

FEDERAL

Federal mahogany inlaid card table, Newport or Providence, Rhode Island, circa 1790, 36in. wide.
(Skinner Inc.) $3,400

Federal mahogany veneered card table, probably Connecticut, circa 1820, the serpentine top with ovolo corners, 36in. wide. $1,650

A Federal inlaid mahogany card table on four tapering legs, Baltimore, 1790-1810, 36¼in. diam. (Christie's) $4,800

A Federal inlaid mahogany card-table, Rhode Island, 1790–1810, the hinged D-shaped top with lightwood banding over a conforming frieze centered by a fluted vase issuing bellflowers and rosettes, 36¼in. wide.
(Christie's) $16,500

A pair of Federal inlaid mahogany card tables, Baltimore, 1790–1810, each with demi-lune hinged top with thumbmolded edge, 35½in. wide.
(Christie's) $14,950

One of a pair of Federal inlaid mahogany card-tables, attributed to John Townsend, Newport, Rhode Island, 1780-1800, each top with serpentine front and sides, 35in wide.
(Christie's) $43,700

Federal mahogany inlaid card table, Concord, New Hampshire, early 19th century, with panels outlined in stringing, 34¾in. wide.
(Skinner) $1,610

A Federal carved mahogany card table, attributed to Henry Connelly, circa 1810, 36in. wide.
(Christie's) $3,300

Federal mahogany inlaid card table, Concord, New Hampshire, 1794–96, probably the work of Choate and Martin, 34⅛in. wide.
(Skinner) $2,070

FEDERAL

Federal mahogany inlaid card table, Rhode Island, circa 1800, old refinish, 35³/₄in. wide. (Skinner Inc.) $5,250

Federal mahogany inlaid card table, Newport, Rhode Island circa 1800, on four square tapering front legs; two back legs swing to support the top. (Skinner Inc.) $25,000

Federal mahogany card table with mahogany and birch veneers, Portsmouth, New Hampshire, circa 1800, 36in. wide. (Skinner Inc.) $11,800

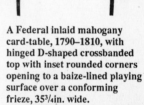

A Federal inlaid and figured mahogany demilune card table, Connecticut, circa 1800, the hinged D-shaped top with radiating inlay, 34¹/₂in. wide open. (Sotheby's) $3,450

One of a pair of Federal inlaid mahogany card tables, Baltimore, 1790–1810, each with radiating veneered demi-lune top with banded edge, 36in. wide. (Christie's) (Two) $222,500

A Federal inlaid mahogany card-table, 1790–1810, with hinged D-shaped crossbanded top with inset rounded corners opening to a baize-lined playing surface over a conforming frieze, 35³/₄in. wide. (Christie's) $8,500

Federal mahogany inlaid card table, probably Maryland, circa 1800, the skirt is divided into three panels outlined in contrasting veneer, 36in. wide. (Skinner) $1,380

A Federal inlaid cherrywood card table, New Hampshire, 1790–1810, the hinged D-shaped top with banded line inlaid edge, 36in. wide. (Christie's) $920

A good Federal inlaid mahogany games table, New England, possibly Rhode Island, circa 1800, the rectangular top with astragal corners and checker-inlaid edge, 36in. wide. (Sotheby's) $4,025

Federal mahogany inlaid card table, probably Maryland, circa 1800, the skirt is divided into three panels outlined in contrasting veneer, 36in. wide. (Skinner) $1,380

A Federal mahogany inlaid card table, probably Mass., circa 1790, 35in. wide. (Skinner)　　$3,400

Federal mahogany veneer card table, Massachusetts, early 19th century, with beaded edges on the table tops, 36in. wide. (Skinner)　　$978

Federal mahogany inlaid card table, Massachusetts, circa 1810, refinished, 35½in. wide. (Skinner Inc.)　　$3,300

A Federal inlaid mahogany card table, North Shore, Massachusetts, 1800–1810, the serpentine top with outset rounded corners and inlaid edge folding above a conforming apron, 35½in. wide. (Christie's)　　$2,500

Federal mahogany and bird's-eye maple card table, probably Massachusetts, circa 1810–1815, on a lyre-form support on down-curving legs, ending in square brass casters, 33½in. wide. (Butterfield & Butterfield)　　$4,150

Federal mahogany veneer carved card table, Salem, Massachusetts, circa 1820, leaf carving on a star punched background, 38¾in. wide. (Skinner Inc.)　　$1,300

A fine Federal inlaid mahogany card table, Massachusetts, 1790-1810, on square tapering line-inlaid legs with inlaid cuffs, 91cm. wide. (Christie's New York)　　$3,025

A good Federal maple-inlaid mahogany serpentine-front card table, Massachusetts, circa 1795, the hinged shaped top with inlaid edge, 36¼in. wide. (Sotheby's)　　$4,887

Federal cherry veneered card table, Southern Massachusetts, circa 1810, on four ring turned reeded tapering legs ending in turned feet, 35¼in. wide. (Skinner Inc.)　　$3,250

Federal mahogany veneer card table, Massachusetts, early 19th century, 37.4in. wide. (Skinner) $1,495

Federal mahogany inlaid card table, probably Massachusetts, circa 1815, 36in. wide. (Skinner) $1,150

Federal mahogany inlaid card table, Boston, circa 1815, on ring-turned reeded tapering legs, 36½in. wide. (Skinner) $5,750

Federal cherry inlaid and carved gaming table, possibly central Massachusetts, circa 1800, folding rectangular top with carved edge, 33in. wide. (Skinner) $920

Federal mahogany veneer carved card table, North Shore Massachusetts, 1815–25, the bowed top with incised leading edge flanked by ovolo corners above legs with colonnettes, 36¼in. wide. (Skinner) $488

Federal mahogany and flame birch veneer card table, Massachusetts, circa 1800, the edge of the top outlined in patterned inlay above inlaid skirt panel, 35¾in. wide. (Skinner) $8,050

A very fine Federal birchwood-inlaid mahogany card table, Northern Coast of Massachusetts, circa 1810, 37in. wide. (Sotheby's) $17,250

A Federal carved and figured mahogany serpentine-front card table, Salem area, Massachusetts, circa 1815, 34¾in. wide. (Sotheby's) $2,000

A Federal inlaid mahogany games table, Massachusetts, circa 1800, the rectangular top with astragal corners and crossbanded edge, 36in. wide. (Sotheby's) $1,610

FEDERAL, NEW ENGLAND

Federal mahogany veneered card table, New England, early 19th century, refinished, 36½ in. wide.
(Skinner Inc.) $950

Federal cherry and bird's-eye maple card table, New England, early 19th century, 36in. wide.
(Skinner) $1,380

Federal mahogany inlaid card table, probably New England, circa 1790, the rectangular folding top with ovolo corners, 36in. wide.
(Skinner) $7,475

Federal inlaid birch and mahogany card table, New England, circa 1800–1810, on square tapering line inlaid legs, 36in. wide.
(Butterfield & Butterfield) $1,650

Federal mahogany card table, New England, early 19th century, the reeded edge shaped hinged top above a conformingly shaped frieze on ring-turned, twisted rope legs on ball feet, length 36¾in.
(Butterfield & Butterfield) $690

A Federal inlaid mahogany demi-lune card table, New England, circa 1810, the D-shaped top with inlaid edge and rectangular inlaid dies, 36¼in. wide.
(Sotheby's) $2,875

A Federal inlaid mahogany card table, New England, circa 1815, the oblong top with inlaid edge, 35¾in. wide.
(Sotheby's) $1,610

Country Federal carved mahogany inlaid card table, New England, 17½in. deep.
(Skinner) $1,320

Federal mahogany and maple veneer card table, New England, circa 1800, old refinish, 35¾in. wide.
(Skinner Inc.) $3,250

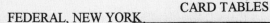

Federal mahogany inlaid card table, New York City, circa 1790 the folding top with serpentine front, 36¼in. wide.
(Skinner) $11,500

A fine Federal inlaid and figured mahogany demi-lune card table, attributed to William Whitehead, New York, circa 1805, 36½in. wide.
(Sotheby's) $17,250

A fine Federal inlaid and figured mahogany bow-front card table, New York, circa 1810, the oblong top with conformingly shaped hinged leaf, 36in. wide.
(Sotheby's) $3,162

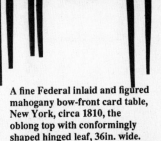

A Federal satinwood and mahogany card-table, New York, 1790–1810, the hinged clover-shaped top with crossbanded edges above a conforming apron centering a raised rectangular inlaid reserve, 35½in. wide.
(Christie's) $8,500

Federal carved mahogany card table, New York, circa 1810–1815, on an acanthus carved pedestal above a quadripartite base, 36½in. wide.
(Butterfield & Butterfield) $4,800

A Federal inlaid mahogany demi-lune card table, New York, 1790–1810, the hinged top centering a ring of inlaid bell flowers above a conforming apron, on square tapering bellflower inlaid legs, 36⅛in. wide.
(Christie's) $5,520

A fine Federal carved mahogany swivel-top card table, New York, circa 1810, on waterleaf-carved reeded and ring-turned legs, 36¾in. wide.
(Sotheby's) $3,000

An important pair of Federal satinwood-inlaid figured mahogany demi-lune card tables, attributed to William Whitehead, New York, circa 1800, 36in. wide.
(Sotheby's) $151,000

A Federal mahogany card table, New York, 1800–1815, the hinged clover-shaped top above a conforming apron, on five reeded cylindrical tapering legs, 36¼in. wide.
(Christie's) $2,530

Late 19th century Renaissance Revival inlaid mahogany center table, America, 45½in. wide. **$1,850**

Renaissance Revival walnut center table, third quarter 19th century, stamped *W. Gertz*, with carved laurel leaf frieze, 28¾in. long. (Skinner Inc.) **$4,050**

Renaissance Revival rosewood and marble center table, third quarter 19th century, 42in. wide. (Skinner Inc.) **$2,600**

A classical stenciled mahogany center table, New York, 1810–1820, the circular marble top above a conforming apron with gilt-stenciled edge over a columnar pedestal on a tripartite base, 37½in. diameter. (Christie's) **$4,830**

Renaissance Revival walnut center table, third quarter 19th century, the inset marble top above a carved pedestal with four fluted supports, 30½in. high. (Skinner Inc.) **$1,250**

A classical mahogany veneer center-table, New York, early 19th century, with a molded circular fossiled black marble top above a crossbanded conforming frieze, with scrolling feet, 29½in. high. (Christie's) **$3,900**

Rennaissance Revival inlaid walnut center table, circa 1870, 42¼in. wide. (Skinner) **$2,250**

Marquetry and laminated wood center table, 20th century, inlaid with various woods, raised on cabriole legs, 29¾in. diameter. (Skinner Inc.) **$950**

A Renaissance Revival marble top parlor table, by T. Brooks Cabinet & Upholstery Warehouse, circa 1865, the white oval top 37in. long. **$2,180**

Rosewood center table, late 19th century, raised on single baluster form pedestal supported by three griffon headed C-scroll legs, 26in. high.
(Skinner) $550

A walnut center table, Pennsylvania, late 18th/early 19th century, on tapering block and ring-turned legs with flattened ball feet, 71in. wide.
(Christie's) $10,350

Rococo Revival walnut center table, mid 19th century, shaped carrara marble top on a base carved throughout with grape clusters and leaves, 39in. long.
(Skinner) $2,530

Classical mahogany veneer center table, New York, 1810–30, marble top on a conforming skirt with canted corners over a four-column pedestal, 33½in. wide.
(Skinner Inc.) $1,400

A classical carved mahogany center table, Philadelphia, 1815–1825, acanthus leaf-carved pedestal with carved gadrooning and cross-hatching flanked by four saber legs, 35¾in. wide.
(Christie's) $1,380

Classical marble and figured veneer center table, Middle Atlantic States, 1835–45, the hexagonal shape with marble center above a three pillar support, 38¼in. wide.
(Skinner) $748

A classical marble-top center table, New York, 1810–20, on a flat tripartite base with acanthus and lobed and melon-carved feet, 36in. diameter.
(Christie's) $5,750

American Renaissance Revival gilt bronze mounted rosewood, marquetry and marble inset center table, third quarter 19th century, attributed to Pottier & Stymus, New York City, 51½in. wide.
(Skinner) $19,550

Carved Lotus center table, executed by John Bradstreet, Minneapolis, circa 1905, original black finish, unsigned, 30in. diam.
(Skinner Inc.) $19,000

A Queen Anne maple dining table with oval drop-leaf top, Rhode Island, circa 1760, 50in. wide open.
(Skinner) $9,300

Arts and Crafts dining table, four octagonal column base, corbels, two leaves, original finish, 60in. diameter.
(Skinner) $3,335

Chippendale mahogany drop leaf table, Massachusetts, circa 1800, 48³/₄in. long extended.
(Skinner) $1,495

A Federal inlaid mahogany three-part dining table, New England, circa 1800, in three parts; with a drop-leaf center section flanked by D-shaped ends, 8ft. 11¹/₂in. long.
(Sotheby's) $74,000

Lifetime oak pedestal dining table, No. 9057, circa 1907, round extension top on square pedestal with four radiating legs, three leaves, Paine Furniture retail tag, 48in. diameter.
(Skinner) $1,035

Chippendale cherry drop leaf table, attributed to Samuel Sewall, York, Maine, 18th century, with molded legs and shaped skirts, 38¹/₂in. deep extended.
(Skinner) $1,955

A Chippendale carved mahogany dining table, Essex County, Massachusetts, circa 1770, angular cabriole legs on claw-and-ball feet, 47in. wide.
(Sotheby's) $5,462

Two American Hepplewhite 'D'-end tables, in mahogany, originally the ends of a larger dining table, 50in. long.
(Eldred's) $1,430

Federal mahogany veneer three part dining table, Boston, Massachusetts, circa 1800, 161¹/₄in. long extended.
(Skinner) $4,600

One-drawer table, Canterbury, New Hampshire, circa 1850, pine, red paint, two board top, mortised case, finely turned tapered legs, 60¾in. long. (Skinner) $2,300

Queen Anne painted maple drop leaf dining table, New England, 1760–80, extended 42¼in. (Skinner Inc.) $4,450

One-drawer table, Enfield, New Hampshire, circa 1840, curly birch and pine, well-shaped deep ogee apron, finely turned legs, 36in. wide. (Skinner) $8,050

Roycroft pedestal base dining table, East Aurora, New York, circa 1910, signed with logo, no leaves, 48in. diam. (Skinner) $3,100

Classical mahogany and mahogany veneer banquet table, probably Massachusetts, circa 1825, the double hinged D-form top on a conforming beaded apron, 172¾in. long extended. (Skinner) $6,900

L. & J.G. Stickley dining table, circa 1912, no. 720, circular top, straight apron, supported on five tapering legs, with four extension leaves, 48in. diameter. (Skinner Inc.) $2,200

"Bonnie" dining table, designed by Ferruccio Tritta, produced by Studio Nove, New York, on three columnar supports, 56in. diameter. (Skinner Inc.) $3,250

A Federal mahogany dining table, circa 1815, 47in. wide. (Skinner) $1,250

Limbert dining table, circa 1910, circular top over arched skirt connecting to four square legs, 51in. diameter. (Skinner Inc.) $1,350

A mixed maple faux bamboo-turned dressing table, possibly R.J. Horner and Company, New York City, 1875–1890, the rectangular pediment with raised and glazed central panel, applied medial shelves and bamboo-turned molding and finials above a conforming surface with hinged and canted rectangular lid opening to reveal a fitted interior, on four bamboo-turned legs embellished with bamboo-turned brackets and joined by similar H-stretchers, 31in. wide.
(Christie's) $3,800

Renaissance Revival walnut and
burl walnut drop-well dresser,
third quarter 19th century,
50⅛in. wide.
(Skinner)   **$1,035**

A mirrored dressing table
with circle pulls, by Gustav
Stickley.   **$3,100**

Federal mahogany carved and
bird's eye maple veneered inlaid
bureau and dressing glass,
Boston, circa 1810–20, old
brasses, 39in. wide.
(Skinner)   **$85,000**

A classical carved mahogany
dressing table, New York,
1810-1815, the upper section
surmounted by acanthus and
rosette-carved serpentine arms
centering a rectangular mirror,
40½in. wide.
(Christie's)   **$4,025**

Federal mahogany veneer
dressing chest, New England,
1810–20, the dressing glass
supported by scrolled supports
above two-tiered drawers,
38¼in. wide.
(Skinner)   **$862**

A very fine and rare Federal,
ormolu-mounted figured
mahogany dressing table with
mirror, attributed to Duncan
Phyfe, New York, circa 1810,
36½in. wide.
(Sotheby's)   **$25,300**

Classical mahogany veneer
dressing bureau, New England
or New York, second quarter
19th century, polished black
marble top above recessed
paneled sides, 39in. wide.
(Skinner)   **$2,185**

Eastlake lockend walnut
chest of drawers, late 19th
century, superstructure of
mirrored cabinet and raised
galleried shelves, 35¼in. wide.
(Skinner Inc.)   **$1,500**

Classical rosewood veneer
cherry and bird's eye maple
bureau with dressing glass,
Orange, Massachusetts, circa
1835, old refinish, old brass
pulls, 41¼in. wide.
(Skinner)   **$1,955**

DRESSING TABLES

A yellow painted pine dressing table with stencil and foliate designs, New England, circa 1825, 34in. wide.
(Skinner) $1,000

Federal mahogany dressing table, New England, circa 1825, 33in. wide.
(Skinner) $750

A fine and rare Federal paint decorated pine dressing table, Salem, Massachusetts, circa 1820, 37¼in. wide.
(Sotheby's) $65,750

A Federal paint-decorated pine dressing table, New England, probably Massachusetts or Maine, circa 1825–1828, the shaped splashboard with brass rosette-mounted scrolls above a shelf incorporating two drawers, 33¼in. wide.
(Sotheby's) $11,500

Art Deco bird's-eye maple vanity and stool, second quarter 20th century, the elevated partially framed mirror plate swiveling within a U-shaped bracket, 38½in. wide.
(Butterfield & Butterfield) $862

A Federal inlaid mahogany Beau Brummel, American or English, 1790-1800, the two-part hinged top opening to a compartmented interior fitted with a ratcheted mirror, 29¾in. wide.
(Christie's) $920

Rare William and Mary japanned maple and pine dressing table, Boston area, 1710-1715 (one leg and foot, an old replacement), 34in. wide.
(Skinner) $50,000

A late Federal red-painted dressing table, New England, early 19th century, the scalloped splashboard enclosing a rectangular top, 30in. wide.
(Christie's) $1,265

A Federal inlaid mahogany Beau Brummel, New York, circa 1800, the hinged rectangular top opening to a tripartite interior, 27¾in. wide.
(Sotheby's) $4,600

American Sheraton stepped vanity, in old yellow and black paint with stenciled decoration, 33½in. wide. (Eldred's) $550

A paint decorated pine bow-front single-drawer diminutive dressing table, New England, circa 1825, 30¼in. wide. (Sotheby's) $3,220

Classical tiger maple and mahogany veneer dressing table, circa 1825, refinished, 36in. wide. (Skinner) $1,840

Grain painted and stencil decorated dressing stand, Maine, circa 1820, old red and black graining with stenciled floral and fruit decoration, 29¼in. wide. (Skinner) $460

A Federal painted dressing glass, Massachusetts or New Hampshire, circa 1810, painted cream with outline of red and gray pinstriping, top with painted foliate devices, 17¾in. wide. (Skinner) $1,092

A Federal bird's-eye maple and mahogany veneered dressing table, New England, circa 1825, the scrolled splashboard with a stepped and conforming bird's-eye maple veneered drawer, 37in. wide. (Christie's) $3,680

An American Federal mahogany and maple dressing bureau in the manner of John and Thomas Seymour of Boston, on turned tapering reeded legs, 38½in. wide. (Christie's) $7,100

A Queen Anne cherry dressing table, Upper Connecticut River Valley, circa 1785, 34½in. wide. (Skinner) $13,750

Federal painted and decorated dressing table, North Shore, Massachusetts, early 19th century, with early sage green paint, stenciled and freehand decoration, 34¼in. wide. (Skinner) $920

Heywood Wakefield five-drawer chest with mirror, original champagne finish, 1952, 34¼in. wide.
(Skinner) $345

A classical mahogany dressing table with mirror, attributed to the workshop of Duncan Phyfe & Sons, New York, circa 1845, 47⅞in. wide.
(Sotheby's) $8,750

Federal bird's eye maple veneer bureau with dressing glass, New England, circa 1815, old glass pulls, 39in. wide.
(Skinner) $1,980

A Federal carved mahogany dressing table, New York, 1800–1815, the stepped rectangular top with four short drawers surmounted by a rectangular frame containing a conforming plate on serpentine dolphin supports, 63¼in. high.
(Christie's) $2,750

Classical mahogany and gilt-bronze mirrored bureau, New York, circa 1820, the rectangular half marble top surmounted by a rectangular mirror frame with gilt-bronze oak leaf border, width 42¼in.
(Butterfield & Butterfield) $2,300

A late Federal carved mahogany dressing table with looking glass, Massachusetts, 1815-1825, the upper section with acanthus carved scrolled arms centering a rectangular looking glass, 37in wide.
(Christie's) $2,070

Federal mahogany carved and inlaid dressing bureau, Boston or North Shore, Massachusetts, circa 1810, supported by fluted posts and scrolled side arms, 38½in. wide.
(Skinner Inc.) $19,000

Roycroft mirrored dressing table, East Aurora, New York, circa 1910, with swing handles, tapering MacMurdo feet, signed with orb, 39in. wide. (Skinner Inc.) $1,300

Classical mahogany and mahogany veneer carved dressing bureau, probably New York State, circa 1825, 38in. wide.
(Skinner) $805

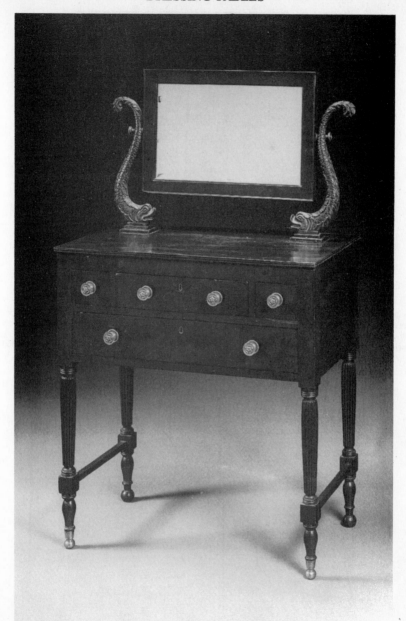

A Federal mahogany veneered dressing chest with mirror, New York City, 1810–1820, the
rectangular frame enclosing a mirror flanked by carved dophin supports above a rectangular top
over a conforming case fitted with three short drawers, the central drawer of greater width, above
a single long drawer, on ring-turned and reeded legs with swelled feet joined by straight stretchers,
33½in. wide.
(Christie's) $5,175

The Samuel Coates fine and rare Chippendale carved and figured walnut dressing table, Philadelphia, Pennsylvania, circa 1760, the rectangular top with molded edge above one long and three short thumbmolded drawers, flanked by fluted quarter-columns, the shaped scrolling apron below on cabriole legs ending in claw-and-ball feet, width of top 35in.
(Sotheby's) $41,400

A very fine and rare Chippendale carved and figured walnut dressing table, Philadelphia, circa 1760, the rectangular thumbmolded top with notched corners above three molded drawers, the central drawer carved with a shell flanked by acanthus leaves, fluted corner columns flanking, the shaped skirt below continuing to shell-carved cabriole legs ending in claw-and-ball feet.
(Sotheby's) $134,500

CABRIOLE LEG

Queen Anne walnut and maple dressing table, probably Massachusetts, circa 1750, old brasses, 30in. wide. (Skinner) $10,350

Tiger maple and maple dressing table, Massachusetts or New Hampshire, circa 1740, old refinish, 32¼in. wide. (Skinner) $6,000

A Queen Anne walnut dressing-table, Massachusetts or Rhode Island, 1740-1760, the overhanging molded top with indented front corners, 34¼in. wide. (Christie's) $50,000

Queen Anne mahogany and mahogany veneered dressing table, probably Rhode Island, circa 1770, the molded overhanging top above cockbeaded case, 30½in. wide. (Skinner Inc.) $12,500

The Morris family Chippendale carved mahogany dressing table, Philadelphia, 1760–80, the rectangular top with molded edge and cupid's-bow front corners, 35½in. wide. (Christie's) $59,700

Chippendale walnut carved dressing table, probably New York, circa 1750, with molded top above drawers, on cabriole legs with carved leafage on the knees, 28in. wide. (Skinner) $20,900

Chippendale carved walnut dressing table, Pennsylvania, circa 1770, with shaped skirt and shell carved legs ending in trifid feet, 35in. wide. (Skinner Inc.) $5,100

The Bennett family Queen Anne mahogany dressing table, three thumbmolded drawers over a shaped skirt, Charleston, Carolina, circa 1750, 31in. wide. (Christie's) $101,500

Queen Anne cherry dressing table, probably Connecticut, circa 1770, the rectangular overhanging top with shaped corners and molded edge, 35¾in. wide. (Skinner) $18,750

CABRIOLE LEG

A Chippendale carved walnut dressing table, Phila., 1765-85, 36in. wide. (Christie's) $290,000

A Queen Anne walnut dressing table, Massachusetts, or Rhode Island, 1740-1760, on cabriole legs with pad feet, 34⅛in. wide. (Christie's) $36,800

Queen Anne cherry dressing table, Connecticut, 1750–80, brass replaced, 33in. wide. (Skinner Inc.) $22,000

A Queen Anne cherrywood dressing-table, Connecticut, 1740-1760, the case fitted with one thumbmolded long drawer over a central shell-carved thumbmolded short drawer, 36½in wide. (Christie's) $13,800

A Queen Anne carved mahogany dressing table, attributed to John Goddard, Newport, Rhode Island, 1750-1770, thumbmolded long drawer over two short drawers, 35½in. wide. (Christie's) $310,500

A Queen Anne cherrywood dressing table, New England, 1740–1760, with a molded rectangular top above a long drawer and three short drawers over an arched apron, 32½in. wide. (Christie's) $11,000

A Chippendale carved mahogany dressing table, Philadelphia, 1760-1780, the rectangular top with molded edge and indented corners above a cavetto molding, 38½in. wide. (Christie's) $85,000

A Queen Anne carved cherrywood dressing table, Connecticut, 1740–60, the rectangular thumbmolded top above one long thumbmolded drawer, 35½in. wide. (Christie's) $13,800

A fine Queen Anne carved mahogany dressing table, Salem, Massachusetts, 1740-1760, on cabriole legs with pad feet, 34in. wide. (Christie's) $75,000

A Queen Anne walnut veneered dressing table, Boston, 1730–1750, the rectangular thumbmolded and veneered top with herringbone surround above a conforming case fitted with two short drawers over three short drawers, each veneered with herringbone borders and cockbeaded surrounds and all enclosed by applied molding, above a shaped and cockbeaded skirt with pendant drops, on cabriole legs with padded disk feet, 30½in. wide.
(Christie's) $9,000

A Queen Anne carved mahogany dressing table, attributed to John Goddard (1723–1785), Newport, 1750–1760, the rectangular top with cove molded edge above a conforming case fitted with a thumbmolded long drawer over two thumbmolded short drawers centering a scalloped carved fan enclosing a spray of fluted petals above a shaped skirt, on cabriole legs with padded disk feet, 31¾in. wide.
(Christie's) $519,500

CABRIOLE LEG

Queen Anne dressing table, New England, 18th century, refinished, replaced brasses, 33in. wide.
(Skinner Inc.) $15,000

Queen Anne walnut dressing table, Massachusetts, 18th century, with molded top above a case thumbmolded drawers, 33¼in. wide overall.
(Skinner) $8,970

A Chippendale tiger maple dressing table on cabriole legs, probably Penn., circa 1780, 33¾in. wide.
(Skinner) $25,000

A Queen Anne maple dressing table, Massachusetts, 1740–1760, the rectangular top with thumbmolded edges above a conforming case fitted with one long thumbmolded drawer above three short thumbmolded drawers, 33½in. wide.
(Christie's) $10,000

A Queen Anne carved and inlaid walnut dressing table, Portsmouth, New Hampshire, 1735–1760, the concave carved shell and arched and scrolled apron centering two acorn drops, 36in. wide.
(Christie's) $103,700

A Queen Anne carved walnut dressing-table, Salem, Massachusetts, 1725–1760, the rectangular top with cupid's bow corners above a conforming case with a long drawer over a pair of short drawers, on cabriole legs with pad feet, 34½in. wide.
(Christie's) $4,950

The Samuel Morris Chippendale carved mahogany dressing table, Philadelphia, 1760–1780, on shell-carved cabriole legs with ball-and claw feet, 36in. wide.
(Christie's) $35,000

A Chippendale walnut dressing table, Philadelphia, 1760-1780, the rectangular top with pinched corners above a fitted case with three thumbmolded graduated drawers, 35½in. wide.
(Christie's) $40,000

A Queen Anne inlaid walnut dressing table, New England, 1730-1750, the rectangular top with molded edge above one long drawer over three short drawers, 32½in. wide.
(Christie's) $3,800

CABRIOLE LEG

A Chippendale carved walnut dressing-table, Philadephia area, 1760–1780, on cabriole legs with carved knees and ball-and-claw feet, 33¹/₂in. wide. (Christie's) $52,000

A Queen Anne carved mahogany dressing table, Philadelphia, 1730–50, the rectangular top with thumbmolded edge with cusped corners, 35¹/₂in. wide. (Christie's) $10,350

A Chippendale mahogany dressing table, Philadelphia, 1760–1780, on four cabriole legs, the knees shell-carved, with claw-and-ball feet, 36¹/₂in. wide. (Christie's) $7,700

Mahogany carved dressing table, probably Massachusetts, circa 1750, overhanging top with chamfered edge, above a central concave carved drawer. (Skinner) $17,250

A Chippendale carved mahogany dressing table, Philadelphia, 1760-1780, the shaped apron centering a carved shell, on cabriole legs with acanthus carved knees, 38⁷/₈in. wide. (Christie's) $68,500

Queen Anne walnut veneer dressing table, Massachusetts, circa 1740, the overhanging top has thumbnail molding and four matched panels of crotch veneer, 29in. wide. (Skinner) $11,500

A rare Queen Anne figured maple dressing table, Delaware River Valley, 1750-1770, on square tapering cabriole legs with Spanish feet, 39in. wide. (Christie's New York) $50,000

A Queen Anne walnut dressing-table, attributed to William Savery, Philadelphia, circa 1770, on cabriole legs with intaglio carved knees, 34¹/₂in. wide. (Christie's) $27,600

A Chippendale carved mahogany dressing table, Philadelphia, circa 1770, the rectangular thumbmolded top above one long and three short molded drawers, 35in. wide. (Sotheby's) $25,000

CABRIOLE LEG

A Queen Anne carved cherrywood dressing table, Connecticut, circa 1765, the rectangular thumbmolded top above one long and three short molded drawers, the shaped skirt below with a central shell-carved device continuing to cabriole legs ending in pad feet. This dressing table is constructed with a two board top, width of case 29⁷/₈in. .
(Sotheby's) $21,850

A fine Queen Anne figured walnut dressing table, Boston, Massachusetts, 1735–50, the oblong top with notched corners above one long and three short molded drawers, the center drawer with a concave arch, the shaped skirt below with later turned pendants continuing to cabriole legs ending in pad feet, width of top 34½in.
(Sotheby's) $26,450

A Queen Anne walnut drop-leaf table, Pennsylvania, 1740–1760, the rectangular top flanked by conforming leaves with cusped corners above a similar frame with shaped apron, on cabriole legs with trifid feet, 57¼in. deep (leaves open).
(Christie's) $2,300

A William and Mary sycamore and birchwood drop-leaf dining table, New England, 1720–1760, the oblong top with two hinged D-shaped leaves above a cyma-shaped skirt fitted with a single drawer on vase-and ring-turned legs joined by turned stretchers, ending in vase-form feet, width extended 16in. (Sotheby's) $11,500

Classical carved mahogany drop leaf table, New England, circa 1825, 50³/₄in. wide (open). (Skinner) **$546**

Pine table, Massachusetts, early 19th century, scrubbed top with single drop leaf over red painted base with paint loss, 47in. wide. (Skinner) **$977**

Tiger maple drop leaf table, New England, early 19th century, 42in. wide. (Skinner) **$3,335**

A William and Mary maple butterfly table, New England, 18th century, refinished, 28in. wide. (Skinner) **$1,150**

A Classical carved mahogany breakfast table, New York, 1815-1825, the clover shaped top with two drop leaves, 29½in. high. (Christie's New York) **$6,800**

Drop leaf maple and pine trestle base table, New England, 18th century, refinished, 37¹/₂in. open. (Skinner) **$4,000**

Bird's-eye and tiger maple drop leaf table, New York or Ohio, circa 1840, rounded leaves on four ring-turned tapering legs, 20in. wide. (Skinner) **$3,450**

Rare and early Gustav Stickley drop leaf table, No. 443, unsigned, through tenons and pegs, deep reddish-brown original finish, 40in. wide. (Skinner) **$5,462**

William and Mary cherry butterfly table, probably Connecticut, early 18th century, the overhanging oval drop leaf top on four splayed block vase and ring-turned legs, 40in. wide. (Skinner) **$2,415**

Maple dining table, New England, late 18th century, refinished, 48in. diameter. (Skinner) **$4,312**

Late Federal rosewood veneer, gilt and brass inlaid breakfast table, attributed to Charles-Honore Lannuier, N.Y., circa 1815, 46in. long, extended. (Christie's) **$85,000**

Antique American Sheraton drop-leaf dining table, in cherry with turned legs, top 46 x 18in. with two 20in. leaves. (Eldred's) **$495**

William and Mary maple turned tuck-a-way table, New England, 18th century, old refinish, 30in. wide. (Skinner) **$6,900**

Classical mahogany veneer breakfast table, probably Boston, circa 1815, the drop leaves over four curving beaded legs, 42in. wide. (Skinner Inc.) **$950**

A William and Mary gumwood trestle drop-leaf table, New York, 1720–1735, the oval top with hinged drop leaves above baluster and ring-turned legs, 33³/₄in. wide. (Christie's) **$20,000**

Fine American custom-made butterfly table in the 17th century style, one drawer, 28in. high. (Eldred's) **$650**

Classical mahogany veneer table, Northern New England, circa 1820, with a single hinged drop leaf in the rear, 28in. wide. (Skinner) **$1,725**

William and Mary maple and pine trestle drop leaf table, New England, early 18th century, 38in. wide. (Skinner) **$6,325**

A Chippendale mahogany drop-leaf table, the molded rectangular top with one hinged leaf above a conforming frame with shaped skirt, on cabriole legs with ball-and-claw feet, 32½in. wide, 32⅜in. deep open.
(Christie's) **$2,300**

CHIPPENDALE

Chippendale cherry carved dining table, possibly Rhode Island, circa 1780, old refinish, 52½in. wide.
(Skinner) $6,900

Chippendale mahogany drop leaf table, Massachusetts, circa 1780, old finish, 52½in. long (open).
(Skinner) $690

A Chippendale maple drop leaf table, New England, 1760–1780, the rectangular top above a scalloped apron, 45¾in. wide (open).
(Christie's) $2,760

A good Chippendale walnut drop-leaf breakfast table, Boston, Massachusetts, circa 1760, the oblong top with two hinged D-shaped leaves, 35¾in. long.
(Sotheby's) $4,000

A fine Chippendale carved and figured walnut drop-leaf dining table, Pennsylvania, circa 1760, on cabriole legs, 4ft. 9in. wide open.
(Sotheby's) $40,250

A fine Chippendale carved mahogany drop-leaf table, Boston or Salem, Massachusetts, circa 1760, the oblong top flanked by rectangular leaves, 44¼in. wide open.
(Sotheby's) $8,050

A Chippendale carved mahogany small drop-leaf table, Massachusetts, 1760–1780, the two drop leaves with cove-molded edges, 35¾in. wide
(Christie's) $51,750

A Chippendale mahogany dining table with two drop-leaves, Phila., 1765-85, 55in. long. $2,500

Chippendale cherry drop leaf table, New England, circa 1780, with beaded edges and replaced brass, refinished, 36in. wide.
(Skinner Inc.) $690

CHIPPENDALE

Chippendale walnut dining
table, Pennsylvania, 1770–90,
with two end thumbmolded
drawers, 49¼in. wide.
(Skinner)   **$5,250**

Chippendale mahogany drop
leaf table, Pennsylvania, 18th
century, 46¼in. wide.
(Skinner)   **$805**

Chippendale cherry drop leaf
table, New England, 1750–80,
41½in. wide extended.
(Skinner)   **$633**

A fine Chippendale carved and
figured walnut drop-leaf table,
Philadelphia, circa 1765, the
two-board top flanked by
rectangular leaves, 4ft. 1in. wide
open.
(Sotheby's)   **$4,312**

Chippendale mahogany carved
drop leaf table, probably Rhode
Island, circa 1780, the
rectangular drop leaf top on
four square molded stop fluted
legs, 47¾in. wide.
(Skinner)   **$1,725**

A Chippendale carved and
figured walnut drop-leaf dining
table, Philadelphia, circa 1770,
the shaped skirt continuing to
cabriole legs, 4ft. 11½in. wide
extended.
(Sotheby's)   **$20,700**

Chippendale walnut drop leaf
dining table, possibly
Pennsylvania, late 18th century,
with shaped skirt and molded
Marlborough legs, 15½in. wide.
(Skinner)   **$1,840**

A Chippendale mahogany drop-
leaf table, Salem, Massachusetts,
1760–1780, the molded oval
twin-flap top above an arching,
shaped skirt on cabriole legs and
ball-and-claw feet, 53in. wide.
(Christie's)   **$11,000**

A Chippendale mahogany drop-
leaf table, Newport, Rhode
Island, 1740-1760, the rectangular top with similarly
shaped drop leaves above a conforming case, 47¾in. wide.
(Christie's)   **$4,500**

A fine Chippendale carved and figured walnut drop-leaf table, Philadelphia, circa 1765, the two-board top flanked by rectangular leaves with shaped corners, the cyma-shaped frieze below on cabriole legs ending in claw and ball feet, width open 4ft. 1in.
(Sotheby's) $10,350

The Boardman Family Chippendale carved mahogany drop-leaf table, Coastal Essex County, Massachusetts, 1760–1775, the rectangular hinged top with drop leaves above a shaped apron, on cabriole legs with ball-and-claw feet, 47in. wide.
(Christie's) $34,500

FEDERAL

Federal tiger maple drop leaf table, New England, circa 1820, 39in. wide.
(Skinner) $2,645

A rare and unusual paint decorated birch drop-leaf dining table, Maine, early 19th century, 60¹/₂in. long.
(Sotheby's) $5,463

Federal cherry inlaid drop leaf table, probably Connecticut, circa 1790, refinished, 36in. wide.
(Skinner) $2,185

A Federal figured maple drop-leaf table, New England, 1800–1820, the rectangular top with two drop leaves above a plain apron, on square tapering legs, 55¹/₂in. wide.
(Christie's) $5,500

A Federal figured maple drop-leaf table, New England, 1790-1810, the rectangular top with conforming hinged leaves with rounded corners, 42in. wide.
(Christie's) $1,265

A Federal inlaid mahogany drop-leaf table, Boston, Massachusetts, 1800-1815, the rectangular top with hinged rounded drop leaves, 39¼in. wide.
(Christie's) $8,000

A Federal curly maple drop-leaf table, New England, 1790–1810, on square tapering line-inlaid legs, 35¹/₂in. wide.
(Christie's) $4,600

A Federal figured mahogany drop-leaf dining table, Baltimore, circa 1815, the rectangular top flanked by hinged leaves with reeded edges, 5ft. 3in. wide open.
(Sotheby's) $4,025

Federal mahogany drop leaf table, New England, early 19th century, the squared leaves fall over turned tapering legs, 46¹/₄in. wide extended.
(Skinner) $460

FEDERAL

Federal cherry inlaid breakfast table, New England, circa 1810, refinished, 18¼in. wide. (Skinner Inc.) $650

Federal mahogany dining table, Rhode Island, circa 1815, 56in. wide. (Skinner) $4,675

Federal tiger maple drop leaf table with drawer, New England, circa 1820, old finish, 35½in. wide. (Skinner) $1,092

A Federal mahogany dining table, New York, 1805-1810, the demi-lune ends above a conforming apron with inlaid tablets, on twelve reeded tapering legs, 88in. wide open. (Christie's) $18,000

A Federal mahogany drop-leaf table, New York, 1810-1815, the rectangular top with conforming hinged leaves, the case fitted with a single drawer, on rope-turned legs with turned and tapering feet with ball socket castors, 29¼in high. 49in. wide open, 36¾in. deep. (Christie's) $690

Federal cherry drop leaf table, Eastern Massachusetts or Rhode Island, circa 1820, with one drawer and old finish, 34½in. wide extended. (Skinner) $1,150

A Federal painted maple dining table with rounded drop leaves, New England, circa 1800, 42in. wide. (Skinner) $5,000

Federal mahogany carved and veneered drop leaf table, Rhode Island, circa 1815, one working and one simulated drawer, 45¼in. wide. (Skinner Inc.) $1,650

A Federal painted birchwood drop-leaf dining table, New England, circa 1810, on square tapering legs, the base painted red, length 39½in. (Sotheby's) $1,495

QUEEN ANNE

A Queen Anne figured mahogany drop-leaf dining table, Massachusetts, 1740–1770, the oblong top with bowed ends flanked by D-shaped leaves above a convex cyma-shaped apron on cabriole legs ending in pad feet, width open 45in.
(Sotheby's) $5,175

A fine and rare Queen Anne figured mahogany six-leg drop-leaf dining table, New York, 1740–1760, the oblong top with two hinged D-shaped leaves above a single-drawer frieze, on circular tapering legs ending in pointed slipper feet. Warm reddish brown color, width extended 5ft. 6in.
(Sotheby's) $18,400

QUEEN ANNE

Queen Anne drop leaf table, York, Maine area, attributed to Samuel Sewall, late 18th century, 31¹/₈in. wide. (Skinner) **$9,200**

Queen Anne maple drop leaf table, Rhode Island, circa 1760, the rectangular top with rounded leaves, 26in. high. (Skinner Inc.) **$2,150**

A good Queen Anne maple drop leaf dining table, Rhode Island, circa 1765, on angular cabriole legs ending in pad feet, width extended 52¹/₂in. (Sotheby's) **$4,250**

Queen Anne red painted cherry and birch dining table, probably Connecticut River Valley, 18th century, 40¹/₂in. wide. (Skinner) **$20,700**

American diminutive Queen Anne drop-leaf table, in cherry, top 11in. wide with two 11in. drop leaves. (Eldred's) **$7,040**

Queen Anne maple and birch dining table, Rhode Island, circa 1760, tapering legs ending in high pad feet, 59in. wide. (Skinner) **$6,100**

A Queen Anne cherrywood drop leaf table, probably Connecticut, 1740-1760, on cabriole legs with pad feet, 28in. high. (Christie's New York) **$2,400**

A Queen Anne mahogany drop leaf dining table, New England, probably Massachusetts, 1750–70, the oblong top with bowed ends. (Sotheby's) **$4,887**

A Queen Anne mahogany drop-leaf table, Newport, 1740-60, 47⅞in. wide. (Christie's) **$6,200**

Maple Queen Anne drop leaf dining table, Massachusetts, mid 18th century, with shaped skirt above cabriole legs, 46in. wide extended.
(Skinner) **$2,530**

Queen Anne walnut dining table, Massachusetts, circa 1760, old finish, 48in. wide.
(Skinner) **$11,500**

Small Queen Anne-style walnut drop-leaf table, Massachusetts, 20th century, with scrolled skirts and cabriole legs ending in pad feet, 30¾in. diameter.
(Skinner) **$4,600**

Queen Anne mahogany drop leaf table, Massachusetts, 1750-1780, with hinged square leaves over a shaped skirt, 27in. high. (Skinner Inc.) **$6,800**

A Queen Anne maple drop leaf table, Massachusetts, 1730-1750, with shaped skirts and cabriole legs, 42½in. wide, extended.
(Skinner) **$72,000**

A Queen Anne walnut drop-leaf table, Salem, Massachusetts, 1740-70, the shaped molded skirt below on cabriole legs ending in pad feet, 41½in. wide open.
(Sotheby's) **$4,025**

A Queen Anne cherrywood drop leaf table, Massachusetts, 1740-1760, on cabriole legs with pad feet, 26½in. high. (Christie s New York) **$6,800**

Queen Anne maple dining table, probably Massachusetts, circa 1770, the overhanging rectangular top with cutout corners on four cabriole legs, 36in. wide.
(Skinner) **$1,495**

A Queen Anne mahogany drop-leaf table, Salem or Boston, Massachusetts, 1740–1760, with two rounded drop leaves, 30½in. wide.
(Christie's) **$50,000**

QUEEN ANNE, NEW ENGLAND

Queen Anne mahogany drop leaf table, New England, 18th century, 45in. long extended. (Skinner) $2,875

Queen Anne maple dining table, New England, circa 1760, 45in. long. (Skinner) $4,125

Queen Anne tiger maple drop leaf table, New England, on cabriole legs ending in pad feet, 48in. wide. (Skinner Inc.) $8,250

A diminutive Queen Anne maple drop-leaf table, New England, 1740–1760, on cabriole legs and pad disk feet, 30½in. wide (open). (Christie's) $74,000

A diminutive Queen Anne drop-leaf table, New England, 1740–1760, the oval top with drop leaves above a conforming rectangular apron, 32in. wide (open). (Christie's) $18,400

A Queen Anne maple drop-leaf dining table, New England, circa 1775, the cyma-shaped skirt continuing to cabriole legs ending in pad feet, length 53in. (Sotheby's) $4,000

Queen Anne maple dining table, southeast New England, late 18th century, the overhanging rectangular top on four block turned legs, 38¾in. wide. (Skinner) $2,760

Queen Anne cherry and maple dining table, New England, circa 1770, 45in. wide open. (Skinner) $1,760

Country Queen Anne maple dining table, New England, mid 18th century, the rectangular drop leaf top above a shaped skirt, 26¾in. high. (Skinner Inc.) $3,750

Queen Anne maple drop leaf dining table, New England, circa 1760, 44³/₈in. wide extended. (Skinner) **$5,463**

A Queen Anne mahogany drop-leaf dining table, New England, 1750-70, 50in. deep with leaves open. (Christie's) **$11,000**

Queen Anne maple drop leaf dining table, New England, circa 1760, 46in. wide extended. (Skinner) **$6,325**

Diminutive Queen Anne maple drop leaf table, New England, circa 1750, on four cabriole legs terminating in pad feet, 25¼in. high. (Skinner Inc.) **$4,400**

A Queen Anne maple drop leaf dining table, New England, 1740-1760, on cabriole legs with pad feet, 44in. wide. (Christie's) **$3,000**

A Queen Anne mahogany drop-leaf table, New England, circa 1750, the hinged oval top with twin drop-leaves over a flat-arched apron and cabriole legs, 46½in. wide. (Christie's) **$3,000**

Queen Anne maple drop leaf table, New England, 18th century, with half-round ends on turned legs, 51¼in. wide extended. (Skinner) **$1,955**

A Queen Anne maple drop-leaf table, New England, 1740-60, the rectangular hinged top with molded edge above a cyma-shaped carved apron, 42in. wide. (Christie's) **$2,990**

Painted Queen Anne maple drop leaf table, southern New England, 18th century, with old red stained top above darkened straight cabriole legs, 40in. wide. (Skinner) **$8,625**

QUEEN ANNE, NEW YORK

A rare Queen Anne figured mahogany drop-leaf dining table, New York, 1750–80, the oblong top with bowed ends, 48in. wide open.
(Sotheby's) $3,737

A fine and rare Queen Anne mahogany single-drawer drop-leaf dining table, New York, 1735–60, on six cabriole legs ending in pointed slipper feet, 42in. wide open.
(Sotheby's) $14,950

A Queen Anne cherrywood drop-leaf dining table, New York, 1750–80, the oblong top with bowed ends flanked by D-shaped leaves, 4ft. 2in. wide open.
(Sotheby's) $5,175

QUEEN ANNE, PENNSYLVANIA

A Queen Anne walnut drop-leaf dining table, Pennsylvania, 1740–60, the circular hinged top with two drop leaves above a shaped apron, 48in. wide.
(Christie's) $2,760

A Queen Anne carved and figured walnut drop-leaf dining table, Pennsylvania, 1730–50, the rectangular top, flanked by notched leaves, 4ft. 6½in. wide open.
(Sotheby's) $3,737

A Queen Anne walnut drop-leaf table, Pennsylvania, 1740–1760, the oval top with two drop leaves above a shaped skirt, on cabriole legs with slipper feet, 65½in. wide.
(Christie's) $11,000

QUEEN ANNE, RHODE ISLAND

Queen Anne maple drop leaf breakfast table, Rhode Island, circa 1760, 38in. wide.
(Skinner) $2,970

A Queen Anne mahogany drop-leaf table, Rhode Island or Pennsylvania, 1740–1760, the hinged oval top with D-shaped drop-leaves, 43¾in. open.
(Christie's) $10,000

A good Queen Anne figured mahogany drop-leaf table, New England, probably Rhode Island, circa 1750, the oblong top with bowed ends flanked by D-shaped leaves, 4ft. 6in.
(Sotheby's) $2,300

A Victorian mahogany drum-top library table, the revolving top with tooled leather insert, on a scroll-carved tripod base with brass castors, 48in. diameter. (Bearne's) $4,000

A classical carved mahogany drum table, New York City, 1810-1825, the circular top with molded edge above a conforming veneered frame, 21¹/₈in. diameter.
(Christie's) $11,500

A George IV oak octagonal library table with leather lined top, 42½in. wide. (Christie's) $4,250

George IV mahogany drum table, second quarter 19th century, the cross-banded circular revolving top above a frieze fitted with alternating drawers and false drawers, 44in. diameter.
(Butterfield & Butterfield) $5,000

A Gothic Revival oak centre table, New York, second quarter 19th century, the octagonal top with green baize lining and molded edge above a conforming frieze with ebonised molding above an octagonal pedestal carved with ogee arches, 48¹/₂in. wide.
(Christie's) $12,500

A classical carved mahogany drum table, New York, 1815-1825, on four saber legs with panel carved knees and brass paw castors, 27in. diameter of top.
(Christie's) $5,250

A Federal mahogany and veneer drum table on a tripod cabriole leg base, 31in. diam, circa 1820.
(Skinner) $1,250

A mid-Victorian mahogany library table, the octagonal molded top with a frieze fitted with four drawers and four false drawers, 57in. wide.
(Christie's) $6,000

A Regency mahogany drum table, on a ring-turned baluster support and channeled hipped downswept legs, 18³/₄in. diameter.
(Christie's) $5,175

William and Mary maple gate leg table, New England, circa 1740, old surface, 41³/₄in. wide. (Skinner) $2,860

A William and Mary walnut gateleg table, probably New England, circa 1740, 56in. wide. (Skinner) $4,600

Maple gateleg table, Massachusetts, circa 1740, old scrubbed top on early base, 42½in. wide. (Skinner Inc.) $4,000

A rare William and Mary turned maple and birchwood diminutive gateleg dining table, New England, 1720–50, on ring-and-vase-turned legs joined by similarly turned stretchers, 4ft. wide open. (Sotheby's) $13,800

A William and Mary maple gateleg table with oval drop-leaf top, New England, circa 1740, 41in. long, 51in. wide. (Skinner) $3,100

A rare William and Mary turned and paint-decorated maple and pine gateleg table, probably Windsor, Connecticut, circa 1760, the rectangular top flanked by D-shaped drop-leaves above a plain skirt, 33¹/₂in. wide, extended. (Sotheby's) $19,550

A very fine and rare William and Mary maple gate-leg dining table, New England, 1730–60, the oblong top with two hinged D-shaped leaves, 50¹/₂in. wide extended. (Sotheby's) $63,000

A very fine and rare William and Mary turned and figured mahogany large gate-leg dining table, Philadelphia, 1710–40, 59½in. wide extended. (Sotheby's) $18,400

A William and Mary maple gate-leg dining table, Massachusetts, 1700–1720, the rectangular top with bowed ends flanked by D-shaped drop leaves, 51in. wide. (Christie's) $88,300

A rare William and Mary turned walnut diminutive gate-leg drop-leaf dining table, New England, 1720–50, 4ft. 2in. wide open.
(Sotheby's) $3,737

Painted gate leg table, New England, 18th century, 43³/₄in. wide.
(Skinner) $1,840

Painted maple gateleg table, New England, 18th century, dark red stain, beaded skirt, 29³/₄in. wide.
(Skinner Inc.) $4,800

A William and Mary maple gate-leg table, New England, 1700–1730, with rectangular top and two hinged rectangular leaves, 36in. wide open.
(Christie's) $6,000

A rare pine gateleg table, probably Southern, 18th century, the rectangular top with two drop leaves, on turned feet, 29¹/₃in. high.
(Christie's New York) $2,750

A William and Mary maple gate-leg dining-table, probably Massachusetts, 1730–1745, with oval drop-leaf top above an apron with single end drawer, 45¹/₂in. deep.
(Christie's) $6,000

A William and Mary maple and birchwood single-drawer gate leg drop-leaf dining table, New England, probably Massachusetts or Rhode Island, 1720–50, 61¹/₄in. wide extended.
(Sotheby's) $79,500

Antique American William & Mary gate-leg table in maple and curly maple, drawer of pine and poplar secondary woods, top open 49in. x 61in.
(Eldred's) $3,500

William and Mary walnut gate-leg table, Massachusetts, 1715-1740, the rectangular top with half round hinged leaves, 28½in. high.
(Skinner) $25,000

A cherry hutch table, Cherry Valley, NY., circa 1750, 45in. diameter.
(Skinner) $1,500

Grain painted chair table, probably New England, early 19th century, the rectangular top above baluster and ring turned supports, 42¼in. wide.
(Skinner) $4,887

Painted chair table, New England, early 18th century, old red painted surface, 44.5in. diameter.
(Skinner) $8,625

Early 18th century pine and maple trestle foot chair table, New England, 55½in. diameter.
(Skinner) $15,000

Painted pine hutch table, New England, circa 1810, 41½in. diameter.
(Skinner) $3,575

Late 19th century New England birch table and pine painted hutch table, 54½in. diameter.
(Skinner) $5,000

Painted birch hutch table, New England, circa 1880, 41½in. diameter.
(Skinner) $3,000

Red painted pine and maple chair table, New England, early 19th century, on ring-turned tapering legs, 41⅛in. wide.
(Skinner) $4,312

Early 19th century painted birch and pine hutch table, New England, 42in. wide.
(Skinner) $5,500

Pine and maple hutch table, New England, 18th century, the circular top tips above block and bulbous turned arms, 27½ in. high. (Skinner Inc.) $2,100

A rare maple hutch table, New York or New England, 1720–50, the hinged oval top tilting to reveal a well, 42in. wide. (Sotheby's) $10,350

Pine and ash shoe foot hutch table, New England, late 18th century, on demi-lune cut-out ends, 46⅜in. diameter. (Skinner) $16,100

A tiger maple hutch table, North America, 18th century, on molded stepped, shoe feet, 45½in. wide. (Skinner) $6,400

Painted pine hutch table, Massachusetts, 18th century, the round two board top above a two board seat, 49in. diam. (Skinner Inc.) $5,500

William and Mary cherry and pine hutch table, Hudson River Valley, circa 1750, 44in. diam. (Skinner) $8,000

Cherry shoe foot hutch table, probably New York, 18th century, 47¹/₂in. diameter. (Skinner) $2,970

Antique American shoe-foot hutch table, in pine with circular top, 40in. diameter. (Eldred's) $1,320

Pine and maple shoe foot hutch table, New England, late 18th century, 45³/₄in. diameter. (Skinner) $2,090

A very fine and rare Federal carved and figured mahogany three-pedestal dining table, Boston, Massachusetts, circa 1810, in three parts; each hinged oblong top tilting above a ring-turned and spirally-reeded urn-form support on molded down-swept legs ending in eagle-decorated brass caps and casters, 11ft. 8in. long.
(Sotheby's) $156,500

A late Classical mahogany veneered dining table, American, 1835-1850, in three parts; the two ends each with a semicircular top with a single hinged rectangular drop-leaf above a conforming veneered apron over paired scrolled supports with outscrolling feet and a single turned fly-leg; the central section comprising a rectangular leaf, 28¾in. high, 45½in. wide, 48in. deep closed.
(Christie's) $11,000

Queen Anne maple dining table, probably Rhode Island, circa 1760, old refinish, 47¼in. wide. (Skinner Inc.) $3,750

Shaker cherry ministry dining table, probably Enfield, New Hampshire or Harvard, Massachusetts, first half 19th century, the cherry two-board scrubbed top above an arched maple base, 84in. long.
(Skinner Inc.) $100,000

Federal pine and cherry harvest table, New England, early 19th century, the rectangular overhanging top on four square tapering legs on casters, 72in. wide.
(Skinner) $4,025

A poplar and pine trestle base dining table, possibly North Carolina, early 19th century, the rectangular top with two chamfered cleats tilting above two trestle supports, 118½in. long.
(Christie's) $35,000

A pine painted table, probably New England, early 19th century, the overhanging scrubbed two board top with breadboard ends, 50in. wide. (Skinner) $2,300

A Federal inlaid mahogany two-part dining table, probably Baltimore, 1800–1810, in two parts, each with D-shaped ends and rectangular drop leaves, on five square tapering legs edged with stringing, 48in. wide.
(Christie's) $17,500

Federal cherry and walnut veneer dining table, New England or New York, circa 1825, with shaped reveneered skirt, above spiral carved legs ending in turned feet, 84¼in. wide extended.
(Skinner) $1,380

Country Federal mahogany two part dining table, New England, circa 1820, the D-end tops with molded edge and hinged drop leaves, extended 91in.
(Skinner Inc.) $5,300

Shaker cherry trestle table, probably Harvard, Massachusetts community, 72in. wide. (Skinner) $6,325

Federal mahogany veneer two-part dining table, circa 1815, refinished, 93in. long. (Skinner Inc.) $2,600

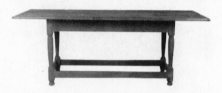

Federal cherry and mahogany veneer two-part dining table, New England, early 19th century, refinished, 88⅝in. wide. (Skinner Inc.) $1,800

Painted pine and maple tavern table, probably New England, 18th century, base with red stain, top scrubbed, 72in. long. (Skinner Inc.) $3,100

A Federal inlaid mahogany three-part dining table, New England, circa 1800, in three parts, the center section with rectangular drop leaves above a crossbanded frieze, 7ft. 6in. long open. (Sotheby's) $5,750

A Federal mahogany inlaid dining table, Mid-Atlantic, 1790–1810, in three sections, the whole forming a rectangular top with demi-lune ends and line-inlaid edge, 117in. deep (open). (Christie's) $9,200

A fine Classical mahogany two part dining table, Boston, 1820-1830, on molded saber legs with cylindrical feet, 29¼in. high. (Christie's New York) $35,000

Drop-leaf table, George Nakishima for Widdicomb Furniture, Grand Rapids, Michigan, circa 1955, 73¾in. wide. (Skinner Inc.) $1,850

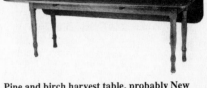

A Country maple and pine painted harvest table, New England, circa 1800, 72in. long. (Skinner) **$3,500**

Pine and birch harvest table, probably New England, circa 1830, 81in. long. (Skinner) **$4,945**

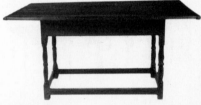

A classical mahogany drop leaf dining table, New England, circa 1830, old refinish, 71$^{1}/_{4}$in. wide extended. (Skinner) **$690**

Walnut and cherry tavern table, probably New York State, 18th century, old surface, 53$^{1}/_{2}$in. wide. (Skinner Inc.) **$2,800**

A classical mahogany three-pedestal dining table, American, circa 1825, comprising a rectangular center section and two D-shaped end sections, length approximately 15ft. 7in. (Sotheby's) **$17,500**

A fine Federal mahogany three-part dining table, American, probably Boston, circa 1810, on turned and reeded tapering legs ending in ball feet, length extended 13ft. 3$^{1}/_{2}$in. (Sotheby's) **$9,000**

A late Federal mahogany three-part dining table, New York, circa 1820, on ring and spirally turned legs on brass casters, length 9ft. 6in. (Sotheby's) **$8,500**

Federal two-part cherry inlaid banquet table, New England, circa 1825, old refinish, 61in. wide. (Skinner) **$3,450**

Large six drawer library table, circa 1915, rectangular top over six drawers, large post legs with side stretchers, 86in. long.
(Skinner Inc.) $1,250

Shaker birch and pine trestle foot table, from Shirley Shaker settlement, 19th century, old refinish, 102in. wide.
(Skinner) $6,900

A mahogany dining-table in three sections, the end-sections with rectangular single drop-leaf, the central section with two drop-leaves, on square tapering reeded legs, 160in. long.
(Christie's) $3,300

The Loockerman family pair of Chippendale carved mahogany drop-leaf tables, Philadelphia, 1760-80, 62½in. wide open.
(Christie's) $310,500

A Federal mahogany accordion-action dining table, New York, 1790–1810, the rounded rectangular top extending to include five extra leaves over a straight apron and baluster and ring-turned supports, on downswept molded saber legs, 147in. wide, extended.
(Christie's) $27,500

Federal carved mahogany two-part dining table, New England, circa 1815–1825, the D-shaped top with one drop leaf, on ring-turned and foliate carved legs, length extended 7ft. 9in.
(Butterfield & Butterfield) $1,950

A fine and rare Federal inlaid and figured mahogany diminutive two-part dining table, New England, circa 1805, comprising two D-shaped end sections, 8ft. 3in. wide extended.
(Sotheby's) $43,125

Painted pine and maple stretcher base table, New England, 18th century, the top with bread board ends overhangs a single drawer, 69¼in. wide.
(Skinner) $10,925

A Classical carved mahogany dining table, New York City, circa 1825, in two parts; each end with a rectangular top with rounded corners with a hinged rectangular drop-leaf above a conforming veneered apron edged by gilt Greek-key banding over a leaf-carved baluster pedestal, on a quadripartite base with waterleaf and scroll-carved legs with animal-paw feet, 96in. wide. (Christie's) $7,500

A Federal mahogany dining table, American, 1805–1820, in two sections; each with a semi-circular top with hinged rectangular leaf above a conforming veneered frame, on ring and reeded column-turned legs with tapering feet fitted with castors, 88in. deep approximately, leaves open. (Christie's) $11,500

A Federal carved and figured mahogany drop-leaf library table, attributed to Duncan Phyfe, or one of his contemporaries, New York, circa 1810, the rectangular top with two hinged D-shaped drop leaves above a single cockbeaded drawer, the skirt with turned ball pendants raised on four spirally-twisted and vase-form ring-turned uprights, the fluted plinth base raised on molded down-curving legs ending in brass animal-paw feet and brass casters, extended width 50in. (Sotheby's)

$24,150

The Marshall Field Renaissance Revival carved mahogany desk, Herter Brothers, New York City, circa 1872, 60in. wide. (Christie's)   **$77,300**

Gustav Stickley hexagonal top library table, circa 1904, no. 625, 48in. diam. (Skinner)   **$9,380**

A Renaissance Revival burled walnut library table, labeled by Alex. Roux, N.Y., circa 1860, 48in. wide.   **$4,000**

L. & J. G. Stickley library table, no. 520, circa 1910, overhanging rectangular top, single drawer with copper hardware elongated corbels inside each leg with medial shelf, 36in. wide. (Skinner)   **$750**

Federal carved and figured mahogany drop-leaf library table, attributed to Duncan Phyfe or a contemporary, New York, circa 1815, 46¹/₂in. wide extended. (Sotheby's)   **$9,200**

Limbert oak one-drawer library table, No. 153, Holland, Michigan, circa 1907, shaped top over blind drawer, panel ends with cut outs and medial shelf, 48in. long. (Skinner)   **$2,645**

Roycroft oak two-drawer library table, No. 75, circa 1906, original medium finish and copper hardware, carved orb mark, 52¹/₈in. long. (Skinner)   **$1,955**

A Gustav Stickley round library table, no. 633, circa 1904, 48in. diam. (Skinner)   **$3,100**

Stickley Brothers library table, attributed, leather top with round tacks, through tenons over bow feet, original dark finish, 42in. wide. (Skinner)   **$1,610**

Red painted table, New Hampshire, early 19th century, 36in. wide.
(Skinner) $2,185

A leather top library table with three drawers, by Gustav Stickley, 66½in. wide. $3,800

A library table with one drawer, by L. & J. G. Stickley, signed with Handcraft label, 42in. wide.
(Skinner Inc.) $1,000

Rare Limbert oak six-drawer library table, Grand Rapids, Michigan, circa 1905, panel sides and each end fitted with three graduated drawers, unsigned, 56in. long.
(Skinner) $2,990

A classical carved mahogany drop-leaf library table, New York, circa 1820, the rectangular top flanked by oblong leaves with notched corners, 48in. wide open.
(Sotheby's) $1,265

Gustav Stickley round library table, circa 1907, no. 636, with diagonal chamfered legs and arched cross stretcher with keyed tenons, unsigned, 48in. diameter.
(Skinner Inc.) $1,800

A Roycroft oak library table, East Aurora, New York, circa 1910, having two drawers and square tapered legs with shaped feet, 48in. wide. $2,500

Fine American Renaissance gilt-incised walnut partner's desk, executed by Herter Brothers, New York, circa 1870, the rectangular top with molded edge, the sides with pull-out slides, width 5ft. 5in.
(Butterfield & Butterfield)
                         $23,000

Limbert oak two-drawer library table, No. 164, circa 1907, original medium finish and copper hardware, branded mark, 48in. wide.
(Skinner) $1,955

A Gothic Revival mahogany marble-top table, New York, 1840–1860, the hexagonal marble top above a conforming turreted mahogany apron over three cluster columns with pierced tracery cage on a flat, tripod plinth on castors 31in. high, 41in. wide, 35½in. deep. The form illustrated here belongs to a group of seven tables, all originating in New York City and almost certainly made by a French cabinetmaker like Charles Baudouine or Alexander Roux. These are among the most refined of the American Gothic Revival furniture forms and to be distinguished from cruder Anglophile furniture made in New York City and Boston.
(Christie's) $70,700

A walnut stretcher-base table, Pennsylvania, 18th century, the rectangular top above a conforming case fitted with two offset thumb-molded drawers, 47³/₄in. wide.
(Christie's) $2,300

Pine and maple stretcher base table, New England, 18th century, tapering ring-turned legs joined by stretchers, 36in. wide. (Skinner) $2,645

Limbert oak occasional table, No. 146, Holland, Michigan, circa 1910, original medium-light finish, branded mark, 45in. long.
(Skinner) $2,300

Mission oak 'knock-down' table, unsigned, circa 1910, 30in. diam.
(Skinner) $344

Painted and decorated Windsor table, New England, early 19th century, later orange paint with buff color accent, 29¹/₄in. wide. (Skinner Inc.) $900

'Quaint Furniture' cafe table with copper top, Grand Rapids, Michigan, circa 1915, no. 2615, signed with metal tag, 18¹/₄in. diameter.
(Skinner Inc.) $880

A Federal maple tripod table, New England, 1790–1810, the oval top above a ring-and-urn turned shaft over a tripod base with arched legs, 21³/₄in. wide.
(Christie's) $460

A rare Queen Anne cherrywood slate-top mixing table, Pennsylvania, 1730–1750, on tapering cylindrical legs with pad feet, 26¹/₄in. wide.
(Christie's) $20,000

A Shaker butternut tripod table, New Lebanon, New York, 1820–40, the circular top above a tapering columnar pedestal, 14³/₈in. diameter.
(Christie's) $3,220

A red painted stretcher-base table, Lancaster County, Pennsylvania, late 18th/early 19th century, on tapering blocked legs joined by flat stretchers, 47¼in. wide. (Christie's) $5,750

A Federal inlaid mahogany marble-top mixing table, New England or New York, circa 1800, rectangular white and gray veined marble top, 41in. wide. (Sotheby's) $35,650

Pine and maple stretcher base table, New England, 18th century, the top overhangs a painted block and ring turned base, 43³/₈in. wide. (Skinner) $3,737

A William and Mary black-painted trestle-base table, New England, 1730–1750, with oval top above double baluster-turned legs, 28¼in. wide. (Christie's) $20,000

Painted cherry table with drawer, Soap Hollow, Pennsylvania, dated 1875, overhanging top above single drawer, 21³/₄in. wide. (Skinner) $1,840

Quaint Furniture spindle-side occasional table, circa 1908, overhanging rectangular top, square tapering legs with three vertical spindles at each side, 30in. wide. (Skinner) $850

Shaker painted butternut and maple table with drawer, New England, circa 1820, the rectangular overhanging top with beveled edge, 19½in. wide. (Skinner) $7,475

Shaker butternut and cherry table, Mt. Lebanon, New York, circa 1860, the two plank butternut top above a drawer, 31in. wide. (Skinner) $4,025

Carved folk art table, possibly Pennsylvania, late 19th century, the circular carved top with sawtooth edge centering a carved star, 21in. diameter. (Skinner) $805

Classical Revival mahogany and mahogany veneer marble top table, circa 1825, 24in. diameter. (Skinner) $6,050

Limbert double oval table with cut out base, Grand Rapids, Michigan, circa 1907 (bangs and stains on surface). (Skinner) $6,250

Shaker birch table with drawer, Canterbury, New Hampshire, 1825–1850, 17in. wide. (Skinner) $935

A rare William and Mary painted and turned cherrywood stretcher table, New York or Connecticut, 1710–50, painted gray over red, length 21¾in. (Sotheby's) $17,500

Rare Chippendale mahogany carved slab table, North Shore, Massachusetts, 1760–80, the rectangular thumbmolded marble top with shaped corners above a conforming mahogany apron, 26in. wide. (Skinner) $222,500

Aesthetic Movement brass mounted rosewood and mixed metal occasional table, fourth quarter 19th century, the top corner with inlay of a spider's web, 20in. wide. (Skinner) $8,625

Round table with caned pedestal base, probably Michigan, circa 1915, unsigned, (refinished), 36½in. diam. (Skinner) $560

Rare oval painted pine sawbuck table, coastal Massachusetts or New Hampshire, 18th century, with scrubbed top on an 'X'-form base, 23¹/₈in. wide. (Skinner) $3,738

Roycroft pedestal base lamp table, East Aurora, New York, circa 1910, with four curving legs joining in the middle, 29½in. high. (Skinner Inc.) $2,500

Natural finish wicker and oak occasional table, late 19th century, 20¼in. diameter. (Skinner) **$259**

A Limbert oval table with cut-out sides, Grand Rapids, Michigan, circa 1907, no. 146, 45in. long. **$1,500**

A Rococo Revival laminated rosewood lamp table, by J. B. Belter, New York, circa 1855, 26in. diam. **$31,000**

A Federal carved and figured mahogany adjustable drawing table, the carving attributed to Samuel McIntire, Salem, Massachusetts, circa 1800, 30½in. long. (Sotheby's) **$189,500**

A Hammond No. 12 American type shuttle machine with Ideal keyboard and reverse hammer action, with original table and swivel chair, 1893. (Auction Team Köln) **$1,089**

A classical gilt-stenciled mahogany architect's table, probably New York, 1820-30, on acanthus carved and reeded legs with rope-twist carved ankles, 37½in. wide. (Christie's) **$12,650**

A Renaissance Revival rosewood gaming table, American, 1860–1880, the carved apron with single drawer over four tapering cylindrical supports, 26³/₈in. diameter. (Christie's) **$1,495**

A rare Queen Anne carved walnut slab-table, Philadelphia, 1730–1750, the rectangular thumbmolded marble top above a conforming walnut apron with shaped multiple lobed skirt, 36½in. wide. (Christie's) **$450,000**

Art Deco maple and veneered occasional table, America, circa 1930, burr walnut and fruitwood veneered octagonal top, five-part pedestal, 28½in. diameter. (Skinner) **$1,495**

STICKLEY

Gustav Stickley oak round table, No. 645, circa 1904, arched crossed stretchers with dome finial, red decal, 36in. diameter. (Skinner) $1,840

A drop-leaf table, by Gustav Stickley, no. 638, circa 1912, 42in. long, 40in. wide, open. (Skinner) $3,500

An L. & J. G. Stickley occasional table, no. 543, circa 1912, 29¼in. diam. (Skinner) $500

Early Gustav Stickley table, circa 1902–03, no. 439, round top with four cut-in leg posts, 30in. diameter. (Skinner Inc.) $1,500

A Gustav Stickley square table with cut corners, no. 612, circa 1905-06, signed with small red decal, 29¾in. sq. (Skinner) $1,500

Gustav Stickley table, no. 441, circa 1903, round overhanging top with apron, on square post legs, arched, stacked cross-stretchers and central round pin, 36in. diameter. (Skinner) $880

Gustav Stickley dining table, no. 632, circa 1904, overhanging round top with apron on five square tapering legs, 49in. diameter. (Skinner) $2,500

L. & J.G. Stickley oak extension dining table, Model 713, 1912–1917, raised on a shaped curved base, with four leaves, 8ft. extended. (Butterfield & Butterfield) $2,300

L. & J. G. Stickley dining table, circa 1912, no. 722, round top, straight apron cross stretcher base tenoned through square legs, with three leaves, 48in. diameter. (Skinner) $2,000

STICKLEY

Gustav Stickley round oak table, circa 1904, 24in. diam. $2,500

A spindle-sided table with lower shelf, by Gustav Stickley, circa 1905, 36in. wide. $7,500

A Gustav Stickley hexagonal leather-top table, no. 624, circa 1910-12, 48in. diam. (Skinner) $10,000

Gustav Stickley table with twelve Grueby tiles, 1902-1904, four flat rails framing 4in. green tiles, 24in. wide. (Skinner Inc.) $25,000

An occasional table with cut corners, possibly early Gustav Stickley, circa 1902-04, 29in. high. (Skinner) $1,500

A Gustav Stickley round leather-top table, no. 645, circa 1907, 36in. diam. (Skinner) $3,100

Gustav Stickley table, circa 1912–16, no. 626, round top on four legs, joined by arched cross stretchers with finial, 40in. diameter. (Skinner Inc.) $1,500

Gustav Stickley round drop leaf table, circa 1912, demi-lune drop leaves, paper label, 32in. long. (Skinner) $2,000

An occasional table, no. 609, by Gustav Stickley, circa 1904-05, unsigned, 36in. diam. (Skinner) $1,250

An inlaid mahogany Pembroke table, the oval kingwood banded top with trailing floral border above frieze drawer, 38in. wide. (Christie's) **$1,072**

Classical carved mahogany veneer Pembroke table, New York, circa 1835, with shaped corners, 56¼in. wide extended. (Skinner) **$1,495**

American Pembroke table, in mahogany with shaped top and one drawer, rope-turned legs with casters, 28½in. high. (Eldred's) **$550**

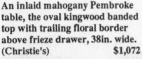

A fine Federal inlaid mahogany Pembroke table, Newport, Rhode Island, circa 1800, the oblong top with hinged D-shaped leaves, width extended 38½in. (Sotheby's) **$50,000**

A pair of Federal cherry drop leaf tables, Nantucket, Massachusetts, circa 1820, 23in. wide. (Skinner) **$978**

Federal mahogany inlaid Pembroke table, Rhode Island, circa 1790-1810, on four square tapering inlaid legs terminating in spade feet, measures 32 x 40½in. (Skinner Inc.) **$5,300**

A George III mahogany Pembroke table, the ebony-inlaid rounded rectangular twin-flap top crossbanded with satinwood, upon square tapering legs with brass caps, 39¼in. wide, open. (Christie's) **$2,367**

Classical mahogany veneer Pembroke table, New York, 1820s, with reeded edges on the falling leaves and cockbeaded end-drawers, one simulated, 39in. wide. (Skinner) **$1,840**

A Federal inlaid mahogany Pembroke table, Rhode Island, 1790–1810, the hinged oval top with molded edge decorated with stringing over a bowed frieze drawer with lightwood banding, 31in. wide. (Christie's) **$16,500**

Cherry inlaid Pembroke table, Connecticut River Valley, circa 1800, refinished, 36in. long. (Skinner Inc.) $4,800

George III mahogany oval Pembroke table, late 18th century, fitted with a drawer and raised on square tapered legs, length 35¼in. (Butterfield & Butterfield) $2,070

Federal cherry inlaid Pembroke table, New England, circa 1810, with stringing on the skirts and legs, 34½in. wide. (Skinner Inc.) $1,650

A Federal inlaid mahogany Pembroke table, Philadelphia, 1790-1810, the rectangular top with conforming hinged leaves with serpentine corners, 37¼in. wide. (Christie's) $1,035

George II satinwood, thuya and rosewood Pembroke table, late 18th century, the oblong top and demilune drop leaves broadly cross banded and line inlaid, raised on straight tapered line inlaid legs, 20in. wide. (William Doyle Galleries) $9,200

A Federal inlaid mahogany Pembroke table, Mid-Atlantic States, probably Baltimore, Maryland, circa 1795, the oblong top with bowed ends flanked by hinged D-shaped leaves, 40in. wide open. (Sotheby's) $3,450

A Federal inlaid mahogany Pembroke table, Rhode Island, 1790–1810, the hinged oval top with molded edge decorated with stringing over a bowed frieze drawer with lightwood banding, 31in. wide. (Christie's) $19,000

George III satinwood and rosewood crossbanded Pembroke table, last quarter 18th century, with a fitted work drawer and candleholder, 38½in. long. (Skinner) $4,370

Federal inlaid mahogany Pembroke table, Rhode Island, circa 1800, the molded oval top with two drop leaves on square tapering legs with bellflower, line inlay, length 30¼in. (Butterfield & Butterfield) $3,450

CHIPPENDALE

Chippendale mahogany
Pembroke table, New England,
late 18th century, old refinish,
37in. wide.
(Skinner) $1,265

A fine Chippendale carved and
figured mahogany Pembroke
table, New England, possibly
Portsmouth, New Hampshire,
circa 1785, extended width 35in.
(Sotheby's) $27,600

Chippendale mahogany
Pembroke table, Rhode Island,
1765–90, with fluted and
chamfered legs, 29in. wide.
(Skinner) $747

A Chippendale carved
cherrywood Pembroke table,
Connecticut River Valley, circa
1800, on square tapering legs
joined by an X-stretcher with
incised scrolling vines, width
extended 36in.
(Sotheby's) $3,000

A fine and rare Chippendale
figured mahogany Pembroke
table, Philadelphia, circa 1780,
hinged rectangular leaves
centering a frieze drawer, width
open 41in.
(Sotheby's) $13,800

A Chippendale cherrywood
Pembroke table, American,
probably Pennsylvania, circa
1785, the rectangular top with
two hinged leaves above a single
molded drawer, width extended
39in.   (Sotheby's) $2,070

Chippendale cherry Pembroke
table, Portsmouth, New
Hampshire, late 18th century,
the rectangular drop leaf top
overhangs a straight skirt, 35in.
wide.
(Skinner) $1,610

A Chippendale mahogany
Pembroke table, possibly
Penn., circa 1780, the shaped
top with serpentine leaves,
31in. wide.
(Skinner) $1,620

Chippendale walnut Pembroke
or breakfast table, probably
Philadelphia, circa 1800,
pierced fret cross stretchers,
28¾in. high.
(Skinner Inc.) $7,500

CHIPPENDALE

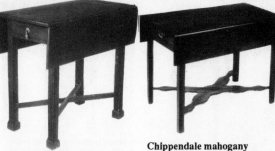

A Chippendale carved mahogany Pembroke table, Portsmouth, New Hampshire, 1760–1780, the serpentine top with two drop leaves above an apron, 33¹/₂in. long. (Christie's) $21,850

Chippendale walnut Pembroke table, probably Maryland, 18th century, with single drawer, 34in. wide extended. (Skinner) $1,150

Chippendale mahogany Pembroke table, Connecticut River Valley, circa 1780, exotically grained drop leaf top on four square legs, 35in. wide. (Skinner) $2,875

A Chippendale mahogany Pembroke table, Massachusetts, 1760–1780, the hinged serpentine top with serpentine drop leaves above a cockbeaded bowed frieze drawer, 27¹/₂in. high. (Christie's) $4,500

A Chippendale figured mahogany Pembroke table, Philadelphia, Pennsylvania, circa 1785, the oblong molded top with bowed ends flanked by serpentine leaves, 41in. long extended. (Sotheby's) $145,500

A Chippendale mahogany Pembroke table, Massachusetts, circa 1770, the rectangular top with bowed ends flanked by serpentine shaped drop leaves, 35⁵/₈in. wide. (Christie's) $5,175

A good Chippendale mahogany Pembroke table, New England, possibly Rhode Island, circa 1780, the oblong top with bowed ends, 36¹/₂in. wide open. (Sotheby's) $4,600

A fine and rare Chippendale figured mahogany Pembroke table, Philadelphia, circa 1780, the rectangular top with bowed ends flanked by hinged serpentine leaves, width open 37³/₄in. (Sotheby's) $9,200

A Chippendale figured mahogany Pembroke table, New England, circa 1780, the rectangular top with two hinged rectangular leaves, 37¹/₂in. wide. (Sotheby's) $2,875

PEMBROKE TABLES

FEDERAL, BALTIMORE

A very fine Federal satinwood-inlaid mahogany Pembroke table, Baltimore, Maryland, circa 1795, on inlaid square tapering legs ending in brass caps, width extended 41¼in. (Sotheby's) $30,000

An inlaid mahogany Pembroke table, Baltimore, Maryland, 1790–1810, the line-inlaid oval top with drop leaves above a conforming apron with line inlaid square tapering legs, 41½in. wide. (Christie's) $25,000

Fine Federal inlaid mahogany Pembroke table, attributed to Levin Tarr, Baltimore, circa 1800, the double line and banded inlaid edge oval top with two drop leaves, length 33¼in. (Butterfield & Butterfield) $48,875

CONNECTICUT

A good Federal inlaid mahogany Pembroke table, Connecticut, circa 1810, the rectangular top flanked by D-shaped leaves, 40in. wide open. (Sotheby's) $2,875

A Federal figured maple Pembroke table, eastern Connecticut or Rhode Island, 1795–1825, on square tapering legs joined by an X-shaped stretcher, 29⅜in. high. (Christie's) $7,500

Federal cherry inlaid Pembroke table, Massachusetts or Connecticut, circa 1800, the serpentine drop leaf top with frieze drawer and string inlay, 20in. wide. (Skinner) $2,645

MASSACHUSETTS

Federal mahogany inlaid Pembroke table, Massachusetts, circa 1800, (minor restoration), 39in. wide. (Skinner) $3,450

Federal mahogany inlaid Pembroke table, probably Massachusetts, circa 1800, the rectangular drop leaf top with ovolo corners, 35¾in. wide. (Skinner) $1,380

Federal mahogany and tiger maple veneer Pembroke table, Massachusetts, circa 1815, old refinish, 42in. wide. (Skinner) $2,310

FEDERAL, MID-ATLANTIC STATES

Federal mahogany inlaid
Pembroke table with drawer,
Middle Atlantic States, circa
1790, old refinish, 40in. wide
(open).
(Skinner) $1,610

NEW ENGLAND

A Federal inlaid mahogany
Pembroke-table, Mid-Atlantic
States, 1790–1810, the hinged
oval top with twin drop-leaves
over a conforming cockbeaded
frieze drawer flanked by tablet
inlay on square-tapering legs,
38¼in. wide.
(Christie's) $3,800

A Federal inlaid mahogany
Pembroke table, Mid-Atlantic
States, 1790–1810, on square
tapering line inlaid legs with
cuffs, 39⅜in. wide (open).
(Christie's) $4,025

A Federal inlaid mahogany
Pembroke table, New England,
circa 1810, the oblong top with
two hinged D-shaped leaves,
42in. wide extended.
(Sotheby's) $1,725

NEW YORK

Mahogany Pembroke table, New
England, late 18th century,
serpentine drop leaf top above a
base with beaded drawer and
four molded Marlborough legs,
18in. wide.
(Skinner) $1,380

A Federal cherrywood
Pembroke table, New England,
1800–1810, the rectangular top
with two D-shaped drop-leaves
above a long drawer, on square
tapering legs, 35½in. long.
(Christie's) $1,375

A Federal inlaid mahogany
Pembroke table, New York,
1790-1810, the rectangular
top with bowed ends and line
inlaid edge, 41in. wide (leaves
open). (Christie's) $6,800

A late Federal figured maple
and cherrywood Pembroke
table, signed by A. J. Baycock,
Brookfield, Madison County,
New York, 1810-1830, on
spirally reeded tapering
cylindrical legs, 28¼in. high.
(Christie's New York) $4,800

Federal mahogany inlaid
Pembroke table, attributed to
William Whitehead, New York,
1790–1810, the line inlaid oval
top above bowed drawers at
either end, 30¾in. wide.
(Skinner) $8,050

FEDERAL, NEW YORK

A Federal inlaid mahogany
Pembroke table, New York,
circa 1800, the oblong top with
two line-inlaid hinged leaves,
length 30³/₄in.
(Sotheby's) $4,500

A Federal inlaid mahogany
Pembroke table, New York,
circa 1810, the rectangular top
with hinged lid.
(Sotheby's) $1,725

Federal mahogany inlaid
Pembroke table, New York City,
1785–1800, with inlaid flutes
and shaded husks and
overlapping ovals, 19¹/₈in. wide.
(Skinner) $18,000

A Federal mahogany Pembroke
table, labeled by Charles
Christian, New York, 1810–
1815, on reeded tapering legs
with baluster and ring turned
capitals and feet, 43³/₄in. wide
(open).
(Christie's) $5,750

A Federal mahogany Pembroke
table, New York, 1790–1810, the
rectangular top with clover-leaf
shaped drop leaves over a frieze
drawer, on square tapering legs,
31in. wide.
(Christie's) $3,300

A Federal inlaid mahogany
Pembroke table, New York,
circa 1795, the oblong line-inlaid
top with bowed ends flanked by
D-shaped leaves, 40¹/₂in. wide
extended.
(Sotheby's) $17,250

A Federal mahogany Pembroke
table, attributed to George
Woodruff, New York, 1800–
1810, the rectangular top with
hinged double-elliptical drop
leaves, 32³/₈in. wide.
(Christie's) $5,520

A Federal inlaid mahogany
Pembroke table, New York,
circa 1795, the oblong
crossbanded top with bowed
ends flanked by D-shaped
leaves, 38in. wide open.
(Sotheby's) $9,775

A fine Federal satinwood-inlaid
mahogany single-drawer
Pembroke table, New York,
circa 1800, the oblong top with
two hinged D-shaped leaves,
44in. wide open.
(Sotheby's) $14,950

FEDERAL, NEW YORK

A Federal inlaid mahogany Pembroke table, New York, circa 1795, the line-inlaid top flanked by rectangular leaves, 40in. wide open.
(Sotheby's) $2,587

A Federal mahogany Pembroke-table, New York, 1790–1810, on square tapering legs joined by serpentine X-stretchers, 31in. wide.
(Christie's) $6,800

A Federal inlaid mahogany Pembroke table, New York, 1790–1810, the circular hinged top with two drop leaves, 31¼in. wide.
(Christie's) $10,350

A Federal mahogany Pembroke-table, New York, 1790–1810, the oval hinged top with molded edge and D-shaped drop leaves over a cockbeaded bowed frieze drawer, on square tapering legs, 31¾in. wide.
(Christie's) $2,200

Federal mahogany Pembroke table, New York, circa 1810, the rectangular top with two clover leaf-shaped drop leaves above a frieze with one long beaded edge drawer, length 36in.
(Butterfield & Butterfield)
                                $1,093

A Federal inlaid mahogany Pembroke table, New York, 1790–1810, the rectangular line inlaid top with two drop leaves and ovolo corners, on square line inlaid legs with cuffs, 37¼in. wide.
(Christie's) $2,760

Federal mahogany and mahogany veneer Pembroke table, possibly New York, circa 1810, rectangular top with rounded leaves above a straight beaded skirt, 23in. wide.
(Skinner) $863

A Federal satinwood inlaid mahogany Pembroke table, attributed to William Whitehead, New York, circa 1795, 41in. wide (open).
(Christie's) $85,000

A Federal figured maple Pembroke table, New York or Bermuda, 1800-1820, the rounded rectangular top with two drop leaves, 28in. high.
(Christie's New York) $3,800

A Chippendale carved mahogany pier table, Newport, 1760–1790, the rectangular top with chip-carved edges above a conforming frame with serpentine aprons with beaded edge over pierced knee returns, on stop-fluted straight legs, 41¾in. wide.
(Christie's) $74,000

A rare pair of classical gilt, stenciled and ormolu-mounted marble-top mahogany pier tables, Boston, Massacusetts, circa 1815, 44¼in. wide.
(Sotheby's) $13,800

Classical mahogany carved and mahogany veneer pier table, attributed to Williams and Everett, Boston, circa 1825, the marble top above a projecting frieze drawer, 45in. wide.
(Skinner) $5,463

One of a pair of Empire mahogany marble-top pier tables, probably Boston, circa 1830, 49in. wide.
(Christie's) (Two) $5,500

A classical carved parcel-gilt rosewood marble-top pier table, Boston, 1820–40, 45in. wide.
(Christie's) $6,900

Classical mahogany veneer and gilt pier table, New York City, 1820-35, with stenciled veneered frieze and antique verte carved front feet, 42¼in. wide.
(Skinner) $3,738

A Classical mahogany veneered and marble-top pier table New York City, 1810-1820, the rectangular marble top above bronze and alabaster columns, 42½in. wide.
(Christie's) $10,350

A classical brass-inlaid and carved mahogany pier-table, stamped *H. Lannuier, New York*, circa 1815, on four waterleaf and hairy-carved animal legs with paw feet, 33in. wide.
(Christie's) $34,500

Classical mahogany, mahogany and burlwood veneer pier table, probably Boston, circa 1825, the rectangular marble top above an applied molded case, 41in. wide.
(Skinner) $2,875

Classical carved mahogany veneer table, possibly mid-Atlantic States, 1830-40, the figured mahogany veneer splashboard supported by marble columns, 37½in. wide.
(Skinner) $3,450

Classical mahogany veneer pier table, Massachusetts, 1835–40, with old carrara marble top with thumb molded edge, 40in. wide.
(Skinner) $2,415

A classical brass inlaid mahogany marble top pier table, N.Y., circa 1810/30, 41½in. wide. $4,250

An important Queen Anne carved walnut serpentine-front marble-top pier table, Boston, Massachusetts, circa 1745, 27½in. high overall. (Sotheby's) $200,500

A Classical rosewood marble top pier table, Philadelphia, 1820-1830, with ormolu medallion and leafage above gilt scrolled supports, 42in. wide. (Christie's New York) $9,600

A classical mahogany pier-table, probably New York, circa 1825, the rectangular crossbanded top above a frieze with brass string inlay and a mirrored back-plate, 42¾in. wide. (Christie's) $3,300

A classical gilt-stenciled mahogany pier-table, New York, 1815–1830, the rectangular white and gray marble top with canted corners over a conforming bolection-molded frieze centered by a rosette, 45in. wide. (Christie's) $8,250

A classical carved mahogany pier table, attributed to Charles-Honore Lannuier, New York, 1810–1819, on guilded acanthus carved and ebonized animal paw front feet and square rear legs, 38¾in wide. (Christie's) $20,700

A fine George II carved and figured mahogany marble top pier table, English, mid-18th century, on cabriole legs ending in claw-and-ball feet, top 30in. wide. (Sotheby's) $6,900

A Classical stenciled mahogany marble-top pier table, American, 1815-1835, the rectangular marble top above a conforming coved frame, 44in. wide. (Christie's) $7,475

A Classical carved and gilt stenciled mahogany marble top pier table, Philadelphia, 1825-1835, on scroll supports with acanthus knees, 42in. wide. (Christie's New York) $5,700

A Federal inlaid mahogany serving table, possibly Maryland, 1790–1810, the rectangular top above a conforming case fitted with two short drawers each inlaid with oblong stringing over two similar doors, flanked by string inlaid stiles, on string-inlaid square legs with cuffed ankles and tapered feet, the rear legs replaced, 34¹/ₛin. wide.
(Christie's) $3,000

A Federal carved mahogany serving table with D-shaped top, 1810-15, 36in. wide. **$5,000**

A classical carved mahogany serving table, New York, 1810–20, the rectangular top with outset rounded front corners and reeded edge, 35in. wide. (Christie's) **$6,900**

A rare Federal carved mahogany marble-top two-drawer server, New York, circa 1815, on acanthus-carved ring-turned legs, 29$\frac{1}{4}$in. wide. (Sotheby's) **$6,000**

A Federal mahogany serving table, attributed to Michael Allison, new York, 1805–1810, the rectangular top with ovolo corners and reeded edge, 36in. wide. (Christie's) **$21,850**

Federal carved mahogany server, New England, circa 1815–1820, on ring-turned, reeded and rope twist legs joined by a serpentine shaped shelf ending in brass casters, 36in. wide. (Butterfield & Butterfield) **$1,500**

A good Federal mahogany three-drawer serving table, New York, dated 1816, on frontal reeded supports joined by a shaped medial shelf, 36$\frac{1}{2}$in. wide. (Sotheby's) **$6,500**

A late Federal carved mahogany serving table, New York, 1815-1825, the reeded rectangular top with outset rounded corners, 36in. wide. (Christie's New York) **$4,100**

Antique American Empire server in pine, one molded drawer over two cupboard doors flanked by turned columns, 32in. wide. (Eldred's) **$750**

A Federal mahogany serving-table, New York, circa 1810, the rectangular top with outset rounded front corners and reeded edge, on turned tapering legs and brass feet, 35$\frac{3}{4}$in. wide. (Christie's) **$4,100**

Rare L. & J.G. Stickley server, three drawers above lower shelf, signed *The work of ...*, 44in. wide.
(Skinner) $2,070

Lifetime Furniture buffet, no. 5272, circa 1910, three short drawers over single long drawer with cabinet doors below, brass hardware.
(Skinner) $1,000

Federal mahogany and mahogany veneer serving table, New York, circa 1800, replaced pulls, 36in. wide.
(Skinner) $4,400

Fine Stickley Brothers server, two drawers over one, mirrored back, lower shelf, paneled sides, Quaint tag, original finish, 48in. wide.
(Skinner) $1,840

Arts & Crafts ebonized oak server inset with Grueby tiles, the server attributed to L. & J.G. Stickley, raised on square posts joined by a platform stretcher, 30$^{1}/4$in. high.
(Butterfield & Butterfield) $1,725

Rare and exceptional Limbert 'Ebon-oak' server, fine original finish and patina to metal fittings, inlaid ebony, paneled sides with through tenons, 38in. wide.
(Skinner) $2,587

Lifetime Furniture buffet server, circa 1915, plate rail on overhanging rectangular top, single long drawer with brass pulls, 39in. wide.
(Skinner) $500

A late Federal mahogany serving-table, Boston, circa 1815, on spirally-turned legs with turned feet and casters, 39$^{1}/2$in. wide.
(Christie's) $5,500

A fine and rare paint and smoke-decorated pine and maple single-drawer serving table, New England, early 19th century, 37$^{1}/2$in. wide.
(Sotheby's) $25,300

A Federal cherrywood and curly maple single-drawer side table, probably New England, circa 1800, on square tapering legs, 21in. wide.
(Sotheby's) $990

Walnut side table with drawer, Lancaster County, Pennsylvania, mid 18th century, 38in. wide.
(Skinner) $3,738

Important American Queen Anne side table, in walnut with one drawer, reeded side panels, 30in. high.
(Eldred's) $12,650

A Federal paint-decorated pine single-drawer side table, New England, circa 1800, the rectangular top with notched corners above a case fitted with a drawer, on square tapering legs, 28in. high.
(Sotheby's) $9,200

A classical green-painted and gilt-stenciled side-table, attributed to John Needles, Baltimore, early 19th century, on a quadripartite base with foliate bracketed X-shaped supports, on turned tapering feet, 37in. wide.
(Christie's) $8,200

An American paint decorated side table with single drawer, New England, circa 1830, on ring-turned tapering legs ending in elongated turnip feet, 18¼in. wide.
(Sotheby's) $3,738

A fine Federal mahogany two-drawer side table, New York, circa 1810, on reeded tapering legs ending in ebonised vase and ball feet, 20½in. wide.
(Sotheby's) $5,000

A maple single-drawer stretcher-base side table, American, probably New York or New England, 1770–1800, 34in. wide.
(Sotheby's) $1,380

A Federal cherrywood single-drawer side table, American, probably New England, first quarter 19th century, 19in. wide.
(Sotheby's) $1,430

A diminutive Federal mahogany side table, Salem, Massachusetts, circa 1790, the oval top with inlaid bordered edge, 23½in. high.
(Christie's) $32,200

A fine and rare Chippendale figured mahogany one-drawer side table, Rhode Island, circa 1780, on square molded legs,
(Sotheby's) $32,200

A fine paint decorated pine side table, New England, early 19th century, the top sponge decorated in tones of green and yellow, 27½in. high.
(Sotheby's) $11,500

A William and Mary turned birchwood and pine single-drawer stretcher-base side table, New England, 1710–40, the rectangular molded top above a single-drawer frieze, 31½in. wide.
(Sotheby's) $6,325

Pair of Frank Lloyd Wright oak side tables, executed for the Aline Barnsdall Hollyhock House, Los Angeles, circa 1917, 30in. wide.
(Butterfield & Butterfield) $10,925

A mahogany veneered side table, designed by Frank L. Wright, circa 1955, 21½in. wide, red decal on back.
(Skinner) $1,050

A classical mahogany poudreuse, Duncan Phyfe, New York, 1812-1825, on double-swelled waterleaf-carved feet with brass castors, 30½in. high.
(Christie's) $40,250

Classical mahogany and mahogany veneer side table, probably Massachusetts, circa 1825, the rectangular top with scrolled gallery, 39in. wide.
(Skinner) $2,530

Regency mahogany console table, circa 1810, D-shaped top raised on circular carved tapering legs, 31¼in. long.
(Skinner) $3,600

Mid 19th century mahogany sofa table, the arched pedestals surmounted by giltwood eagle heads, 126cm. wide.
(Finarte) $9,000

Classical Revival mahogany and mahogany veneer sofa table, probably New York, circa 1820, 36in. wide.
(Skinner) $3,025

Classical carved mahogany veneer sofa table, probably Boston, 1830's, 42in. wide.
(Skinner) $4,675

Classical painted sofa table, Baltimore, Maryland, circa 1830, the rectangular drop leaf top above two short drawers, 31in. wide closed.
(Skinner) $1,725

A Classical carved mahogany and mahogany veneer sofa table, probably New York, circa 1820, 35½in. wide.
(Skinner) $9,300

A fine and rare classical brass-mounted carved and figured-mahogany sofa table, Philadelphia, circa 1820, width extended 5ft. 2½in.
(Sotheby's) $54,625

Classical mahogany veneer sofa table, probably New York, 1820–40, with two veneered cockbeaded drawers, 23³/₈in. wide.
(Skinner) $4,025

A mahogany and boxwood lined sofa table, of George III design, the reeded rounded rectangular twin-flap top above a frieze with two drawers, 55in. wide.
(Christie's) $2,362

A classical mahogany sofa table, the working drawer with a brass lion head pull, circa 1810/20, Phila., 42in. wide. $7,000

A turned and figured walnut two-drawer tavern table, Pennsylvania, 1740–80, the rectangular removable top above a frieze, 4ft. 10in. wide. (Sotheby's) $6,900

A Masonic carved maple tavern table, table desk, and accompanying ceremonial box, early 20th century, 27¼in. wide. (Sotheby's) $3,500

A turned walnut two-drawer stretcher-base tavern table, Pennsylvania or Mid-Atlantic States, 1775–1800, 4ft. 6½in. wide. (Sotheby's) $4,312

A painted 'Windsor' tavern table, possibly Rhode Island, circa 1780, 28in. wide. (Skinner) $7,500

Painted poplar and pine table, Pennsylvania, 1780–1810, with removable top having carved pins doweled through the supporting battens, two thumb-molded drawers, 30½in. wide. (Skinner) $6,440

Queen Anne figured maple tavern table, New England, 18th century, the oval top above a rectangular case on circular tapering legs, 36½in. wide. (Butterfield & Butterfield) $2,100

A Queen Anne painted maple oval-top tavern table, New England, 1750-1780, the oval top above a plain frieze, 36in. long. (Sotheby's) $8,050

A turned maple and pine tavern table, New England, 1740-1770, the rectangular cleated top above a conformingly shaped frieze, 30in. wide. (Sotheby's) $6,325

Antique American tavern table in pine and other woods, oval top, cut-out apron, molded square tapered legs, 25in. high. (Eldred's) $240

Painted Queen Anne tavern table, Rhode Island, 18th century, scrubbed top on original red washed base, 38in. wide. (Skinner Inc.) $15,000

William and Mary maple tavern table, New England, 18th century, on four block vase and ring turned legs, 38½in. wide. (Skinner) $2,415

Pine and oak table, Pennsylvania, 1760–80, with thumb-molded top and single drawer with old replaced brass, 55½in. wide. (Skinner) $2,760

A fine Queen Anne walnut single-drawer tavern table, Pennsylvania, circa 1780, the rectangular top above a single molded drawer, 35¼in. wide. (Sotheby's) $5,500

A Queen Anne tavern table, Pennsylvania, 1730-50, the rectangular top with breadboard ends above an apron fitted with a thumbmolded drawer, 31¾in. wide. (Christie's) $14,950

A Queen Anne figured maple single-drawer tavern table, New England, circa 1740–80, the oblong molded top above a frieze drawer, 22in. wide. (Sotheby's) $8,050

William and Mary painted tavern table, New England, early 18th century, the rectangular overhanging top on four block, vase and ring-turned legs, 43in. wide. (Skinner) $6,325

Walnut tavern table, Pennsylvania, early 18th century, the overhanging rectangular top above a molded skirt containing a thumbmolded drawer, 32in. wide. (Skinner) $2,530

A rare grain-painted poplar one-drawer tavern table, Pennsylvania, 1740–80, the removable two-board rectangular top pegged to a conformingly shaped frieze, 41in. wide. (Sotheby's) $4,600

NEW ENGLAND

An 18th century maple tavern table with breadboard ends, New England, the top 40 x 24½in.
(Skinner) $3,400

Pine tavern table, New England, 18th century, old refinish, oval top, 34in. long.
(Skinner Inc.) $2,000

Painted pine and maple tavern table with drawer, New England, 18th century, top with old varnish and base with old red paint, 37½in. wide.
(Skinner) $2,070

A painted and turned maple and pine oval-top tavern table, New England, 1730–70, the oval top above a molded frieze raised on vase- and reel-turned legs, 23in. wide.
(Sotheby's) $6,900

A gray-painted and turned pine tavern table, New England, 1730–60, the oval top above a rectangular frieze, 21in. wide.
(Sotheby's) $3,162

A very fine and rare Queen Anne maple 'butterfly' tavern table, New England, 1730–60, the oblong top with two hinged D-shaped leaves, width extended 37¼in.
(Sotheby's) $12,500

A good figured maple oval-top tavern table, New England, 1750–80, on circular turned and tapered legs, 26¼in. wide.
(Sotheby's) $10,000

Painted pine and maple tavern table, northern New England, mid-18th century, scrubbed top with breadboard ends, 37¾in. wide.
(Skinner) $1,840

Pine and maple tavern table, New England, 18th century, oval top, molded stretchers, 28in. wide.
(Skinner) $4,888

WILLIAM & MARY

William and Mary painted
tavern table with drawer,
Newbury Massachusetts, early
18th century, painted old red,
39in. wide.
(Skinner) $9,200

A William and Mary maple
tavern table, New England,
circa 1730, 34in. diam.
(Sotheby's) $7,500

William and Mary walnut
tavern table, possibly Boston,
early 18th century, 31¹/₂in. wide.
(Skinner) $8,050

William and Mary maple tavern
table, New England, 18th
century, old natural surface on
the top, dark red painted base,
23.4in. wide.
(Skinner) $6,325

A rare William and Mary
turned birchwood and pine
tavern table, New England,
1730–50, the oval top above a
molded rectangular frieze,
32¹/₂in. wide.
(Sotheby's) $4,025

A William and Mary painted
pine and maple tavern table,
New Hampshire, 1740–1770, the
oval top above a straight apron
on double baluster-turned legs,
31in. long.
(Christie's) $16,100

A William and Mary turned
maple tavern table, New
England, 1740–80, the
rectangular two-board top
above a conformingly-shaped
molded frieze, 34½in. wide.
(Sotheby's) $2,300

A fine and rare William and
Mary red-painted pine, hickory,
and maple tavern table, New
England, 1730–50.
(Sotheby's) $5,462

A William and Mary turned
birchwood and pine tavern
table, New England, the
rectangular molded top above
a frieze drawer, 23in. wide.
(Sotheby's) $4,600

Painted maple and cherry tea table, probably Massachusetts, mid 18th century, 28¾in. wide. (Skinner) $4,887

Painted tea table, New England, 18th century, old surface with red paint, 32in. wide. (Skinner) $9,200

Maple tea table, Rhode Island, 1740–90, refinished, 36⅞in. wide. (Skinner Inc.) $3,750

A very fine and rare William and Mary turned and carved maple and pine 'Spanish-foot' tea table, Massachusetts, possibly Ipswich, 1720–50, 35in. wide. (Sotheby's) $29,900

Federal cherry inlaid tea table, Massachusetts or Connecticut, late 18th century, the serpentine top centering a compass inlay of contrasting woods, top 31¾in. square. (Skinner) $4,313

Fine painted country maple tea table, New England, circa 1800, rectangular top with shaped corner overhangs, 27in. high. (Skinner) $12,500

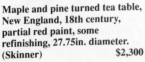

Maple and pine turned tea table, New England, 18th century, partial red paint, some refinishing, 27.75in. diameter. (Skinner) $2,300

Painted maple tea table, probably Massachusetts, mid 18th century, four-block turned splayed legs, 23in. wide. (Skinner) $4,025

Country maple and pine tea table, New England, 18th century, on tapering turned legs, 25½in. high. (Skinner) $1,500

CHIPPENDALE

TEA TABLES

Chippendale walnut tea table, Pennsylvania, circa 1780, 33in. diameter.
(Skinner) **$1,320**

A very fine and rare early Chippendale carved mahogany piecrust tilt-top tea table, Philadelphia, circa 1745, height 27in.
(Sotheby's) **$55,000**

Chippendale mahogany dish top tip table, New England, circa 1780, 19in. diameter.
(Skinner) **$1,870**

Chippendale mahogany dish top bird-cage tea table, Philadelphia, circa 1760, the single board above a ring turned and compressed ball standard raised on cabriole legs, diameter 35¹/₄in.
(Butterfield & Butterfield) **$3,450**

Chippendale carved mahogany tilt-top tea table, Massachusetts, late 18th century, the molded edge serpentine shaped top tilting above a vase form standard, width of top 31¹/₄in.
(Butterfield & Butterfield) **$6,325**

A Chippendale mahogany dish-top table, attributed to John Goddard, Newport, Rhode Island, circa 1760–1770, the circular dished top tilting above a reeded cylindrical support, 30¹/₈in. diameter.
(Christie's) **$7,475**

Chippendale walnut tilt-top birdcage tea table, New England, late 18th century, circular top on a birdcage platform, 33¹/₄in. diameter.
(Skinner) **$2,300**

Chippendale mahogany tilting and turning tea table, American, third quarter 18th century, the circular dish top above a bird-cage over a tapering vase-turned support on cabriole legs, diameter 17¹/₄in.
(Butterfield & Butterfield) **$1,035**

Chippendale mahogany tilt-top tea table, Massachusetts, circa 1780, the shaped top with serpentine sides, 28³/₄in. wide.
(Skinner) **$1,610**

CHIPPENDALE

Chippendale mahogany tilt top tea table, New England, circa 1780, the circular top above a birdcage support, 34in. diam.
(Skinner) $2,500

Chippendale mahogany tilt-top tea table, southern New England, late 18th century, 33in. wide.
(Skinner) $1,092

Chippendale mahogany carved tea table, Newport, Rhode Island, 1760–80, old surface, 33in. diameter.
(Skinner Inc.) $13,750

Chippendale mahogany tilt-top tea table, probably Massachusetts, late 18th century, serpentine top with molded edge on a vase and ring turned post, top 33 x 31³/₄in.
(Skinner) $2,300

Chippendale walnut dish-top tea table, Pennsylvania, 18th century, the top tilts above the birdcage and pedestal on cabriole leg base, 33¹/₂in. diameter.
(Skinner) $863

Chippendale cherry tilt top tea table, Norwich, Connecticut, 1760-1790, on cabriole leg tripod base, 26½in. high.
(Skinner Inc.) $1,650

Chippendale walnut tea table, Pennsylvania, circa 1780, the circular molded top on a birdcage platform and vase and ring-turned post, 35¹/₂in. diameter.
(Skinner) $2,300

A Chippendale carved and figured maple piecrust tilt-top tea table, in the Pennsylvania manner, on acanthus leaf-carved cabriole legs, 29in. high.
(Sotheby's) $5,462

An early Chippendale carved walnut tilt-top tea table, Philadelphia, circa 1760, the circular dished top tilting and swiveling above a bird-cage support, 32¹/₂in. diameter.
(Sotheby's) $805

CHIPPENDALE

Chippendale walnut tilt-top tea table, Pennsylvania, 1750–80, 34in. diameter.
(Skinner) $1,093

Chippendale carved walnut tilt top tea table, Connecticut, 1760-1780, on a cabriole leg tripod base, 34in. diam.
(Skinner Inc.) $4,000

Chippendale tiger maple bird cage tilt top tea table, on tripod cabriole leg base, 19½in. diam. (Skinner Inc.) $4,000

A Chippendale carved mahogany scallop top tea table, Pennsylvania, 1765-1785, on tripod cabriole legs with ball and claw feet, 28in. high. (Christie's New York)
$16,500

A Chippendale cherrywood large tilt-top tea table, Connecticut, circa 1780, the circular top above a birdcage support, 41in. diameter.
(Sotheby's) $2,587

A rare Chippendale mahogany tilt top tea table, attributed to John Goddard, Newport, Rhode Island, 1760-1790, on three arched legs, 69.5cm. high. (Christie's New York)
$35,000

Chippendale walnut tilt top table, Middle Atlantic States, circa 1800, refinished, 28½in. diameter.
(Skinner Inc.) $750

A Country Chippendale maple tea table, New England, circa 1780, 33½in. wide.
(Skinner) $1,050

Chippendale walnut tilt-top tea table, Pennsylvania, late 18th century, old surface, 27½in. diameter.
(Skinner Inc.) $1,100

470

CHIPPENDALE

A rare Chippendale carved and figured mahogany tilt-top birdcage tea table, New York, circa 1770, 31³/₄in. diameter. (Sotheby's) $11,500

Chippendale mahogany carved tilt top tea table, probably Connecticut, circa 1780, 34¹/₂in. wide. (Skinner Inc.) $3,100

The Edwards family Chippendale carved mahogany tilt-top tea table, Boston, 1760–80, 36in. diameter. (Christie's) $46,000

A Chippendale carved mahogany tea table, Philadelphia, 1765–85, the circular top with molded scalloped edge tilting and turning above a birdcage support, 35¹/₂in. diameter. (Christie's) $121,300

A fine Chippendale carved mahogany tea table, Philadelphia, 1760–1780, with circular dished and molded rim top revolving and tilting above a tapering columnar and compressed ball-turned pedestal, 27¹/₂in. high. (Christie's) $35,000

A very fine and rare Chippendale turned and carved cherrywood tilt-top tea table, Lancaster County, Pennsylvania, circa 1765, 33³/₄in. diameter. (Sotheby's) $288,500

Chippendale mahogany carved tilt-top tea table, Boston, 1760–80, old surface, 35in. diameter. (Skinner Inc.) $5,100

A Chippendale carved mahogany piecrust tilt-top tea table, Philadelphia, Pennsylvania, circa 1770, 33in. diameter. (Sotheby's) $530,500

Chippendale mahogany carved tilt top table, Philadelphia, circa 1765, old refinish, bird cage fixed in place, 32in. diameter. (Skinner Inc.) $13,750

QUEEN ANNE

A good Queen Anne figured maple oval-top splayed-leg tea table, New England, 1760–90, 35¹/₂in. wide. (Sotheby's) **$9,775**

Queen Anne mahogany tilt-top tea table, New England, 1760–80, 29¹/₄in. diameter. (Skinner) **$633**

A Queen Anne figured maple octagonal tilt-top tea table, Conn., 1730-40, 33in. wide, 26in. high. (Christie's) **$23,000**

A Queen Anne cherrywood tea-table, probably Northampton or Hatfield, Massachusetts, 1740–1760, the deeply scalloped molded top above a rectangular frame, 35in. wide. (Christie's) **$45,000**

A Queen Anne cherry and walnut tea table, probably Rhode Island, circa 1760, the rectangular breadboard overhanging top with exposed tenons, 30in. wide. **$36,000**

A good Queen Anne maple and pine tea table, New York State, probably Long Island, 1780–1800, the rectangular top above a cyma-shaped skirt, 25¹/₂in. wide. (Sotheby's) **$2,875**

A rare Queen Anne gumwood tea table, New York, circa 1750, the rectangular thumbmolded top above a plain molded frieze, 30¹/₄in. wide. (Sotheby's) **$6,325**

A rare Queen Anne walnut tea table, Pennsylvania, 1730-80, the rectangular top above a shaped apron on cabriole legs, 35in. (Sotheby's) **$22,425**

Queen Anne maple tea table, New England, mid 18th century, the overhanging oval top on four block turned tapering legs, 28in. wide. (Skinner) **$2,875**

TRAY TOP

A good Queen Anne red- and green-painted maple and pine tray-top tea table, New England, 1740–60.
(Sotheby's) $13,800

Queen Anne style mahogany tray table, with a brass gallery tray top with shell and foliate design, 24in. wide.
(Du Mouchelles) $500

A Chippendale mahogany tray-top tea table, probablyNew York, 1750–70, the rectangular dished top with cusped corners, 32in. wide.
(Christie's) $63,000

A Queen Anne cherrywood tray top tea table, New England, 1740–60, the rectangular top with cove molding, 28¾in. wide.
(Sotheby's) $32,200

A Queen Anne mahogany tray-top tea table, Connecticut, 1740-1760, the rectangular tray top with concave molded edges above a cavetto molded apron, 27¾in. wide.
(Christie's) $57,500

Queen Anne walnut carved tea table, Williamsburg, Virginia area, mid 18th century, with the tray top over-hanging the slightly shaped skirt, 27½in. wide.
(Skinner) $5,750

A fine Queen Anne mahogany tray-top tea table, Goddard-Townsend School, Newport, Rhode Island, circa 1750–80, on cabriole legs, 20¾in. long.
(Sotheby's) $28,750

Eldred Wheeler Queen Anne-style tea table, in tiger maple with molded top and scalloped apron, candle slides, top 31½ x 20in.
(Eldred's) $1,045

A good Queen Anne carved walnut tray-top tea table, Boston, Massachusetts, 1740–60, slender cabriole legs ending in pad feet, 27½in. wide.
(Sotheby's) $63,000

A rare Classical rosewood-veneered, ormolu-mounted carved and figured mahogany work table, probably Boston, Massachusetts, circa 1820, the rectangular cross-banded top supported on four free-standing colonettes centering a baize-line writing slide and two graduated drawers, with a ring-turned and leaf-carved standard below on a concave sided rectangular plinth with canted corners on volute- and feather-carved paw feet below ending in casters, 20in. wide. (Sotheby's)

$3,737

A rare and important paint decorated single-drawer work table, South Paris Hill, Maine, early 19th century, 29in. high.
(Sotheby's) **$37,950**

American Renaissance figured maple and rosewood sewing table by Herter Brothers, New York, circa 1872, on stylized feet, 34½in. wide.
(Butterfield & Butterfield) **$1,300**

An Academy painted tiger maple work table, New England circa 1815, the rectangular overhanging top edged in tiny flowers, 43,5cm. wide.
(Skinner) **$9,000**

A Gustav Stickley work cabinet, circa 1905-7, with two cabinet doors over two drawers with square wooden pulls, 36in. high.
(Skinner) **$18,750**

Unusual Roycroft sewing table, East Aurora, New York, circa 1910, incised with logo, (some stains, one knob broken) 30in. wide.
(Skinner) **$2,500**

A paint-decorated pine two-drawer work table, made by Erastus Grant, Westfield, Massachusetts, decorated by Eliza G. Halam, dated *1827*, 19in. wide.
(Sotheby's) **$3,737**

A fine paint decorated pine work table, American, early 19th century, the rectangular top with notched corners, 18½in. wide.
(Sotheby's) **$3,680**

Painted and grained work table, possibly Pennsylvania, second quarter 19th century, with smoke grained top, 25½in. wide.
(Skinner Inc.) **$2,750**

Stickley Brothers flip-sided sewing table, Grand Rapids, Michigan, circa 1912, rectangular box with applied handle, 18in. wide.
(Skinner) **$530**

CLASSICAL

Classical tiger maple work table, Middle Atlantic States, circa 1825, the rectangular top above two graduated drawers, 21in. wide.
(Skinner) $1,092

Classical mahogany veneer sewing table, New England, circa 1820, replaced brass, 21in. wide.
(Skinner) $1,210

Classical cherry and rosewood veneer gilt-stenciled worktable, Middle Atlantic States, circa 1815, 20³/₄in. wide.
(Skinner Inc.) $1,870

A classical carved mahogany work table, Philadelphia, 1815–1825, on four saber legs with carved scrolled knees and cast foliate brass casters, 20in. wide. (Christie's) $4,800

A classical carved mahogany work-table, attributed to A. Quervelle, Philadelphia, 1815–1825, the hinged rectangular top with molded edge above a fitted interior, on four carved paw feet with waterleaf-carved knees and casters, 23in. wide.
(Christie's) $4,800

Classical mahogany and mahogany veneer work table, Rhode Island, circa 1830, on a veneered swiveling pedestal, 20³/₄in. wide.
(Skinner Inc.) $560

Classical carved mahogany veneered work table, Boston, 1820–30, the central fitted veneered drawer above similar frame drawer for the wooden work bag, 30¹/₂in. high.
(Skinner Inc.) $2,200

A classical cherry and mahogany veneer two-drawer work stand, New England, circa 1820, with opalescent glass pulls, refinished, 18in. wide.
(Skinner) $1,035

Classical mahogany and mahogany veneer carved sewing stand, attributed to Isaac Vose and Isaac Vose Jr., Boston, circa 1824, 20¹/₂in. wide.
(Skinner) $3,738

A rare Classical carved and figured mahogany and birchwood work table, Boston, Massachusetts, circa 1815, the rectangular molded top above four frieze drawers and a sliding sewing bag flanked by birchwood-inlaid dies and turned reeded-lyre-form supports, 20in. wide. (Sotheby's) $71,250

A Classical carved and inlaid mahogany work table, Boston, 1815–1830, the rectangular top with sliding tray inlaid with a chessboard and opening to an interior compartment above a conforming veneered case flanked by relief-carved rectangular rosettes over a semi-cylindrical case fitted with a conforming sliding upholstered drawer above double-scroll and leaf-carved supports over rectangular plinths joined by a cylindrical and waterleaf-carved stretcher, on scrolled saber legs fitted with castors, 23½in. wide.
(Christie's) $11,500

Classical mahogany carved and mahogany veneer work table, Massachusetts, circa 1833, 20in. wide.
(Skinner) $1,955

Classical carved mahogany and mahogany veneer work table, Boston, early 19th century, 22½in. wide.
(Skinner) $12,650

Classical mahogany veneer work stand, Massachusetts, 1815–25, 19¼in. wide.
(Skinner) $690

Classical mahogany and mahogany veneer work table, probably Massachusetts, circa 1825, refinished replaced brasses, 18¼in. wide.
(Skinner) $1,840

Classical mahogany carved and veneer work table, possibly Isaac Vose Jr., Boston, circa 1830, the rectangular top with rounded leaves above two drawers, 22½in. wide.
(Skinner) $1,840

Classical mahogany carved and mahogany veneer work table, Massachusetts, circa 1825, the rectangular top above two cockbeaded drawers, 22¾in. wide.
(Skinner) $2,070

Classical mahogany and mahogany veneer work table, probably Massachusetts, circa 1825, 21in. wide.
(Skinner) $1,092

A classical mahogany worktable, Massachusetts, 1800–20, on four baluster-turned reeded legs, 18¾in. wide.
(Christie's) $3,450

Classical mahogany and mahogany veneer work table, probably Massachusetts, circa 1825, 18.25in. wide.
(Skinner) $805

CLASSICAL, NEW YORK

A classical mahogany worktable, New York, 1815–1820, on four reeded saber legs with reeded castors, 20¹/₂in. wide. (Christie's) **$5,520**

A classical inlaid and veneered mahogany worktable, New York, 1815–30, on tapering reeded legs, 22¹/₄in. wide. (Christie's) **$6,900**

Classical carved mahogany veneer worktable, New York, circa 1820, on base with carved feet on castors, old refinish, 29in. high. (Skinner) **$770**

A classical mahogany lyre-based work table, New York, 1810–1820, the rectangular top with outset rounded corners over a conforming case fitted with two drawers, on a quadripartite base with downswept legs and brass paw feet, 20¹/₂in. wide. (Christie's) **$1,210**

A classical mahogany work-table, New York, circa 1830, the square top with outset polygonal hinged ends opening to deep compartments over two cockbeaded small drawers, 30¹/₂in. high. (Christie's) **$1,100**

A classical carved mahogany two-drawer work table, New York, circa 1825, on acanthus-carved and vase-turned legs joined by a platform stretcher, 22¹/₂in. wide. (Sotheby's) **$2,185**

Classical Revival mahogany veneered carved work table, probably New York or New Jersey, circa 1830m, with brass inlay, 24in. wide. (Skinner Inc.) **$880**

A Classical stenciled rose-wood work table, New York, 1815-1825, on four gilt acanthus leaf carved lion's paw feet, the top and corners with gilt stenciling, 29¼in. high. (Christie's New York) **$8,000**

A Classical grain painted and stenciled work table, New York, 1825-1835, the rectangular top with drop leaves, 28¾in. high. (Christie's New York) **$3,300**

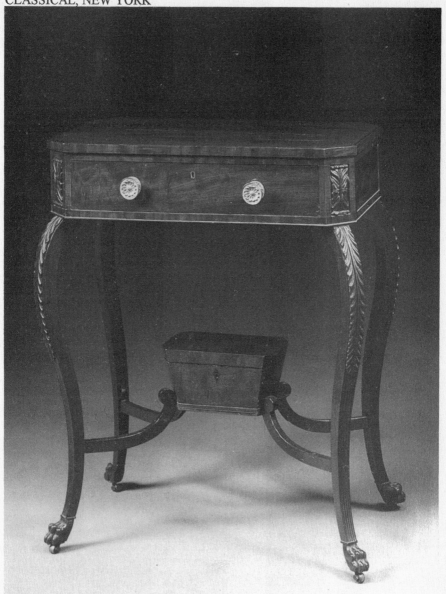

A Classical carved mahogany work table, attributed to the shop of Duncan Phyfe, New York City,
1810–1820, the rectangular top with canted corners and band inlaid edge above a conforming case
fitted with a drawer and an opposing sham drawer flanked by acanthus-carved panels, on tapering
waterleaf-carved and reeded saber legs with paw carved feet and castors joined by scrolled
supports centering a tapering octagonal shaped hinged spool box, 25½in. wide.
(Christie's) $107,000

A Classical mahogany veneered work table, Boston or North Shore, 1810–1820, the banded and
veneered rectangular top with outset ring-turned corners above a conforming case fitted with two
veneered drawers over a lyre-carved pedestal above a rectangular base, with scrolled saber legs
fitted with castors, 23in. wide.
(Christie's) $7,475

CLASSICAL, NEW YORK

Classical cherry carved bird's eye maple and mahogany veneer work table, possibly New York, circa 1825, 21³/₄in. wide. (Skinner)   **$1,610**

Classical carved mahogany veneered work table, probably New York, 1820s, two working and two simulated drawers, 15¹/₂in. wide. (Skinner Inc.)   **$530**

A classical mahogany two-drawer worktable, New York, 1805-1815, the rectangular top above a conforming case fitted with two drawers, 21¹/₂in. wide. (Christie's)   **$1,840**

A classical carved mahogany and stenciled work table, attributed to Roswell A. Hubbard (active 1834-1837), New York, with rectangular top above two drawers flanked by freestanding columns, 21¹/₂in. wide. (Christie's)   **$1,955**

A classical mahogany work table, New York, 1820–1830, the octagonal top with reeded edge over a conforming frieze fitted with two drawers, on saber legs with brass paw feet and casters, 29¹/₂in. high. (Christie's)   **$1,650**

A Classical gilt stenciled mahogany work table, New York, 1820-1830, on acanthus carved lion's paw feet with casters, 23in. wide. (Christie's New York)   **$4,400**

A classical carved mahogany worktable, New York, 1815–1825, the rectangular top above conforming case with two graduated drawers on reeded tapering legs, 21in. wide. (Christie's)   **$4,250**

A rare classical stencil-decorated and parcel-gilt carved mahogany swivel-top work table, New York, circa 1820, 25in. wide. (Sotheby's)   **$1,955**

A classical carved mahogany two-drawer work table, New York, circa 1825, on acanthus-carved supports joined by a concave-fronted platform stretcher, 20¹/₂in. wide. (Sotheby's)   **$2,530**

FEDERAL

A late Federal mahogany work-stand, Philadelphia, 1800-1820, on baluster turned and reeded legs on peg feet, 16¾in. wide. (Christie's) $2,600

A Federal inlaid mahogany and birch work table, New Hampshire, 1790-1810, the scalloped top with gilt-decorated conforming band, 16½in. wide. (Sotheby's) $36,800

A satinwood and mahogany Federal octagonal sewing table, attributed to John and Thomas Seymour, Boston, 1800–1810, 20½in. wide. (Christie's) $25,300

A Federal brass-mounted and inlaid mahogany two-drawer work table, Philadelphia, circa 1810, with ring-turned three-quarter-round columns at each corner, width 20in. (Sotheby's) $5,000

A Federal mahogany work table, Newport, Rhode Island, 1790–1810, the case fitted with two cockbeaded drawers flanked by fluted sides, on cylindrical tapering reeded legs, 20⅛in. wide. (Christie's) $1,840

Federal mahogany veneer work stand, Portsmouth, New Hampshire, 1708–1815, with bird's-eye maple and flame birch veneer, mahogany crossbanding, 17in. wide. (Skinner) $2,760

A fine Federal penwork-decorated tiger maple two-drawer work table, Massachusetts or New Hampshire, early 19th century, 18⅝in. wide. (Sotheby's) $28,750

Federal mahogany veneer serpentine work stand, Boston, 1790, possibly the Seymour Workshop, with side opening bag drawer, original turned pulls, 19.25in. wide. (Skinner) $6,325

A Federal inlaid birch and mahogany two-drawer work table, Judkins and Senter, Portsmouth, New Hampshire, 1816, 16⅜in. wide. (Christie's) $43,700

A Federal mahogany work table, Salem, 1810–1820, the rectangular top with outset rounded corners surmounted by bosses with a beaded edge above a conforming case fitted with two cockbeaded drawers flanked by water-leaf carved posts, on turned and reeded legs with swelled cylindrical feet, 21¼in. wide.
(Christie's) $2,760

A Federal mahogany two-drawer work table, Massachusetts, probably Salem, circa 1820, the oblong top with turret corners, 21in. wide.
(Sotheby's) $2,530

Federal mahogany and mahogany veneer work table, Massachusetts, circa 1800, the rectangular top with ovolo corners, 21½in. wide. $3,500

A Federal mahogany two-drawer work table, Boston, Massachusetts, circa 1810, the rectangular top above a case with two drawers, 21in. wide.
(Sotheby's) $3,850

A late Federal carved mahogany work-table, Salem, Massachusetts, 1800–1820, the rectangular top with outset rounded corners, on spirally-turned tapering legs and ball feet, 21¾in. wide.
(Christie's) $1,650

A Federal mahogany sewing-table, Salem, Massachusetts, 1790–1810, the serpentine top above a conforming case with a cockbeaded drawer fitted with a velvet-lined writing surface over an additional drawer and sliding work-bag, 19½in. wide.
(Christie's) $10,300

A Federal paint-decorated figured maple and pine work table, decorated by Sarah Eaton-Balch, at Mrs. Rowson's School, Roxbury, Massachusetts, circa 1798–1810, 18¼in. wide.
(Sotheby's) $17,250

A fine Federal inlaid mahogany and maple work table, Massachusetts, circa 1800, the square top serpentine on all sides with checkered-inlaid edge, 17¼in. wide.
(Sotheby's) $9,200

A fine and rare Federal maple-inlaid mahogany sewing table, Boston, Massachusetts, circa 1795, the hinged octagonal top with inlaid edge above a conforming frieze, 19¾in. wide.
(Sotheby's) $11,500

A fine and rare Federal paint decorated pine work table, Salem, Massachusetts, circa 1820, painted and decorated with birds and sprays of leaves, 47in. high.
(Sotheby's) $24,150

FEDERAL, MASSACHUSETTS

Federal mahogany and mahogany veneer work table, probably Massachusetts, 18.5in. wide.
(Skinner) $862

A Federal mahogany work table, Boston, Massachusetts 1810-1820, on molded saber legs with castors, 51.1cm. wide, closed. (Christie's) $4,100

A Federal mahogany two-drawer sewing table, Massachusetts, circa 1820, the oblong top flanked by hinged D-shaped leaves, 38in. wide open.
(Sotheby's) $2,530

A Federal mahogany worktable, Massachusetts, 1800–1810, the rectangular top with outset rounded corners above three cockbeaded drawers flanked by ring-turned engaged colonettes, 20³/₄in. wide.
(Christie's) $1,150

Federal mahogany and flame birch veneer inlaid sewing stand, Boston or Salem, Massachusetts, 1790–1800, the rectangular top with canted corners and crossbanded veneer edge, 21in. wide.
(Skinner) $3,450

A Federal satinwood and burlwood inlaid sewing table, attributed to John and/or Thomas Seymour, Boston, Massachusetts, circa 1800, 21in. wide.
(Sotheby's) $189,500

Federal mahogany carved, bird's-eye maple and mahogany veneer work table, probably Massachusetts, 1815–20, 20¹/₂in. wide.
(Skinner) $2,875

A rare Federal mahogany veneered inlaid work table, probably Seymour workshop, Boston, Massachusetts, 1795-1810, 18in. wide.
(Skinner) $50,000

A Federal carved mahogany work table, attributed to Samuel McIntire, Salem, Massachusetts, 1810–1815, on spiral carved legs, 22in. wide.
(Christie's) $2,990

FEDERAL, MASSACHUSETTS

A Federal inlaid and figured mahogany serpentine sewing table, Massachusetts, circa 1820, the shaped oblong top with turret corners and checker-inlaid edge, 20in. wide.
(Sotheby's) $10,350

Federal mahogany and satinwood veneer worktable, Massachusetts, circa 1810, old finish, 19³/₄in. wide.
(Skinner) $5,500

A Federal veneered mahogany and satinwood sewing table, North Shore, Massachusetts, 1790-1810, the octagonal top with veneered edge, 20½in. wide.
(Sotheby's) $7,475

A late Federal figured mahogany two-drawer work table, Salem, Massachusetts, circa 1825, on star-punch-decorated reeded tapering legs ending in tapered feet, 22in. wide.
(Sotheby's) $2,070

A fine and rare Federal carved and figured mahogany work table, Salem, Massachusetts, circa 1810, the octagonal case fitted with a single drawer, 21in. wide.
(Sotheby's) $26,450

A Federal carved mahogany sewing table, Massachusetts, circa 1820, the rectangular top with turret corners above two drawers, 18³/₄in. wide.
(Sotheby's) $1,495

A Federal mahogany work table, Massachusetts, 1790-1810, the octagonal top with outset rounded corners, molded roundels, and reeded edge, 20½in. wide.
(Christie's) $10,925

Federal mahogany veneered work table, Boston or North Shore, circa 1800, the mahogany veneered top with four carved ovolo corners, 18½in. wide.
(Skinner) $3,750

A Federal mahogany work table, Massachusetts, 1795-1815, the rectangular serpentine top with outset rounded corners, 19in. wide.
(Christie's) $4,600

FEDERAL, NEW YORK

A Federal figured mahogany two-drawer work table, New England, circa 1810, the rectangular top above a two drawer frieze, 18½in. wide. (Sotheby's) $3,220

Federal mahogany veneer work stand, New England, circa 1810, old refinish, 16½in. wide. (Skinner Inc.) $4,150

Federal tiger maple work stand, New England, circa 1820, the two drawers with original glass pulls, 19in. wide. (Skinner) $1,495

A Federal mahogany sewing table, New England, 1800-15, the rectangular top with drop leaves above a case fitted with three cockbeaded drawers, 30½in. wide, open. (Christie's) $1,265

A Federal figured cherrywood and pine four-drawer work table, New York or New England, circa 1810, the rectangular top above four drawers, 17in. wide. (Sotheby's) $4,312

Federal painted and decorated tiger maple work table, New England, circa 1815, the rectangular top with a red and black chain border above two long drawers, width 20¼in. (Butterfield & Butterfield) $7,475

A Country Federal inlaid cherry work table, New England, circa 1800, top 20 x 19¼in. (Skinner) $4,300

Country Federal tiger maple and mahogany veneer table, New England, circa 1810, top 16½ x 20in. (Skinner) $715

A late Federal mahogany drop leaf work table, New England, 1810-1830, on spirally reeded and ring turned legs, 44½in. wide, leaves open. (Christie's) $1,500

A Federal veneered mahogany worktable, New York, 1790–1810, the rectangular top with two drop leaves and molded edge, 35in. wide open. (Christie's) **$1,725**

A Federal carved mahogany two drawer work table, New York, circa 1815, the oblong top above a two-drawer frieze, 20in. wide. (Sotheby's) **$2,070**

Federal mahogany veneered work table, New York, 1810–30, top drawer fitted, replaced brasses, 22½in. wide. (Skinner Inc.) **$5,000**

A Federal mahogany work-table, New York, 1805-1810, the rectangular top with canted corners above a conforming case with three drawers, 17¾in wide. (Christie's) **$1,725**

A Federal mahogany work-table, New York, 1800–1815, on a turned pedestal and quadripartite base on downswept molded legs, on paw feet with casters, 25¼in. wide. (Christie's) **$4,100**

Federal mahogany veneer carved astragal-end work table, New York, circa 1815, the hinged top above a fitted interior, 26½in. wide. (Skinner) **$2,000**

A Federal figured mahogany two-drawer lift-top work table, New York, circa 1815, on circular reeded tapering legs, 20¾in. wide. (Sotheby's) **$2,875**

A Federal carved and figured mahogany astragal-end work table, attributed to Duncan Phyfe or a contemporary, New York, circa 1815, 25½in. wide. (Sotheby's) **$12,650**

A Federal figured mahogany work table, New York, circa 1810, the rectangular top with reeded edge, 21¾in. wide. (Sotheby's) **$4,025**

SHAKER

Shaker butternut walnut and cherry sewing table, Mt. Lebanon, New York, circa 1830, one-board butternut top, 30in. wide.
(Skinner) $6,500

Shaker butternut sewing box, the drawers with ebonised diamond escutcheon and turned ivory pull, New England, circa 1820, 7½in. wide.
(Skinner) $7,750

Shaker cherry drop leaf sewing case, probably Hancock, circa 1820, the overhanging rectangular top with a single drop leaf, 35½in. wide.
(Skinner) $18,400

A Shaker pine worktable, New York, signed *Anderson*, early 20th century, with detachable long compartmented double shelf above a rectangular top with breadboard ends, 29¾in. wide. (Christie's) $1,725

A Shaker figured-maple sewing cabinet, possibly Watervliet, New York, first half of the 19th century, 32½in. wide.
(Christie's) $77,300

Sewing desk, Canterbury, New Hampshire or Sabbathday Lake, Maine, circa 1840, pine, fruitwood pulls, salmon paint, plank-sided case with ogee-shaped base, 26in. wide.
(Skinner) $8,625

Shaker one-drawer work table, 19th century, in pine with square tapered legs, ivory-inlaid escutcheon and turned wooden pull, top 21 × 17½in.
(Eldred's) $1,320

Shaker cherry and butternut sewing case, probably Enfield, Connecticut, circa 1840, on square tapering legs, 27in. wide.
(Skinner) $23,000

Shaker washed cherry workstand, Enfield, Connecticut, circa 1840, the classic one drawer stand with overhung hinged compartment, 26in. wide.
(Skinner) $9,200

A good Chippendale figured walnut tall chest of drawers, Pennsylvania, circa 1770, the rectangular overhanging cornice above five short and four graduated thumbmolded long drawers, the base molding below on spurred bracket feet, 42in. wide. (Sotheby's)

$7,475

Maple and pine tall chest, New England, circa 1800, refinished, replaced brasses, 36in. wide. (Skinner Inc.) $4,120

Maple tall chest, probably New York state, circa 1800, refinished, replaced brasses, 41¼in. wide. (Skinner Inc.) $2,300

Cherry tall chest, Pennsylvania, circa 1800, refinished, on splayed bracket feet, 41¾in. wide. (Skinner) $3,575

Antique American Chippendale seven-drawer tall chest, circa 1750, in maple and curly maple with graduated drawers, molded cornice, scrolled bracket base, 40in. wide. (Eldred's) $7,150

Cherry and maple tall chest of drawers, New England, circa 1800, the case of six thumbmolded graduated drawers on cut-out bracket base, 36in. wide. (Skinner) $1,840

Painted chest on frame, New Hampshire, circa 1830, with six graduated thumb molded drawers, on cabriole legs with arris pad feet, 36in. wide. (Skinner Inc.) $160,000

Antique American seven-drawer tall chest in cherry, molded top with dentil molding, molded drawer fronts, 40in. wide. (Eldred's) $1,540

William and Mary red-brown painted tall chest over drawers, New England, first half 18th century, 35¼in. wide. (Skinner) $4,312

Cherry and maple tall chest, Thetford, Vermont, circa 1800, refinished, replaced brasses, 38¼in. wide. (Skinner Inc.) $5,000

CHIPPENDALE

A Chippendale figured walnut tall chest of drawers, Chester County, Pennsylvania, circa 1780, 40½in. wide.
(Sotheby's) $4,600

A Chippendale figured walnut tall chest of drawers, Pennsylvania, circa 1780, 42¾in. wide.
(Sotheby's) $4,887

Chippendale walnut tall chest of drawers, Pennsylvania, circa 1780, old refinish, replaced brasses, 38½in. wide.
(Skinner) $1,955

A Chippendale walnut tall chest of drawers, Pennsylvania, circa 1770, the molded cornice above two short and four long graduated molded drawers, 45¼in. wide.
(Sotheby's) $5,750

A Chippendale tiger maple tall chest on bracket feet, replaced brasses, New England, circa 1790, 38½in. wide.
(Skinner) $6,800

A good Chippendale walnut tall chest of drawers, Pennsylvania, circa 1780, the overhanging stepped cornice above three short and five long graduated molded drawers, 45in. wide.
(Sotheby's) $13,800

Antique American Chippendale six-drawer tall chest in maple, graduated drawers, molded cornice, bracket base, 38in. wide.
(Eldred's) $2,350

Chippendale maple tall chest, Rhode Island, late 18th century, the flat molded dentil cornice above the thumbmolded drawers, 36in. wide.
(Skinner) $8,337

A Chippendale mahogany tall chest-of-drawers, Pennsylvania, 1770-1790, the rectangular flaring cornice above a conforming case, 40½in. wide.
(Christie's) $1,750

CHIPPENDALE

Chippendale butternut and maple tall chest of drawers, New England, circa 1780, 36in. wide. (Skinner) **$4,400**

Chippendale maple tall chest with six thumbmolded drawers, New England, circa 1770, 38in. wide. **$3,750**

Red painted Chippendale maple tall chest, New England, circa 1780, 36in. wide. (Skinner) **$8,500**

Chippendale applewood carved tall chest of drawers, probably Concord, Massachusetts, circa 1780, the flat molded cornice above a case of six graduated drawers, 35½in. wide. (Skinner) **$4,025**

A Country Chippendale pine blanket chest, New England, circa 1780, the molded lift top above a case of two false thumb-molded drawers and three working drawers, 36¾in. wide. (Skinner) **$1,875**

Chippendale maple tall chest of drawers, southeastern New England, late 18th century, case of two thumbmolded short drawers and five long drawers on bracket feet, 36in. wide. (Skinner) **$1,725**

Chippendale tiger maple tall chest, Rhode Island, late 18th century, the cornice molding over a seven-drawer thumbmolded case, 37in. wide. (Skinner) **$10,350**

A Chippendale maple tall chest-of-drawers with original pulls, circa 1780, 36in. wide. (Skinner) **$8,120**

Chippendale maple tall chest of drawers, Rhode Island, late 18th century, the molded cornice above the thumb-molded edge, on bracket feet, 39¼in. wide. (Butterfield & Butterfield) **$4,400**

FEDERAL

TALL CHESTS

A Federal tiger maple tall chest, Pennsylvania, circa 1810, the rectangular top with flaring cornice, 40in. wide.
(Skinner) $4,600

A Federal inlaid walnut tall chest of drawers, Pennsylvania, 1790-1810, on flared French feet, 43¾in. wide.
(Christie's) $6,600

Federal birch tall chest of drawers, New England, late 18th century, top drawer with two drawer façade, 38³/₄in. wide.
(Skinner) $2,185

A Federal inlaid figured maple tall chest of drawers, New England, 1790-1810 with cove molded cornice, on French feet, 44½in. wide.
(Christie's New York) $11,000

A fine Federal paint-decorated poplar tall chest of drawers, probably Schwaben Creek Valley, Pennsylvania, circa 1830, the rectangular top with dentil-carved tympanum, 41in. wide.
(Sotheby's) $31,050

Federal tiger maple tall chest of drawers, probably Pennsylvania, circa 1800, case of two cockbeaded short drawers above four graduated long drawers, 37¹/₂in. wide.
(Skinner) $4,025

QUEEN ANNE

A Queen Anne walnut chest-on-stand, feather-banded overall, the molded cornice above three short and three graduated long drawers, 40¹/₂in. wide.
(Christie's) $9,677

A Queen Anne maple highboy, New Jersey, circa 1730, 37in. wide. $14,000

A Queen Anne style walnut veneered highboy on hipped cabriole legs with Spanish type feet, 62¼in. high. $2,600

QUEEN ANNE

A good Queen Anne maple chest-on-frame, New Hampshire, 1750–80, in two parts, on cabriole legs, 41in. wide.
(Sotheby's) $9,775

A rare early Queen Anne walnut tall chest of drawers, Philadelphia, Pennsylvania, 1730-60, 40½in. wide.
(Sotheby's) $10,350

Queen Anne maple tall chest of drawers, probably Rhode Island, circa 1750, on bracket feet, 33⅜in. wide.
(Skinner) $2,645

A good Queen Anne figured walnut chest-on-frame, Chester County, Pennsylvania, circa 1750, in two parts, 44in. wide.
(Sotheby's) $34,500

A Queen Anne maple high chest of drawers, New England, 1740-1760, the upper case with molded swan neck pediment centering three ball and spire finials, 38⅜in. wide.
(Christie's New York) $29,000

Queen Anne maple tall chest, Salisbury, New Hampshire area, School of Bartlett Cabinetmaking, circa 1800, refinished, 36in. wide.
(Skinner Inc.) $5,000

A Queen Anne painted maple tall chest on a tall bracket base, New England, circa 1750, 36in. wide.
(Skinner) $8,000

Queen Anne maple chest of drawers, New England, 18th century, flat molded top, 36in. wide.
(Skinner) $3,738

Queen Anne maple chest on frame, New Hampshire, circa 1760, old refinish, brasses probably original, 38in. wide.
(Skinner Inc.) $9,000

A Federal inlaid and carved mahogany wardrobe, New York, 1800-1820, on short reeded baluster turned legs, 56½in. wide. (Christie's) **$7,000**

A Chippendale carved mahogany wardrobe, in two sections, New York, 1760-80, 53in. wide. **$7,500**

A bamboo-turned figured maple wardrobe, attributed to R.J. Horner & Company, New York City, 1870–85, in three parts, 33in. wide. (Christie's) **$10,925**

Fine American Renaissance parcel-gilt, stained and burled maple armoire by Herter Brothers, New York, circa 1872, the mirrored door above a single drawer, 46½in. wide. (Butterfield & Butterfield) **$6,800**

Classical mahogany carved and mahogany veneer wardrobe, labeled *Manufactured ... at Mathews Cabinet and Chair Factories ... New York*, circa 1820, 55in. wide. (Skinner) **$4,400**

A classical mahogany armoire, Duncan Phyfe, New York, 1815-1825, the flared cornice above paneled doors with reeded brass edging and cornucopia escutcheons, 66¾in. wide. (Christie's) **$32,200**

Lifetime oak two-door wardrobe, Grand Rapids, Michigan, circa 1910, original medium finish, fitted interior, decal, 38in. wide. (Skinner) **$4,370**

A classical carved mahogany wardrobe, New York City, 1820–40, the molded cornice above a veneered band over an inset veneered frieze, 64in. wide. (Christie's) **$2,990**

A Federal blue-painted cupboard, New England, late 18th/early 19th century, with deeply molded rectangular cornice over a fielded panelled cupboard door, 40½in. wide. (Christie's) **$7,250**

A good cut-decorated paneled pine trastero, Penasco, New Mexico, circa 1850, the molded rectangular cornice surmounted by a shaped scrolling pediment, 37½in. wide. (Sotheby's) $24,150

American oak wardrobe, early 20th century, paneled full-length door alongside a small mirrored door, 45in. wide.
(Du Mouchelles) $350

A fine classical gilt-stenciled mahogany wardrobe, New York, possibly by Joseph Meeks and Sons, circa 1820, with stylised carved paw feet, 54½in. wide.
(Sotheby's) $12,500

A classical figured mahogany armoire, labeled by Joseph Meeks & Sons, New York, circa 1835, two lancet-arched panelled doors flanked by free-standing columnar supports, 5ft. 9in. wide.
(Sotheby's) $6,325

Pine wardrobe or Kas, Hudson River Valley or Delaware, circa 1750, on large turnip feet painted black, 59½in. wide.
(Skinner) $8,000

Grain painted pine wardrobe, coastal Massachusetts, circa 1830, the molded cornice above a door with two raised panels opening to an interior of hooks with shelves to the right, 44in. wide. (Skinner) $1,032

Gustav Stickley two-door wardrobe, circa 1907, two paneled doors with copper pulls opening to reveal two compartments, 34⅛in. wide.
(Skinner Inc.) $6,250

Chippendale cherry carved linen press, Kent, Connecticut area, circa 1780, the scrolled and pierced crest above recessed panel doors, opening to a two shelved interior, 41½in. wide.
(Skinner) $16,500

A glazed-surface pine trastero, Aniceto Garundo, Chacon, New Mexico, circa 1870, the rectangular over-hanging dentil molded cornice above two field paneled doors, 4ft. wide.
(Sotheby's) $1,265

A Federal mahogany wash-
stand, circa 1795, 39in.
high, 23in. wide. $1,050

Antique American dry sink in
pine, with two paneled doors
and one drawer, 40in. high.
(Eldred's) $825

A Federal mahogany carved
washstand, probably Mass.,
circa 1815, 20in. wide.
                      $3,750

A late Federal curly maple
single-drawer washstand,
Pennsylvania or Middle Atlantic
States, circa 1825, 21¼in. wide.
(Sotheby's) $3,250

Antique American kitchen
cupboard in pine, backsplash
top, two small drawers over two
paneled cupboard doors,
bracket feet, 48in. high.
(Eldred's) $850

A Federal mahogany basin
stand, Boston, Massachusetts,
circa 1820, the shaped
splashboard above a projecting
pierced basin, 20½in. wide.
(Sotheby's) $2,013

A late Federal mahogany washstand, New York, 1815-1825,
the shaped splashboard above
a medial shelf over a pierced
and fitted D-shaped top. $2,180

A late Federal fancy painted
washstand, New England, 1810–
1820, with rectangular splashboard above a rectangular top,
27¾in. wide.
(Christie's) $1,265

Country Federal tiger maple
corner washstand, New
England, circa 1810, the
shaped backboards above cut
out shelf, 40½in. high.
(Skinner Inc.) $3,100

Federal mahogany corner washstand on splay feet, 21½in. wide, circa 1800.
$1,500

Grain painted chamber stand, New England, circa 1830, 39in. wide.
(Skinner) $550

A Classical Revival mahogany washstand, probably Boston, circa 1815, 17½in. diam.
$25,000

A Federal inlaid mahogany and birch-veneered wash-stand, Portsmouth, New Hampshire, 1790–1810, the rectangular top pierced with three circular openings and edged with a three-quarter gallery, 35½in. high.
(Christie's) $27,500

Shaker painted pine washstand, Harvard, Massachusetts, 19th century, the hinged lid opens to a storage compartment above a cupboard, 36in. wide.
(Skinner Inc.) $13,000

A Federal carved mahogany wash basin stand, Boston, 1800–1810, with reeded and shaped splash board above a rectangular top with reeded edge fitted for three wash bowls, 30½in. wide.
(Christie's) $1,430

Federal mahogany and bird's-eye maple veneer corner chamber stand, Massachusetts, early 19th century, 21in. wide.
(Skinner Inc.) $2,600

Tiger maple chamberstand, probably New York State, the shaped gallery above a rectangular top and long drawer, 34in. wide.
(Skinner) $2,415

A Federal mahogany and mahogany veneer inlaid one-drawer wash stand, probably Massachusetts, circa 1800, with tambour door, 18½in. wide.
(Skinner) $1,495

501

WASHSTANDS

Red painted pine and maple corner chamberstand, New England, 1820s, with scrolled backsplash, 16¾in. wide. (Skinner) $2,415

Antique American Sheraton washstand in mahogany, shaped backsplash, drawer in base, turned legs, 18½in. wide. (Eldred's) $280

A painted and decorated washstand, New England, circa 1830, 15¼in. wide. $630

A Chippendale mahogany washstand, American, circa 1780, the hinged two-part top opening to a pierced surface within a cyma-shaped molding, 30in. wide (open). (Sotheby's) $3,162

Federal mahogany veneered Beau Brummel, probably Eastern United States, circa 1820, on turned tapering legs, 40in. high. (Skinner) $7,500

A Federal inlaid mahogany and birch veneered washstand, attributed to Langley Boardman, Portsmouth, New Hampshire, 1800–1810, 16½in. wide. (Christie's) $19,550

A fine Federal inlaid mahogany corner washstand, Northeastern Shore, New England, circa 1805, the convex surface pierced with three circular holes, 22in. wide. (Sotheby's) $3,000

A Federal figured maple washstand, Mid-Atlantic States, circa 1830, the three-quarter scrolling back-splash above a rectangular top, 23in. wide. (Sotheby's) $4,600

A very fine Federal bird's eye maple veneered mahogany corner basin stand, Boston, Massachusetts, circa 1805, height 40½in. (Sotheby's) $8,250

Federal mahogany and flame birch veneer basin stand, Boston, circa 1800, old surface. (Skinner) $3,105

Shaker pine, tiger maple and butternut washstand, 20¼in. wide. (Skinner) $12,500

A Federal inlaid mahogany corner stand, the top with a pierced brass gallery, probably New York, 1800-15, 34½in. high. $3,750

A Federal inlaid mahogany corner washstand, New England, 1790–1810, the shaped splashboards with shelf above a convex top fitted with three holes for basin and dishes, 18³/₄in. wide. (Christie's) $1,500

Shaker pine painted wash stand, circa 1850, retains original chrome yellow wash, 45¹/₄in. wide. (Skinner) $8,000

A Federal carved mahogany wash basin stand, Boston, 1800–1810, with reeded and shaped splash board above a rectangular top with reeded edge fitted for three wash bowls, 30¹/₂in. wide. (Christie's) $1,750

A late Federal fancy-painted washstand, New England, 1820–1830, the rectangular recessed shelf on shaped supports, 20in. wide. (Christie's) $1,093

A rare classical mahogany washstand, Boston, Massachusetts, circa 1815, the hinged square molded top opening to three circular recesses, 18¹/₂in. wide. (Sotheby's) $1,955

A 19th century painted pine washstand, painted old pink over other colors, America, 15½in. wide. (Skinner) $1,000

A Federal inlaid mahogany wine cooler with lift top, 22in. wide. $5,750

A late classical carved mahogany cellaret, New York, 1820–40, the rectangular peaked or hinged lid with rounded edge, 39³/₄in. wide.
(Christie's) $3,450

Classical Revival mahogany and mahogany veneer cellaret, possibly New York, circa 1825, 33in. wide.
(Skinner) $1,045

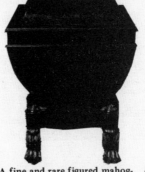

A rare Federal inlaid cherrywood cellaret, Southern, circa 1795, the hinged rectangular top with molded edge opening to a well, 31³/₄in. wide.
(Sotheby's) $4,600

A fine and rare figured mahogany veneer cellaret, attributed to Duncan Phyfe, New York, 1815-1825, of sarcophagus form, with gilt leaf carved lion's paw feet, 25¼in. high. (Christie's New York) $16,500

A Federal inlaid and figured mahogany cellaret, Mid-Atlantic States, circa 1795, the rectangular molded top section fitted with a crossbanded door, 19¹/₄in. wide.
(Sotheby's) $2,185

Limbert cellaret, circa 1908, no. 751, rectangular top projecting over single drawer with square copper pulls, 24³/₄in. wide.
(Skinner) $1,300

Federal mahogany veneer cellaret, New York City, 1815–25, with cross-banded mahogany veneer outlining the octagonal shaped top, 24¹/₂in. wide.
(Skinner) $2,530

A classical carved mahogany sarcophagus cellaret, New York, 1810-1820, the flattened-dome hinged top opening to reveal a well, 20⁵/₈in wide.
(Christie's) $3,680

INDEX

Academy 475
Adelheim, T.F. 223
Aesthetic 38
Aesthetic Movement
28, 59
Alexander, Wm. 341
Allison, Michael 458
American Cabinet Co.
58
American Periods 11
Ampico mechanism
294
Ampico player 295
Anderson 491
Ansonia Clock Co. 198
Apthorp, Charles 94
Arts & Crafts 22, 38,
59, 311
Atkins Clock Mfg. Co.
197
Atkins Whiting & Co.
208

B & H 257
Babcock, Alpheus 295
Bailey, John 199
Baily, I 273
Baird Adv. Clock Co.
209
Baird Clock Co. 208
Baldwin 295
Banjo Clocks 188-191
Barjon, D. 20
Barry, Joseph 26, 320
Bartholomew, E. and
G.W. 200
Bartram, James 97
Baudouine, Charles 439

Baycock, A.J. 451
Beds 20-29
Belden, George 158
Belter, J.B. 443
Belter, John Henry 137,
313, 314, 333
Belter,J.H. 111
Bembe and Kemmel
110
Bennett Family 403
Billings, Jonathan 191
Birge, Mallory & Co.
197
Birge & Fuller 200
Birge and Fuller 197
Bishop and Bradley
194
Blacker, Robert R. 80
Blanket Chests 30-36
Bliss and Horswill 134
Bloom, M. 106
Boardman Family 416
Boardman, Langley
502
Bond & Sons, Wm. 205
Bookcases 37-41
Boston Beer Co. 208
Boxes 42-51
Boyer, John 155
Brackett, O. 198
Bradstreet, John 393
Breakfast Tables
374-375
Brewster & Ingrahams
197, 199
Brierly, Ernest 297
Brokaw, Isaac 203
Brooks Cabinet &
Upholstery
Warehouse, T. 392

Bryant & Loud 384
Bucher, Heinrich 51
Burden, J. 331
Bureaux 52-56
Butler, Peter 30

Cabinets 57-59
Cable Midget 294
Cahoon, R. 299
CAHR 30
Candle Stands 60-71
Canterburys 72
Card Tables 376-391
Center Tables 392-393
Cermenati & Monfrino
291
Chairs 73-149
Chalet, Toby 337
Chandler, A. 192
Chandler, Abiel 286
Chapin Family 66
Chelsea Clock Co. 208
Cheney, Asahel 205
Chests 150-153
Chests on Chests
180-185
Chests of Drawers
154-179
Chests over Drawers
186-187
Chickering 294
Choate and Martin 386
Christian, Charles 452
Churchill, Lemuel 134
Claggett, William 204
Clark, Joseph 174
Clark, Sylvester 198
Clocks 188-209
Coates, Samuel 402

Coca Cola 209
Collins and Alkman
Corporation 373
Collins, James 192
Compos, Foster S. 190
Connelly, Henry 386
Cornell, Edward 280
Corner Chairs 73-75
Corner Cupboards
210-212
Cornwall, NY Foundry
315
Courting Chair 121
Cradles & Cribs 218
Credenzas 219
Crosby & Vosburgh
208
Cummens, William 207
Cupboards 220-227
Curtis, Lemuel 189,
190
Cutler & Son, A. 232

Davenport, A.H. 111
Davis, Joseph 238
Demeritt, Powder
Major John 267
Derby, Elias Hasket 89
Derby Family 184
Derwallis, John 115
Desks 228-230
Dining Chairs 76-107
Dining Tables 394-395
Display Cabinets
252-253
Dixon & Sons 259
Dolan, John T. 229
Dominy 91
Dower 152
Downes, Ephraim 195
Downs, Ephraim 193

Dressing Tables
396-401
Drop Leaf Tables
410-424
Drum Tables 425
Dummer, Governor 82
Dunlap Family 69, 185
Dunlap, Lieutenant
Samuel 261
Dunlap, Major 185
Dunlap, Robert 353
Dunlap School 63, 177,
261

Eames, Charles and
Ray 111
Eastlake 21, 110, 397
Easy Chairs 108-114
Eaton-Balch, Sarah 486
Edwards 204
Edwards Family 471
Edwards, Timothy 119
E.H. 49
Elbow Chairs 115-129
Elliot, John 284
Ellis, Harvey 29, 40,
41, 228, 251, 297,
350
EMD 46
Emmons and Archibald
339
Esterlie, John 204
Ever Ready Safety
Razor 208

Field, Marshall 437
Filley Family 43
Finley, John and Hugh
79
Fireplace Furniture
254-257

Fireplaces 258-259
Fisk, William 290
Forrestville
Connecticut Clock
Manufactory, The
196
Forrestville
Manufacturing Co.
199
Fortier, Andrew 178
Foster, Samuel 202
Friedrich, Wenzel 109
Furnace, Mary Anne
256
Furness, Frank 112
Furniture Designers 13

Gaines, Thomas 78
Gains, John 199
Gamble House, D.B. 79
Gateleg Tables 426-427
Gentso? 314
Gerrish, Oliver 189
Gertz, W. 392
Gibson and Davis 295
Gilbert Family 265
Gillingham, James 82
Goddard, John 82, 404,
406, 468, 470
Goddard, Nicholas 206
Goddard Townsend
School 473
Goddard-Townsend
232, 271
Goddard-Townsend
School 20, 182
Gostelowe, Jonathan
156
Gould Jr., John 329
Grant, Erastus 475

Green, Beriah 104
Greene & Greene 79, 80
Grinnell & Son, Peter 287
Grueby 445, 459
Hahn, Henry 206
HAJ 46
Halam, Eliza G. 475
Hall, Peter 79, 80
Hammond 443
Hancock, Holden and Adams 365
Handcraft 29, 58
Handcraft Furniture 116
Haneye, Nathaniel 204
Hansen, Peter Heinrich 198
Harbeson, Benjamin and/or Joseph 256
Harden 136, 311, 340, 371
Harden & Co. 116, 373
Harden Co. 136
Harland, Thos. 205
Harrold, Robert 84
H.C.S. 187
Hedges, Stephen 229
Henzey, Joseph 105
Heritage-Henredon Furniture Co. 77
Herter Brothers 22, 27, 28, 38, 59, 109, 112, 115, 154, 219, 228, 354, 437, 438, 475, 498
Heywood Brothers 72, 112, 130
Heywood-Wakefield 369
Hickory 127

High Chairs 130-131
High Chests of Drawers 260-266
Highboys 267-271
Hill Wells & Co. 198
Hinckley, Henry A. 191
Hixon & Co, Edward 219
Hoadley, S. 202
Hoadley, Silas 198, 199, 206, 207
Hodges, Erastus 195
Holl II , Peter 35
Holl III, Peter 226
Holl, Peter 35
Horner & Company, R.J. 498
Horner and Company, R.J. 396
Horner, R.J., & Company 93
Hotchkiss & Benedict 192
Howard & Co., E. 190, 208
Howard & Davis 204
Howard, E & Co. 189
Howard, Thomas Jnr. 119
Howell, Silas W. 201
Hubbard Family 377
Hubbard, J.C. 332
Hubbard, Roswell A. 483
Hutch Cupboards 226
Hutch-Chair Tables 428-429
Hutchins, Levi 207

IS 90
Ives, C. & L.C. 192

Ives, Joseph 199, 208

Jackson, Edward 299
Jenkins, Anthony H. 301
Jeromes & Darrow 194
John, Major 261
John Needles 460
Judkins and Senter 484

Kas 272
Keene 54
Kendal, David 136
Kimbal and Cabus 212
King, Daniel 254
King Jr. , William 321
Kittinger 122
KK 30
Kneehole Desks 232-233

Lamb's-Tongue 23
Lannier, Charles Honoré 381
Lannier, Charles-Honore 92
Lannuier, Charles-Honore 382, 412, 456
Lannuier, H. 383, 455
Large Tables 430-435
Lehn, Joseph Long 44, 281
Library Tables 436-438
Lifetime 110, 394, 498
Lifetime Furniture 311, 340

Limbert 38, 39, 111, 136, 253, 292, 311, 336, 339, 348, 354, 358, 365, 369, 372, 395, 437, 438, 440, 442, 443, 459, 504
Linen Presses 273
Lively, Geo 202
Lloyd Wright, Frank 461
Lockerman Family 434
Lolling Chairs 132-135
Loomis, Asa 155
Lothrop, E. 286
Loud Brother, 294
Lowboys 274-277

McArthur, Warren 111
McHugh, Joseph, and Co. 92
McIntire, Samuel 181, 184, 257, 443
McIntire, Samuel F. 52
McIntire, Samuel Field 184
Maher, George Washington 150
Marcy Foundry Co. 359
Maris-Gregg 82
Marlborough 20
Marlen, William 385
Marsh, Gilbert & Co. 192
Marshall Field 437
Marshall and Wendell 295
Masonic 51, 463
Mathews Cabinet and Chair Factories 498
Matteson, Thomas 154
Meeks and Company, Joseph 324

Meeks, J. and J.W. 370
Meeks and Sons, Joseph 499
Meyers, Jacob 123
Michigan Chair Company 357
Miffin Family 261
Mills & Co., J.B. 199
Mills, John 185
Miniature Furniture 278-282
Mirror Clocks 192
Mirrors 283-293
Mitchell, G. 193
MN 50
Molesworth, Thomas 296
Molineux, John 255
Morris 111
Morris, Benjamin 202
Morris Family 403
Morris, Samuel 181, 407
Munger, Asa 192
Munger and Benedict 191
Murdoch Foundry 259
Musgrove, James 286

Nakashima, George 21
Nakishima, George 432
New Haven Clock Co. 208, 209
Newlin, Joseph 156
Nutting, Wallace 276
Nye, Elihu 175

Occasional Tables 439-445
Old Hickory 115

Pabst, Daniel 112
Paine Furniture 229, 332, 394
Paine Furniture Co. 234, 372
Peloupet, Pelton & Company 294
Pembroke Tables 446-453
Pencil-post 23, 28
Perry, Henry G. 367
Phoenix Furniture 136
Phyfe, Duncan 22, 72, 91, 92, 93, 112, 119, 319, 322, 325, 326, 328, 364, 374, 382, 383, 397, 400, 436, 437, 461, 481, 490, 504
Phyfe, Duncan, School of 249
Pianos 294-295
Pier Tables 454-456
Pillar & Scroll Clocks 193-195
Plail & Co. 369
Plail Brothers 112, 116, 137
Pleasant Furnace 254
Plycraft 115
Potter, Louis 254
Pottier and Stymus 78
Potts, Thomas 182
Pratt & Company, N. 254
Pratt, J.D. 137
Prince & Co., Geo. 295

Quaint Furniture 340, 440, 441
Quervelle 323

Querville, A. 476

Ranck, Johannes 35
Rank, Johannes 33, 35
Rice, Jabez 279
Rocking Chairs
136-139
Rockwell,Samuel 202
Rodman Family 277
Rogers, Abner 206
Rohlfs, Charles 229,
353
Roman Bronze Works
254
Roux, Alex 437
Roux, Alexander 439
Rowson's, Mrs., School
486
Royce, Elijah 172
Roycroft 20, 152, 154,
315, 336, 337, 357,
359, 365, 395, 400,
437, 442, 475

Sabbathday Lake 225
St. Stephen's Park 46
Sala, John Snr. 153
Salisbury Family 320
Salmon, Thomas 126
Savery, William 33, 95,
98, 408
School of Bartlett
Cabinetmaking 497
Schott, N. 313
Schrenk & Co. 232
Screens 296-297
Seavers, William 80
Secretaries 298-299
Selzer, John 150
Serving Tables 457-459
Settees & Couches
310-334

Sewall, Samuel 394,
420
Seymoor, John or
Thomas 202
Seymour & Son, John
385
Seymour, John and/or
Thomas 487
Seymour, John and Son
303
Seymour, John and
Thomas 307, 384,
399, 484
Seymour Workshop
484

Shaker 44, 47, 51, 62,
63, 100, 138, 178,
222, 224, 353, 431,
434, 440, 441, 442,
491, 501, 503
Shakespeare, 58
Shaw, John 302
Shearer, John 235
Shelf Clocks 196-201
Shelves & Brackets
336-338
Shimnway, W.D. 178
Ship Eagle, E.O'Brien,
Curling Master 34
Shop of the Crafters 38,
252
Shop-O'-The Crafters
291
Shoshone Furniture
Company 296
Side Tables 460-461
Sideboards 339-350
Six Board 153
Slant Top Desks 234
Slover & Taylor 326,
328

Smith and Goodrich
200
Sofa Tables 462
Spangler, W.H.,
Ephrata. Pa., 54
Splitler, Johannes 35
Stands 351-359
Stanyan, J. 366
Starck 294
Starret House of
Warren 57
Step Back Cupboards
360-363
Stephenson-Phillips
Family 266
Stewart, Daniel 105
Stickley 219, 445
Stickley Bros 335
Stickley Brothers 49,
101, 125, 179, 350,
353, 359, 368, 437,
475
Stickley, Charles 125
Stickley, Gustav 28, 40,
41, 57, 101, 113, 114,
124, 125, 139, 151,
179, 200, 202, 203,
228, 250, 251, 253,
255, 287, 290, 297,
334, 335, 336, 337,
338, 349, 350, 354,
357, 358, 359, 365,
368, 411, 437, 438,
444, 445, 475, 499
Stickley, L. & J.G. 29,
40, 58, 101, 113, 114,
124, 125, 139, 198,
250, 251, 253, 334,
335, 336, 349, 350,
354, 356, 357, 367,
368, 395, 437, 438,
444, 459

Stillman, William 204
Stools 364-368
Stow & Davis 219
Street, Nathaniel 126
Studio Nove 22, 395
Suites 369-373

Tables 374-491
Tady 22
Tall Case Clocks
  202-207
Tall Chests 492-497
Tarr, Levin 450
Tavern Tables 463-466
Tea Tables 467-473
Terry & Sons, E. 193,
  195, 197
Terry, Eli 194
Terry, Eli & Samuel
  193
Terry Jnr., Eli 209
Texas 20
TH 131
Thomas Clock Co.,
  Seth 197, 209
Thomas, Daniel 294
Thomas, Seth 193, 194,
  195, 198, 208, 209
Tiemann Co., G. 43
Tiffany & Co. 197
Toby 357
Toby Furniture Co. 114
Towensend Workshops
  232
Tower, Reuben 198,
  206
Tower, Ruben 207
Townsend, Edmund
  233

Townsend, John 386
Tramp Art 285, 353
Tray Top 473
Tritta, Ferruccio 395
Tritta, Feruccio 22
Trotter, Daniel 118
 Van Vechten Family
378
Vedder, Elihu 257, 259
Vose & Son, Isaac 320,
  380
Vose, Isaac 476, 479
Vose Jr., Isaac 476

Wakefield, Heywood
  228, 400
Wakefield Rattan Co.
  137
Wall Clocks 208-209
Wall Cupboards 227
Wallace Nutting
  Reproductions 232
Waltham Clock Co.
  189
Wardrobes & Armoires
  498-499
Washstands 500-503
Waterbury 209
Weber, Jacob 45, 48,
  150
Weber-Aeolian 295
Welch Company 209
Welch, John 94
Wellford, Robert 258
Wharton, Joseph 133
Whitcombe, A. 199
White, Charles 324
White, White 323
Whitehead, William
  391, 451, 453

Whitehorne, Samuel
  233
Whiting, Riley 194,
  195, 200, 203; 206,
  207
Whiting, Samuel 189
Wilder, Joshua 192
Willard, A. Jnr. 189
Willard, Aaron 188,
  190, 197, 202, 203,
  204, 209
Willard, Aaron Jnr. 191
Willard, Alex J. 205
Willard, Benjamin 203
Willard, Simon 205
Williams, David 188,
  191
Williams and Everett
  455
Winchester, Ziba 222
Wine Coolers &
  Cellarets 504
Wing Chairs 140-149
Wire, John 331
Wittingham, Richard
  257
Wood, David, 198
Woodruff, George 452
Wooton Desk Co. 229
Wooton Desk
  Manufacturing
  Company 228
Work Tables 474-491
Worshipful Master's
  Chair 78

Young & Co., J 110
Young, J.M. 315, 366
Youngs, Stephen and
  Moses 382